Culture, Mind, and Society

Series Editor
Peter G. Stromberg
Anthropology Department
University of Tulsa
Tulsa, Oklahoma, USA

The Society for Psychological Anthropology—a section of the American Anthropology Association—and Palgrave Macmillan are dedicated to publishing innovative research that illuminates the workings of the human mind within the social, cultural, and political contexts that shape thought, emotion, and experience. As anthropologists seek to bridge gaps between ideation and emotion or agency and structure and as psychologists, psychiatrists, and medical anthropologists search for ways to engage with cultural meaning and difference, this interdisciplinary terrain is more active than ever.

More information about this series at
http://www.springer.com/series/14947

Robert Lemelson • Annie Tucker

Afflictions

Steps Toward a Visual Psychological Anthropology

Robert Lemelson
University of California
Los Angeles, California
USA

Annie Tucker
University of California
Los Angeles, California
USA

Culture, Mind, and Society
ISBN 978-3-319-59983-0   ISBN 978-3-319-59984-7   (eBook)
DOI 10.1007/978-3-319-59984-7

Library of Congress Control Number: 2017946191

Cover image © Elemental Productions
Cover design by Samantha Johnson

Printed on acid-free paper

This Palgrave Macmillan imprint is published by Springer Nature
The registered company is Springer International Publishing AG
The registered company address is: Gewerbestrasse 11, 6330 Cham, Switzerland

To Dorothy Lemelson: With the deepest respect, admiration, and love

PREFACE

Photo 1   Anthropologist Robert Lemelson at a *jathilan* performance in 2006

In 1996, as a graduate student in psychological anthropology, I went to Indonesia to conduct doctoral research exploring the influence of cultural context on the experience and trajectory of mental illness. The question I was interested in, addressed in a series of research projects by the World

Health Organization (WHO) (the International Pilot Study on Schizophrenia and the Determinant of Outcome of Severe Mental Disorders) in the 1970s forward, seemed straightforward enough: why people who have developed a psychotic illness in the developing world have a better outcome or recovery than those in the West. This has been termed "The Outcome Paradox." How could it be that people living in societies that had few dollars, or national resources, devoted to the care and treatment of people with serious mental illness, like Indonesia, would get better more quickly, than in the West, where large sums are devoted to the care and treatment of people living with mental illness?

The WHO researchers defined outcome as the ability to return home after an initial hospitalization, return to work, and have fewer severe symptoms, re-hospitalizations, and relapses. After engaging in the largest transcultural psychiatric epidemiologic research project in history exploring this important public health concern, they identified a number of domains that were related to differential outcome and recovery from mental illness. These included attributional models of etiology for illness, labeling of symptoms and syndromes, the relative flexibility of daily routines; types of treatment available and accessible, the degree and types of social support, and the family emotional climate a patient returns to, among others. However, they struggled to fully answer this question, in part because the clinical and epidemiological emphasis of the research, while being able to identify these important domains, in some ways lacked the textured specificity to parse out these factors, in particular cultural places and times. One of the needs cited for future research in the WHO final report, in reference to recovery factors for schizophrenia in the developing world, was a call for greater integration of ethnographic findings. They called for qualitative and anthropological research to tease out the contextualized specifics.

In addition to "The Outcome Paradox" seeming to be an important and complex question with real life implications, it was this call for ethnographic approaches that I responded to after taking a seminar on this issue with one of my mentors, Prof. Robert Edgerton, who had done foundational work on the relation of psychosis and culture. I picked Bali as a field site, following the suggestion of another of my mentors, Prof. Douglas Hollan, who had extensive research experience on the neighboring island of Sulawesi, among the Toraja.

Bali, Indonesia, is one of the most well-examined societies in the world by anthropologists. For over a hundred years they (alongside the now millions of tourists) have come to this beautiful and culturally elaborate society to explore a wide range of topics. In anthropology proper, Bali is now seen as a place that is well understood, even overdone, and thus perhaps lacking in contemporary ethnographic interest. However, since I wanted to investigate the impact of culture on mental illness experience, a well-examined culture such as Bali seemed a good fit; there was already ample information about the myriad aspects of the ceremonial, ritual, and social life that might be relevant.

To conduct such a study I knew I would need to explore such diverse areas as explanatory models, local ways of understanding unusual sensory experiences, cultural shaping of putative psychiatric syndromes, and traditional and biomedical/psychiatric treatment systems. My conceptual toolkit included participant observation of locally available treatments; utilizing etic models such as psychiatric nosological and diagnostic systems to separate symptom and syndrome, disease and illness; and exploring the lifeworlds and life histories of my subjects via in-depth interviews. I also planned to use clinical and ethnographic forms of data collection including culturally contextualized diagnostic interviews; structured, semi-structured, and open-ended interviews; person-centered interview schedules; and community and clinical surveys. In my dissertation proposal, I briefly mentioned that I was interested in videotaping some of my research.

I was lucky at this early stage in my research career (1995–1997) to meet a Balinese psychiatrist, Dr. Luh Ketut Suryani, who had been involved with the WHO research and had done her own sophisticated work on culture and mental illness. In the mid-1980s she had spent a year collecting first hospitalizations for acute psychosis, and had a sample of 115 cases, which she investigated using a mixed method approach of clinical evaluation, interviews, and structured questionnaires. After meeting and discussing my interests with her, she agreed to have me work with four of her residents to re-contact these original patients, re-interview them, and do one of the first ten-year follow-up studies in this area. Over the course of a year and a half in 1996–1997, 95 of the original 115 were re-contacted and re-interviewed.

Toward the latter part of this fieldwork I received a letter from a colleague who was a researcher at the National Institute of Mental Health (NIMH), who wondered if I would be interested in participating in a pilot research program at the NIMH attempting to find cases of neuropsychiatric disorders in the developing world. The impetus for this research was the then-recent finding about the pediatric autoimmune neuropsychiatric disorders associated with streptococcus infection, also known as the PANDAS hypothesis. Briefly, this was a theory that some cases of specific neuropsychiatric disorders, such as obsessive-compulsive disorder and Tourette Syndrome, had their origins in multiple streptococcus infections in children who were genetically predisposed. The research team believed that in a place like Indonesia, with high rates of infectious diseases, it should be possible to find cases of neuro-psychiatric disorders, and then link these back to elements related to the PANDAS hypothesis.

After multiple presentations were made to local psychiatric professionals about this research, one of the local psychiatrists, I Gusti Putu Panteri, who ran a private psychiatric hospital in Denpasar, Bali, approached me about collaborating on this project. He had been in practice for decades and had an extensively documented clinical caseload; several dozen of these patients were identified who fit the NIMH criteria. We then spent six months re-contacting these patients in their villages scattered throughout Bali.

Several months into this new research project, a friend and graduate student in anthropology who had some experience in the film world, came to Bali to stay with my family for several weeks. We agreed she would film me conducting my fieldwork. Beyond that, I did not give much thought to how I might use these films.

In the following few weeks, we gathered approximately thirty-five to forty hours of video with a dozen or so of my research subjects. Some of these were truncated interviews shot largely for their visual quality, while others were more complete ethnographic interviews. Upon returning to the United States, I put the videos aside and spent the next year and a half completing my dissertation. While writing, I was contacted by a young Javanese psychiatrist, Mahar Agusno, and his wife, psychologist, and English teacher, Ninik Supartini, who were interested in my research and potential collaboration.

After finishing my dissertation in 1999, I started a project with a genet-icist who was exploring various aspects of the genetic basis of common neuropsychiatric disorders. She was interested in finding cases of Tourette disorder in Indonesia. My collaborators Mahar and Ninik assisted us with this project, initially collecting cases drawn from Mahar's clinical case log and then conducting a community-based study to find additional cases by going through villages in Gunung Kidul, a poor region of Central Java where Ninik was from and where many in her extended family still resided. Mahar had just finished his residency in psychiatry, which had required him to serve a large region of rural South-Central Java. This made him the ideal person to do the required community surveys. In late 1999 and early 2000, they conducted a detailed survey of several regencies. Mahar and Ninik videotaped some of their subjects for research purposes. The genetics project soon foundered due to a lack of funding, but the anthropological project, which was a logical extension of my work in Bali, continued.

At this point, I also began teaching at UCLA, and I thought about the thirty-five to forty hours of film footage gathered in 1997. Around the same time, a young documentary filmmaker approached me, to give my anthropological opinion of a recent film he was directing. I thought the material and his approach interesting, and asked if he was able to work with me on editing the footage I had into small teaching pieces, for my classes. He agreed, and we produced several short videos. They turned out to be a big success with my students, and I decided to go back to Indonesia, re-contact the people in the footage, and follow them up, both for research and to expand upon the teaching films.

In the summer of 2000 I therefore returned to both Bali and Java. In addition to the young documentary filmmaker, I worked closely with Wayan Sadha, a cartoonist and journalist who provided an indispensable lens into the daily life of the average Balinese, and later with his daughter Sri. Unfortunately my collaborator on the neuropsychiatric research, Dr. Panteri, had had a stroke in 1999, making collaboration difficult. I was also able to work with Dr. Made Nyandra, a much younger Balinese psychiatrist "on his way up." As a Christian, Dr. Nyandra offered some interesting perspectives on the dominant Balinese Hindu community. In Java, my initial collaboration with Mahar and Ninik deepened into what became my closest and most longstanding professional relationship and friendship in Indonesia. I discovered that Mahar was deeply interested in the interplay between Javanese and Indonesian culture and the experience and outcomes of the people living with the different forms of mental illness he was treating on a daily basis. Ninik, as a psychologist with an interest in cultural psychology, provided great insight into many different aspects of Javanese culture.

In these early years, however, my understanding of film and filmmaking was still rather minimal. Having grown up on a television diet of documentaries made in the 1960s and 1970s, ranging from Mike Wallace's *Biography* series, to the Mutual of Omaha's *Wild Kingdom* and *National Geographic* specials, I had a very naïve understanding of just what good cinema or good documentary, let alone good ethnographic film, entailed. As an undergraduate and graduate student in anthropology I had been exposed to the typical if rather sparse set of classic ethnographic films, from John Marshall's

The Hunters to Timothy Asch's *A Man called Bee* and *The Ax Fight*, a range of other ethnographic snippets, typically focused on some aspect of technology, subsistence, or ritual life; and the occasional more complex film, such as *Ongka's Big Moka*. But my understanding of films was largely gained through watching and discussing them with my friends, and through the general diffusion of knowledge that permeates life in Los Angeles, where so many work in the film industry.

At this early stage, in 2000, I did not foresee the visual ethnography becoming extended beyond short teaching pieces. I simply hoped that if I could visually document the lives of my participants, this might bring my students into the world I was immersed in as an ethnographic researcher. Accordingly, as I traveled in Bali and Java continuing my ethnographic explorations of culture and mental illness, I saw the camera as little more than "an extension of my eyes," recording my ethnographic encounters while documenting the rich cultural life of the communities in Bali and Java.

In the following years, my experience, ambition, and love of filmmaking grew. I returned to Indonesia every year once or twice a year for two to four weeks at a time to continue this work. In the intervening months, footage would be edited and assembled into basic narratives; as I first began making teaching films with the materials shot, I designed the structure of the films around key research topics of interest in the field, such as cultural differences in the symptomatology and expression of illness, rather than around individuals or their personal stories and what was of primary interest to *them* in their lives. Yet, through filming subjects on repeated trips, I developed deeper relationships with the participants. Through these relationships I began forming a new understanding of the issues brought to the field with research question and hypotheses; ultimately, I realized that the footage collected was full of interesting *personal* stories, and that these stories eloquently articulated not just themes of my original research but wider issues in psychological anthropology.

With each successive shoot, my interest in film and filmmaking deepened and widened. Over the next five years or so, I began to read more extensively about film theory, the history of ethnographic film, explorations in storytelling, narrative, and character development, and many of the related technical issues involved in contemporary filmmaking. My understanding of what "good filmmaking"—and more specifically, good storytelling and good narration—entailed became more informed and nuanced.

Much has been made of the "Cambridge turn" in ethnographic film, and certainly a number of visionary filmmakers and anthropologists have come out of the Boston area. Los Angeles is much less known as a center for ethnographic filmmaking. This is somewhat odd, as UCLA has an esteemed anthropology program and a famous film school, while USC has the visual anthropology program initially founded by Timothy Asch, which remains a rich source of young ethnographic filmmakers. Outside of these centers for training in ethnographic film, Los Angeles is also of course a global center of the film industry. Yet relatively few, if any, anthropologists have turned toward the film industry here as a resource or a source of knowledge, let alone inspiration or collaboration. In any case, it was not difficult for me to find thoughtful professionals in the film industry with an interest in ethnographic film; some had taken courses in anthropology or even had degrees in visual anthropology. Independent filmmakers in particular can share concerns with anthropologists, committed as they often are to "telling the truth," about the difficulties of contemporary life and including the voices and stories of those not included in mainstream films.

In 2006 I founded the documentary production company Elemental Productions, and have finished over a dozen films: *40 Years Of Silence: An Indonesian Tragedy* (2009) about the long-term effects of the 1965–1966 mass killings; the six films in the *Afflictions* series (2010–2011); *Jathilan* (2011), a film about possession performance; *Ngaben: Emotion and Restraint in a Balinese Heart* (2012), addressing the personal experience of funerary ritual; *Standing on the Edge of a Thorn* (2012), a film about the complicated pathways to sex work implicating personal vulnerability and social response; *Bitter Honey* (2014), a film about polygamy and gender-based violence in Bali; and finally *Tajen* (2015), on the Balinese cockfight, and other audio-visual projects, with additional projects in various stages of pre-production or production.

In 2009 I hired a graduate student, Annie Tucker, as a research assistant and writer to help develop study guides for the films. Annie received her PhD at UCLA in 2015, researching the interpretation and treatment of autism spectrum disorder in Java; her training in Disability Studies, experience living, working, and conducting research in Indonesia, and her fluent Bahasa Indonesia made her a natural fit as a collaborator. She is the second author of this book.

Through all of this, the project, most longstanding, foundational, and closest to my heart, stems from the original research on culture and mental illness in Bali and Java—the six films of the *Afflictions* series,[1] which are the subject of this book. One of the main purposes of this book is to complement the stories told and themes explored in the *Afflictions* series with both a deep dive into a written ethnography and more practical guidelines about filmmaking in general. While there are often linkages between ethnography proper and ethnographic film on the same subject, works that specifically link the two are quite rare. Even rarer are efforts to not only connect these two but toprovide descriptive, reflexive accounts of the projects themselves, and the related issues of film production, issues of ethics and participant/collaborator/team relationships, and finally to advocate for film as a potentially equal partner to classic ethnography.

This bringing together of ethnographic film and the concerns and domains of psychological anthropology we term "visual psychological anthropology".

One of the stated goals of a visual psychological anthropology is the rendering of textured, person-centered life history narrative that instantiates these elements into a multi-sensory expression that feels "lived" to the viewer. Another is to connect the domains and the theory in psychological anthropology to the actual lives of participants in our research, and embed these in understandable and emotional stories. Tracking these themes and story, over time, is also key. Linking the visual aspect to the written work, so that each complement and add to each other, further strengthens this new endeavor. Integrating the visual, whether whole films, scenes and clips, or related material, with the written in an interactive digital format helps bring together the fields of ethnographic film and psychological anthropology. Another, more distal goal is to make the research of psychological anthropology available to a much larger, public audience, through the medium of film. This book attempts to address all of these issues.

NOTE

1. The films are available, for a discount to purchasers of this book, at www.elementalproductions.org

SERIES PREFACE

Psychological anthropologists study a wide spectrum of human activity: child development, illness and healing, ritual and religion, selfhood and personality, political and economic systems, just to name a few. In fact, as a discipline that seeks to draw the lines connecting persons and culture, it would be difficult to come up with examples of human behavior that fall outside the purview of psychological anthropology. Yet beneath this substantive diversity lies a common commitment. The practitioners of psychological anthropology seek to answer broad questions about how peoples' inner worlds are interwoven with their outer ones. And while psychological anthropologists may focus on emotions or human biology, on language or art or dreams, they rarely stray far from the attempt to understand the mental and physical possibilities and limitations that ground human experience.

Afflictions: Steps Toward a Visual Psychological Anthropology is a companion to the *Afflictions* film series, six ethnographic films about the experience of mental illness in various cultural settings in Indonesia. In proposing visual psychological anthropology, the authors introduce a sub-discipline centered on the implications of film for theory, ethnography, and the lives of the subjects who anthropologists study. As in much anthropology, the present book works simultaneously on two levels. The chapters here reflect both on the films in the series and on broader questions about ethnographic film, anthropology, and the practical and ethical implications of films that depict mental illness. The authors are attuned—among other issues—to the humanizing possibilities of films that remind us that their subjects are examples neither of a particular culture nor of a diagnosis, but rather that they are human beings with day-to-day lives in families and communities. Overall, these chapters serve to consolidate and welcome a new area of inquiry in psychological anthropology, one that will undoubtedly help to determine the direction of the field in the coming years.

Tulsa, OK   Peter G. Stromberg
USA   Editor of *Culture, Mind, and Society*

Acknowledgments

In a project that spans twenty years, in the research, the film, and the written form, there are many people to acknowledge and thank.

First my writing partner and friend, Anne Tucker, always a source of steady and calm good feelings, combined with hard work and brilliance as a scholar. *Rajin pangkal pandai*. Thank you.

The following organizations for their assistance in getting the research accomplished and guidance along the way: the American-Indonesian Exchange Foundation, the Foundation for Psychocultural Research, the Indonesian Consulate General, Los Angeles, the Indonesian Department of Health, the JW Fulbright Foreign Scholarship Board, Lembaga Ilmu Pengetahuan Indonesia, the National Institute of Mental Health, Rumah Sakit Jiwa Bangli, Rumah Sakit Jiwa Magelang, Rumah Sakit Umum Wangaya, the Society for Psychological Anthropology, the Society for the Study of Psychiatry and Culture, the UCLA Department of Anthropology, the UCLA Medicine, Mind and Culture Group, the UCLA International Studies Overseas Program, Udayana University Department of Psychiatry, USC Center for Visual Anthropology, and the World Health Organization.

Thanks to the copy editor of this work, Anne Greenberger.

I would like to thank my psychiatric colleagues in Bali—I Made Nyandra, I Gusti Nyoman Sastradi, Ni Anak Agung Indriani, and I Gusti Nyoman Mahayasa, especially my two main colleagues I Gusti Putu Panteri and Luh Ketut Suryani, without whom this project would never have started.

To Judith Rapoport and Allan Fiske for helping launch the neuropsychiatric research component.

I would like to thank the people I have worked with in the many phases of the film production, both in the United States and Indonesia. Kathy Huang, Darwin Nugraha, Carolyn Rouse, Mieke Douridas, Luis Lopez, Luh Putu Artini, Anak Agung Indra Kusuma, Darwin Nugraha, Luis Lopez, Rachmi Diyah Larasati, Leslie Dwyer, Ayu Martiani, Degung Santikarma, Anak Agung Gede Putra, Agung Alit, Anak Agung Ngurah Termana, Juliana Wijaya, Upadi Yuliatmo, and Handi Ilfat.

Thanks to Dag Yngvesson and Wing Ko, for all the work they put in as directors of photography and other work related to *Afflictions*. And to my first mentor in anthropology, Barbara Yngvesson.

On the Elemental stateside, I would like to thank my long (and shorter) term staff Yee Ie, Putu Robin Geni Wijaya, Alessandra Pasquino, Riawaty Jap, Putu Surmiasih, Chin Rodger, Briana Young, Emily Ng, Martha Stroud, Yulin Sun, and Irine Prastio.

To the *Afflictions* composer Malcolm Cross, for his phenomenal scores, and to music editor and friend Richard Henderson, for our long discussions about R. Crumb and Frank Zappa. Also for Pak Nyoman Wenten, for bringing the complexity of Balinese music to our soundtrack.

Editors are the unsung heros of filmmaking, and I would like to thank Sandra Angeline, Heidi Zimmerman, Herbert Bennett, and Michael Mallen for their work editing *Afflictions*.

In particular, I would like to thank my long-time editor Chisako Yokoyama for her effort not just on *Afflictions*, but also on other related projects. And to my friend and consulting editor Pietro Scalia—strength and honor.

To my friends and colleagues Mahar Agusno and Ninik Supartini, for many years of dedicated work and close abiding friendship.

To my numerous colleagues and friends in the Department of Anthropology at UCLA and beyond who have given me guidance and feedback over the years on this emergent project, including Mary-Jo DelVecchio Good, Byron Good, Cameron Hay-Rollins, Alex Hinton, Jason Throop, Devon Hinton, Janet Hoskins, Laurence Kirmayer, Hildred Geertz, Abby Ruddick, Unni Wikan, Eileen Anderson-Fye, Jill Korbin, Tom Weisner, Jason Throop, Aomar Boum, Linda Garro, Carol Worthman, Mel Konner, Gilbert Herdt, Rick Shweder, Geoff Robinson, Deena Newman, Charles Stewart, Romo Baskara Wardaya, Adrian Vickers Alan Tobin, and Emeran Mayer.

My long-time colleagues at The Foundation for Psychocultural Research: Connie Cummings, Mamie Wong, and Irene Sukwandi; and the Board of the FPR: Beate Ritz, Marie Françoise Chesselet, Douglas Hollan, Marvin Karno, Steve López, Carole Browner, and Marjorie Kagawa-Singer. All with very great affection. I am most lucky to have such a committed and wonderful board, and most particularly staff, as I have had for these many years.

To Peter Singer, for friendship in the time remaining to both of us.

To my dearest of friends and wise advisor Caitlin Mullin whose loss is still felt most keenly.

To Wayan Sadha, my best friend in Bali. *Saya merasa kehilangan kamu.* And his daughter Ni Luh Gede Sri Pratiwi, for many years of friendship. And to Nyoman Asug, for our long talks while driving. To Made Reni and Ketut, for lifelong friendship. *Saya merasa kehilangan kamu juga, Bu Made.*

Special thanks are due to the participants of the films in the *Afflictions* series. Ni Ketut Kasih, Nyoman Kereta, Bambang Rujito, Gusti Ayu Suartini, I Wayan Yoga Adi Suwarduana, Estu Wardhani, and their respective families to whom I have an abiding respect and gratitude.

To my dissertation committee Robert Edgerton, Allen Johnson, and particularly Douglas Hollan and Marvin Karno for mentorship and abiding friendship.

To Shihan Tsutomu Ohshima, and my seniors at Shotokan Karate of America, especially Marion Taylor and Brian Maeda, who taught me the meaning of "The Way- who will pass it on straight and well".

To my friends in Los Angeles (and elsewhere), but especially to Sam Nichols, David Yoshimaru, David Hertz, Stewart Norman, and Mike Massey for enduring friendship.

To my mother, Dorothy Lemelson, to whom this book is dedicated, brother Eric, and nephew Jeremiah and his mom Jennifer Bruml.

To the rest of my large and supportive family.

To my children Noah and Zoe, the source of my joy, love, and respect, and their mother Susan Morse who helped raise these amazing people.

To my beautiful, brilliant, and always sweet and supportive wife Seinenu Thein, without whom this book would not have been written.

As always, to the memory of my father Jerome Hal Lemelson.

Anne Tucker would like to thank her co-writer Robert Lemelson for his ongoing mentorship and enduring support. She would also like to thank

Constance Cummings, Mamie Wong, and Yee Ie for their crucial feedback and assistance during the preparation of this book.

Both authors would like to thank Rachel Krause and Kyra Saniewski, our editors at Palgrave, and Peter Stromberg, the series editor for the Culture, Mind, and Society series, for ushering the book to publication. We would also like to thank our anonymous reviewer, whose comments and suggestion provided us the opportunity to clarify and expand certain key aspects of our arguments.

CONTENTS

LIST OF ABBREVIATIONS

AAA	American Anthropological Association
ADHD	attention deficit/hyperactivity disorder
APA	American Psychiatric Association
B.B.	Bahasa Bali
B.I.	Bahasa Indonesia
B.J.	Bahasa Java
BGTC	basal-ganglia-thalamocortical circuits
CBT	cognitive behavioral therapy
CD	compact disc
CSTC	cortico-striatal-thalamo-cortical pathways
DER	Documentary Educational Resources
DOSMD	determinants of outcome of severe mental disorder
DSLR	digital single lens reflex
DSM	*Diagnostic and Statistical Manual of Mental Disorders*
DVD	digital versatile disc or digital video disc
ECT	electroconvulsant therapy
EE	expressed emotion
fMRI	functional magnetic resonance imaging
HIV	human immunodeficiency virus
ICD	International Classification of Diseases
IDA	International Documentary Association
IPSS	International Pilot Study of Schizophrenia
IRB	Institutional Review Board
KPSI	Keluarga Pasien Schizofrenia Indonesia??
KPSI	Komunitas Peduli Skizofrenia Indonesia??
MMAC	Medicine, Mind, and Culture, at UCLA

NAMI	National Alliance on Mental Illness
NGO	non-governmental organization
NIMH	National Institute of Mental Health
OCD	obsessive-compulsive disorder
OK	okay
PANDAS	pediatric autoimmune neuropsychiatric disorder
PCE	person-centered ethnography
PKI	Indonesian Communist Party
PKI	Partai Komunis Indonesia
PKK	*Pembinaan Kesejahteraan Keluarga*
PLOS	Public Library of Science
PNI	Indonesian Nationalist Party
PPDGJ	Pedoman Penggolongan dan Diagnosis Gangguan Jiwa
PSE	Present Status Exam
PTSD	posttraumatic stress disorder
RAID	redundant array of independent disks
RSJM	Rumah Sakit Jiwa Magelang
SSRI	selective serotonin reuptake inhibitor
SVA	Society for Visual Anthropology
TS	Tourette Syndrome
UCLA	University of California, Los Angeles
USC	University of Southern California
VPCE	visual person-centered ethnography
WHO	World Health Organization

LIST OF FIGURES

PART I

Steps Towards a Visual Psychological Anthropology

Photo 1 Arjuna meditates, beset by beautiful women (From the Mead Bateson collection)

CHAPTER 1

Visual Psychological Anthropology: A Vignette and Prospectus

1.1 THE MULTIPLE AFFLICTIONS OF GUSTI AYU, "THE BIRD DANCER"

Surrounded by her family, Ni Gusti Ayu Suartini sat cross-legged on the front veranda of her house in rural Central Bali. She was being shot on video by a cameraman and interviewed by a foreign anthropologist and an Indonesian psychiatrist. It was the year 2000, and three years had passed since the anthropologist had originally interviewed her. Gusti did not look well. A baggy red t-shirt swallowed her slight frame and her hair, which had once been shoulder length, was shorn, practically down to the scalp. Her forehead and arms were covered with scabs. At times seeming shy but curious and other times looking down at the floor despondently, Gusti began to tell her story to the small research team and film crew, as her family chimed in.

Gusti looked self-conscious and uncomfortable as her siblings urgently described how Gusti shouted dirty words, seemed compelled to hit herself, moved her body in strange ways, and most troubling, frequently spit copious amounts of saliva. The neighbors called her crazy, possessed, or cursed. Her mysterious illness was embarrassing to her family and shamed them deeply. They believed Gusti had damaged the family's reputation, hurting their own chances of finding marriage partners, and brought financial misfortune. Quietly, Gusti asserted that she had no control over her behavior, but she joined her family in begging for a cure. Even though Gusti had been formally diagnosed with Tourette Syndrome by a respected Balinese psychiatrist several years previously and prescribed medication, she and

© The Author(s) 2017
R. Lemelson, A. Tucker, *Afflictions*, Culture, Mind, and Society,
DOI 10.1007/978-3-319-59984-7_1

her family struggled with what her disorder meant and how to respond to it, and desperately wished it would just go away.

During follow-up ethnographic fieldwork and videography over the course of many years, Gusti continued to struggle, sometimes saying that she felt she was disgusting and even asking for help committing suicide. As time passed, however, and she continued to search for satisfying explanations and effective cures for her disorder, she also began to distance herself from the social environment that excluded, rejected, and devalued her. Gusti left her natal village and established friendships with peers who were not bothered by her symptoms; she gained self-confidence and self-worth; she found work. Her life began to change and she had ongoing conversations, both on- and off-screen, about these changes.

Almost two decades after she first joined the research and filming project, in a smart white blouse, Gusti set out from her hotel room in Indonesia's capital city of Jakarta, making her way through a bustling landscape of escalators, taxicabs, and skyscrapers toward a packed screening room on the campus of the illustrious University of Indonesia. Together, Gusti and the audience of students, professors, clinicians, counselors, and community members watched *The Bird Dancer* (Lemelson 2010a), a film about her life that located her struggles not just in her bizarre symptoms, but in her social world. After the screening, Gusti sat on a panel for a Q&A session. With a firm voice that still showed a hint of her original shyness, Gusti used a pointed metaphor to describe how she believed prevalent attitudes toward people with neuropsychiatric disorders and mental illness could be re-oriented. She said:

> Let's say you have eight eggs, and one looks rotten from the outside, but on the inside this egg is actually just fine, not rotten at all, then how do you solve this problem to make sure you don't throw it away by mistake? Because the owner of this particular egg really cares about it.

In a person-centered interview in 2009, Gusti sat in the hot Balinese sun, in a friend's courtyard, and talked about her life and its recent twists and turns. Gusti had made several good friends, people she could "share her heart" with (B.I. *mencurahkan isi hati*). She said:

> If I think about it, now it seems better, because I found work and so I'm free from the house. I wasn't so happy at home, often hearing things from people in the village, you know, insulting me. Now I have a job here, I have many friends. I'm so happy.

At this point, Gusti had been involved in longitudinal visual ethnographic research on mental illness and neuropsychiatric disorder for almost twenty years. This project was an experiment in what could be called visual psychological anthropology, an effort to bring the topics and insights of psychological anthropology to bear upon ethnographic film. While the research team and film crew were working toward developing this approach, Gusti had been filmed going about her daily tasks, having painful and contentious discussions with her family, addressing existential and spiritual concerns about her life and her condition, daydreaming about finding a true love, and growing into her new identity as an activist for people with Tourette Syndrome and other neuropsychiatric disabilities. Representative moments from parts of her entire adult life had been captured on film and edited into a feature-length visual ethnography which has been screened not only at the event in Jakarta, but first privately for Gusti and her immediate family, then her village community, Indonesian mental health advocacy organizations, universities, conferences, and film festivals in Indonesia, the United States, and beyond. The changes in her life have been profound, as she transformed from a depressed and outcast teenager into a self-assured and self-advocating woman.

This impact on Gusti's life would probably not have resulted from participating in a standard written ethnographic project that could be written, read, and disseminated without her participation, understanding, or input. Nor would the film have become what it was—or reached such a wide audience—without learning with and from Gusti about her life and following her lead as to how it should be represented on-screen. She was an active participant in shaping the evolving understanding of her story, quietly but emphatically moving away from an early narrow focus on her symptoms to a much more complete investigation of her compelling life concerns. The experience of filming Gusti taught invaluable lessons about developing relationships with subjects, understanding their life histories, and representing their stories in a sensitive and empathetic manner. The collaborative and bidirectional process of shaping this initial film about Gusti was a powerful experience, and—because of the visual element—one for which there were few precedents in psychological anthropology, but the process revealed much about the practice and application of the discipline. To most fully understand not only Gusti's subjective and inflected reality but also how this was both influenced by and influential to the *Afflictions* film project,[1] one needs to understand the history and theory of visual psychological anthropology.

1.2   Ethnographic Film and Psychological Anthropology: Points of Connection and Disjuncture

Psychological anthropology is the subfield of anthropology concerned with the intersection of the psychological and the cultural. This fundamental focus undergirds the exploration of a diverse range of topics including perception, emotion, personality, mental illness, extraordinary psychological experience, and child development. Psychological anthropology has deep roots in the broader field of anthropology; indeed, some early eminent anthropologists at a number of anthropology departments throughout the United States had an interest in issues still relevant to contemporary psychological anthropologists. For example, Irving Hallowell, one of the founders of the University of Pennsylvania anthropology department, was explicitly concerned with issues of self and identity central to the exploration of the "Culture and Personality" school, an earlier formulation of psychological anthropology. Cora Dubois (the first tenured female faculty in Harvard's anthropology department) collaborated with psychiatrist Abram Kardiner to explore culture and psychopathology, and later went on to do groundbreaking fieldwork in the Dutch East Indies (now Indonesia), utilizing psychological tests and interviewing to explore culture and "temperament." Walter Goldschmidt and Robert Edgerton, founders of the UCLA anthropology department, were psychological anthropologists who explored a broad spectrum of topics, including the self and identity, subsistence practices and personality, deviance, and stigma. And finally Margaret Mead, inarguably the most famous American anthropologist, studied adolescent development, mental illness, sexuality, and infant care and development and experimented with visual approaches in her investigations. These founding "ancestors" had many students whose research and careers brought about the development of contemporary psychological anthropology (R. Shweder, address at Society for Psychological Anthropology (SPA) annual meeting 2017).

The research described in this book was deeply influenced by this history of psychological anthropology and grows out of the basic theoretical and methodological concerns of the field. These concerns now arguably suffuse the entire discipline of cultural anthropology to a greater or lesser extent with broader and ongoing investigations of empathy, care, "the suffering subject," and the "anthropology of the good" (Robbins 2013). The visual component of the research—encompassing videography, films, and still photography—began in the late 1990s, right on the cusp of the digital film revolution, and has continued for almost two decades. It has witnessed the rise of affordable handheld personal camcorders, and more recently video-enabled mobile phones, social media, streaming content, and more. In part, therefore, the visual aspect of this research traces the stunning changes in and widespread accessibility of film and visual materials in everyday life. More pointedly, it traces some of the developments of visual methods in the field of anthropology and provides material with which to think through some of the significant questions and debates in visual anthropology and ethnographic film, in particular: How should film and video be used in psychological anthropological research, if it is to be used at all? What makes a film ethnographic and what counts as ethnographic film, when making films about mental illness, neuropsychiatric disorder, or other concerns relevant to psychological anthropology? What are the benefits and risks in different methodologies of filmmaking—be they observational, representational, illustrative, sensory, etc.? And finally, if one is to take film seriously as a medium that can both capture and convey cultural information and that is always at once a record of and a discourse about culture, what strategies and techniques might best enact the theories that the ethnographers or filmmakers are attempting to illuminate in their work? Are some of these strategies and techniques more prescient for psychological anthropology in particular? These questions are relevant to a number of sub-disciplines in anthropology—visual, medical, psychological, and critical ethnography studies, for example—but are not restricted to the central issues in those specific subdisciplines; rather, they hone in on the points of overlap and resonance, but also the disjunctures, interstitial zones, and disagreement between them, and most particularly the voids and spaces yet to be fully articulated or theorized.

Put most simply, the question this book seeks to answer is: What can ethnographic film offer psychological anthropology and what can the theories and methods of psychological anthropology offer ethnographic film? This introduction sketches out some provisional answers. The rest of the book will delve much deeper into the methodology of making visual psychological anthropology and the issues that arise during the process to come up with fruitful synergistic practices at the intersection of visual and psychological anthropology, encapsulated in what could be called visual psychological anthropology.

A visual approach toward domains specific to psychological anthropology distinguishes itself from either visual anthropology or psychological anthropology significantly enough to warrant designation as a unique intersectional subfield of both. Take, for example, the study of mental illness. While psychological anthropology proper has explored this domain in great detail and complexity, visual representations from a cross-cultural perspective are extremely scarce, and few come specifically from the concerns of psychological anthropology.

But the relationship between the visual and psychological subfields of anthropology cultivated in visual psychological anthropology is more reciprocal than simply bringing visuals to the field of psychological anthropology. It also explicitly incorporates the foci, theory, and methods developed in psychological anthropology within its visual strategy. As this book will demonstrate, psychological anthropology's increasing focus on the subjective, phenomenological, intrapsychic, and intersubjective aspects of experience opens up a range of visual approaches not often utilized in ethnographic film that focus on character, narrative, and emotion. With its focus on character development and the dramatic presentation of the conflicts and concerns in a character's life, visual psychological anthropology meshes well with compelling mainstream cinematic conventions and styles. Its related focus on more vivid and emotional representation of an individual and their context allows for the creative integration of cinematic elements such as soundtracks, dramatic arcs, and creative editing approaches. These elements link the psychological anthropological research, the visual storytelling, and the content of the stories themselves to create descriptive and affective ethnographic films.

1.3   Visual Psychological Anthropology and Ethnography

We begin to see that visual psychological anthropology is a unique endeavor within filmmaking, one more specialized than making films about individuals, as many canonical ethnographic films are (from *Nanook* [Flaherty 1922] to *N!ai* [Marshall 1980]), and more specific than making films with a powerful affective or emotional element, as many contemporary ethnographic films have, no matter their particular topical focus (such as cultural confrontation between Australians and native peoples in the highland of New Guinea in *First Contact* [Connolly and Anderson 1983] or trauma and loss in the "lost boys" of the Sudan in *Benjamin and his Brother* [Howes 2002]). While we will argue, particularly in Chap. 2, that such films are in fact an additional resource to the study of psychological anthropology and advocate for better incorporating them into the subfield's curriculum as such, we go beyond this exhortation to flesh out a distinct approach toward filmmaking.

One key aspect of visual psychological anthropology is its incorporation of tried-and-true methodology in psychological anthropology. This begins with espousing and adapting the methodology of "person-centered" ethnography developed in the field of psychological anthropology in the 1970s–1990s by anthropologists such as Robert Levy and Douglas Hollan (Levy 1973; Levy and Hollan 1998), and still prevalent in the field up until the present. Derived from techniques in both psychiatry and psychoanalysis, person-centered ethnography (PCE) is both a methodologically and theoretically distinct process from other forms of interviewing and data gathering in anthropology. Methodologically, PCE involves a number of approaches and techniques. One is long-term interviewing, engaging with the subject for an hour or more, weekly or monthly over the course of months, or even years. The interviews themselves, while directed and focused on particular domains outlined in their Checklist of Open-Interview topics, are generally open-ended, subject-driven and non-directive. Theoretically, the interviews and material gathered have a focus on the internal, emotional, embodied, and idiosyncratic subjective meaning for the interviewee, while situating these meanings and experiences in a particular cultural setting. In addition, PCE focuses not only on phenomenological and experiential meaning for the participant themselves, but on psychoanalytically based concepts such as defense mechanisms, parapraxes, transference, and countertransference. At the end of this inductive approach, a complex, multileveled, individualized account of a particular subject in a particular cultural place and time emerges. In terms of subject matter, Levy and Hollan's form of PCE is extremely wide ranging, exploring issues such as childhood experience, key relationships, dreams, and adolescence (Levy and Hollan 1998).

Person-centered ethnography, with its focus on open-ended interviews done over months or even years, allows for more textured unfolding of personal issues that can be analyzed utilizing the interpretive tools and methods of psychological anthropology. In a review of the current state of PCE near the turn of the new millennium, Douglas Hollan outlined the three general kinds of PCEs being made: there were those that primarily focused on what people *say* about their subjective experience, those that focused on what people *do* that behaviorally enacts their subjective experience, and those exploring how people *embody* their subjective experience (Hollan 1997). He noted that the first of these were overrepresented in the field, and called for more ethnographies addressing the latter two.

Ironically, though, even as person-centered methodology has pushed ethnographers to observe and attend to more than what people can say verbally by focusing on or cross-checking with bodies and behavior, the medium has not intersected much with the visual. This format of research presentation is limited in the same ways that focusing only on what respondents say is limited: Written ethnographies excel at "telling" and can cause readers to reflect, empathize with another's experience, and at times feel something deeply emotional while taking in the material. Visual methods, on the other hand, can communicate information about what people do or how they embody their experience much more directly; a viewer can experience some of this visually, aurally, kinesthetically (Foster 2010), and, still most importantly, emotionally.

Visual representation complements other research methods when it comes to recording body mechanics and analyzing how these mechanics relate to emotional expression and social communication; film specifically can capture crucial elements of this expression such as sequencing, speed, and rhythm. Some ethnographic filmmakers have focused on body language in their work, both capturing physical behavior as data and editing this material into films to illustrate key aspects of social organization, interpersonal relationships, and embodied habitus. For example, in John Marshall's film *A Joking Relationship* (1962), the subjects are framed in extreme closeups, emphasizing body language to the exclusion of other information, a strategy used to convey the casual intimacy between a particular young wife and her great-uncle in a ritualized Ju/'hoan kinship form.

Yet, while moving images have been incorporated somewhat into the fieldwork and data collection and analysis process, editing these moving images into narrative films has been viewed with suspicion in anthropology. So perhaps in advocating for the extension of PCE into the visual realm, it is helpful to review certain basic key components of PCE in relation to adaptation or application for visual or film work.

One main principle of PCE is that it takes the individual as the point of reference and the vessel of understanding; rather than providing an overview of a culture or community study, person-centered ethnographers want to know what it feels like to live as an individual in a particular cultural setting. The natural extension of this principle into film work is to have a single participant or, in film terms, the "main character," who is understood as a unique individual, with his or her own particular history, strengths, challenges, beliefs, idiosyncrasies, etc. In fulfilling this principle, it might be that film complements written material in a variety of ways. Taylor (1998, 535) says:

> [E] thnographic film is tied to the particularities of the person before it is to the generalities of culture [...] While film's reticence about culture has tended to be a source of frustration for (and so cause for its disparagement by) word-oriented anthropologists, its indexical attachment to its subject prevents it from playing fast and loose with the person in ways that are par for the course with expository prose.

Furthermore, PCE always strives to be "experience near": In other words, description and analysis try to remain as faithful as possible to the sensations and meanings and lived experience of the individual, rather than getting too abstract and theoretical, coming to conclusions that might make elegant academic points but would not be relevant to life as lived. As such, any "statement" an anthropologist is making needs the "supporting testimony of a tangible person or persons to whom such a statement is of real value in his system of interrelationship with other beings" (Sapir 1958, 574).

Being oriented toward individual experience has meant taking emotion seriously and forefronting it in ethnographic inquiry and representation, moving past interpretivist approaches and deconstructing the idea of "objectivity" in the field, and advocating for a more affective and "forceful" anthropology (Rosaldo 1989). Film can illustrate the interplay of emotions as individuals interact, but the viewer can also take in the play of emotions on the faces of the subjects as they subtly shift or change. From an ethnographic standpoint, the effects of cultural shaping of emotional experience and its expression make this interpretive process—parsing out, for example, what is either universal or culturally specific in emotional expression and experience, and the individual variation therein—a more complex, subtle, and rich experience in the mind of the viewer.

Another emphasis in PCE has been gathering and analyzing internal, deeply felt, and at times ineffable worlds—dreams, sensations, fantasies, and memories. Visual methods provide another avenue to realize the mission of psychological anthropology in accessing and presenting such content, because rather than simply interviewing people about these internal worlds, the visual anthropologist can use creative and multimodal sensory film techniques to evoke, re-create, or re-enact them. While ethnographers have always engaged the senses throughout fieldwork, filming can capture visual attention and interest in new, different, and at times unexpected ways, from individual shot composition to scene construction.

Along with these foci on elements of the research participants' experience, PCE has also taken the intersubjective aspects of fieldwork seriously, reflexively considering the anthropologist's own feelings and reactions to fieldwork and including these in the presentation. Psychological anthropologists strive to be aware of emotional engagement, relationships, and the shifting intersubjective reality as an integral part of the ethnographic process that should be accounted for in methodology and research results. They also seek to understand the relationship between subjective experience and social, cultural, and political economic contexts, including the context of the interview or research setting itself (Lutz 1988). Film is a vehicle for offering up more of the research setting for scrutiny, directly depicting the anthropologist at work.

1.4   Making Films About Culture and Mental Illness: From Symptomatology Toward Lived Human Experience

So, a person-centered ethnographic film would depict individuals, evoking their lived experience, taking their emotions seriously as a fundamental aspect of meaning-making, and creatively bringing their internal worlds to light while being transparent about the fieldwork process. But what about making such films specifically to explore the lived experience of very specific domains, in particular that of mental illness in a cultural context?

Prior to and aside from visual methods, psychological anthropology and PCE methodology in particular are crucial to understanding the cultural contexts and lived experiences of mental illness and neuropsychiatric disorders. Specifically, PCE provides a framework for embodiment and sensation, crucial for understanding the way the sensorial system is impacted by processes of mental illness; similarly, its focus on emotion helps analyze the experience of emotional dysregulation common to many neuropsychiatric and mood disorders. Its attention to dreams, fantasies, and personal symbolic systems provides insight into the ways these impact individuals in the interpretation of their illness and the progression of their illness experience and personal lives, and an emphasis on intersubjectivity deepens the contextual field to include not just cultural but also interpersonal elements.

Integrating all this into film presents a number of challenges. One challenge is balancing the subjective, experiential, and phenomenological concerns of the participants with clinical, research, and contextual domains, but while doing so, avoiding simplifying and objectifying the film participants as representatives of a disease category. How can the lived experience and the particularities of any one individual be best represented? How might deepening relationships and deepening understanding of the film participants as people and not just "case studies" be represented?

A second challenge is situating these issues within a film that meets the demands and conventions of filmic narrative styles, so that personal stories about actual individuals with active emotional lives come across as such. It can be difficult to strike a balance of adapting conventional ethnographic filmmaking tools to the needs of psychological anthropology while avoiding the conventions of the genre that might render the films dry or disengaged. These challenges, and the insights gained from struggling to create new forms of explication and storytelling to address them, can significantly influence the development of forms of narrative and character development in visual psychological anthropology.

In making films specifically about culture and mental illness, methods such as PCE may need to be adapted to the particular domains explored. For example, classic PCE was not developed to address Western, biomedically oriented categories of mental disorder such as those found in the *Diagnostic and Statistical Manual of Mental Disorders* (*DSM*; American Psychiatric Association [APA] 2013), categories integral to understanding and framing first the experience of mental illness by subjects and psychiatric care providers, and second the multiple contexts, psychiatric and otherwise, in which these subjects are embedded. As another example, in classic PCE the issues of stigma and exclusion are not typically explored at length. But as these experiences are common for people living with mental illness, they must be considered in a much more textured way than in more standardized person-centered interviews.

Despite this extended focus on particular aspects of the experience of mental illness, a key lesson to be learned from person-centered visual ethnographies of mental illness is that, ultimately, the most significant issues in people's lives will *not* be diagnoses, treatment concerns (both primary domains of contemporary psychiatry), nor even the most painful aspects of their symptoms, but rather the more fundamental aspects of their lives, such as family support, love, partnership, and a sense of respect and meaning—or lack thereof. In other words, while certainly incorporating the phenomenological experience of symptoms and treatment, such films should not be primarily symptom- or treatment-focused.

This approach follows theoretical shifts in the anthropology of mental illness. Psychological anthropology has moved away from the psychiatric "exotica" of culture-bound syndromes (Simons and Hughes 1985; Simons 1982, 2001; Good 2012) or unusual symptoms that once fascinated the field toward individual phenomenology and experiential material, paying more attention to people's subjectivity than psychiatric nosology (Jenkins and Barrett 2004; Jenkins 2015) explicitly focused on phenomenological approaches in the cross-cultural study of severe mental illness. In medical anthropology also, there has been a movement toward a deeper engagement with aspects of illness experience besides a categorical and descriptive focus on bizarre or unusual symptomatology. Works like Kleinman and Good (Kleinman and Good 1985) and Kleinman's monographs on depression in China (Kleinman 1986, 1980; Kleinman et al. 2011), as well as numerous other research projects (Becker 1995; O'Nell 1996), set the stage for a more subjectivity—and phenomenologically—oriented approach, focusing on social embedding and understanding of attribution of various disorders while developing a language to examine personal experience in relation to severe mental illness.

Widening the scope away from an exclusive focus on those isolated aspects of ethnographic inquiry that relate most directly to their mental illness diagnosis and symptomatology lets the wider human experiences and particular voices of ethnographic subjects to be better heard. This "experiential turn" (Willen and Seeman 2012) orients the focus of person-centered ethnographic film about culture and mental illness toward other components of the film subjects' lives and the issues most pressing for them, which more often than not include basic human experiences of loss, fear, love, and desire.

This orientation toward the internal struggles, motivations, desires, phenomenological experience, and subjectivity of an individual (Biehl et al. 2007; Csordas 2004; Desjarlais and Throop 2011; Fuchs 2010; Kirmayer and Sartorius 2007) to a certain extent puts psychological anthropology at odds with the conventions of traditional ethnographic film. Ethnographic film has often purposefully avoided conventional narrative structures and to a large extent emotion and even at times artistry (Apley and Tamés 2005).

This has been in part due to visual anthropology's original intention to be objective, scientific, and educational (Michaelis 1956) in capturing the reality of others, but has also been explicitly to avoid forcing a Western framework onto the experience of non-Western peoples (Worth and Adair 1972). Ironically, this orientation may have led to some ethnographic films that are actually *less* faithful to the lived experience of the participants, particularly because they are missing a key element of that experience, namely, emotion and emotional force.

Person-centered approaches to ethnographic films place a concerted emphasis on the subjects' emotions as the focal point of the narrative. There are established film techniques to convey and evoke emotion, from shot composition and angles and distances that focus the viewer's attention on what the director wants to convey, to using a narrative structure that addresses conflict and resolution in character development, to editing techniques that highlight interpersonal dynamics and illness progressions, to the use of an evocative soundtrack to highlight the emotional experience of the subject by heightening it for the viewer. Similar to the new forms of ethnographic writing that emerged in the 1980s and 1990s in response to the call for a more affective anthropology that applied stylistic conventions of fiction, memoir, and even poetry (e.g., Clifford and Marcus 1986) to evoke and invite emotional engagement, so might the psychological anthropology call for a new kind of ethnographic film, one that in highlighting emotion more accurately conveys, not distorts, the experience of others (Damasio 1994, 1999, 2010). Such filmic strategies will be explored throughout this book.

1.4.1 Afflictions: *A Person-Centered, Emotionally Focused, and Domain-Specific Film Series*

The *Afflictions* film series (Lemelson 2010–2011), which includes *The Bird Dancer* (Lemelson 2010a), marks a movement toward person-centered visual ethnography, an effort to craft a visual psychological anthropology. As such, it is situated at the point of confluence between topics and themes in the study of psychological anthropology, visual anthropology, and global mental health. While each field has its own distinct history and driving concerns, they are united here in the service of a methodology that will enable a better understanding of the social and cultural components of mental health and effective current visual storytelling strategies for capturing and presenting these.

As an ensemble, the series explores classic areas of inquiry in the cross-cultural study of mental illness. It investigates how cultural values, beliefs, and practices play out in individual biographies to color the experience and course of mental illness, whether protectively buffering individuals in distress or acting as stressors that can exacerbate their illness experience. It depicts individuals embedded in family systems and highlights how attribution, negative or positive emotional interactions, and daily routines influence outcome and recovery. It considers the uses and efficacy of traditional healing and biomedical treatment, portraying the benefits and challenges of each. It exemplifies the heterogeneity of major mental illness and neuropsychiatric disorder and above all employs an inductive approach that looks beyond mental illness per se to determine "what is at stake" in the subjects' lives. The attempt to situate mental illness as part of the totality of lived experience, work inductively, and focus on the subjects' own perspective of their illness has determined the structure and approach of the films, which de-emphasizes clinical diagnoses, which the viewer comes to understand as the subjects do, as just one aspect of their illness experience, and situated within the multiple contexts of their lives.

The series then goes beyond these classic questions to engage in a more reflexive line of questioning, pondering: How does the act of filming and then editing of raw footage into a coherent finished film about a participant's life influence their self, their subjectivity, their relationships with their kin network, and their relationships with the anthropologist, who is often an interrogator, supporter, counselor, and friend? How does this process influence the anthropologist as a theorist, practitioner, and person? What are some of the complex aspects of fieldwork that do not usually make it to the page or the screen? What are the stakes in such a working relationship and what are some of the long-lasting results on the ground?

Afflictions: Culture and Mental Illness in Indonesia is divided into two sections of three films each: Part One focuses on neuropsychiatric disorders and Part Two psychotic disorders. While the films explore many issues beyond these general psychiatric categories, this two-part division is useful for translational purposes and follows the delineations of the lead author's two research projects, which as described in the preface preceded the visual ethnography and through which the film subjects were recruited. In particular, the films explore themes (stigma, attribution of illness, family environment, social support, globalization, etc.) that address the issue of differential outcome for mental illness in the developing world, following the WHO DOSMD studies (World Health Organization 1973, 1979).

1.5   ORGANIZATION OF THE BOOK

This volume is ordered in three distinct but interrelated sections. The first section lays out the issues and domains involved in the six *Afflictions* films, but also addresses the larger issues pertaining to visual psychological anthropology. The second section explores the life progression of each of the main participants in *Afflictions* and the multiple issues raised and highlighted in the films about their lives.[2] The third section involves both practical aspects of visual psychological anthropology and the more textured issues of collaboration, intervention, and ethics.

Throughout the volume, insights from written ethnographic material, visual research, and edited films are reviewed. These insights are considered alongside a reflexive account of the methodology behind the films, revealing how the interpersonal dynamics involved in making longitudinal visual psychological anthropology are relevant to discussions of the issues they seek to understand and considering how the process has revealed methodology salient to the situation.

In the first section, Chap. 2, "Perspectives on Integrating Visual Content into Psychological Anthropology," reviews the literature and filmography that provide a basis for understanding the history and promise of the confluence of visual ethnography and psychological anthropology. While often thought of as discrete, these two subgenres have laid the groundwork for anthropologists seeking to make emotional and person-centered films about neuropsychiatric disorder and mental illness. Some of the cross-cutting issues in visual psychological anthropology are introduced. Timeless classics, as well as more recent ethnographic films, will be referenced here and throughout the volume. A vast array of ethnographic films have been made in the last fifty years, yet a much smaller number of older works remain touchstones for many, having been screened in numerous anthropology courses throughout the university system for decades. They remain useful as references because of their comparative familiarity, even to those who may not follow film closely, and therefore are returned to throughout the book.

Chapter 3, "The Lived Experience of Culture and Mental Illness in Indonesia," will provide background information on the experience, treatment, and cultural context of mental illness in Java and Bali useful to understanding the stories of the participants depicted in the *Afflictions* series and discussed in Part Two of the book, which includes a chapter on each of the films in the *Afflictions* series.

Making longitudinal person-centered visual psychological anthropology about the lived experience of mental illness is a complex process that requires ongoing theoretical and interpersonal negotiation and reflection. What is captured on film and finally shared with audiences is of course only part of visual ethnography. The interpersonal working dynamics, ever-shifting intersubjective realities, and relationships that are built and change throughout the process of filming are central to the process.

This section foregrounds the films while extending and elaborating on those numerous aspects of the fieldwork and ethnography that could not fit into the frame or scope of the films proper, which have their unique requirements in terms of structure and content. Material in each of these chapters will include detailed information about the participant's life story; ethnographic elaboration and analysis; and an in-depth consideration of the filmmaking process, how this process influenced thoughts about methodology, contributed to the final structure of the film, and impacted the participants. Due to the inductive and person-centered approach, each of the films delves beyond mental illness and neuropsychiatric disorder per se to speak to different domains in psychological anthropology that emerged from the material, and these domains provide the unifying concern for each chapter.

Chapter 4, "The Bird Dancer: Social Rejection and Social Suffering," revisits the life of Gusti Ayu and the making of the film *The Bird Dancer* (Lemelson 2010a). Ultimately, Gusti's Tourette symptoms were in and of themselves a minor concern. Rather, her troubles arose from her surroundings: the meaning ascribed to her difference, the reactions it engendered, and the way the interpretations of her illness intersected with the restrictions and expectations of her gendered caste position to limit and marginalize her. This troubling context gives rise to questions about the role of the film and research team in understanding and interpreting alternative frameworks with which to understand Gusti's life concerns, and the extent to which reflexive concerns and debates appear in the finished visual ethnography. The chapter will address the repercussions of attempting to "help" a film subject and propose that the role of a visual psychological anthropology is to focus on the participant's own voice, perspective, and pressing concerns. While there are significant limits to "doing good" in a fieldwork context, ethnographic dialogue does open up a space for "alternative narratives of self." Perhaps a side effect of filmmaking in psychological anthropology is helping the participants "see" themselves in a new light, different from the way they have previously been seen by their immediate family and community.

Chapter 5, "Shadows and Illuminations: Interpreting and Framing Extraordinary Experience," addresses the role of trauma in the life story of Nyoman Kereta and the making of the film *Shadows and Illuminations* (Lemelson 2010c). To determine what Kereta was actually experiencing, and how his visions might be understood—as a symptom of illness or expression of defiant withdrawal from a hostile and dangerous world—an understanding of complex Balinese cosmology was needed. Furthermore, local idioms of distress, the cultural shaping of affect, and the tangible and immediate danger involved in talking about political violence may have compounded both Kereta's lived experience and what he felt comfortable discussing onscreen. One of the central filmmaking challenges addressed is how to create emotional impact across cultural conventions of communication and, more importantly, how to mitigate any psychological harm that might potentially result from participation in a film project.

Chapter 6, "Family Victim: Encountering Deviance and Representing Intersubjectivity," uses the experience of making *Family Victim* (Lemelson 2010b) to explore how researchers, family members, and subjects create an understanding of themselves, their relationships, and the filmmaking situation that can shift over the course of a project; how to include these shifts within the structure of the film; and whether these shifts should influence the final narrative structure, film style, and choices made about film distribution. Estu's problems eluded clear categorization, making "deviance" perhaps the most salient way to understand his behavior—a model that is not clearly based on mental illness, but can include it. As the filmmaking and fieldwork progressed, and a deep friendship with Estu and his family members developed, the researchers entered into the process of trying to label Estu's behavior and understand the implications for his filmic representation. Did it matter to the film whether he was mentally ill? Was it just his own behavior that was up for representation? How much did his family want to include or obscure about their *own* thoughts and beliefs about their son and brother? Ultimately, in centering in on the very complexity of Estu's case, the film and the ethnography seek to demonstrate the forms of analytic consciousness an anthropologist goes through in attempting to make sense of a complex situation, balancing different models of understanding deviance, including psychiatric, traditional Javanese, forensic, and finally interpersonal and personal insight models.

In Chap. 7, "Memory of My Face: Globalization, Madness, and Identity Onscreen," the experience of making *Memory of My Face* (Lemelson 2011) is mobilized to reconsider ideas about mental illness that have been pushed aside with the ascendance of biological psychiatry and delve deeper into the ways an engagement with the filmic representation of an individual during episodes of mental illness and remission can deepen an understanding of the subjective role that mental illness experience plays in the life course—and indeed, in a broader historical context. When initially filmed, Bambang was in the throes of a manic schizoaffective episode, so at first glance he seemed logically incoherent and classically "mad." It was only through repeated viewings and analysis of this initial film footage that the research team came to realize how prescient and poignant the content of Bambang's "mad" speech was, lamenting not just his own condition but that of the post-colonial and rapidly globalizing nation of Indonesia. Concurrent with efforts to "make meaning" out of what contemporary psychiatrists might label as the meaningless result of disordered neurochemistry was Bambang's own effort to make meaning out of his illness episodes and the way they had impacted his life. It was in part through interacting with his filmed image that Bambang and his family came to develop a particular stance on his illness episodes. This chapter explores how film can therefore lead to considerations of personal and even national identity for participants who wish to purposefully engage in their own self-fashioning on-screen.

Chapter 8, "Ritual Burdens: Culturally Defined Stressors and Developmental Progressions," addresses the role of narrative and the possibilities and limitations of film to address the impact of early life history, trauma, and life cycle events on recurrent mental illness. Ni Ketut Kasih's episodes of distress were triggered most evidently by her culturally specific ritual responsibilities; but longitudinal fieldwork revealed how these were intimately connected to other aspects of her life narrative as she and her family understood it. Various strategies were used to depict these elements of her history, in all its complexity and texture. The chapter examines the challenges of making a film about a vulnerable subject; over time, certain interview topics related to Ni Ketut Kasih's traumatic past were determined to be "off limits" by her family, in order to protect and preserve her piece of mind, while Ni Ketut Kasih herself grew increasingly self-conscious about the physical side effects of her medication and her aged appearance. This chapter depicts filmmaking as a balancing act between probing the multifaceted triggers for mental illness while respecting the needs, wishes, and sensitivities of the family unit and their own understanding of their story.

The final chapter in this section is Chap. 9, "Kites and Monsters: Continuity in Cultural Practices." This last film in the series comes from a quite different perspective, illustrating how cultural practices such as dance, folklore, music, and art can create a continuity, both as a guiding concept for filmmaking methodology and in the developmental progression toward health and maturity in the main participant.

Part Three outlines the multiple issues involved in the making of visual psychological anthropology films. This section begins with Chap. 10, "The Process of Visual Psychological Anthropology," which discusses the fieldwork, filming methodology, and representational techniques used to capture and present the experiences of individuals on film. There is analysis of filmmaking techniques that developed or were adopted to a particular style of visual psychological anthropology and description of the working methodology in terms of fieldwork, pre-production, production, and post-production, sharing "teachable moments" and problem-solving from the history of the series. This is a long chapter, as it overviews many practical and technological issues involved in creating a visual psychological anthropology. Readers are encouraged to use this chapter as a reference guide for their own filmmaking.

Chapter 11, "Collaboration, Intervention, Compensation, and Ethics," provides behind-the-scenes, process-oriented discussions weaving together personal and ethnographic content, representational strategies, and methodology for collaborating in the field, on- and off- camera. The benefits and pitfalls of collaboration with fellow researchers, film crew, and film participants are covered and thorny ethical questions in conducting fieldwork and filmic representation are addressed. Similar to the previous chapter, Chap. 11 includes much specific, contextualized material and examples drawn from many years of resolving ethical issues in the field.

Finally, Chap. 12, "Visual Psychological Anthropology: Implications for Teaching and the Future," synthesizes the material covered in previous chapters, and offers some theoretical, pedagogical, and practical advice for students and colleagues. Psychological anthropology is critical for gaining ethnographic perspectives on mental illness, and PCE has been crucial to the development of contemporary psychological anthropology, providing a methodology, an orientation, and a set of values: The field now has an opportunity to expand its methodology and reach into the visual and auditory. Psychological anthropologists may find an engagement with visual methods to be illuminating and satisfying because of the visual, aural, kinesthetic, and affective impact multimodal ethnography can have in illustrating and communicating its key tenets.

NOTES

1. Additional written and visual material relating to this book, as well as information on purchase of the six *Afflictions* films, can be found at www. afflictionsbook.com. Other films by the lead author can be purchased at http://www.elementalproductions.org
2. N.B. The chapters in the second section are of variable lengths, reflecting the variable lengths of the films themselves.

REFERENCES

American Psychiatric Association. 2013. *Diagnostic and Statistical Manual of Mental Disorders*. 5th ed. Washington, DC: Author.

Apley, Alice, and David, Tamés. 2005. Remembering John Marshall (1932–2005). *New England Film*. Retrieved from http://www.newenglandfilm.com/news/archives/05june/marshall.htm

Becker, Anne. 1995. *Body, Self, and Society: The View from Fiji*. Philadelphia: University of Pennsylvania Press.

Biehl, João G., Byron J. Good, and Arthur Kleinman, eds. 2007. *Subjectivity: Ethnographic Investigations, Ethnographic Studies in Subjectivity*. Berkeley: University of California Press. https://doi.org/10.1525/california/9780520247925.001.0001

Clifford, James, and George E. Marcus. 1986. *Writing Culture: The Poetics and Politics of Ethnography*. Berkeley: University of California Press.

Connolly, Bob, and Robin, Anderson. 1983. *First Contact*. 54 min. Watertown: Documentary Educational Resources. http://www.der.org/films/first-contact.html

Csordas, Thomas J. 2004. Asymptote of the Ineffable: Embodiment, Alterity, and the Theory of Religion. *Current Anthropology* 45 (2): 163–185. doi:10.1086/381046

Damasio, Antonio R. 1994. *Descartes' Error: Emotion, Reason, and the Human Brain*. New York: G.P. Putnam.

———. 1999. *The Feeling of What Happens: Body and Emotion in the Making of Consciousness*. New York: Harcourt Brace.

———. 2010. *Self Comes to Mind: Constructing the Conscious Brain*. New York: Pantheon Books.

Desjarlais, Robert R., and C. Jason Throop. 2011. Phenomenological Approaches in Anthropology. *Annual Review of Anthropology* 40: 87–102. doi:10.1086/381046

Flaherty, Robert J. 1922. *Nanook of the North*. 1 hr, 19 min. Pathé Exchange.

Foster, Susan Leigh. 2010. *Choreographing Empathy: Kinesthesia in Performance*. London: Routledge.

Fuchs, Thomas. 2010. Phenomenology and Psychopathology. In *Handbook of Phenomenology and Cognitive Science*, ed. D. Schmicking and S. Gallagher. New York: Springer. doi:10.1007/978-90-481-2646-0_28

Good, Byron J. 2012. Theorizing the 'Subject' of Medical and Psychiatric Anthropology. *Journal of the Royal Anthropological Institute* 18 (3): 515–535. doi:10.1111/j.1467-9655.2012.01774.x

Hollan, Douglas. 1997. The Relevance of Person-Centered Ethnography to Cross-Cultural Psychiatry. *Transcultural Psychiatry* 34 (2): 219–243. doi:10.1177/136346159703400203

Howes, Arthur. 2002. *Benjamin and His Brother*. 87 min. Watertown: Documentary Educational Resources. http://www.der.org/films/benjamin-and-his-brother.html

Jenkins, Janis H. 2015. *Extraordinary Conditions: Culture and Experience in Mental Illness*. Oakland: University of California Press.

Jenkins, Janis H., and Robert J. Barrett. 2004. *Schizophrenia, Culture, and Subjectivity: The Edge of Experience, Cambridge Studies in Medical Anthropology*. New York: Cambridge University Press.

Kirmayer, Laurence J., and Norman Sartorius. 2007. Cultural Models and Somatic Syndromes. *Psychosomatic Medicine* 69 (9): 832–840.

Kleinman, Arthur. 1980. *Patients and Healers in the Context of Culture: An Exploration of the Borderland between Anthropology, Medicine, and Psychiatry*. Berkeley: University of California Press.

———. 1986. *Social Origins of Distress and Disease: Depression, Neuraasthenia, and Pain in Modern China*. New Haven: Yale University Press.

Kleinman, Arthur, and Byron Good. 1985. *Culture and Depression: Studies in the Anthropology and Cross-Cultural Psychiatry of Affect and Disorder*. Berkeley: University of California Press.

Kleinman, Arthur, Yunxiang Yan, Jing Jun, Sing Lee, Everett Zhang, Tianshu Pan, et al. 2011. *Deep China: The Moral Life of the Person – What Anthropology and Psychiatry Tell Us About China Today*. Berkeley: University of California Press.

Lemelson, Robert. 2010–2011. *Afflictions: Culture and Mental Illness in Indonesia Series*. 182 min. Watertown: Documentary Educational Resources. http://www.der.org/films/afflictions.html

———. 2010a. *The Bird Dancer*. 40 min. Watertown: Documentary Educational Resources. http://www.der.org/films/bird-dancer.html

———. 2010b. *Family Victim*. 38 min. Watertown: Documentary Educational Resources. http://www.der.org/films/family-victim.html

———. 2010c. *Shadows and Illuminations*. 35 min. Watertown: Documentary Educational Resources. http://www.der.org/films/shadows-and-illuminations.html

————. 2011. *Memory of My Face*. 22 min. Watertown: Documentary Education Resources. http://www.der.org/films/memory-of-my-face.html

Levy, Robert I. 1973. *Tahitians: Mind and Experience in the Society Islands*. Chicago: University of Chicago Press.

Levy, Robert I., and Douglas Hollan. 1998. Person-Centered Interviewing and Observation. In *Handbook of Methods in Cultural Anthropology*, ed. H.R. Bernard, 333–364. Lanham: Alta Mira Press.

Lutz, Catherine. 1988. *Unnatural Emotions: Everyday Sentiments on a Micronesian Atoll & Their Challenge to Western Theory*. Chicago: University of Chicago Press.

Marshall, John. 1962. *A Joking Relationship*. 13 min. Watertown: Documentary Educational Resources. http://www.der.org/films/joking-relationship.html

————. 1980. *N!Ai, Story of A !Kung Woman*. 59 min. Watertown: Documentary Educational Resources. http://www.der.org/films/nai-kung-woman.html

Michaelis, Anthony. 1956. *Research Films in Biology, Anthropology, Psychology and Medicine*. New York: New York Academic Press.

O'Nell, Theresa D. 1996. *Disciplined Hearts: History, Identity, and Depression in an American Indian Community*. Berkeley: University of California Press.

Robbins, Joel. 2013. Beyond the Suffering Subject. *Journal of the Royal Anthropological Institute* 19 (3): 447–462.

Rosaldo, Renato. 1989. Grief and a Headhunter's Rage. In *Culture and Truth: The Remaking of Social Analysis*, 1–21. Boston: Beacon Press.

Sapir, Edward. 1958. *Culture, Language and Personality: Selected Essays*. Berkeley: University of California Press.

Simons, Ronald C. 1982. *Latah: A Culture-Specific Elaboration of the Startle Reflex*. 38 min. Bloomington: Indiana University Audiovisual Center.

————. 2001. Introduction to Culture-Bound Syndromes. *Psychiatric Times* 18 (11): 283–292.

Simons, Ronald C., and Charles C. Hughes. 1985. *The Culture-Bound Syndromes: Folk Illnesses of Psychiatric and Anthropological Interest*. Dordrecht: D. Reidel.

Taylor, Lucien. 1998. Visual Anthropology Is Dead, Long Live Visual Anthropology! [Book Review]. *American Anthropologist* 100 (2): 534–537. doi:10.1525/aa.1998.100.2.534

Willen, Sarah S., and Don Seeman. 2012. Introduction: Experience and Inquiétude. *Ethos* 40 (1): 1–23. doi:10.1111/j.1548-1352.2011.01228.x

World Health Organization. 1973. *Report of the International Pilot Study of Schizophrenia*. Vol. 1. Geneva: Author.

————. 1979. *Schizophrenia: An International Follow-up-Study*. Chichester: John Wiley & Sons.

Worth, Sol, and John Adair. 1972. *Through Navajo Eyes: An Exploration in Film Communication and Anthropology*. 2nd ed. Bloomington: Indiana University Press.

CHAPTER 2

Perspectives on Integrating Ethnographic Film into Psychological Anthropology

Visual psychological anthropology is informed by two streams of thought and practice: the visual methods of popular documentary and ethnographic film heritage, which have sometimes been quite disparate, and the theory and methods of anthropology—specifically, the developments of the subdiscipline of psychological anthropology. Yet these streams have only occasionally flowed together. In the rich history of innovative methods and techniques employed by documentary filmmakers there is little direct engagement with the findings of psychological anthropology. This is unfortunate. Today, most people are navigating a multimedia landscape of written text, audio, video, and interactive content. Moving images are now a ubiquitous and expected part of information sharing, and their impact cannot be understated. It will be argued in this book that psychological anthropology, which aims to provide a contextualized, nuanced, and in-depth view of human experience, can benefit from an engagement with visual methods. This engagement could be helpful in meeting the goal codified in the American Anthropological Association's "Statement of Purpose" which promotes "the dissemination of anthropological knowledge and its use to solve human problems."

The digital revolution and the profound changes in how information is accessed and understood point to the increasing salience of visual forms of narrative and storytelling. As David MacDougall noted, "images

© The Author(s) 2017
R. Lemelson, A. Tucker, *Afflictions*, Culture, Mind, and Society,
DOI 10.1007/978-3-319-59984-7_2

and written texts not only tell us things differently, they tell us different things" (1998, 257). By reviewing the different historical, theoretical, and technological movements that have led to the present opportunity for a visual psychological anthropology, it becomes clear that visual psychological anthropology offers a synergistic practice that extends the toolkit of psychological anthropologists and fulfills the goals of their discipline while offering an engaged approach toward ethnographic film.

2.1   HISTORICAL PRECEDENTS AND PROSPECTS
FOR A VISUAL PSYCHOLOGICAL ANTHROPOLOGY: A REVIEW
OF RELEVANT FILMOGRAPHY

There are numerous excellent works describing and analyzing the history of ethnographic film (Asch et al. 1973; Barbash and Taylor 1997; Heider 1976; Rony 1996). This section overviews and explores the history of ethnographic films and related research with an orientation relevant to the concerns and domains of visual psychological anthropology.

In the realm of popular cinema, before the genre of ethnographic film was even conceptualized, there were early precedents for making films "about culture"—indeed, some have drawn direct parallels between the histories of early film and early ethnography, which shared overlapping concerns and even field practices despite not being in direct communication with one another (Ruby 1980). The silent film *Nanook of the North* (Flaherty 1922), now universally recognized as one of the first ethnographic or documentary films, was produced for a popular audience and achieved commercial success. Other films from the dawn of the "talky" era were made with the technical and narrative cinematic conventions of the time. For example, *Legong, Dance of the Virgins* (De la Falaise 1935) was shot on location in Bali with an entirely native cast by one of the most well-known Hollywood cinematographers of that era, Howard Green. The film extensively recorded Balinese ritual and social activities, showcasing several dance performances and elements of betrothal and funerary customs. At the time of its release, it was praised for including many details of anthropological interest, yet the character-driven story, which revolved around a romantic love triangle, was scripted.

During the years following these early experiments, concurrent with the explosion of film for news, entertainment, and educational purposes, interest in the documentation and representation of "culture," or at least the depiction of what was believed to be the cultural "other" continued. Colonial-era newsreels highlighted popular conceptions of "the native." There were more evocative visual explorations of non-Western settings, such as the beautifully shot *Grass* (Cooper and Schoedsack 1925), which depicted transhumance migration in what-is-now Iran. There were "adventure" films depicting Western explorers in foreign lands, such as the technically groundbreaking, visually amazing and profound *The Epic of Everest* (Noel 1927) portraying the tragic Mallory and Irvine expedition of the 1920s. During the same period, adventurer couple Martin and Osa Johnson contributed to the popular allure of the "exotic savage" by showing their footage of peoples during their travels around the world, from Borneo to Africa, depicting them as headhunters and cannibals (Talley 1937).

In the years after these early experiments in documentary film in non-Western settings, there was an explosion of visual forms of representation. The documentary form was used for many purposes, such as propaganda in the service of nation states, as the massive amount of material produced on all sides during World War II attests to. Many documentaries made for education and entertainment purposes were set in "foreign lands" and were in the service of multiple agendas of colonialism, imperialism, and corporate promotion. Others were made for sheer visual spectacle, such as the first films in the "exploitation" or shockumentary genre. Of these, the memorable *Mondo Cane* ("A Dog's World" [Jacopetti et al. 1962]) featured a montage of graphic footage collected across the globe—from drunken Germans to Taiwanese butchering dogs to cargo cults in the Pacific to bull fights in Portugal—juxtaposed for prime shock value.

Anthropologists had been using visual methods since the late 1800s, graphically documenting dress, physical behavior, art, textiles, and vernacular architecture—and more problematically race and ethnicity (Rony 1996)—with drawing, photography, and film (Banks and Ruby 2011; Muybridge 1979; Edwards 2001). "Salvage ethnography"(Gruber 1970; Haddon et al. 1901) in particular sought to collect a visual and material archive of lifeways and aesthetic culture that were feared to be lost soon, such as Edward Curtis's massive, if problematic, documentation of Native American societies (Curtis and Adam 2014; Curtis and Hodge 1970). Yet, for decades, for the most part, anthropologists did not make films. The few that did sought to create a supposedly "neutral" depiction of the culture in which the anthropologist/filmmaker was embedded. Ethnographic film further distinguished itself from commercial film of this era by presenting some exegesis and analysis, rather than blatantly exoticizing or exploiting its subjects, as the colonialist project had. Some of these films were relevant to psychological anthropology, whether or not consciously identifying as such. A brief review of some of the most significant projects follows.

Margaret Mead and Gregory Bateson went to Bali in the mid-1930s to explore (Curtis and Adam 2014; Curtis and Hodge 1970) among other things the "configuration" (Erickson et al. 2013) of Balinese culture, the relation of Balinese child socialization to adult "character" (Jensen and Suryani 1992), and the relationship of Balinese cultural practices to the development of a "schizoid character." As part of their methodology, they chose to experiment with emergent photographic and film technologies, becoming some of the first ethnographers to explicitly integrate visual and psychological anthropology. They produced both monographs and films. Their main monograph, "Balinese Character," though today somewhat underutilized and perhaps underappreciated, was groundbreaking in its ethnographic description and analysis paired side by side with photographs illustrating particular subjects and domains. They also made a series of influential films: *Trance and Dance in Bali* (1952), *Bathing Babies in Three Cultures* (1954), and *Karba's First Years* (1950). Mead became an advocate for integrating visual approaches into psychological anthropology proper. This pioneering work is still useful for teaching anthropology and anthropological methods, though some of the overarching conclusions of the research (Jensen and Suryani 1992) and films (Rony 2006) have been roundly criticized.

While not an anthropologist, Maya Deren, the avant-garde filmmaker and artist, explored her interests in culture and subjective psychology by making films about voodoo trance dancers in Haiti. She was inspired by Bateson's Bali material, and her Guggenheim grant renewal called for a "cross-cultural fugue" of visual productions (Deren and Bateson 1980) between Bali and Haiti. Deren took her first trip to Haiti in 1947, and over the course of six years took multiple trips to complete her ethnographic film on ritual possession, *The Divine Horsemen: The Living Gods of Haiti* (1953). As an early film exploration of the self and personality in relation to possession, alternative states of consciousness, and their cultural contexts, this film is quite relevant to psychological anthropology's interests (Nichols and Deren 2001).

Subsequent to Mead, Bateson, and Deren, and following a dearth of ethnographic films relevant to psychological anthropology in the 1940s–1950s, three American filmmakers stand out as giants of ethnographic film: John Marshall, Timothy Asch, and Robert Gardner. Marshall's work was carried out primarily with the Ju/'hoansi Bushmen of the Kalahari, for a remarkable fifty years (1951–2002). Over the span of Asch's noteworthy career, he most famously collaborated with Napoleon Chagnon in the Amazon (*The Yanomamo Series*, 1968–1971) and Linda Connor in Indonesia (the *Jero Tapakan* series, 1979–1983). Asch's integration of ethnographic films with supplemental teaching materials is a useful pedagogical model. Gardner's groundbreaking and evocative films about the Dani in highland New Guinea (*Dead Birds*, 1963), the Nuer in Sudan (*The Nuer*, 1971), the Hamar of Ethiopia (*Rivers of Sand*, 1973), and the city of Benares, India (*Forest of Bliss*, 1986) exposed several generations of college students to a diverse range of topics and cultures.

While Marshall, Asch, and Gardner's foundational works in visual anthropology were not explicitly made under the rubric of psychological anthropology, there are parallels in their methodology and main concerns. For example, Marshall and Asch initially aimed to capture sequences of spontaneous interactions, and tried to film "integral" or "real" events from their natural beginning to their natural conclusion without what they considered to be disruption from non-essential editing (Connor et al. 1986; Marshall 1993; Asch 1979). This "sequence" method aimed to present "whole single units of behavior" which anthropologists could then study (Asch et al. 1973). Such a focus on daily life and routines connects well with basic tenets of psychological anthropology methodology, such as "ecocultural pathways of development" (Weisner 2002).

The films of all three anthropologists explored core issues for psychological anthropology. Marshall was fascinated by the intersection of personal experience with history, political economy, and cultural change, both in his shorter studies (e.g., *N!ai, Story of a!Kung Woman* [1980]) and in his deeply moving six-hour magnum opus *A Kalahari Family* (1951–2002). The latter remains a unique contribution to ethnographic film because of its longitudinal focus on one family transitioning from subsistence family-level hunting and gathering to forced resettlement and integration into state-level society. All of the filmmakers were interested in interpersonal conflict (e.g., Asch's *The Ax Fight* [1975]), healing, and extraordinary states of consciousness, evident in Marshall's *Num Tchai: The Ceremonial Dance of the !Kung Bushmen* (1969b) and *A Curing Ceremony* (1969a); Asch's *Jero Tapakan* series and several of his Yanamamo films; and Gardner's *Forest of Bliss* (1969a). All the filmmakers produced work in classic anthropological areas of gender, kinship, child development, ritual life, and cosmology

(Connor et al. 1979–1983, 1981, 1986; Fox et al. 1989; Lewis et al. 1992; Gardner 1971, 1974; Marshall 1969b, 1980).

Although the ethnographic films of Marshall, Asch, and Gardner offered breadth and depth, disciplinary concerns with "visual evidence" often precluded a more intimate—and, some might argue, accurate—look into their subjects' internal worlds. By the mid-1970s, ethnographic film was exploring elements of narrative and artistry outside of purportedly "scientific" documentation (Banks 2001; Banks and Ruby 2011); however, these were often critiqued as too subjective, raising debate over what criteria of content, structure, and intent needed to be fulfilled in order to be appropriately considered "ethnographic" (Ruby 1975; Heider 1976). Gardner, the most experimental of the three, was criticized for emphasizing the aesthetic, sensory, and symbolic aspects of his work rather than the lived realities of the people in his films (e.g., Ruby 1993).

Responding in part to these critiques, Asch came to question the objectivity of events and grew interested in his subjects' interiority; by the time he made his later film *Jero Tapakan: Stories from the Life of a Balinese Healer* (1986), he was more concerned with the respondent's use of cultural narrative conventions than in the factual validity of her autobiography (Acciaioli 2003).

Marshall, too, exhibited a move toward individual subjectivity through the course of his filmmaking career. It was apparent that he was concerned with experiential or subjective aspects of Ju/'hoansi individuality from the beginning; the first film he released, *The Hunters* (1957), focuses on the leader of the small band of bushmen the Marshall family had been working with, a man by the name of Tsoma Tsamko, who would ultimately reappear multiple times in other films and become the chief protagonist of his magnum opus, as well as his good friend. In this early film, while much of the voice-over Marshall wrote focuses on the landscape, ecological, and cultural contexts of the giraffe hunt (the ostensible *raison d'être* of the film), it also renders Tsoma's experiences and those of his small band of hunters, while refraining, unlike Gardner in *Dead Birds* (1963), from intuiting what the main characters are thinking. Decades later, Marshall moved beyond voice-over to include the voices of his subjects. He interviewed Tsoma about that hunt in 1953 on camera. Tsoma, now an older man, beautifully recollected and narrated the hunt, including reflexive elements about Marshall's behavior and the experience of shooting it. Marshall artfully interwove this new narration into the original film to render a fully fleshed-out, complex, relationally and reflexively presented account of an individual (*A Kalahari Family* [1951–2002]).

After the invention of portable 16-mm cameras with sync sound in the early 1960s, which allowed for greater freedom and spontaneity in film-making, documentarians explored issues of relevance to psychological anthropology in innovative ways. In the 1960s and 1970s in North America, filmmakers explored Direct Cinema, an observational style fascinated with the subjective nature of truth. Allan King filmed "actuality dramas" (Feldman 2002) featuring content from therapies for emotionally disturbed children (*Warrendale* [1967]) as well as the psychodynamic intricacies of married life (*A Married Couple* [1969]). D.A. Pennebaker, Richard Leacock, and Albert and David Maysles created dynamic, "fly on the wall," "Direct Cinema" films on politics such as *Primary* (1960) and *Crisis* (1963), analyzed the social context for emerging musical trends in films such as *Don't Look Back* (1967) and *Gimme Shelter* (1970), and portrayed other aspects of contemporary American life. The Direct Cinema approach was certainly in line with early ethnographic filmmakers, such as Margaret Mead, who emphasized the importance of an unobtrusive "objective" approach, where the camera was merely documenting factual reality.

In related developments, Barbara Kopple, who worked for the Maysles, captured the personal toll of corrupt corporate policy on the lives of mine workers in *Harlan County, USA* (1976). Frederick Wiseman captured human behavior in institutional settings such as welfare offices (*Welfare* [1975]), schools (*High School* [1968]), and most relevant for this volume, a hospital for the criminally insane in *Titicut Follies* (1967)—interestingly enough shot by John Marshall. *An American Family* (1973) was ground-breaking when aired on public television, documenting the personal life of a California family as they negotiated divorce and their son's homo-sexuality. Across different contexts, the subjective and experiential focus of Direct Cinema proved a useful model for capturing "life as lived" (Bruner 1984, 7).

Outside of North America, other notable filmmakers were investigating similar ideas and topics. From France, Louis Malle evocatively captured ritual life in India (*Calcutta* [1969]), and interestingly, applied the insight he gained from working in ethnographic film to his fiction films. Paralleling the rise of French New Wave Cinema and the American Direct Cinema approach were Jean Rouch's experiments with Cinema Verité and "Ethnofictions" (Stoller 1992; Henley 2010), which touched on topics relevant to psychological anthropology, from trance and possession (*Les maitres fous* [1954]) to autobiography (*Moi, un noir* [1968]) to the complexities of memory and daily and work routines in his masterpiece "Chronicle of a Summer" (*Chronique d'un été* [Rouch and Morin 1961]). In Japan, Kazuo Hara directed intimate documentaries about physical disability (*Goodbye CP* [1972]), obsessive love (*Extreme Private Eros: Love Song* [1974]), and the lingering traumas of war (*The Emperor's Naked Army Marches On* [1987]).

The 1980s and 1990s saw a rise in genres of "new autobiography" (Renov 1989) and "experimental ethnography" (Russell 1999). Following an earlier venture by Saul Worth and John Adair, who taught filmmaking techniques to a group of Navajo in order to explore film's potential to reveal an indigenous structuring of reality free from the "unconscious domination" of the anthropologist (Worth and Adair 1972), these genres further blurred the lines between documentary, storytelling, and ethnography. While some of these films used post-modern methods to critique colonialist ethnography rather than advancing psychological anthropology per se, their overarching investment in indigenous and transnational viewpoints opened new avenues for representing unique subjectivities (Behar 1993). In parallel, the advent of inexpensive digital technology in the late 1990s and early 2000s led to an explosion of mainstream personal documentaries (Borshay Liem 2000; Poeuv 2008; Orgeron and Orgeron 2007), some of which could also crossover as ethnographic film (MacDonald 2013), such as Ross McElwee's *Time Indefinite* (1993).

The filmmakers discussed above were, to variable degrees, influenced by methodologies or insights derived from anthropology theory and practice, whether or not these were drawn from psychological anthropology per se. Yet, many contemporary psychological anthropologists seem relatively unaware of the contributions of these different filmmakers to anthropology and, other than showing a few ethnographic films in their classes, rarely reference or utilize this body of work in their own studies. But this may be changing.

In the past fifteen years, there has been a growth of interest in film approaches in anthropology, largely following the technological advances in shooting and editing technologies. Cameras have gotten smaller, lighter, cheaper, and more powerful. The 4 K video cameras now taken for granted on a $200-smart phone would have cost tens of thousands of dollars even five years ago and would not have been technologically possible ten years ago. Video editing systems, restricted to professional editors and costing $100,000 or more twenty years ago, now come included not only in laptop and desktop computers, but also in tablets and smart phones. These advances over the past few years, which cut the costs of production by many multiples, have made filmmaking much more affordable. However, few psychological anthropologists are making films, because training and education in the field have not kept pace with these technological advances, and many are perhaps unaware of the benefits of a visual approach. There are meaningful reasons for this deferment, and yet, the time has come to rethink these and orient toward visual methods.

2.2   PSYCHOLOGICAL ANTHROPOLOGY'S MOVE TOWARD SUBJECTIVITY

Parallel to these developments in methods and approaches in ethnographic film are the changes in psychological anthropology proper. One of the directions in the last several decades in the history of the field has been a movement toward subjectivity, phenomenology, experientialism, and in a more contemporary turn of phrase, "what is at stake," in the ethnographic enterprise and, more specifically, in the understandings and perceptions of the main form of "data," which is a complex human being in a specific cultural setting.

When looking at the understanding and representation of "subjects" in the differing decades of psychological anthropology's history, what is noticeable in the early decades, from the 1930s to 1970s, is the *lack* of a particular subject as an individual in a cultural setting. Certainly in the work of Mead, Dubois, Kardiner, and even Irving Hallowell (Mead 2001; Bateson and Mead 1942; Du Bois et al. 1944, Kardiner and Linton 1974; Hallowell 1955), there are rarely individuals' portraits or voices per se, just representatives of a "modal personality" or its opposite, the "deviant." With the discarding of the culture and personality movement, configurationalism and national character studies, and the subsequent rise of more behaviorally oriented comparative approaches such as the Whiting's psychocultural model (Whiting 1963), there remained a similar lack of individualized subjects, even in the form of textured case studies.

Since this foundational ethnographic fieldwork, psychological anthropologists have been free to move away from the broad theorizing of the earlier schools and develop a more specific and discrete focus on the subtle and textured complexities involved in the study of individual subjectivity. It is now rarer to find a contemporary ethnography or a psychological anthropology that *doesn't* have textured and individualized accounts of specific subjects rather than more generalized, broader stroke depictions of cultural types, such as "The Javanese" or "The Balinese." More recent psychological anthropology introduces us to individuals—Wikan's Suriati, mourning her lover with a bright face (Wikan 1990); Crapanzano's complex and disturbed character Tuhami (Crapanzano 1980); Biehl's Catarina, creating a dictionary of personal meaning even though left abject in the zone of abandonment (Biehl 2005); or Behar's raging but powerful street peddler, Esperanza (Behar 2003). Even anthropological work that is not strictly psychological per se is concerned with individual biography and subjectivity (see Chernoff's books about Hawa the Ghanaian bar girl [2003, 2005] and more recently Michael Jackson's work on migration, *The Wherewithal of Life* (2015)).

These ethnographies have helped to sow a fertile field, allowing for an ethnographic film to engage in similar exploration and analysis of individual subjectivity. It also created an audience primed to watch a film with such structure and direction, meaning psychological anthropologists can explore many directions and topical domains in their visual research and tell compelling stories to not only their colleagues but also the wider world. Without these developments, making films focused on individuals would be an unlikely, if not impossible, prospect. But in order for psychological anthropologists to move forward in their attempts to integrate their research with film, a number of key issues need to be addressed.

2.3   Issues Confronting a Visual Psychological Anthropology

Outside of visual anthropology proper, most anthropologists from the other subdisciplines have not tended to make films, and many even avoided visual methods of any kind. In his work "Iconophobia," Taylor (1996) has tracked a history of distrust of the visual within the field, showing how anthropologists have often rejected visual methods of research presentation. One persistent argument is that film images are decontextualized and make totalizing decisions[1] for the viewer—foreclosing multiple interpretations rather than letting them come to their own conclusions, therefore becoming simplistically "thin" rather than appropriately complex and "thick" (e.g., Hastrup 1992).

The viability of ethnographic film, as a subfield of a more inclusive visual anthropology, continues to be debated within the field of anthropology, which is, as Margaret Mead noted, "a discipline of words" (Mead 1995). Take, for example, how most anthropologists present their data at conferences. While there is an increasing use of presentation software like PowerPoint or Keynote that allows for a visual component, many presentations involve reading papers. This can be seen most clearly at multidisciplinary conferences; when researchers from diverse disciplines such as neuroscience, psychiatry, psychology, philosophy, history, and anthropology come together, it is usually anthropologists who still maintain the practice of directly reading from a written document, often without any supporting visuals. If the piece is well written, evocative, and powerful, then this form of presentation can be profound. At the same time, anthropology should reconsider its elevation of the written word above all other modes of representation to integrating and raising the status of visual elements in respected research.

Anthropologists are generally aware of what the visual brings to data collection, analysis, and research presentation. However, visual forms of narrative and storytelling, as opposed to written ethnographies that accomplish the same goals, are generally not as well recognized. Yet different mediums influence the way stories can be discovered through fieldwork and the way anthropological research is presented. Film and photography can provide valuable counterpoints in certain kinds of visual, occupational, and material ethnography and have fairly long histories in these subfields. Since its inception, ethnographic film has historically been biased toward what David MacDougall calls "the filmable" (1992), documenting topics with an explicitly visual progression and appeal, from the mundane, such as a house construction (Heider's *Dani Houses* [1974]), to the spectacular, such as a ritual warfare (Gardner's *Dead Birds* [1963]).

The catalog of the best-known ethnographic film distributor, Documentary Educational Resources (DER) (http://www.der.org/), has very few films based on psychological anthropology. This is not to say that many of its films are irrelevant to the discipline; quite the contrary. For example, Kildea's *Celso and Cora* intimately portrays a poor Filipino couple struggling to support themselves and their infant when the mother becomes depressed, thematically addressing the possible sequelae of structural violence in the form of mental illness. Identity, masculinity, and mourning are all explored in Hoskins' beautiful film *Horses of Life and Death* (Hoskins 1991), shot on the island of Sumba in Eastern Indonesia.

Transgenderism, ritual life, and possession are explored in Merrison's *Friends in High Places* (Merrison 2001) on Nat Kadaw spirit mediums in Burma. Clearly, numerous filmmakers and anthropologists, while not self-identified specifically as psychological anthropologists, are making films relevant to the subdiscipline's concerns. But these films are rarely utilized or referenced in contemporary practice in psychological anthropology.

The deferment of visual methods in psychological anthropology may be because its subject matter is by definition psychological, and therefore not thought of as being conducive to visual representation as material culture, art and performance (Fruzetti et al. 2005), ritual life (Getzels and Gordon 1985; Hoskins and Whitney 1991), or festivals (Willis 2009; Zemp 2001–2002) would be. Psychological anthropology often explores topics such as subjectivity and phenomenology, and other internal and intersubjective processes that are more challenging to portray on screen.

Out of the numerous topics psychological anthropology explores, mental illness in particular presents unique representational challenges in film regarding chronology, interiority, alternative states of consciousness, psychoanalytic domains such as defense mechanism and conflicts, and multiple vectors of difference. The experience of mental illness is significantly caught up in those aspects of experience that John Marshall called "reality-invisible content" (1993), that is, content not immediately visually apprehensible, including subjective states, hallucinations, flashbacks, memories, and subtle changes in perception or sensation (Csordas 2004; Hinton and Kirmayer 2013; Hollan and Wellankamp 1994; Jenkins and Barrett 2004; Kirmayer and Sartorius 2007; Luhrmann 2012). Perhaps paradoxically, these elements of experience do often have observable physical and behavioral counterparts—such as physical dysregulation or amplified affect—but these have made the visual representation of mental illness an even *more* sensitive issue. Representations of neuropsychiatric disorder and disability in the mainstream media, including both journalism and fiction film, have been well critiqued, with the general consensus that for the most part depictions have contributed to stigma by their mobilization of stereotype, myth, and misinformation (Anderson 2003; Klin and Nemish 2008; Wahl 1995).

One area where psychological anthropologists have utilized film is as a useful tool for raw data collection in the field. Visual methods are increasingly included in a fieldworker's toolkit as a pneumonic and a source of data to be analyzed. With the new ubiquity and ease of video technology, even edited video footage—pieces that go beyond simple field notes and audio recordings—is now frequently used in accompaniment to all kinds of ethnographic research in many subfields, and there are a number of good recent texts providing instructions on how to do so (Marion and Crowder 2013; Barbash and Taylor 1997; Heider 1997; Grimshaw and Ravetz 2009).

For example, visual methods are being used in the field to record interviews and other events being ethnographically observed, either in addition to or in lieu of written field notes. There are certainly some advantages to using film in this way. Filmmaking can enhance and advance the process of taking field notes since with film one can not only record complete interviews, but also visually capture the gestalt in which interviews took place, as well as other areas of interest in psychological anthropology such as parapraxes, body language, proxemics, kinesthetic, and eye gaze (Prost 2003). Indeed, some of the earliest footage shot by Muybridge (Muybridge et al. 2010) was used for postural and movement analysis in the late 1800s. The ability to visually record a respondent and take field notes about the footage later frees one up during the interview to focus on the respondent, rather than turning away and busily scribbling notes or going off in a corner and writing up observations.

When capturing data in the field, one of the earliest, and still relevant, debates regarding the use and utility of film in psychological anthropology is over how one views the camera—as a neutral observer or a subjective extension of the filmmaker's perspective. In some ways, the purpose and application of film as understood by people like Margaret Mead—who was very clear that film could provide a rich, eminently descriptive part of a researcher's armamentarium—typify a certain perspective on how visual "data" should be gathered, interpreted, and utilized. Her position, and the argument against it, can be seen clearly in an at-times contentious conversation between Mead and Bateson (Brand 1976), held long after their divorce and toward the end of both of their lives, as they discussed their Balinese material and debated how to use the camera as a research tool. Mead believed film data could be as objective and "scientific" as possible. In fact, she believed that unaltered footage, such as the kind you might get by setting up a tripod in the corner of a room, would provide the most accurate visual record, unbiased by what the filmmaker/anthropologist might "think" was happening. She believed that "artful" films were useless for research, whereas objective films were useful as "proof" for the claims and hypotheses of anthropologists that would withstand the test of time, as they were available to be examined and re-examined in light of new theoretical developments. She also believed such tripod footage could capture information that the anthropologist did not even know was important at the time of recording, hence revealing key insights when viewed at a future date by the filmmaker, team members, or other researchers.

Bateson held that it was impossible for any visual record to be "unaltered" by the subjectivity of the filmmaker/anthropologist, and therefore believed that "the photographic record *should* be an art form" (Brand 1976). He was a proponent of the hand-held, interactive, and "responsive" camera, arguing that the camera disconnected from the artful direction of the anthropologist/filmmaker was nothing but "a dead camera [that] sees nothing."

To this day the basics of Mead and Bateson's opposing positions remain operative, frequently echoed in critiques of "positivist" positions in visual ethnography that reject the idea that one "truth" of any situation exists, let alone is available to be captured on a video camera (Pink 2001; Ruby 1980) and the waning interest in the "accuracy" of data in favor of the situated perspective that data might illuminate (Holliday 2000). Congruent with the interpretivist and post-modern turn in anthropology, most contemporary cultural anthropologists would be in agreement with Bateson in terms of their approach to their written field notes, seeing these as an obvious extension of the anthropologist's viewpoint. But when it comes to film, Bateson's theoretical stance does not translate well, and due to the lack of exposure of most non-visual anthropologists, many would still agree with Mead's position of the camera as a "naïve observer." When many anthropologists approach the use and potentialities of film and video, they tend to use these forms essentially as further methods to "objectively" document what is happening, rather than as an expression of what they are subjectively framing and seeing. As has been noted in allied fields of social science, "Visual inquiry has for the large part failed to connect with the wider currents in social theory" which has meant there is a "widespread tendency to use visual materials... in a purely illustrative, archival, or documentary way rather than giving them a more analytic treatment" (Emmison and Smith as quoted in Pink 2001, 587). This disjunction can be rather puzzling and startling, and is most clearly evident in how people both write up field notes and utilize their recordings for that purpose.

Still, there are strengths and weaknesses to using film in the field. When filming, in the past one could not include any of the immediate reflections, personal thoughts, queries, or insights that emerge when writing up field notes, therefore video recordings could not supplant such notes (unless perhaps one also made a video diary). That may be changing; there are now technologies that allow one to write notes as the camera is live, so the notes are linked to a specific time code of the camera. However, without utilizing such emergent technologies, the fresh and immediate generation of ideas that occurs along with taking field notes could be lost if one is relying on recorded footage, waiting until after the day is done and reviewing the footage in the evening—or more likely, another day. However, some of the solitary and reflective activity of written field notes can be mirrored and even expanded later in the video editing process. The process of reviewing footage can return one in some very direct ways to the experience of "being there" and the thoughts and feelings one had during the interview or observation can be re-accessed; in fact filming may actually allow the ethnographer to remember the context and sensory experience of fieldwork *more* accurately, without the mediation of memory, with all its vicissitudes and distortions.

Of course, this is not to say that what one gets on video is at all a totalistic account, and the issue of the camera's presence shaping, distorting, or closing off certain forms of data or expression is always operant. But video or film does yield a wealth of contextual information that would be almost impossible to replicate in its entirety with written field notes. Footage can be viewed multiple times, concentrating on different aspects, and it also can be slowed down and coded. It can be played for interview subjects to elicit further information and insight (Collier and Collier 1986; Harper 2002), and this elicitation can be used to bridge visible, tangible, or external information with internal or conceptual worlds (Connor et al. 1981).

Given the affordability of videotapes and the lightness and ease of use of video cameras, it seems an obvious choice to incorporate at least some amount of filming into fieldwork and even minimally edited recordings can be used to enhance the presentation of anthropology projects for classroom, fundraising, and translational purposes.

In addition to the potential ways film or video can enhance data collection in the field of the subject proper of ethnographic inquiry is the way it might enhance the depiction of the complex interactions between film participants, the anthropologist, and the filmmaker. Within the psychological anthropology corpus, there is relatively little material about the direct nature of the responses of a subject or informant vis-à-vis their reactions to their representation in a written ethnography, particularly among non-native English-speaking populations. Within a standard written ethnography, there are multiple levels of mediation of direct experience, particularly as it is filtered through the anthropologist's writing process; even then it is not a given that the subject will access the final product, depending on whether they are literate or fluent in stylized academic prose in which a typical ethnography is written. In any case, time and space intercede so that the participant's direct and immediate reaction to and understanding of the material and their representation are often lost or greatly truncated. This is not the case when the subjects watch themselves onscreen or in a film, where there is an opportunity for a more direct reaction that could be profitably analyzed for insights.

In the field of ethnographic film, interestingly enough, right from the beginning there was an interest in including a representation of how the subjects engage with the film recordings of themselves in the finished product. In *Nanook of the North* in the title cards at the beginning of the film, there are notes about how Nanook's family enjoyed watching the "moving pictures" of themselves as they went about their dramatized daily activities. In later decades, while subjects were shown footage and even were filmed commenting on it, it was not until the *Jero Tapakan* films by Tim Asch that the reaction of the character was made the entire focus of the film, in *Jero on Jero* (Connor et al. 1981). Since that time it has become commonplace for filmmakers to show a representation of their participants reacting to rough cuts or even finished cuts of the film about them.

For all these reasons, visual anthropology practitioners or would-be practitioners have a sense that visual and multimedia modes of anthropology are the future of the field, best situated to bridge the gap between the academy and the lay person, especially now as most anthropology journals are going completely digital. It is important to note here, though, that visual components are not intended to replace writing, but to complement work in concert with it. Even to some of visual anthropology's most enthusiastic apologists, visual ethnography is seen as additive. No one considers it a substitution for written ethnography, and people who do not do written ethnography in addition to their visual work are not calling themselves anthropologists, but rather practitioners of ethnographic or documentary film (Tucker 2014).

What is needed, therefore, for a visual psychological anthropology are person-centered, participant- and narrative-driven, emotionally focused films in specific places, contexts, and domains to enhance and complement the outstanding written work being done. Ethnographic methods and the concerns of psychological anthropology have actually paved the way for such films, and therefore they could be a natural extension of the pre-existing ethnographic repertoire. Finally, it is in the integration of visual and written forms, as explored and enacted in this book, that should be the future goal of visual psychological anthropology.

NOTE

1. Roger Ebert, in his review of Stanley Kubrick's *Barry Lyndon* (Ebert 2009) makes the point that "Kubrick was such a master at getting, there are *not* multiple ways in which to interpret what Kubrick is trying to say, there is *only* Kubrick's interpretation. In other words, we don't simply see Kubrick's movie, we see it in the frame of mind he insists on—unless we're so closed to the notion of directorial styles that the whole thing just seems like a beautiful extravagance (which it is). There is no other way to see Barry than the way Kubrick sees him."

REFERENCES

Acciaioli, Gregory. 2003. Grounds of Conflict, Idioms of Harmony: Custom, Religion and Nationalism in Violence Avoidance at the Lindu Plain, Cental Sulawesi. *Indonesia* 72: 81–114.

Anderson, M. 2003. 'One Flew over the Psychiatric Unit': Mental Illness and the Media. *Journal of Psychiatric and Mental Health Nursing* 10 (3): 297–306.

Asch, Timothy. 1979. Making a Film Record of the Yanomamo Indians of Southern Venezuela. *Perspectives on Film* 2: 4–9.

Asch, Timothy, and Napoleon Chagnon. 1968–1971. *The Yanomamo Series.* 7 hrs, 8 min. Watertown: Documentary Educational Resources. http://www.der.org/films/yanomamo-series.html

———. 1975. *The Ax Fight.* 30 min. Watertown: Documentary Educational Resources. http://www.der.org/films/ax-fight.html

Asch, Timothy, John Marshall, and Peter Spier. 1973. Ethnographic Film: Structure and Function. *Annual Review of Anthropology* 2: 179–187.

Banks, Marcus. 2001. *Visual Methods in Social Research.* London: Sage.

Banks, Marcus, and Jay Ruby, eds. 2011. *Made to Be Seen: Perspectives on the History of Visual Anthropology.* Chicago: University of Chicago Press.

Barbash, Ilisa, and Lucien Taylor. 1997. *Cross-Cultural Filmmaking: A Handbook for Making Documentary and Ethnographic Films and Videos.* Berkeley: University of California Press.

Bateson, Gregory, and Margaret Mead. 1942. In *Balinese Character: A Photographic Analysis*, Special Publications of the New York Academy of Sciences Vol II, ed. W.G. Valentine. New York: The New York Academy of Sciences.
———. 1950. *Karba's First Years*. 20 min. New York: New York University Film Library.
———. 1954. *Bathing Babies in Three Cultures*. 11 min. University Park: Pennsylvania State University.
Behar, Ruth. 1993. *Translated Woman: Crossing the Border with Esperanza's Story*. 10th Anniversary Edition. Boston: Beacon Press.
———. 2003. *Translated Woman: Crossing the Border with Esperanza's Story*. 10th Anniversary Edition. Boston: Beacon Press.
Biehl, João G. 2005. *Vita: Life in a Zone of Social Abandonment. Photographs by Torban Eskerod*. Berkeley: University of California Press. https://doi.org/10.1525/california/9780520247925.001.0001
Borshay Liem, Deann. 2000. *First Person Plural*. 1 hr. Berkeley: Mu Films.
Brand, Stewart. 1976. For God's Sake, Margaret [A Conversation Between Stewart Brand, Gregory Bateson, and Margaret Mead]. *CoEvolutionary Quarterly* 10: 32–44.
Bruner, Jerome. 1984. Interaction, Communication, and Self. *Journal of the American Academy of Child Psychiatry* 23 (1): 1–7.
Chernoff, John M. 2003. *Hustling Is Not Stealing: Stories of an African Bar Girl*. Chicago: University of Chicago Press.
———. 2005. *Exchange Is Not Robbery: More Stories of an African Bar Girl*. Chicago: University of Chicago Press.
Collier, John, and Malcolm Collier. 1986. *Visual Anthropology: Photography as a Research Method*. Minneapolis: University of Minnesota Press.
Connor, Linda, Patsy Asch, and Timothy Asch. 1981. *Jero on Jero: A Balinese Trance Seance Observed*. 17 min. Watertown: Documentary Educational Resources. http://www.der.org/films/balinese-trance-seance.html
———. 1986. *Jero Tapakan: Balinese Healer*. Cambridge: Cambridge University Press. http://der.org/films/jero-tapakan-series.html
Connor, Linda, Timothy Asch, and Patsy Asch. 1979–1983. *Jero Tapakan Series*. Watertown: Documentary Educational Resources. http://der.org/films/jero-tapakan-series.html
Cooper, Merian C., and Ernest B. Schoedsack. 1925. *Grass [Iran]*. 71 min. Los Angeles: Paramount Pictures.
Crapanzano, Vincent. 1980. *Tuhami: Portrait of a Moroccan*. Chicago: University of Chicago Press.
Csordas, Thomas J. 2004. Asymptote of the Ineffable: Embodiment, Alterity, and the Theory of Religion. *Current Anthropology* 45 (2): 163–185. doi:10.1086/381046

Curtis, Edward S., and Hans-Christian Adam. 2014. *The North American Indian: The Complete Portfolios.* Cologne: Taschen. still image.

Curtis, Edward S., and Frederick Webb Hodge. 1970. *The North American Indian, Being a Series of Volumes Picturing and Describing the Indians of the United States and Alaska.* 20 vols, *Landmarks in Anthropology.* New York: Johnson Reprint Corp.

De la Falaise, Henry. 1935. *Legong, Dance of the Virgins.* 65 min. DuWorld Pictures (US) and Paramount International.

Deren, Maya, 1953. *The Divine Horseman: The Living Gods of Haiti.* 52 min. Boston: Howard Gottlieb Archival Research Center.

Deren, Maya, and Gregory Bateson. 1980. An Exchange of Letters Between Maya Deren and Gregory Bateson. *October* 14: 16–20. doi:10.2307/778528

Drew, Richard. 1963. *Crisis: Behind a Presidential Commitment.* 52 min. New York: Criterion Collection.

Du Bois, Cora Alice, Abram Kardiner, and Emil Oberholzer. 1944. *The People of Alor; A Social Psychological Study of an East Indian Island.* Minneapolis: The University of Minnesota Press.

Ebert, Roger. 2009. Barry Lyndon [Film Review]. http://www.rogerebert.com/reviews/barry-lyndon-1975

Edwards, Elizabeth. 2001. *Raw Histories: Photographs, Anthropology and Museums.* Oxford: Berg.

Erickson, Paul A., Liam D. Murphy, and Paul A. Erickson. 2013. *Readings for a History of Anthropological Theory.* 4th ed. North York: University of Toronto Press.

Feldman, Seth, ed. 2002. *Allan King: Filmmaker.* Bloomington: Indiana University Press.

Flaherty, Robert J. 1922. *Nanook of the North.* 1 hr, 19 min. Buffalo: Pathé Exchange.

Fox, James, Patsy Asch, and Timothy Asch. 1989. *Spear and Sword: A Ceremonial Payment of Bridewealth.* 25 min. Watertown: Documentary Educational Resources. http://www.der.org/films/spear-and-sword.html

Fruzzetti, Lina, Akos Ostor, and Aditi Nath Sarkar. 2005. *Singing Pictures.* 40 min. Watertown: Documentary Educational Resources. http://www.der.org/films/singing-pictures.html

Gardner, Robert. 1963. *Dead Birds.* 83 min. Watertown: Documentary Educational Resources. http://www.der.org/films/dead-birds.html

———. 1971. *The Nuer.* 73 min. Watertown: Documentary Educational Resources. http://www.der.org/films/the-nuer.html

———. 1974. *Rivers of Sand.* 85 min. Watertown: Documentary Educational Resources. http://www.der.org/films/rivers-of-sand.html

———. 1986. *Forest of Bliss.* 90 min. Watertown: Documentary Educational Resources. http://www.der.org/films/forest-of-bliss.html

Getzels, Peter, and Harriet Gordon. 1985. *In the Footsteps of Taytacha*. 30 min. Watertown: Documentary Educational Resources. http://www.der.org/films/footsteps-of-taytacha.html

Gilbert, Craig (Producer). 1973. *An American Family*. Arlington: PBS.

Grimshaw, Anna, and Amanda Ravetz. 2009. *Observational Cinema: Anthropology, Film, and the Exploration of Social Life*. Bloomington: Indiana University Press.

Gruber, Jacob W. 1970. Ethnographic Salvage and the Shaping of Anthropology. *American Anthropologist* 72 (6): 1289–1299. doi:10.1525/aa.1970.72.6.02a00040

Haddon, Alfred C., W. H. R. Rivers, C. G. Seligman, Charles Samuel Myers, William McDougall, Sidney Herbert Ray, and Anthony Wilkin. 1901. *Reports of the Cambridge Anthropological Expedition to Torres Straits*. 6 vols. Cambridge: The University Press.

Hallowell, Alfred I. 1955. *Culture and Experience*. Philadelphia: University of Pennsylvania Press.

Hara, Kazuo. 1972. *Goodbye Cp [Sayonara Cp]*. 1 hr, 22 min. Tokyo: Shisso Productions.

———. 1974. *Extreme Private Eros: Love Song*. 98 min. Tokyo: Shisso Productions.

———. 1987. *The Emperor's Naked Army Marches On*. 122 min. Tokyo: Shisso Productions.

Harper, Douglas. 2002. Talking About Pictures: A Case for Photo Elicitation. *Visual Studies* 17 (1): 15–26.

Hastrup, Kirsten. 1992. Anthropological Visions: Some Notes on Visual and Textual Authority. In *Film as Ethnography*, ed. Peter I. Crawford and David Durton. Manchester: University of Manchester Press.

Heider, Karl. 1974. *Dani Houses*. 35 min, 9 min extras. Watertown: Documentary Educational Resources. http://www.der.org/films/karl-heider-dani-films.html

———. 1976. *Ethnographic Film*. Austin: University of Texas Press.

Heider, Karl G. 1997. *Seeing Anthropology: Cultural Anthropology Through Film*. Boston: Allyn and Bacon.

Henley, Paul. 2010. *The Adventure of the Real: Jean Rouch and the Craft of Ethnographic Cinema*. Chicago: University of Chicago Press.

Hinton, Devon E., and Laurence J. Kirmayer. 2013. Local Responses to Trauma: Symptom, Affect, and Healing. *Transcultural Psychiatry* 50 (5): 607–621.

Hollan, Douglas, and Jane C. Wellankamp. 1994. *Contentment and Suffering: Culture and Experience in Toraja*. New York: Columbia University Press.

Holliday, R. 2000. We've Been Framed: Visualising Methodology. *The Sociological Review* 48 (4): 503–522.

Hoskins, Janet, and Laura Whitney. 1991. *Horses of Life and Death*. 28 min. Los Angeles: Center for Visual Anthropology. http://www.der.org/films/horses-of-life-and-death.html

Jackson, Michael. 2015. *The Wherewithal of Life: Ethics, Migration, and the Question of Well-Being*. Berkeley: University of California Press.

Jenkins, Janis H., and Robert J. Barrett, eds. 2004. *Schizophrenia, Culture, and Subjectivity: The Edge of Experience*. Cambridge: Cambridge University Press.

Jensen, Gordon D., and Luh Ketut Suryani. 1992. *The Balinese People: A Reinvestigation of Character*. New York: Oxford University Press.

Kardiner, Abram, and Ralph Linton. 1974. *The Individual and His Society: The Psychodynamics of Primitive Social Organization*. Westport: Greenwood Press.

King, Allan. 1967. *Warrendale*. 1 hr, 40 min. New York: The Criterion Collection.

———. 1969. *A Married Couple*. 1 hr, 37 min. New York: The Criterion Collection.

Kirmayer, Laurence J., and Norman Sartorius. 2007. Cultural Models and Somatic Syndromes. *Psychosomatic Medicine* 69 (9): 832–840.

Klin, Anat, and Dafna Nemish. 2008. Mental Disorders Stigma in the Media: Review of Studies on Production, Content, and Influences. *Journal of Health Communication* 13 (5): 434–449.

Kopple, Barbara. 1976. *Harlan County, USA*. 1 hr, 43 min. New York: The Criterion Collection.

Lewis, E. Douglas, Timothy Asch, and Patsy Asch. 1992. *A Celebration of Origins*. 45 min. Watertown: Documentary Educational Resources. http://www.der.org/films/celebration-of-origins.html

Luhrmann, T.M. 2012. *When God Talks Back: Understanding the American Evangelical Relationship with God*. New York: Alfred A. Knopf.

MacDonald, Scott. 2013. *American Ethnographic Film and Personal Documentary: The Cambridge Turn*. Berkeley: University of California Press.

MacDougall, David. 1992. 'Photo Wallahs': An Encounter with Photography. *Visual Anthropology Review* 8 (2): 96–100.

———. 1998. *Transcultural Cinema*. Edited and with an Introduction by Lucien Taylor. Princeton: Princeton University Press.

Malle, Louis. 1969. *Calcutta*. 105 min. Paris: Nouvelle Éditions de Films.

Marion, Jonathan S., and Jerome W. Crowder. 2013. *Visual Research: A Concise Introduction to Thinking Visually*. English edition. London: Berg.

Marshall, John. 1957. *The Hunters*. 1 hr, 12 min. Watertown: Documentary Educational Resources. http://www.der.org/films/hunters.html

———. 1969a. *A Curing Ceremony*. 9 min. Watertown: Documentary Educational Resources. http://www.der.org/films/curing-ceremony.html

———. 1969b. *N/Um Tchai: The Ceremonial Dance of The !Kung Bushmen*. 20 min. Watertown: Documentary Educational Resources. http://www.der.org/films/num-tchai.html

———. 1980. *N!Ai, Story of A !Kung Woman*. 59 min. Watertown: Documentary Educational Resources. http://www.der.org/films/nai-kung-woman.html

———. 1993. Filming and Learning. In *The Cinema of John Marshall*, ed. Jay Ruby, 1–134. Philadelphia: Harwood.

Marshall, John, and Claire Ritchie. 1951–2002. *A Kalahari Family.* 360 min. Watertown: Kalfam Productions and Documentary Educational Resources. http://www.der.org/films/a-kalahari-family.html

Maysles, Albert, David Maysles, and Charlotte Zwerin. 1970. *Gimme Shelter.* 91 min. New York: Criterion.

McElwee, Ross. 1993. *Time Indefinite.* New York: First Run Features.

Mead, Margaret. 1995. Visual Anthropology in a Discipline of Words. In *Principles of Visual Anthropology*, ed. Paul Hockings, 3–10. Berlin: De Gruyter.

———. 2001. *Coming of Age in Samoa: A Psychological Study of Primitive Youth for Western Civilisation.* 1st Perennial Classics edition. New York: Perennial Classics.

Mead, Margaret, and Gregory Bateson. 1952. *Trance and Dance in Bali.* 22 min. New York: New York University Film Library.

Merrison, Lindsay. 2001. *Friends in High Places.* Watertown: Documentary Educational Resources. http://www.der.org/films/friends-in-high-places.html

Muybridge, Eadweard. 1979. *Muybridge's Complete Human and Animal Locomotion: All 781 Plates from the 1887 Animal Locomotion.* 3 vols. New York: Dover Publications. Publisher description http://www.loc.gov/catdir/enhancements/fy0709/79051299-d.html

Muybridge, Eadweard, Hans-Christian Adam, Stephen Herbert, Eadweard Muybridge, and Eadweard Muybridge. 2010. *Eadweard Muybridge, the Human and Animal Locomotion Photographs.* Köln/London: Taschen.

Nichols, Bill, and Maya Deren. 2001. *Maya Deren and the American Avant-Garde.* Berkeley: University of California Press.

Noel, John B.L. 1927. *The Epic of Everest.* 1 hr, 27 min. London: BFI.

Orgeron, Marsha, and Devin Orgeron. 2007. Family Pursuits, Editorial Acts: Documentaries After the Age of Home Video. *The Velvet Light Trap* 60: 47–62.

Pennebaker, D.A. 1960. *Primary.* 60 min. Los Angeles: Academy Film Archive.

———. 1967. *Bob Dylan: Don't Look Back.* 1 hr, 36 min. New York: Leacock-Pennebaker.

Pink, Sara. 2001. More Visualizing, More Methodologies: On Video, Reflexivity, and Qualitative Research. *The Sociological Review* 49 (4): 586–599. doi:10.1111/1467-954X.00349

Poeuv, Socheata. 2008. *New Year Baby.* 1 hr, 20 min. Arlington: PBS.

Prost, J.H. 2003. Filming Body Behavior. In *Principles of Visual Anthropology*, ed. Paul Hockings, 285–313. Berlin: Mouton de Gruyter.

Renov, Michael. 1989. The Subject in History: The New Autobiography in Film and Video. *Afterimage* 17(1): 4–7.

Rony, Fatimah Tobing. 1996. *The Third Eye: Race, Cinema, and Ethnographic Spectacle.* Durham: Duke University Press.

———. 2006. The Photogenic Cannot Be Tamed: Margaret Mead and Gregory Bateson's "Trance and Dance in Bali". *Discourse* 28 (1): 5–27. http://www.jstor.org/stable/41389738

Rouch, Jean. 1954. *Les Maitres Fous [Not Capitalized] [The Mad Masters]*. 36 min. Paris: Editions Montparnasse.

———. 1968. *Moi, Un Noir*. 70 mins. New York: Icarus Films.

Rouch, Jean, and Edgar Morin. 1961. *Chronique D'un Été [Chronicle of a Summer]*. 1 hr, 25 min. Neuilly sur Seine: Argo Films.

Ruby, Jay. 1975. Is Ethnographic Film a Filmic Ethnography. *Studies in the Anthropology of Visual Communication* 2 (2).

———. 1980. Exposing Yourself: Reflexivity, Anthropology, Film. *Semiotica* 301 (2): 153–179. https://doi.org/10.1515/semi.1980.30.1-2.153

———, ed. 1993. *The Cinema of John Marshall*. Philadelphia: Harwood.

Russell, Catherine. 1999. *Experimental Ethnography: The Work of Film in the Age of Video*. Durham: Duke University Press.

Stoller, Papul. 1992. *The Cinematic Griot*. Chicago: University of Chicago Press.

Talley, Truman H. 1937. *Borneo* [Martin and Osa Johnson]. 76 min. Turner Classic Movies.

Taylor, Lucien. 1996. Iconophobia: How Anthropology Lost It at the Movies. *Transition* 69: 64–88.

Tucker, Annie. 2014. The State of Visual Anthropology and Multi-Modal Ethnography: A Report from the Screening Scholarship Media Festival 2014. *Psychocultural Cinema*. http://psychoculturalcinema.com/the-state-of-visual-anthropology-and-multi-modal-ethnography-a-report-from-the-screening-scholarship-media-festival-2014-part-1-of-2/

Wahl, Otto F. 1995. *Media Madness: Public Images of Mental Illness*. New Brunswick: Rutgers University Press.

Weisner, Thomas S. 2002. Ecocultural Understandings of Children's Developmental Pathways. *Human Development* 45: 275–281.

Whiting, B.B., ed. 1963. *Six Cultures: Studies of Child Rearing*. New York: Wiley.

Wikan, Unni. 1990. *Managing Turbulent Hearts: A Balinese Formula for Living*. Chicago: University of Chicago Press.

Willis, Artemis. 2009. *Da Feast!* 22 min. Watertown: Documentary Educational Resources. http://www.der.org/films/da-feast.html

Wiseman, Frederick. 1967. *Titicut Follies*. 84 min. Cambridge: Zipporah Films.

———. 1968. *High School*. 75 min. Cambridge: Zipporah Films.

———. 1975. *Welfare*. 2 hr, 47 min. Cambridge: Zipporah Films.

Worth, Sol, and John Adair. 1972. *Through Navajo Eyes: An Exploration in Film Communication and Anthropology*. 2nd ed. Bloomington: Indiana University Press.

Zemp, Hugo. 2001–2002. *Masters of the Balafon Series*. 221 min. Watertown: Documentary Educational Resources. http://www.der.org/films/masters-of-the-balafon.html

CHAPTER 3

The Lived Experience of Culture and Mental Illness in Indonesia

Now that some of the fundamentals of both psychological anthropology and ethnographic film have been presented, and various linkages and directions proposed, the question arises over just how these are related to the topic at hand, the *Afflictions* film series (Lemelson 2010–2011). This chapter reviews the multiple contexts of culture, mental illness, and outcome relevant to the ethnographic literature on Bali and Java, and then relates these to their multilayered representation in the *Afflictions* series.

3.1   Ethnography and Mental Illness: A Brief Review

There have been many anthropological works, both ethnographic and theoretical, devoted to defining culture's influence on factors crucial to mental health or disturbance such as developmental processes, family emotional environments, explanatory models and idioms of distress, and the treatment and interpretation of illness and distress. The traditional interests of the field such as kinship, subsistence patterns, cosmology, and ritual life also contribute to a broader understanding of the multiple contexts of health and illness. Anthropology's primary method of research, ethnographic fieldwork, offers a broad and holistic perspective that expands and refines an understanding of an individual's lived experience across multiple domains.

Within anthropology, the study of mental illness has largely been the domain of psychological anthropology, which began with "culture and personality" and has developed ever more sophisticated methodology for

© The Author(s) 2017   49
R. Lemelson, A. Tucker, *Afflictions*, Culture, Mind, and Society,
DOI 10.1007/978-3-319-59984-7_3

studying the complex dynamics of subjectivity, intersubjectivity, and phenomenology that shape discrete areas of cultural life (Desjarlais and Throop
2011, 240). Recent transcultural psychiatric research has shown that mental
illness experience is an interactive and interpretive enterprise constructed in
social situations based on cultural models and understandings of illness and
social behavior (Csordas 2004; Fuchs 2010; Kirmayer and Sartorius 2007;
White and Marsella 1984). Current theory in psychological anthropology
posits, for example, that "culture" pervades the subjective experience of
psychotic illness and mediates those aspects which might be more "hard-
wired" by influencing the content of fantasy, hallucination, obsessions, and
anxieties (Luhrmann and Marrow 2016; Luhrmann et al. 2015) and offering available local frameworks for personal idioms of distress (Hinton and
Lewis-Fernández 2010); shaping the expression of cognition, affect, and
the interpretation of the meaning of illness (Makanjuola et al. 2016; Hecker
et al. 2016); structuring certain events that may act as triggers (Boehnlein
et al. 2004; Kinzie and Boehnlein 1989); and inflecting the personal narratives and embodied associations that draw these together. Family and the
immediate psychosocial environment also play key roles in the degree of
disability, morbidity, and mortality associated with major mental illness, and
are major factors influencing outcome and recovery (Subandi 2015a; Gone
2013; Burns 2009; Ng et al. 2008). These are some of the ways in which
psychological anthropology understands culture to influence the multiple
facets of mental illness experience.

These multiple perspectives are useful in understanding an individual's
phenomenological experience and course of mental illness within a specific
cultural group at a specific point in time. Ethnography explores meaning
systems and explanatory models, investigating the contexts of major mental
illness and the local categories of experience and meaning that frame symptomatology. An ethnographic understanding, measured over multiple
months or years of community-based fieldwork and deriving categories of
analysis relevant to the "lifeworlds" of patients, can provide the theory,
methodology, and vocabulary for addressing culture that neurobiological,
clinical, and even phenomenological models of major mental illness struggle
to explain fully.

Anthropologists have provided theoretical and applied models in these
areas, using anecdote, case studies, and in-depth cultural biographies
(Jenkins 2015; Luhrmann and Marrow 2016) to complement and illuminate more data-driven work in cross-cultural psychology and psychiatry,
such as the World Health Organization (WHO) global comparative study

on schizophrenia (Hopper et al. 2007). A range of ethnographies have explored psychotic illnesses and culture. In *Saints, Scholars, and Schizophrenics* (Scheper-Hughes 1979), Nancy Scheper-Hughes presented an interactionist perspective of mentally ill members of an Irish community that sought to reconcile medical understandings of schizophrenia with the social context and particular stressors that might render certain men vulnerable to developing the disorder. João Biehl's groundbreaking *Vita* (2005) is a textured, in-depth ethnography of a "mad" individual left to die in a "zone of abandonment" in Brazil, which in its recent re-issue is complemented by visual ethnography in the form of a photo-essay by Torban Eskerod. In her work on Bethel, the experimental North Japanese center for community members with mental illness, Karen Nakamura chose to do what she termed an "old-school" community study, for both her written (Nakamura 2013) and visual (Nakamura 2007) ethnographies. Emily Martin's *Bipolar Expeditions* (Martin 2007) combines auto-ethnography with cultural studies to better understand the role of mania in popular culture and individual lives. The collaborative works by Byron Good, Mary-Jo Del Vecchio Good, and Subandi (Good 2012; Good et al. 2008, 2007; Good and Subandi 2004) provide compelling examples of shorter clinical case studies of individuals with mental illness. Each of these forms provides different insights and of course works within different limitations, yet all address the complexity of the lives of people diagnosed with mental illness. This requires covering a broad field, investigating their relationships with their families and communities, their occupations, and their unique biographies. All of these elements in the lives of people with mental illness are situated within local beliefs and practices, societal structures, broader socioeconomic changes, and even political systems.

3.2   Mental Illness in Indonesia, Java, and Bali

An ethnographic approach to the complex issue of the relationship of culture to outcome needs to be grounded in specific time and place to be contextualized and relevant. This section examines what psychological anthropology brings to the study of mental illness in a specific location, which is also the focus of this book—mental illness in Indonesia, and particularly on the islands of Java and Bali. The anthropological interest in mental illness on Java and Bali dates back to some of the earliest ethnographic research conducted there (Steinberg 2015; Kulhara and Chakrabarti 2001; Pols 2007, 2006). Margaret Mead and Gregory Bateson

went to Bali as part of their research into the impact of culture on development specifically because they thought Balinese childrearing practices and
cultural values may have contributed to a "schizoid" personality, prone to
dissociation and trance-like states; indeed their research was sponsored by
the "Committee for the Study of Dementia Praecox," an abandoned psychiatric term viewing what is now labeled thought disorder, psychosis, or
schizophrenia as a chronic and degenerative disease (Jacknis 1988).

In contrast to Mead's hypothesis of culture contributing to a "schizoid
character" (read personality) in Bali, early comparative psychiatric observation in Java conducted at the turn of the twentieth century by the "father of
modern psychiatry" Emil Kraepelin suggested that aspects of Indonesian
culture might actually be protective. A focus on symptomatology intrigu-
ingly suggested that compared to those of European descent, symptoms of
schizophrenia were less severe in indigenous patients, their recovery
quicker, and their long-term prognosis better, although they often
displayed high volubility and emotionality while in the throes of
illness (Pols 2007). However, this early research on major mental illness in
Indonesia was colored by paternalistic colonialist views which asserted that
mental illnesses were diseases of civilization and that native Indonesians,
being less "civilized" and less developed mentally, were therefore less prone
to such illnesses (Pols 2007).

The understanding of the subjective experience of mental illness in
contemporary Java has been significantly deepened by the work of Subandi,
Byron and Mary-Jo Del Vecchio Good, and Kevin Browne (Biehl et al.
2007; Good and Subandi 2004; Good et al. 2007; Subandi 2009, 2015b;
Browne 2001a, b), among others. Their findings, with regard to explanatory models of mental illness, subjective experience of illness and treatment,
and sociocultural aspects of recovery, echo and complement one another.

In Bali, the most significant research on the subjective experience and
cultural interpretation of mental illness has been carried out by Linda
Connor (Connor 1982a, b), Luh Ketut Suryani (1984), and Suryani and
Gordon Jensen (Suryani and Jensen 1992), whose individual and collaborative work strives to situate extraordinary psychological, mental, and sensory experiences both within a culturally specific context and a framework of
clinical diagnostic criteria. In addition to the visual ethnography, collaborative work with Suryani also contributed to an understanding of the
subjective experience of psychiatric disorder and its treatment and the
cultural shaping of symptoms on Bali (Lemelson 2014; Lemelson and

Suryani 2006). These accounts have also been supplemented by more personal accounts such as that by Denny Thong (Thong et al. 1993).

Javanese and Balinese logics of health, well-being, illness, and suffering are operant in explanatory models and idioms of distress about and reactions to people with schizophrenia, schizoaffective disorder, psychotic illness, and neuropsychiatric disorders. There are some areas of overlap in these domains on the two islands, but notable variation as well.

Various—and often shifting or multiple—etiologies for psychotic illness reported include a lack of awareness or "daydreaming" (B.I. *melamun*); shock; a case of "nerves" (B.I. *syaraf*); exhaustion; family stress and a loss or disruption of a calm and harmonious family atmosphere (B.J. *tentrem*); possession by an angry spirit; improper care of spiritually meaningful ancestral items; improperly carried out rituals or neglect of spirits; divine curse (B.B. *keponggor*); exposure to powers that were too great via spiritual practice; and disappointment or unfulfilled wishes in almost any sphere—political, economic, romantic, or artistic (Browne 2001a; Good and Subandi 2004; Hobart 1997; Subandi 2009).

While interaction with spirit beings has the potential to be dangerous or cause harmful effects, Indonesian families and communities tend to feel greater concern about changes in external behavior and comportment, particularly aggression or disturbance in socialization and self-care, rather than the reported experience of unusual sensory phenomena, such as hearing voices or experiencing the presence or interference of unseen beings (Zaumseil and Lessmann 2007).

Terms commonly used to describe disordered or distressed ways of thinking, feeling, or behaving include: a sense of dizziness, disorientation, and feelings of being overwhelmed (B.I. *bingung, pusing*; B.J. *mumet*; B.B. *paling, inguh, lengeh*); fear or timidity (B.B. *nyeh*); disordered speech or "raving" (B.I. *mengoceh*, B.B. *ngumikmik*); or being overcome with feelings of aggression or anger (B.B. *gedeg*), sometimes associated with physical violence or going on a "rampage" and sometimes indicative of spirit possession (B.J. *ngamuk*) (Browne 2001a; Good 2012; Zaumseil and Lessman 1995). Mental illness can at times be experienced and interpreted as spirit possession, with onset triggered by intense praying or passing by spiritually charged places (Good 2012; Subandi 2009), or as a religious problem, resulting from a loss of faith, devotion, or self-regulation so that treatment involves restoring of physical, physiological, and religious order (Horikoshi 1980). With forgiving models of disrupted behavior, however, these problems must be ongoing, recurring, or of significant severity to be labeled as mental illness (B.I. *sakit jiwa, gangguan jiwa*) (Browne 2001a).

Despite the cultural specificity of idioms of distress and etiological factors, the phenomenological experience of psychotic symptoms in Bali and Java may not be radically different from that in the United States; Balinese patients reported hearing voices and feeling like they were under the voices' control, although they sometimes received conflicting demands. Hearing these voices made it difficult to have normal relationships and stressed their family, but learning to ignore them made daily life easier (Suryani et al. 2013).

3.3   Sociocultural Aspects of Recovery in Java and Bali

Certain aspects of Javanese culture might support recovery from schizophrenia, schizoaffective disorder, and transient psychosis. For example, the emphasis on harmony (B.J. *rukun*) and peace (B.J. *tentrem*) contributes to comparatively low expressed emotion (EE) in Javanese families, in accordance with their ethnographic profile. EE encompasses critical, hostile, or overinvolved reactions to the person with mental illness—high EE can lead to treatment dropout and increased relapse, while low EE or a warm family environment or relationship with caregivers contributes to better long-term outcomes, regardless of cultural context or specific diagnosis, although schizophrenia has received the most attention (Chambless and Steketee 1999; Leff et al. 1990; Lopez et al. 2004; Singh et al. 2013; Tarrier et al. 1999).

The Javanese practice of "caring for gently" (B.J. *ngemong*) can be considered to be an indigenous model of the "warmth and positive remark" that according to the EE concept is so critical to recovery and good prognosis (Lopez et al. 2004). The *ngemong* approach is used for children or for someone who appears to be "acting like a child" and encompasses tolerance of aggressive and impulsive behavior; an absence of criticism, blame, or hostility; an indulgence or fulfilling of needs while demanding or requesting little in return; and constant supportive and protective companionship (Subandi 2011; Tucker 2015; Zaumseil and Lessman 1995).

In the few Javanese families where EE was found to be high, it was accompanied by high levels of warmth and positive remark; furthermore, Subandi reports that in Javanese families high EE was not exclusive of ongoing inclusion in family activities and support of the patient in pursuing care and treatment, and was often quickly resolved to return the family to a low-EE atmosphere. In certain cases, patients interpreted their family member's high EE as evidence of their deep care, which may have mitigated its effects (Subandi 2011). In instances where covert rather than overt devaluation is not enough for the family to cope with differences in behavior—such as in cases of extreme aggression—they may resort to physically restraining the individual in locked rooms, chains, pens, or stocks, known in Indonesia as *pasung* (Suryani et al. 2011).[1]

Other sociocultural aspects of recovery that may support Javanese people who have experienced episodes of acute mental illness include orientations of *bangkit*, a return to awareness, a restoration of *rukun*, social and occupational re-engagement, and a re-ordering of physical living space (Subandi 2009). *Bangkit* is a salient term which can be glossed as "getting up again" and at once references national political histories of recovery and revitalization and a personal stance of assuming an active position, experienced tangibly in the body through physical exercise, daily practices of spiritual effort, and attempts to "keep busy" in the family and community.

In addition to restoring *rukun* through daily interactions between the ill person and his or her family members, and making amends for any potentially upsetting behavior that either preceded the illness episode or occurred during it, household peace and harmony can be restored through spiritual ministrations, such as appeasing ancestral spirits, ritually purifying and handling family heirlooms, preparing ritual offerings, or visiting graveyards where powerful spirits dwell. Muslims may drink water that has been prayed over, pray every night at midnight (*sholat tahajud*), or reinvigorate their religious piety (Browne 2001a; Subandi 2009).

For those episodes of mental illness described as confusion (B.I. *bingung, bengong*) (Browne 2001a; Subandi 2009; Zaumseil and Lessman 1995) or a loss of awareness, a returning of awareness—of surroundings, of one's own role and responsibilities—is both a symptom of and support for recovery. A key part of this awareness and recovery is re-engaging with the social world and returning to work. It is notable that Javanese individuals in Subandi's (2009) and Browne's (2001a) studies faced little discrimination in returning to work; despite illness episodes, they were welcomed back to old occupations and given new ones, trusted to return to previous responsibilities.

In Bali, causes for major mental illness included natural causes (brain disorder), relationship problems or financial stress, exhaustion, and supernatural causes (God's will or fate, witchcraft, or disturbance by the spirits). Most families reported witchcraft, fate, and family stress as the most significant causes. This attribution meant that psychiatric treatment was infrequently sought, a choice associated with poorer long-term prognosis; however, it also meant that families did not hold their disturbed members responsible and responded to them warmly and with low levels of EE, which is associated with comparatively positive long-term outcomes (Kurihara et al. 2006). In one longitudinal study, almost half of patient participants exhibited partial or total remission after eleven years (Kurihara et al. 2005b).

As in Java, certain sociocultural factors in Bali may contribute to the recovery process. For many, the spiritual interpretation of the unusual behavior associated with mental illness may allow sympathetic readings of symptoms. Balinese even recognize some "madness" as spiritual inspiration (B.B. *buduh kedewadewaan*), believing that certain forms of unusual experience and behavior are an indication of a "divinely ordained state of knowledge, rather than a degradation of the person" (Connor 1982a, 784). Some who experience such divine madness may themselves become revered healers upon their recovery.

Even for those whose illness is not labeled as divine, spiritual practices often play an important role in recovery; this may be both due to their symbolic restoration of well-being and the socially pragmatic elements of treatment. For example, a pilgrimage to a holy site simultaneously attends to the spiritual elements of illness and practically removes the sufferer from a potentially triggering or upsetting home environment that may have been contributing to or exacerbating symptoms. Dialoging with spirits via a medium similarly comforts the sufferer via direct contact with the divine, but interpreting and responding to the messages relayed through the medium also provides a safe outlet for families to vent and work through any interpersonal conflicts that may have been a part of the illness experience, sometimes leading to permanent change in family dynamics that is beneficial to the ill member (Connor 1982a).

3.4   HISTORY OF MENTAL HEALTH CARE IN BALI AND JAVA

Indigenous approaches to mental illness in Indonesia have been historically tolerant, with traditional healing and family intervention as outlined above being the sole or primary recourse for many. In addition to the ongoing use of traditional healing in contexts of mental illness or disturbance, there has been a process of change with regard to how mental illness is treated in Indonesia.

By the first decade of the twentieth century, the official government-sponsored medical system was based mostly on European allopathic medicine, used in conjunction with traditional healing (Connor 1982a, McCauley 1984). The Dutch colonists established the first psychiatric institutions in Indonesia, with both acute care and long-term facilities providing a primarily custodial function for those who were disturbing the social order and declared insane by a practicing physician. A limited number of agricultural colonies were established for those considered unlikely to improve (Pols 2006). Throughout the first half of the twentieth century, all of these facilities were understaffed and overcrowded, and some custodial care spilled over into the prison system (Porath 2008).

The 1960s–1980s saw the development of modern psychiatry in Indonesia, alongside the development of the medical field more broadly, and the national Directorate of Mental Health's establishment of *Tri Upaya Bina Jiwa*, or "The Three Pillars of Mental Health": prevention, treatment, and rehabilitation (Wahyuni et al. 2012). Public and private mental hospitals were established and a quarterly psychiatric research journal, *Jiwa*, was founded in 1968. Mental health education improved, and during this period, Indonesian psychiatry was a model for other Southeast Asian countries.

The economic crises of the 1990s saw a decline in care, which is now variable depending on individual institutional funding and capacity (Pols 2006). In his work on mental illness in the early 2000s, Kevin O. Browne observed that in concert with antipsychotic, anti-depressant, and other medications, electroconvulsive therapy (ECT) was routinely used to treat severely depressed, aggressive, and/or psychotic patients. ECT was a preferred method of treatment because it reduced symptoms quickly and allowed the patient to return home sooner. This is significant because hospitalization and medications are expensive and many families go into debt in order to provide institutionalized care for their relatives; many patients may be discharged with the designations of "improved" (B.I. *membaik*) or "socially recovered" (B.I. *sembuh sosial*) while still exhibiting significant impairment in functioning (Browne 2001a).

Psychiatric institutionalization still carries significant stigma for Indonesian families. Therefore, many still try other treatments first, such as home care, traditional healing, or boarding at local clinics or religious boarding schools (B.I. *pesantren, asrama*) (Horikoshi 1980). There are benefits in being treated by family members; home placement avoids the feelings of isolation, loneliness, or uselessness that often accompany a hospital stay

(Nurjannah et al. 2009), and family treatment harmonizes with traditional Indonesian folk models of well-being and communal approaches to illness. The home environment, particularly in a small town where people know a patient's history and might be more tolerant, might prove more supportive or safe than an anonymous urban center where psychiatric hospitals are often located. However, there are significant challenges to home care; people with major mental illness experiencing mania, for example, may be disruptive or upsetting to the local community. If the presentation of mental illness does not fit with vernacular models of spirit possession or other forms of locally recognizable or coherent disturbance, people may not believe that the ill person is truly ill, and therefore their behaviors will not necessarily be met with tolerance. Finally, family members may not know how to respond to mental illness, which in extreme cases can lead to confinement or shackling of people with mental illness in the home (B.I. *pasung*), even within families with the best intentions (Suryani et al. 2011; Zaumseil and Lessman 1995).

Many Indonesian mental health professionals promote new supportive and integrative models of outpatient treatment, where families are given training in how to care for their ill family member, utilizing community placement as an integral part of psychiatric care alongside ongoing therapy and pharmacological treatment (Jensen and Suryani 1992; Stratford et al. 2013; Suryani et al. 2011). Through outreach campaigns, psychiatric professionals educate general practitioners about mental illness and promote early intervention and kinds of treatment with complementary programming that educates families about the causes of mental illness. This approach seeks to dispel the idea that mental illness is the result of black magic, and to promote the use of state mental health institutions either instead of traditional healers or alongside them.

Institutional psychiatric care remains limited due to a lack of facilities. In 2006 Bali had 260 psychiatric beds for approximately 3,050,000 people (Kurihara et al. 2006), while the prevalence of people with major mental illness was estimated at 4.2 out of 1000 (Kurihara et al. 2005a, b). In 2007 Yogyakarta was reported to have more beds than the national average, with 1 for every 10, 000 inhabitants (Zaumseil and Lessmann 2007). A recent boom in hospital development (Bellman 2012) is likely to impact the kinds of care available to those with mental illness.

Similarly, the lack of available and reliable medications may negate the efficacy of biomedical treatment for psychiatric disorders. Psychotropic drugs were introduced to Indonesia in the mid-1950s, primarily for schizophrenia, depression, anxiety, and insomnia. Currently, there are fifteen major anti-depressants, twelve antipsychotics, seven anti-anxiety drugs and four hypnotics most commonly used for treatment (Iskandar 2004). However, throughout the developing world there is trafficking and sales of counterfeit medication. Upwards of 50% of medications sold openly in pharmacies in the developing world may be counterfeit (Cockburn et al. 2005). This means that the active ingredients are present in the wrong amounts, contaminated, replaced by similar acting substances, or entirely missing.

A biomedical approach to psychiatric care is one part of a wider globalized hegemonic process affecting discourses, understandings, and treatment practices and their relation to mental illness, the arrival of which should be heralded with caution. Through both sweeping changes in strategies of mental health care and targeted campaigns by mental health organizations, it has become accepted in the United States to view and treat mental illnesses, such as depression or bipolar disorder, as "brain diseases" over which the ill person has no more control than they might over an infection or other organic illness. The rationale behind this conceptual shift is that by revealing the biological underpinning of psychic suffering, blame and therefore stigma can be relieved from those experiencing it, which in turn might translate into less social isolation and marginalization, yet the lived realities of such a biological model are much more complicated, as the ethnographic case studies in this book illustrate.

3.5   THE *AFFLICTIONS* SERIES

In sum, some of the most salient cultural and local factors in the diagnosis and treatment of mental illness in Bali and Java include collective and holistic approaches to health and well-being which account for emotional and moral etiologies of illness, the use of traditional healers who have elaborated systems of health and disruption or disturbance, a shared animist background and history, Islamic and Hindu healing therapeutics, colonial and post-colonial histories of psychiatric care, and the spread of both a local and globalized popular psychology and psychiatry. In addition, the issues that the WHO researchers identified as salient to differential outcome and recovery from major mental illness, such as labeling, attribution, work routines, social support, family emotional climate, and access to different forms of treatment, are all deeply shaped by Balinese, Javanese, and national Indonesian culture. All of these affect the course of treatment and the long-term outcomes of mental illness for the people portrayed in the *Afflictions* series, becoming common threads traced through all the films. What is the best method to reflect these issues on-screen?

The *Afflictions* ethnographic project presents and analyzes its findings on these themes and topics using a character-based case study structure for six individuals. This particular approach has a number of benefits for exploring this subject matter, especially when using multi-modal and visual psychological anthropology.

Film is well suited to character-based studies because one can imbue them with emotion, conflict, and other forms of "real life" drama. A case-based approach highlights themes in psychological anthropology but embeds these themes in a biographical storyline of a real person and illustrates the impact of dynamics and concepts identified and articulated by psychological anthropology in people's actual lives—both their inner worlds and the everyday practicalities of their lives. In general, the biographical approach makes complex ideas tangible and relatable to an audience.

The comparative case study approach espouses a person-centered, biographical, bottom-up, and inductive heuristic, shown to be suitable to the topic as new research into different forms of mental illness demonstrates the idiosyncratic nature of the experience, a finding supported by the emerging neuroscience on plasticity (Cacioppo et al. 2014; Kendler 2012; Kirmayer et al. 2015; Luhrmann et al. 2015; McKenzie and Shah 2015). This idiographic approach can be further illustrated through the focal points and key themes that ultimately emerged and consolidated in the films that were all putatively about mental illness; through trial and error, the anthropologist and filmmaker learned how to look at what was important to each individual subject or "character" in the film, a process discussed in depth in this book and ultimately argued as key to a *psychological* visual ethnography. During the process of editing the six participant-based narratives, it became clear that each film addressed a particular domain, or even perhaps more narrowly illustrated a "point" about outcome and recovery issues in the lives of people living with mental illness, which were emphasized in each film's narrative, combining a biographical approach with an emergent topical focus. In other words, each of the films had a biographical arc, but also engaged much more deeply with one of the singular domains related in some way to understanding the "Outcome Paradox" (Waxler 1979; Jablensky and Sartorius 2008; Cohen 1992).

At the same time, having a collection of longitudinal case studies allows for comparison between experiences of people with similar diagnoses and symptoms, which in turn illustrates which aspects of their disorder or disturbance may be most significant to themselves or others, and why, and to what effect, demonstrating the importance of an intersectional analysis (Meekosha 2006). Comparison between subjects allows for a deeper understanding of underlying social, economic, and cultural dynamics that shape the experience of mental illness, rather than getting distracted by surface symptoms—in other words, certain reactions, interpretations, or accommodations may have a similar effect no matter what the diagnosis. As such, the group of case studies has implications for psychiatrists, clinicians, applied anthropologists, and others seeking a more idiographic understanding of major mental illness to inform best practices in policy and practice. Due to the nature of film, the integration and comparative analysis of the themes could not occur in the films themselves, but are in the supplementary written material.

3.6   THEMES ACROSS FILMS

In psychiatry, a groundbreaking effort to account for culture in relation to long-term course and outcome of mental illness began in the late 1970s. Two major studies addressed the role of culture in mental illness from the wide-angle lens of transcultural psychiatric epidemiology: the International Pilot Study of Schizophrenia (IPSS) in the 1970s and the Determinants of Outcome of Severe Mental Disorder (DOSMD) in the 1980s, both funded by the WHO. These longitudinal studies established that severe mental illness is a global problem, that thought disorders are "universal," and that, in general, outcome and recovery from schizophrenia and related illnesses were demonstrably better in the "developing" world—the aforementioned "Outcome Paradox"(Eaton 1985; Angst 1988; Jablensky et al. 1992). This research determined that "cultural effects" linked to larger socioeconomic (Warner 1985) and social structural issues (Scheper-Hughes 1982; Waxler 1979) play vital roles in the long-term outcomes of people with major mental illness (Hopper et al. 2007). However, given their epidemiological emphasis using hospital-based samples, standardized diagnostic instruments, and semi-structured interviews focused on discrete domains hypothesized by researchers as significant to outcome, the global WHO studies could not fully explain the cultural effects they identified on recovery and outcome, and thus the study organizers subsequently articulated the need for further research using ethnographic approaches (Hopper et al. 2007)—as did those critiquing the studies' findings (Cohen et al. 2008, 240).

All of the films address, to a greater or lesser degree, some aspect of the "Outcome Paradox" for why people seem to recover more swiftly once they have been "afflicted" with a disorder; while the WHO refers to a population-based level, the films illustrate outcome via individual stories. Again, the factors the WHO research believed were significant[2] include: attributional models of etiology for illness and labeling of symptoms and syndromes; the relative flexibility of daily and work routines; types of treatment available and accessible; the degree and types of social support; and the family emotional climate to which a patient returns. As will soon become clear through the chapters in Part 2, the *Afflictions* series addressed these directly. *The Bird Dancer* (Lemelson 2010) engages with social support, labeling, and the family emotional environment; *Ritual Burdens* (Lemelson 2011b) with daily work routines, family support, and attributional models of illness; and *Memory of My Face* (Lemelson 2011a) with daily routines, different forms of treatment, social support, and so forth. While ultimately there are no definitive answers to the "Outcome Paradox," the *Afflictions* series does provide some pointed insights into the differential salience of such factors, as refracted through the lens of the camera and the lens of the individual participants and their families.

Each of the individual films in the *Afflictions* series also includes variations on the theme that a significant social experience often influences outcome—whether that outcome is social suffering or the onset of extraordinary psychological states. Some participants experienced backgrounds of trauma and some suffered stigma as a response to their mental illness. Many participants sought local and biomedical treatments but also experienced the healing that comes from discovering—or re-discovering—a valued role in their community and society, perhaps through meaningful employment, family support, or even activism. Much as the outcome variables are spread across the different films, in different degrees of relevance, these experiential themes also cut across the films. The films explicitly enter into dialogue with biomedical protocols for treating mental illness, but flesh out the complexity of this in individual lives by presenting longitudinal case studies that strive to provide depth and elicit empathy.

There are also shared themes with regard to the respondents' experience of and relationship to the ethnographic process and product, namely, the relationship of participants to the ethnographic film process and to the anthropologist, local researchers, and crew. For example, there is the question of whether or not participation in visual ethnography can be considered therapeutic in the way it may reposition the participant with regard to their experience, or re-shape a sense of themselves through telling their story, and the role a friendship and work relationship with an outside researcher might play in these processes of re-envisioning their experience. In this way, their participation in the ongoing film process itself yields interesting insights into the role engagement, self-reflection, and reflected representations might play primarily in the life course and development of the participants, and secondarily in their relation with illness experience itself.

Further related issues arise with regard to the anthropologist's or ethnographer's own experience conducting visual anthropology and crafting ethnographic films about mental illness. How the intersubjective reality of fieldwork and film is shaped may have repercussions for the anthropologist's relationship with participants, and the participants' relationship to the edited film. This seems to raise more questions than answers, however: For example, how does the act of filming deepen, complicate, or amplify the researcher-collaborator-respondent relationship? Does the ethnographer have a responsibility to intervene in troubling situations and try to make the participants' lives better? When conducting research with subjects who are struggling with both the symptoms and social context of mental illness, it is difficult to determine if, how, and when to intervene in difficult situations. Sometimes, over the course of research, participants received direct financial assistance to pay for medications they reported to be helping, were provided free medical consultations, ongoing periodic counseling, or received help finding appropriate mental health care. This has often been motivated by concern for the well-being of the participants and an understanding that, with highly limited infrastructure and high price points, medical care and medications are often very difficult to come by for many Indonesians, while as psychological anthropologists, the team had access to these limited mental health care resources that might prove beneficial.

Finally, there are the ongoing considerations about how all these themes, all this complexity, can be portrayed on-screen: how to render internal experience, acknowledge intersubjectivity, and develop unique narrative strategies and visual style that will be faithful to the lived reality of the participant and the ethnographer while communicating complex anthropological concepts to the viewer.

The next section of the book engages with the ethnographies underpinning each individual film, providing the necessary factual and theoretical background for the cultural material and frameworks of each ethnographic study. Each chapter details the history of the individual who is the center of the film, provides an ethnographic analysis that highlights the issue most at stake, and then addresses the interplay of the filmmaking process within the context of psychological anthropology theory.

NOTES

1. See also the recent film on *pasung* by Erminia Colucci (2014).
2. While the WHO research specifically explored outcome for psychosis, many of the same factors can be applied to neuropsychiatric disorders as well.

REFERENCES

Angst, Jules. 1988. European Long-Term Followup Studies of Schizophrenia. *Schizophrenia Bulletin* 14: 501–513. doi:10.1093/schbul/14.4.501

Bellman, Eric. 2012. Indonesia Writes Script for Medical Sector: Country Promises Rich Market as Jakarta Backs Universal Health Care. *Wall Street Journal*, October 18. Retrieved from http://www.wsj.com/articles/SB10000872396390444657804578048153386598438

Biehl, João G. 2005. *Vita: Life in a Zone of Social Abandonment. Photographs by Torban Eskerod*. Berkeley: University of California Press. https://doi.org/10.1525/california/9780520247925.001.0001

Biehl, João G., Byron J. Good, and Arthur Kleinman, eds. 2007. *Subjectivity: Ethnographic Investigations, Ethnographic Studies in Subjectivity*. Berkeley: University of California Press. https://doi.org/10.1525/california/9780520247925.001.0001

Boehnlein, James K., J. David Kinzie, Utako Sekiya, Crystal Riley, Kanya Pou, and Bethany Rosborough. 2004. A Ten-Year Treatment Outcome Study of Traumatized Cambodian Refugees. *The Journal of Nervous and Mental Disease* 192 (10): 658–663. doi:10.1097/01.nmd.0000142033.79043.9d

Browne, Kevin O. 2001a. (Ng)Amuk Revisited: Emotional Expression and Mental Illness in Central Java, Indonesia. *Transcultural Psychiatry* 38 (2): 147–165. doi:10.1177/136346150103800201

———. 2001b. Cultural Formulation of Psychiatric Diagnoses. *Culture, Medicine, and Psychiatry* 25 (4): 411–425. doi:10.1023/A:1013072904827

Burns, Jonathan. 2009. Dispelling a Myth: Developing World Poverty, Inequality, Violence and Social Fragmentation Are Not Good for Outcome in Schizophrenia. *African Journal of Psychiatry* 12 (3): 200–205.

Cacioppo, John T., Stephanie Cacioppo, Stephanie Dulawa, and Abraham A. Palmer. 2014. Social Neuroscience and Its Potential Contribution to Psychiatry. *World Psychiatry* 13 (2): 131–139. doi:10.1002/wps.20118

Chambless, Dianne L., and Gail Steketee. 1999. Expressed Emotion and Behavior Therapy Outcome: A Prospective Study with Obsessive-Compulsive and Agoraphobic Outpatients. *Journal of Consulting and Clinical Psychology* 65 (5): 658–665.

Cockburn, Robert, Paul N. Newton, E. Kyeremateng Agyarko, Dora Akunyili, and Nicholas J. White. 2005. The Global Threat of Counterfeit Drugs: Why Industry and Governments Must Communicate the Dangers. *PLOS Medicine* 2 (4): e100. doi:10.1371/journal.pmed.0020100

Cohen, Alex. 1992. Prognosis for Schizophrenia in the Third World: A Reevaluation of Cross-Cultural Research. *Culture, Medicine, and Psychiatry* 16: 53–75.

Cohen, Alex, Patel Vikram, R. Thara, and Oye Gureje. 2008. Questioning an Axiom: Better Prognosis for Schizophrenia in the Developing World. *Schizophrenia Bulletin* 34 (2): 229–244. doi:10.1093/schbul/sbm105

Colucci, Erminia. 2014. *Breaking the Chains*. Manchester: Granada Center for Visual Anthropology.

Connor, Linda. 1982a. Ships of Fools and Vessels of the Divine: Mental Hospitals and Madness—a Case Study. *Social Science and Medicine* 16 (7): 783–794. doi:10.1016/0277-9536(82)90231-3

———. 1982b. The Unbounded Self: Balinese Therapy in Theory and Practice. In *Cultural Conceptions of Mental Health and Therapy*, ed. Anthony J. Marsella and Geoffrey M. White, 251–267. Dordrecht: D. Reidel.

Csordas, Thomas J. 2004. Asymptote of the Ineffable: Embodiment, Alterity, and the Theory of Religion. *Current Anthropology* 45 (2): 163–185. doi:10.1086/381046

Desjarlais, Robert R., and C. Jason Throop. 2011. Phenomenological Approaches in Anthropology. *Annual Review of Anthropology* 40: 87–102. doi:10.1086/381046

Eaton, William W. 1985. Epidemiology of Schizophrenia. *Epidemiologic Reviews* 7 (1): 105–126.

Fuchs, Thomas. 2010. Phenomenology and Psychopathology. In *Handbook of Phenomenology and Cognitive Science*, ed. D. Schmicking and S. Gallagher. New York: Springer. https://doi.org/10.1007/978-90-481-2646-0_28

Gone, J.P. 2013. Redressing First Nations Historical Trauma: Theorizing Mechanisms for Indigenous Culture as Mental Health Treatment. *Transcultural Psychiatry* 50 (5): 683–706. doi:10.1177/1363461513487669

Good, Byron J., and M.A. Subandi. 2004. Experiences of Psychosis in Javanese Culture: Reflections on a Case of Acute, Recurrent Psychosis in Contemporary Yogyakarta, Indonesia. In *Schizophrenia, Culture, and Subjectivity*, ed. Janis H. Jenkins and Robert J. Barrett, 167–195. Cambridge: Cambridge University Press.

Good, Byron J. 2012. Phenomenology, Psychoanalysis, and Subjectivity in Java. *Ethos* 40 (1): 24–36. doi:10.1111/j.1548-1352.2011.01229.x

Good, Byron J., M. A. Subandi, and Mary-Jo DelVecchio Good. 2007. Psychosis, Mad Violence, and Subjectivity in Indonesia. In *Subjectivity: Ethnographic Investigations*, ed. João G. Biehl, Byron J. Good, and Arthur Kleinman. Berkeley: University of California Press.

Good, Mary-Jo DelVecchio, Sandra T. Hyde, Sarah Pinto, and Byron J. Good, eds. 2008. *Postcolonial Disorders: Reflections on Subjectivity in the Contemporary World*. Berkeley: University of California Press.

Hecker, Tobias, Eva Barnewitz, Hakon Stenmark, and Valentina Iversen. 2016. Pathological Spirit Possession as a Cultural Interpretation of Trauma-Related Symptoms. *Psychological Trauma: Theory, Research, Practice, and Policy* 8 (4): 468–476. doi:10.1037/tra0000117

Hinton, Devon E., and Roberto Lewis-Fernández (eds.). 2010. Trauma and Idioms of Distress [Special Issue]. *Culture, Medicine, and Psychiatry* 34.

Hobart, Angela. 1997. *The People of Bali*. London: Blackwell.

Hopper, Kim, Glynn Harrison, Aleksandar Janca, and Norman Sartorius. 2007. *Recovery from Schizophrenia: An International Perspective*. A Report from the Who Collaborative Project: The International Study of Schizophrenia. Oxford: Oxford University Press.

Horikoshi, Hiroko. 1980. Talking About Pictures: A Case for Photo Elicitation. *Social Science & Medicine. Part B: Medical Anthropology* 14 (3): 157–165.

Iskandar, Yul. 2004. The History of Psychotropic Drugs in Indonesia. In *Reflections on Twentieth-Century Psychopharmacology*, ed. Thomas A. Ban, David Healy, and Edward Shorter, 133–134. East Kilbride: CINP.

Jablensky, Assen, and Norman Sartorius. 2008. What Did the Who Studies Really Find. *Schizophrenia Bulletin* 34 (2): 253–255. doi:10.1093/schbul/sbm151

Jablensky, Assen, Norman Sartorius, Gunilla Ernberg, Martha Anker, Ailsa Korten, John E. Cooper, et al. 1992. Schizophrenia: Manifestations, Incidence and Course in Different Cultures: A World Health Organization Ten-Country Study. *Psychological Medicine Monograph Supplement* 20: 1–97. doi:10.1017/S0264180100000904

Jacknis, Ira. 1988. Margaret Mead and Gregory Bateson in Bali: Their Use of Photography and Film. *Cultural Anthropology* 3 (2): 160–177.

Jenkins, Janis H. 2015. *Extraordinary Conditions: Culture and Experience in Mental Illness*. Oakland: University of California Press.

Jensen, Gordon D., and Luh Ketut Suryani. 1992. *The Balinese People: A Reinvestigation of Character*. New York: Oxford University Press.

Kendler, Kenneth S. 2012. The Dappled Nature of Causes of Psychiatric Illness: Replacing the Organic–Funcitonal/Hardware–Software Dichotomy with Empirically Based Pluralism. *Molecular Psychiatry* 17 (4): 377–388. doi:10.1038/mp.2011.182

Kinzie, J. David, and James J. Boehnlein. 1989. Post-Traumatic Psychosis among Cambodian Refugees. *Journal of Traumatic Stress* 2 (2): 185–198. doi:10.1007/BF00974158

Kirmayer, Laurence J., and Norman Sartorius. 2007. Cultural Models and Somatic Syndromes. *Psychosomatic Medicine* 69 (9): 832–840.

Kirmayer, Laurence J., Robert Lemelson, and Constance A. Cummings, eds. 2015. *Re-Visioning Psychiatry: Cultural Phenomenology, Critical Neuroscience, and Global Mental Health.* New York: Cambridge University Press.

Kulhara, Parmanand, and Subho Chakrabarti. 2001. Culture and Schizophrenia and Other Psychotic Disorders. *Psychiatric Clinics of North America* 24 (3): 449–464.

Kurihara, Toshiyuki, Motoichiro Kato, Robert Reverger, I. Gusti R. Tirta, and Haruo Kashima. 2005a. Never-Treated Patients with Schizophrenia in the Developing Country of Bali. *Schizophrenia Research* 79 (2–3): 307–313.

Kurihara, Toshiyuki, Motoichiro Kato, Robert Reverger, and I. Gusti R. Tirta. 2005b. Eleven-Year Clinical Outcome of Schizophrenia in Bali. *Acta Psychiatrica Scandinavica* 112 (6): 456–462.

Kurihara, Toshiyuki, Motoichiro Kato, Robert Reverger, I. Gusti, and R. Tirta. 2006. Beliefs About Causes of Schizophrenia among Family Members: A Community-Based Survey in Bali. *Psychiatric Services* 57 (12): 1795–1799.

Leff, Julian, N.N. Wig, Harinder S. Bedi, David K. Menon, Liz Kuipers, Ailsa Korten, et al. 1990. Relatives Expressed Emotion and the Course of Schizophrenia in Chandigarh. A Two-Year Follow-up of a First-Contact Sample. *British Journal of Psychiatry* 156: 351–356. doi:10.1192/bjp.156.3.351

Lemelson, Robert. 2010–2011. *Afflictions: Culture and Mental Illness in Indonesia Series.* 182 min. Watertown: Documentary Educational Resources. http://www.der.org/films/afflictions.html

———. 2010. *The Bird Dancer. 40 min.* Watertown: Documentary Educational Resources. http://www.der.org/films/bird-dancer.html

———. 2011a. *Memory of My Face.* 22 min. Watertown: Documentary Education Resources. http://www.der.org/films/memory-of-my-face.html

———. 2011b. *Ritual Burdens.* 25 min. Watertown: Documentary Educational Resources. http://www.der.org/films/ritual-burdens.html

———. 2014. 'The Spirits Enter Me to Force Me to Be a Communist': Political Embodiment, Idioms of Distress, Spirit Possession, and Thought Disorder in Bali. In *Genocide and Mass Violence: Memory, Symptom, and Recovery,* ed. Devon E. Hinton and Alexander L. Hinton, 175–194. New York: Cambridge University Press.

Lemelson, Robert, and Luh Ketut Suryani. 2006. The Spirits, Ngeb, and the Social Suppression of Memory: A Complex Clinical Case from Bali. *Culture, Medicine, and Psychiatry* 30 (3): 389–413. doi:10.1007/s11013-006-9026-y

Lopez, Steven R., Kathleen N. Hipke, Antonio J. Polo, Janis H. Jenkins, Marvin Karno, Christine Vaughn, and Karen S. Snyder. 2004. Ethnicity, Expressed Emotion, Attributions, and Course of Schizophrenia: Family Warmth Matters. *Journal of Abnormal Psychology* 113: 428–439.

Luhrmann, Tanya M., and Jocelyn Marrow, eds. 2016. *Our Most Troubling Madness: Case Studies in Schizophrenia across Cultures.* Oakland: University of California Press.

Luhrmann, Tanya M., R. Padmavati, Hema Tharoor, and Akwasi Osei. 2015. Hearing Voices in Different Cultures: A Social Kindling Hypothesis. *Topics in Cognitive Science* 7 (4): 646–663. doi:10.1111/tops.12158

Makanjuola, Victor, Yomi Esan, Bibilola Oladeji, Lola Kola, John Appiah-Poku, Benjamin Harris, et al. 2016. Explanatory Model of Psychosis: Impact on Perception of Self-Stigma by Patients in Three Sub-Saharan African Cities. *Social Psychiatry and Psychiatric Epidemiology* 51 (12): 1645–1654. doi:10.1007/s00127-016-1274-8

Martin, Emily. 2007. *Bipolar Expeditions: Mania and Depression in American Culture.* Princeton: Princeton University Press.

McCauley, Ann P. 1984. Healing as a Sign of Power and Status in Bali. *Social Science and Medicine* 18 (2): 167–172. doi:10.1016/0277-9536(84)90037-6

McKenzie, Kwame, and Jai Shah. 2015. Understanding the Social Etiology of Psychosis. In *Re-Visioning Psychiatry: Cultural Phenomenology, Critical Neuroscience, and Global Mental Health,* ed. Laurence J. Kirmayer, Robert Lemelson, and Constance A. Cummings. New York: Cambridge University Press.

Meekosha, Helen. 2006. What the Hell Are You? An Intercategorical Analysis of Race, Ethnicity, Gender and Disability in the Australian Body Politic. *Scandinavian Journal of Disability Research* 8 (2–3): 161–176. doi:10.1080/15017410600831309

Nakamura, Karen, 2007. *Bethel: Community and Schizophrenia in Northern Japan.* 40 min. Manic Films.

———. 2013. *A Disability of the Soul: An Ethnography of Schizophrenia and Mental Illness in Contemporary Japan.* Ithaca: Cornell University Press.

Ng, Roger M., Veronica Pearson, Lam May, C.W. Law, Cindy P.Y. Chiu, and Eric Y.H. Chen. 2008. What Does Recovery from Schizophrenia Mean? Perceptions of Long-Term Patients. *International Journal of Social Psychiatry* 54 (2): 118–130.

Nurjannah, Intansari, Mary FitzGerald, and Kim Foster. 2009. Patients' Experiences of Absconding from a Psychiatric Setting in Indonesia. *International Journal of Mental Health Nursing* 18 (5): 326–335. doi:10.1111/j.1447-0349.2009.00611.x

Pols, Hans. 2006. The Development of Psychiatry in Indonesia: From Colonial to Modern Times. *International Review of Psychiatry* 18 (4): 363–370. doi:10.1080/09540260600775421

————. 2007. Psychological Knowledge in a Colonial Context: Theories on the Nature of the 'Native Mind' in the Former Dutch East Indies. *History of Psychology* 10 (2): 111–131. doi:10.1037/1093-4510.10.2.111

Porath, Nathan. 2008. The Naturalization of Psychiatry in Indonesia and Its Interaction with Indigenous Therapeutics. *Bijdragen tot de Taal-, Land- en Volkenkunde* 164 (4): 500–528. http://www.jstor.org/stable/27868521

Scheper-Hughes, Nancy. 1979. *Saints, Scholars and Schizophrenics: Mental Illness in Rural Ireland*. Berkeley: University of California Press.

————. 1982. Anthropologists and the 'Crazies'. *Medical Anthropology Quarterly* 13 (3): 1–11. doi:10.1525/maq.1982.13.3.02a00000

Singh, Swaran P., Kath Harley, and Kausar Suhail. 2013. Cultural Specificity of Emotional Overinvolvement: A Systematic Review. *Schizophrenia Bulletin* 39 (2): 449–463. https://doi.org/10.1093/schbul/sbr170

Steinberg, Holger. 2015. Emil Kraepelin's Ideas on Transcultural Psychiatry. *Australas Psychiatry* 23 (5): 531–535. doi:10.1177/1039856215590253

Stratford, Anthony, Nursyamsu Kusuma, Margaret Godling, David Paroissien, Lisa Brophy, Yeni R. Damayanti, et al. 2013. Introducing Recovery-Oriented Practice in Indonesia: The Sukabumi Project—an Innovative Mental Health Programme. *Asia Pacific Journal of Social Work and Development* 24 (1–2): 71–81.

Subandi, M.A. 2009. Indigenous Processes of Recovery from Psychosis in Java. Workshop on Mental Health System Development for Severe Mental Illness in Asian Countries.

————. 2011. Family Expressed Emotion in a Javanese Cultural Context. *Culture, Medicine, and Psychiatry* 35 (3): 331–346. doi:10.1007/s11013-011-9220-4

————. 2015a. Bangkit: The Processes of Recovery from First Episode Psychosis in Java. *Culture, Medicine, and Psychiatry* 39 (4): 597–613. doi:10.1007/s11013-015-9427-x

————. 2015b. Bangkit: The Processes of Recovery from First Episode Psychosis in Java. *Culture, Medicine, and Psychiatry* 39 (4): 597–613. doi:10.1007/s11013-015-9427-x

Suryani, Luh Ketut. 1984. Culture and Mental Disorder: The Case of Bebainan in Bali. *Culture, Medicine, and Psychiatry* 8 (1): 95–113. doi:10.1007/BF00053103

Suryani, Luh K., and Gordon D. Jensen. 1992. Psychiatrist, Traditional Healer and Culture Integrated in Clinical Practice in Bali. *Medical Anthropology* 13 (4): 301–314. doi:10.1080/01459740.1992.9966054

Suryani, Luh Ketut, Cokorda B.J. Lesmana, and Niko Tiliopoulos. 2011. Treating the Untreated: Applying a Community-Based, Culturally Sensitive Psychiatric Intervention to Confined and Physically Restrained Mentally Ill Individuals in Bali, Indonesia. *European Archives of Psychiatry and Clinical Neuroscience* 261 (Suppl 2): 140. doi:10.1007/s00406-011-0238-y

Suryani, Suryani, Anthony Welch, and Leonie Cox. 2013. The Phenomena of Auditory Hallucination as Described by Indonesian People Living with Schizophrenia. *Archives of Psychiatric Nursing* 27: 312–318. doi:10.1016/j.apnu.2013.08.001

Tarrier, Nicholas, Claire Sommerfield, and Hazel Pilgrim. 1999. Relatives' Expressed Emotion (Ee) and Ptsd Treatment Outcome. *Psychological Medicine* 29 (4): 801–811. doi:10.1017/S0033291799008569

Thong, Denny, Bruce Carpenter, and Stanley Krippner. 1993. *A Psychiatrist in Paradise: Treating Mental Illness in Bali.* Bangkok: White Lotus.

Tucker, Annie. 2015. Interpreting and Treating Autism in Javanese Indonesia: Listening to Folk Perspectives on Developmental Difference and Inclusion. In *Diagnosing Folklore: Perspectives on Disability, Health, and Trauma,* ed. Trevor Blank and Andrea Kitta, 115–136. Jackson: University Press of Mississippi.

Wahyuni, Sri, Sri N. Yuliet, and Veni Elita. 2012. Hubungan Lama Hari Rawat Dengan Kemampuan Pasien Dalam Mengontrol Halusinasi. *Jurnal Ners Indonesia* 1 (2): 69–76.

Warner, Richard. 1985. *Recovery from Schizophrenia: Psychiatry and Political Economy.* New York: Routledge and Kegan Paul.

Waxler, Nancy. 1979. Is Outcome for Schizophrenia Better in Nonindustrial Societies? The Case of Sri Lanka. *Journal of Nervous and Mental Disease* 176: 144–158. doi:10.1097/00005053-197903000-00002

White, Geoffrey M., and Anthony J. Marsella, eds. 1984. *Cultural Conceptions of Mental Health and Therapy.* Dordrecht: D. Reidel.

Zaumseil, Manfred, and Hella Lessman. 1995. Dealing with Schizophrenia in Central Java (unpublished manuscript). https://pdfs.semanticscholar.org/7c4f/2688731f44442d8519d6bcf006677ff52c9e.pdf

Zaumseil, Manfred, and Hella Lessmann. 2007. Dealing with Schizophrenia in Central Java. *Forum Gemeindepsychologie* 12 (1): 1–19. http://www.gemeindepsychologie.de/fg-1-2007_05.html

PART II

Afflictions: Culture and Mental Illness in Indonesia

Photo 1   Ritual ceremony in a family temple (From the Mead Bateson collection)

CHAPTER 4

The Bird Dancer: Social Rejection and Social Suffering

Photo 4.1   Gusti Ayu Suartini

4.1   STORY SUMMARY

Gusti Ayu Suartini is a petite Balinese woman born to a high-caste family in the late 1970s in a small rural village in Central Bali. Gusti is the youngest of four siblings with one older brother and two older sisters. She grew up helping around the family compound, feeding the pigs and cows, cooking meals, and preparing the many offerings required for Balinese religious life.

© The Author(s) 2017
R. Lemelson, A. Tucker, *Afflictions*, Culture, Mind, and Society,
DOI 10.1007/978-3-319-59984-7_4

She attended elementary school and as a little girl was known for being a bright and diligent student.

However, when she was nine, Gusti began exhibiting behaviors that seemed bizarre and totally inappropriate, such as suddenly yelling out obscene or shocking words like "bastard dog." Her normal calm physical demeanor became punctuated with strange and twitching movements, and these odd behaviors slowly increased and magnified until Gusti was frequently spitting, clicking her teeth, and hitting herself. Her family and community were shocked and had no idea what was wrong with her. They thought perhaps she was ill, but she said she felt fine. Despite her protestations to the contrary, her family decided that she was purposefully misbehaving. She was frequently punished by her classroom teacher for her actions, and because of her perceived defiance in "refusing" to stop, as well as her family's embarrassment at her condition, in the fourth grade Gusti was taken out of school, never to return.

Over time it became clear to her family that the behaviors were out of Gusti's control. This led to more worry; Gusti's jerky movements looked like those of trance dancers who are temporarily possessed by spirits in certain Balinese dances such as *Manuk Rawa*, or the Swamp Bird Dance. Neighbors openly mocked her by calling her "the bird dancer," and people speculated as to whether she was permanently possessed, insane, or spiritually unwell. Others in the village feared that her mysterious illness was contagious and began to shun her.

Gusti suffered as she moved into adolescence and watched her friends pull away and her family grow increasingly frustrated. Her siblings suffered as well, as the stigma of an unknown illness in the family tainted their lineage and rendered them undesirable as marriage partners. In the face of these social difficulties, Gusti and her family steadfastly searched for a cure. They consulted with multiple traditional Balinese healers, known as *balian*. Most of these healers agreed that Gusti's problems were the result of black magic (B.B. *kena gelah anak*), a common diagnosis in Bali. They suggested that perhaps someone was jealous of Gusti's goodness and had therefore cursed her. Other healers suggested that the family had displeased an ancestor with improper ritual offerings. They prescribed treatments according to Balinese theories of disturbance and well-being in order to restore Gusti to health, none of which seemed to offer her any lasting relief.

In addition to seeking help from healers, Gusti consulted psychiatrists and neurologists. Finally, when she was in her late teens she was diagnosed with Tourette Syndrome (TS) by Dr. I Gusti Putu Panteri, a psychiatrist working in a private psychiatric hospital. TS is a neurological disorder that manifests in uncontrollable physical movements or vocalizations called tics. Before the late 1800s, TS was unheard of, but it is now a fairly familiar, if still rare, condition increasingly recognized across the globe.

Dr. Panteri prescribed medication, including the antipsychotic Haloperidol and the tri-cyclic anti-depressant Imipramine. While these alleviated symptoms to a degree, they also caused nausea and excessive fatigue, which prevented Gusti from carrying out her everyday activities. Gusti felt these side effects were more impairing and unpleasant than the symptoms they were intended to cure. Furthermore, because the family could not always afford ongoing treatment due the medication's expense, Gusti experienced only partial alleviation of her symptoms. These interminable efforts to resolve Gusti's problem significantly stressed the family. Her brother accused Gusti of not trying hard enough to "control" herself, occasionally mocked Gusti's behaviors, and sometimes even physically lashed out at her in a futile attempt to end her tics.

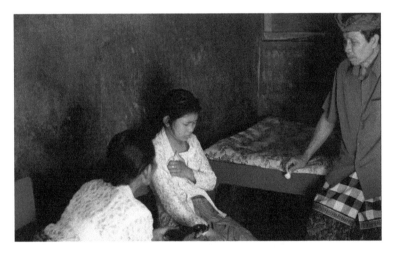

Photo 4.2 Gusti Ayu gets treated by a *balian* who uses massage therapy

A potential opportunity for reprieve presented itself when Gusti developed a romance with a young man in her village. They dated for about three months. He treated her kindly, brought her gifts, and said he did not mind

Gusti's movements. He proposed marriage, and she longed to accept, but he was of a lower caste than her family, and therefore her parents forbade the union. Gusti regretfully acquiesced. A few times in desperation she tried to run away, but her family locked her up to prevent her escape. Feeling increasingly trapped and anguished, struggling with the symptoms of her disorder and the ensuing frustration of inefficacious cures, filled with grief from feeling like a burden to her family yet simultaneously boxed in by them, on multiple occasions Gusti considered killing herself so that her parents could be free of her as the source of their troubles, and she could be free of them too.

Over time, Gusti became certain that to ease her suffering she needed to establish her independence. She moved to the capital city of Denpasar and found work as a maid. She made new friends who accepted her tics and encouraged her to accept them as well, to be kind to herself, and not to isolate herself in shame. This new situation was a highly positive change for Gusti. She was newly proud and confident to be taking care of herself without being a financial "burden" on anyone. She was happy to be out of the oppressive environment of her village, only occasionally making the trip back for major ceremonies. With the support of her new friends she developed effective coping mechanisms to respond to the teasing and stares that she encountered at times in the city. The comfort and focus her new life afforded her eased her anxiety, which in turn seemed to lessen her tics—a commonly observed phenomenon for those with TS.

The challenge that persists for Gusti, despite her change of milieu and increased independence, is her search for a husband. Her longing for love and marriage is simultaneously deeply personal and socially motivated: Gusti wants a soul mate to share her life with, but she also wants to fulfill her responsibility as a Balinese woman by marrying someone of her caste and bearing children, in order to continue her family line and ensure the reincarnation of her soul. While she is proud of her hard-earned independence and thankful for her supportive friends, Gusti's smile often is imbued with a certain sadness. Her deepest wish is to find a life partner to love and with whom she might start a family, a future that increasingly seems like it will slip through her fingers since she is now in her thirties, a decade past the age when most Balinese women get married and have children.

4.2   AN ETIC EXPLANATION: TOURETTE SYNDROME

One of Gusti's pressing concerns is what is causing her disordered movements and vocalizations. One way to determine this is to place them in a biomedical, and more specifically psychiatric, framework or "etic grid." The section below elaborates on this model.

Gusti was diagnosed by both Javanese and American psychiatrists as having TS. TS is a neurological disorder characterized by multiple, repetitive, involuntary physical movements and verbal outbursts known as tics that occur many times a day, causing some impairment in social or occupational functioning (Serajee and Mahbubul Huq 2015; McNaught and Mink 2011; Swain et al. 2007). Tics usually appear in childhood but their anatomical location, frequency, and severity may change over time (Serajee and Mahbubul Huq 2015; Freeman 2015). The first symptoms are often bouts of a single visible tic, most frequently eye blinking or small facial twitching. Other initial symptoms can include tongue protrusion, squatting, sniffing, hopping, skipping, throat clearing, stuttering, shouting or barking, or complex full-body motions (Fernandez et al. 2015; Swain et al. 2007). Verbal tics may often entail the involuntary use of obscenity, known as "coprolalia" (Ganos et al. 2016; Kobierska et al. 2014). Tics may be suppressed with a degree of voluntary control; however, such suppression often brings feelings of increasing tension only relieved by completing the tic. Some people with TS report repetitive thoughts or compulsions to perform particular movements; the syndrome can be associated with family histories of attention deficit/hyperactivity disorder (ADHD), which is indicated by impulsivity, hyperactivity, and distractibility, or obsessive-compulsive disorder (OCD), which is indicated by recurrent and persistent thoughts, impulses, or images perceived as intrusive, inappropriate, and anxiety-provoking, and may be accompanied by either clinical or sub-clinical levels of these conditions (Yu et al. 2015; O'Rourke et al. 2011). Besides these co-morbid disorders there are no additional impairments associated with TS and no inherent barriers to success or achievement for those with the condition. While symptoms can range from mild to severe, most people with TS fall into the "mild" category. Tics can wax and wane, most commonly exacerbated by stress, fatigue, and negative emotional states and ameliorated by stress relief, pleasure, or intense focus (Nagai et al. 2009; Singer and Walkup 1991).

TS is a neurobiological disorder with a genetic component. Although the etiology, primary site, mechanism, and pattern of transmission still remain to be determined (Crane et al. 2011; Ercan-Sencicek et al. 2010; McMahon et al. 2003; Saka and Graybiel 2003; Yoon et al. 2007), both structural and functional abnormalities of the brain have been implicated, including dysfunctional dopamine receptors and disinhibition in the sensorimotor and limbic basal-ganglia-thalamocortical (BGTC) circuits and the corticostriatal-thalamo-cortical (CSTC) pathways (for a review of these findings, see Felling and Singer 2011). Various medications can help reduce symptoms (Scahill et al. 2006), while cognitive behavioral therapy (CBT) may help channel disruptive tics into more socially acceptable behaviors (O'Connor et al. 2009), and stress relief therapies, such as biofeedback, may decrease their incidence (Nagai et al. 2009).

Research into TS increasingly suggests that it is a neurodevelopmental disorder; two of the largest functional magnetic resonance imaging (fMRI) studies of TS to date identified age-related abnormalities in neurological networks and connectivity, suggesting atypical maturational changes in the brain (Marsh et al. 2008; Church et al. 2009). However, tics and symptoms of TS can often subside in young adulthood (Felling and Singer 2011), even if the individual with TS receives little targeted treatment or therapy.

Interest and research in TS have increased markedly in the last twenty years. Once thought of as one of the rarest disorders (incidence of one in a million), TS is now recognized as considerably more prevalent. Epidemiologic literature suggests there are similar rates cross-culturally (Staley et al. 1997). Some medications, in categories as diverse as anti-psychotic, benzodiazepine, selective serotonin reuptake inhibitors (SSRI), anti-seizure, central adrenergic inhibitors, and stimulant medications, have been tried in cases of TS and have proven variably helpful in reducing symptoms (Lizano et al. 2016; Serajee and Mahbubul Huq 2015; Lan et al. 2015; Rice and Coffey 2015; Budman 2014; Yamamuro et al. 2014; Lewis et al. 2010; Ghanizadeh 2010; Weller and Weller 2009; Arana-Lechuga et al. 2008; McKay and Storch 2009). CBT may also help a person with disruptive tics channel these into more socially acceptable actions (McKay and Storch 2009). Various stress relief therapies, such as biofeedback, may also decrease the incidence of tics (Hawksley et al. 2015; Nagai et al. 2014).

Given the increasingly sophisticated understanding of TS neurobiology, transcultural psychiatric and medical anthropology research contends that even the most "hard-wired" or "biological" of neuropsychiatric disorders will be culturally shaped in terms of symptom expression, recognition and labeling, and social context and outcome (Lemelson 2003a; Desjarlais et al. 1995). Family and community response plays a central role in the subjective experience and outcomes of people with TS,[1] underscoring the importance of positive support and illustrating the painful and harmful long-term effects of stigma, particularly during crucial stages of development (Hodes and Gau 2016; Bharadwaj et al. 2015). Gusti's TS symptoms were moderate, but because these symptoms were unfamiliar in her rural village, they elicited grave concern from herself and her family, significantly affecting both the daily and long-term course of her life. Gusti struggled for many years to overcome the suffering that resulted from the web of cultural significance spun around TS in the context of rural Balinese values and beliefs, social and familial structure, and health care practices. Frameworks of meaning that rendered Gusti cursed, possessed, contaminated, contaminating, or at fault in her illness actively contributed to her suffering while offering little relief for her symptoms, and ultimately compelled her to leave her community.

4.3   TRADITIONAL HEALING, EXPLANATORY MODELS, AND THERAPEUTICS FOR NEUROPSYCHIATRIC DISORDERS IN BALI

The questions of illness, meaning-making, and efficacious response beg a deeper discussion of local models of health care, in particular the networks of traditional healing and therapeutics which are still commonly used in Bali. These treatments are often beneficial, and are frequently successfully integrated with Western medicine and modalities (Ferzacca 2001; Thong et al. 1993). In some areas they are the only or predominant form of health care and treatment (Hay 2001). Anthropologists have suggested that traditional healers often help make meaning out of an illness episode and thus may in certain cases be more equipped to cure it, an idea that fits well with anthropological notions that exploring a culture's explanatory models, structures of meaning, belief systems, and so forth will generate a more meaningful and efficacious way to look at illness experience (Jilek 1993). Drawn from the same culture of their patients, indigenous explanatory models often provide the meaning that Western or biomedical explanatory models lack. Yet, while traditional explanatory models for illness may provide an understandable and integrated system of meaning for these disorders, they may be unsuccessful in relieving symptoms or effecting cure. What if, as in the case of TS, the indigenous explanations are not syntonic with the phenomenological reality of differing psychopathological states, such as the repetitive, meaningless tics of TS? What if the available systems of meaning do little to relieve symptoms or suffering? What if the practices themselves are deleterious to the physical and/or psychological health of the sufferer (Edgerton 1992)?

Balinese healing mobilizes complex intertwined explanatory models for illness or ill fortune: magic and sorcery, reincarnation, poisoning, improper enactment of rituals, and imbalance (Lemelson 2003b), and healers use a cornucopia of transformational symbols in their practices (Csordas and Lewton 1998). However, these complex, multilayered, and multivalent explanatory models were not particularly helpful for Gusti. She visited over a dozen *balian* (Keeney and Mekel 2004; Connor 1982; Connor et al. 1986; Mustar 1985) who offered competing explanatory models for her illness: she had been poisoned (B.B. *kena cetik*); her home was ritually impure (B.B. *leteh*); her illness was supernatural in origin and her family had to make an offering to appease the spirits. Healers variably asked her to create a rice offering; go to the ocean to pray to spirits; gather "filthy things" such as the hair of a monkey, a black dog, and a black cat, to be used in a purifying ritual; drink her own urine; and go to a graveyard at midnight—a terrifying and spiritually dangerous place for Balinese—and pray. Herbal specialists prescribed tinctures made from roots and barks and others submitted her to a series of often painful massages, spinal adjustments, and other physical treatments, some of which involved the placement of burning hot metal on her skin, leaving scars, and the application of caustic substances to her eyes. One massage therapist asked Gusti to remove her shirt for a massage, seemed to be touching her in a sexualized manner, and made her deeply uncomfortable.

if I said something wrong, he'd get upset, then he'd hurt me.

Photo 4.3   Gusti laments her brother's treatment of her

For Gusti, some treatments were neutral or occasionally positive experiences. For example, she met with one healer who said that her symptoms were caused by a spirit occupying a grinding stone in her compound yard and that this spirit had been neglected and needed offerings to be appeased and exorcised. Gusti, while somewhat skeptical, said that the healer's diagnosis seemed credible because it echoed other interpretations provided by previous healers. The sense that this diagnosis was of divine origin was underscored by the healer's otherwise inexplicable knowledge of the grinding stone. Perhaps also in part responding to this healer's kindness and empathy in listening to her story, Gusti said that after that healing her "heart was opened" and she felt encouraged by knowing that if she followed the procedure as detailed by the healer, she might feel better. In other cases, the traditional treatments caused Gusti additional suffering in the form of physical pain, disgust, or shame, some so awful that she "felt like she was going to die." Ultimately, neither Gusti nor the other Balinese with TS described above reported long-lasting or significant improvement or relief from such diagnosis or labeling or the corresponding treatments (Lemelson 2003b).

In the case of a neuropsychiatric disorder such as TS, a neurobiological perspective may offer the opportunity for treatments that are both more faithful to the patient's experience of their symptoms and more efficacious in alleviating them, suggesting that to relieve the symptoms of the disorder, neurotransmitter systems would have to be altered. This perspective frees people from the quest for meaning in their illness experience wherein symptoms are experienced as meaningless. While perhaps counterintuitive, in the case of TS such a biological model may in and of itself bring great relief, but is still not a perfect or foolproof solution: The neuroleptic medications often used in the biological treatment at times have disruptive or unpleasant side effects. For Gusti, aside from being physically unpleasant, these side effects made her unable to work and stressed her already tense relationship with her family.

4.4   QUESTIONS OF GENDER, CASTE, AND KINSHIP

Gusti's case raises the question of the role gender plays in the interpretation and long-term ramifications of having a neurological disorder: what constraints are imposed, what opportunities are afforded to men and women in Bali, and how these intersect with neurological disorder. An intersectional analysis underscores the significance of gender and caste in Gusti's story.

Gendered expectations for behavior may affect the way a neuropsychiatric disorder such as TS may be experienced and interpreted on an embodied level. Cultural context provides corporeal scripts, constructing a habitus of physical postures, behaviors, and comportment (Bourdieu 1977). This habitus may be significantly gendered (McNay 1999); put simply, men and women are taught and allowed to move in different ways. Throughout Bali, women are expected to move smoothly and gracefully (Belo 1970; Wikan 1990) and master their emotions—even subtle expressions of anger or displeasure may be shameful. The female ideal is contained and submissive (Jennaway 2002; Parker 1997). Men, while also called upon to maintain a composed demeanor, are allowed a wider range of dynamic physical expression, normatively socially self-projecting, bolder, and noisier (Parker 1997). A distillation of these differences can be found in Balinese performing arts and the way women and men move in the dances and dramas for which they are internationally renowned. In traditional productions, women typically play the roles of princesses, nymphs, temple attendants, or birds of paradise. Their movements are sinuous, refined, and often incorporate gestures of obeisance (McPhee 1956). One of the few times women are freed of these constraints is during moments of trance possession, when they perform with stiff, jerky, or otherwise unruly movements (Belo 1960). When exhibited outside the confines of sanctioned ritual performance, such movements may still be interpreted as signs of possession but so-called peripheral possession (Seligman and Kirmayer 2008), which reflects a disturbance in cosmological order and vulnerability in the one possessed. Suryani (1984) described the Balinese phenomenon of *bebainan*, "attacks" believed to be caused by malignant spirits sent through sorcery to prey on young women, causing brief episodes of screaming, rude speech, and physical rigidity or loss of control. Those considered most vulnerable to such an attack are those thought to be "mentally weak" or sinful. These gendered interpretations of physical comportment appear to have been at play in the response to Gusti's non-normative movements and vocalizations; some villagers negatively compared her to possessed performers while others thought she might be *bebai*.

The structure of marriage in the caste system in Bali offers more nuance to issues of gender in the context of neuropsychiatric disorder. Until the present day, the Balinese have organized according to clan, ancestral kinship groups known as *dadia*, and caste (Geertz and Geertz 1975a). There are four main castes in Bali. Sudras make up approximately 90% of the population and are generally laborers and farmers. The other 10% are divided into the gentry castes, which include Wesyas, who were traditionally merchants; Satrias, who were traditionally warriors and kings; and Brahmans, who were traditionally priests and teachers. The adherence to the caste system varies throughout Bali; nevertheless, it still influences certain aspects of behavior and affiliation. People of different castes receive different names and titles; for women, Ida Ayu is the title for women of Brahman caste, and Gusti is the title for those of Satria castes (Lansing 1995).

The caste system comes into play in marriage. Marriage is of primary importance because it provides extended kin networks of support, economic stability, status, and ideally a loving partnership, but also because it leads to children. Children are important in Balinese culture due to beliefs that the reincarnation of ancestors, crucial to the liberation of the soul in Balinese Hindu beliefs (Geertz and Geertz 1975b; Pringle 2004), occurs through the patrilineal family line (Hobart et al. 2001; Lemelson 2014). In seeking a mate, men are permitted to marry a woman of a lower caste, in which case the woman is given a new title and experiences a rise in status, but women are discouraged from marrying lower-caste men (Geertz and Geertz 1975b). If a woman chooses to marry an unsuitable partner despite this proscribed prohibition, she must leave her home and elope (B.B. *ngerorod*), potentially jeopardizing her relationship with her family; in the contemporary context, she may only be temporarily ostracized (Geertz and Geertz 1975b; Jennaway 2002). This may help explain why Gusti's parents forbade her to marry a man of lower caste (B.B. *nyerod*), even though it represented both a chance for love and relief for their family. If Gusti had been a man, she could marry a woman of lower caste, a match that might have been desirable for such a woman, who would rise in status despite being married to someone with a visible "disorder" or "sickness."

In Balinese society, men have more agency than women in determining their own marital fate because men, with the input of their families, actively choose their mates, asking for the woman's hand in marriage, while women must wait to be chosen. This is compounded by a pervasive fear of spinsterhood, which in women's minds is associated with a lack of offspring, the threat of financial instability or destitution, and a lack of social power (Jennaway 2002; Lemelson 2014).

In Gusti's case, TS may act as a lens that magnifies the vulnerabilities of her structural position within kin and broader social networks (Yang et al. 2014). Gusti's TS has been met with frustration and at times violence in her family because they believe her problem may be due, for example, to black magic or ancestral curse, but also because of her position in her family. She is an unmarried and perhaps an unmarriageable woman, and as such is perceived as a burden on the family. This structurally vulnerable position opens her up to the threat of gender-based violence and abuse, which exacerbates her condition.

Gusti's case also raises compelling questions about the nature of suffering in the context of difference. The film *The Bird Dancer* opens with the questions "What is the nature of suffering? How much of the pain and despair people feel is caused by processes internal to them, and how much are they affected by their interactions with the social world they live in?" Can the suffering caused by physical or neurological impairments be distinguished from the suffering caused by how these impairments are interpreted?

Scholarship on mental illness, difference, and disability has provided theoretical frameworks for distinguishing these. Kleinman famously introduced the difference between disease, what is biomedically wrong with the patient, and illness, the "innately human experiences of symptoms and suffering"(Kleinman 1991) encompassing explanatory models and reactions to disease based on life histories, values, and personal narratives. Global disability scholars Ingstad and Whyte (Whyte and Ingstad 1995) applied the framework of "local moral worlds" to examining disability in global contexts, arguing that "concepts of personhood, causality and value" (p. 281) are crucial to understanding the interpretation of any difference or impairment in any cultural place. These frameworks parse the basic biological fact of human variation from the exclusion or marginalization that so often accompanies it, addressing how this variation gets labeled, shaped, and responded to, and what the effects and choices are for people caught in these webs of significance.

Writing specifically about TS, Buckser terms these issues of interpretation as "semantic symptoms" or "symbolic discontinuities between particular cultural systems and particular disease processes" that can create conflicts and challenges as disabling as physical symptoms (Buckser 2006). Buckser suggested that while TS is neurological in origin, it is primarily a dialogic condition defined by "the ongoing need to attach meaning to what are quite literally empty gestures" (Buckser 2006).

Hollenbeck, a neuroscientist who has TS, called it "a disease of the onlooker," asserting that those with TS who do well are those surrounded by "compassionate onlookers" (Hollenbeck 2003). In Gusti's case, attention must be paid to the structural and cultural elements that might challenge an activation of compassion in onlookers. The social, corporeal, and psychocultural world Gusti was living in shaped the reaction to her TS's symptoms as views about health, witchcraft, physical demeanor, gender roles, and the caste system and marriage customs in a rural location combined to lend a disturbing significance to Gusti's TS symptoms. These sociocultural elements were the most pressing elements of the illness experience for Gusti, not her tic symptoms, and yet this sociocultural context may have worsened her symptoms. Family rejection, stress, and negative affect—also known as high levels of EE (Jenkins and Karno 1992)—can exacerbate neuropsychiatric disorders and negatively impact long-term prognosis, including for developing children and adolescents (Asarnow et al. 1994) and those with TS specifically (Lin et al. 2007). Focus on meaningful activities and stress relief often leads to a decrease in tic symptoms, while anxiety or inactivity may cause an increase in tic frequency and severity as well as contribute to mood disorders such as depression, which can be co-morbid with TS (Robertson 2006). It is possible that the family judgment and frustrating quest for a cure Gusti endured contributed to a stress-response syndrome (Horowitz and Reidbord 2014; Wilson and Raphael 2013) and exacerbated her symptoms, as did her removal from school and the foreclosing of opportunities for other potentially positive activities. Gusti's tics have persisted, although waxing and waning; they often subside when she is surrounded by her friends and co-workers, but flare up when she anticipates making a visit to her home village for ritual celebrations (cf Ni Ketut Kasih's story in Chap. 8), perhaps because she anticipates returning home or is under more internal pressure thinking about offerings and responsibilities, indicating how oppressive and anxiety-provoking this milieu was.

Perhaps unsurprisingly, over the course of many years, what is at stake in Gusti's life has changed, as have her key concerns. Initially, finding a label, explanation, and cure for her troubling symptoms was primary. After more than a decade of stress, stigma, and ineffective treatments, Gusti's priorities changed. She no longer focused on finding a cure, but instead she longed to find relief from her family's judgment and pressure. When given the opportunity, Gusti chose to leave her family and natal village to find work and a measure of independence. From Gusti"s perspective, she flourished in her new city environment, and while her TS's was not cured by moving to the city, much of her emotional distress was. It was not traditional treatment or medication that brought Gusti relief, but a change of environment. As she explains it:

> Now things seem better because I found work and so I'm free from my family's home. I wasn't happy at home, often hearing things from people in the village, you know, insulting me like that. Now, I feel very calm. When I'm home and I'm insulted, I get upset again, and I think about my illness.

Gusti is delighted by the level of social support she has in her community of "compassionate onlookers," namely, her co-workers, and the kindness they show her. Almost with amazement she recounts how these co-workers share their food with her, give her rides, spend their free time with her, and sometimes prepare her a meal.

As of 2013, Gusti still frequently feels itchy, needs to spit, and in quiet moments or during casual conversation she hits her own face and body. However, she has accepted herself and no longer considers her tics a health concern.

4.5   The Complexities of Psychiatric Treatment and the Value of Empathy

When conducting clinically oriented research in cultural psychiatry, or PCE in the field, respondents and researchers may have divergent understandings about the activities and purposes of research, and different goals for its outcome. These disparate ideas and orientations may lead to miscommunication.

Gusti and her family entered the research with hopes that the research team would provide a cure for Gusti's mysterious affliction. Despite having been informed that the researchers (B.I. *peneliti*) and anthropologists were interested in Gusti and her illness, but were not there to provide treatment, for this first and several subsequent interviews the family believed the lead researcher was a doctor—in fact, Gusti initially believed that the lead researcher was the head of the WHO. From the family's perspective, the participation of a Western "doctor" in the interview raised their hopes. They asked numerous questions about the symptomatology and etiology of Gusti's illness, and Dr. Panteri provided information about TS, including its causes, symptoms, and the types of treatment available in America and elsewhere in the world.

The medically oriented nature of the initial interviews may have compounded the family's view of the researchers and what they thought could be done for them. When Gusti or her family had questions for the researchers about causes, symptoms, and prognosis, it was important to re-orient them toward local resources, such as community health centers (*Pusat Kesehatan Masyarakat*, known as *Puskesmas*), local psychiatrists and neurologists, and other medical resources.

The lead author would receive an update from Gusti and her family on the progression of her illness, and if asked, would frame this for them within the discourses of the clinical and research literature on TS and similar disorders. While the research team was exploring multiple factors beyond treatment for Gusti's condition, there was mounting pressure to find a "cure."

While reviewing the footage in the interim between film shoots, it became apparent that there were scenes with Gusti and her family being interviewed, but no interviews or material with Gusti alone. Indeed, interviews where family members were participants in the interview process with patients or subjects were the norm, not the exception, when shooting in Indonesia, but it seemed that conducting an interview with Gusti apart from her family might allow deeper insight into the way their anxiety over a cure was influencing her experience of her tics. While there are not strict gendered prohibitions against a man and an unmarried young female being alone together, it would be culturally non-normative and would not occur as a matter of course. A specific request needed to be made for such an interview. Under the guise of following Gusti into the field to film her daily farming chores, she was able to be interviewed by herself.

This more intimate setting led to a productive interview with more information about Gusti's private desires and fervent hopes for a partner, which would at once meet her needs for loving companionship while releasing her family from the burden of trying to cure her, as Balinese patrilocal kinship meant Gusti could move out of her natal compound and become part of her husband's patriline (Lemelson 2014). She also disclosed how some family members had become increasingly angry and critical (if not outright violent) toward her. These disclosures were compelling because they highlighted issues that were more "at stake" for Gusti than the drier clinical discussions of her illness. Gusti was quite intelligent and an acute observer of the complex familial and community dynamics of which she was a victim.

After interviewing and filming Gusti for over a decade, she had become close friends with the lead author and local collaborators. In 2009, we took Gusti out to dinner after interviewing her about her illness and her life. As Gusti was saying goodbye at the end of the evening, she began to cry and asked, "Why are you friends with me? Don't you feel ashamed to be seen with me? Don't you find me disgusting?" These poignant statements struck us quite deeply. Gusti was assured she was cared for very much; the local collaborators and crew were proud to be her friends, and were genuinely impressed by her fortitude and dignity in the face of her difficult circumstances.

To those living outside Gusti Ayu's daily reality, the symptoms of her TS might not seem so significant, but her emotional outcry indicated an internalization of the local interpretation of her difference, which had turned her into an outcast and contributed to the feelings of low self-worth and hopelessness that were such a significant part of her experience. It became important to determine a narrative structure for the film that would communicate how her comparatively minor symptoms could be so devastating and all-consuming.

During subsequent private interviews, Gusti began disclosing other material about her life that previously would have been difficult to discuss in front of her parents and siblings, such as her feelings of resentment toward her brother, her lingering affection for a potential mate who was of a different caste, and her feelings of despair and hopelessness and being a continual burden on her family that had grown unbearable to the extent that she had considered suicide. Ultimately, these concerns were so significant that it turned out that Gusti's story was about stigma and social suffering and not so much about her symptoms. But Gusti was in very real distress.

In the first interview after returning to the field in 2000, it was apparent that Gusti's condition had deteriorated. Her older brother plaintively asked, "I beg you, with all my respect, we want her to get well, or at least 90%. What is the method by which she can be healed?" Because TS is a biologically based neuropsychiatric disorder, the symptoms can, at times, be relieved or at least well managed by medication. If medications could reduce Gusti's symptoms, they could potentially also alleviate the family problems that were a reaction to these symptoms, and as a result, soothe her emotional anguish.

At this point Gusti's original treatment provider, Dr. Panteri, had had a stroke and was unavailable for home visits, so Gusti was encouraged to see another of the several neurologists on Bali for a consultation, and was provided a small sum of money for the visit. A return team research visit to Bali later that year included the Javanese psychiatrist Dr. Mahar Agusno, who evaluated Gusti Ayu. Although Dr. Mahar is perhaps unfamiliar with the specifics of Balinese culture, he is a sensitive and well-trained psychiatrist and is very interested in cultural psychiatry. After interviewing and diagnosing Gusti, Mahar prescribed her several medications and offered to supervise her remotely from his home in Yogyakarta, Central Java. Unfortunately, hopes for ongoing long-distance treatment were not realistic, so on another return trip to Bali the support of Dr. Made Nyandra, a thoughtful and caring local Balinese psychiatrist, was sought.

Despite these adjustments, and while well-intentioned, such forms of medical intervention can be both inadequate and even potentially harmful. In this instance, offering of this kind of care reinforced Gusti's family's narrative that her problems really did stem from her disordered biology (seen in Indonesia as "*penyakit syaraf*" or a "nerve illness") (Wicaksana 2008), as expressed in her TS symptoms, and perhaps even seemed to capitulate to the idea that the real and best way to ameliorate her suffering would be to reduce these symptoms—an approach that perhaps seemed to concur with her family's desperate quest to "cure" her. This replicated some of the attributional problematics of biomedical psychiatry, where the cause of the illness is located in the patient's self and biology; most importantly, it went against the alternate narrative Gusti was slowly and bravely trying to construct for herself—that perhaps her most significant difficulties were social, and resided in how her family and community were reacting to her difference.

4.6   LAST ENCOUNTERS

Ultimately, after long-term fieldwork, Gusti's key goals of working with the lead author were based on her initial understanding of his role in the research—specifically, the clinical reduction of her symptoms, if not a cure—were in fact little impacted by the relationship. As the research continued, Gusti's main concern repeatedly returned to the intractability of her condition, and her inability to get married and achieve the culturally valued role of wife and mother and fulfill associated responsibilities; those aspects of her role fulfillment were most important for Gusti's sense of satisfaction and her overall happiness.

That being said, there were other, perhaps more intangible effects of the relationship Gusti formed with the lead author, local research team, and to some extent, the crew that did contribute to her feeling that she was valued and had a supportive social world. Through conversations, Gusti discussed the multiple dilemmas she was situated in because of her gender, family position, and illness status (although of course she did not use those terms and concepts in interpreting her own experience). Over the course of many interviews, Gusti gained a sympathetic ear, achieved insight that the repeated exploration of her condition afforded, and earned—and after she moved out of her family home, actually kept or spent as she saw fit— the small amounts of cash that she was paid for each interview.

In one of the earliest interviews with Gusti Ayu, when her sense of isolation, social rejection, and family conflict was at its worst, she revealed she had made these sorts of prayers:

> 'God, if I'm like this forever I can't stand it anymore. It's better if I die. If you still want me to be alive, please give me . . . tell me the medicine I must take so that I can recover soon.' That's how I pray.

A decade later, after moving out of her family compound, working a meaningful job in a fair trade factory, finding a new group of friends, both at work and in the community, Gusti had this to say about her community:

> Before, when I went out people used to laugh at me, mocked me, sweared at me, but (after watching the film) now they seem to realize and regret, 'Ah, why did we humiliate her, she is seriously ill.'

About her friends:

> My friends care for me—they give me attention; when I want to drink something they make it for me.

About her work:

> I feel really grateful that I work here. I have my salary that I can save, I have my own life now.

Regarding her family:

> I go home and bring my mom a little money from my work. I avoid my brother.
> He is too ashamed to ask me for money.

And finally about her future:

I have my own life here; I'm free. My future is now a bright road for me, and I'm very grateful. I can take care of my own finances... I don't have to get stressed out and confused.... My life feels more comfortable. Because all I was doing before was looking for treatments and cures.... Now, no one has control over my life, my life doesn't feel oppressed, and that's what makes me happy...Yes, the future seems so bright for me now.

NOTE

1. A culturally informed reader interested in TS in Indonesia may wonder at the overlap between TS and Latah, a culture-bound syndrome found throughout Southeast Asia sometimes called the hyperstartle syndrome. Latah involves a hypersensitivity to sudden stimulation or fright, with associated behaviors including echopraxia, the involuntary repetition of another's actions; echolalia, or the automatic repetition of another's vocalizations; coprolalia; and dissociative response (see Simons (1996) for a complete review). Jilek (Jilek 1995) notes that even in the nineteenth century, neurologists noticed a phenomenological similarity between TS and Latah, and Gilles de la Tourette himself erroneously assumed Latah-type reactions to be cases of TS, a belief echoed by later psychological anthropologists (Devereux 1980). Although the Balinese recognize Latah (in Bali known as *gigian*), it is not as common as in other areas of Indonesia, such as Java, and has apparently declined in frequency in the last two decades (Simons 1996).

REFERENCES

Arana-Lechuga, Yoaly, Oscar Sanchez-Escandón, Nancy de Santiago-Treviño, Carlos Castillo-Montoya, Guadalupe Terán-Pérez, and Javier Velázquez-Moctezuma. 2008. Risperidone Treatment of Sleep Disturbances in Tourette's Syndrome. *Journal Neuropsychiatry Clin Neurosci* 20 (3): 375–376. doi:10.1176/appi.neuropsych.20.3.375

Asarnow, Joan Rosenbaum, Martha Tompson, Elizabeth Burney Hamilton, Michael J. Goldstein, and Donald Guthrie. 1994. Family-Expressed Emotion, Childhood-Onset Depression, and Childhood-Onset Schizophrenia Spectrum Disorders: Is Expressed Emotion a Nonspecific Correlate of Child Psychopathology or a Specific Risk Factor for Depression? *Journal of Abnormal Child Psychology* 22 (2): 129–146. doi:10.1007/BF02167896

Belo, Jane. 1960. *Trance in Bali*. New York: Columbia University Press.
———. 1970. *Traditional Balinese Culture; Essays*. New York: Columbia University Press.

Bharadwaj, Prashant, Mallesh M. Pai, Agne Suziedelyte, and National Bureau of Economic Research. 2015. Mental Health Stigma. In *NBER Working Paper*

Series No 21240. Cambridge, MA: National Bureau of Economic Research. http://dx.doi.org/10.3386/w21240

Bourdieu, Pierre. 1977. *Outline of a Theory of Practice.* Vol. 16. New York: Cambridge University Press.

Buckser, Andrew. 2006. The Empty Gesture: Tourette Syndrome and the Semantic Dimension of Illness. *Ethnology* 45 (4): 255. doi:10.2307/20456601

Budman, Cathy L. 2014. The Role of Atypical Antipsychotics for Treatment of Tourette's Syndrome: An Overview. *Drugs* 74 (11): 1177–1193. doi:10.1007/s40265-014-0254-0

Church, Jessica A., Damien A. Fair, Nico U.F. Dosenbach, Alexander L. Cohen, Francis M. Miezin, Steven E. Petersen, and Bradley L. Schlaggar. 2009. Control Networks in Paediatric Tourette Syndrome Show Immature and Anomalous Patterns of Functional Connectivity. *Brain* 132 (1): 225–238.

Connor, Linda. 1982. The Unbounded Self: Balinese Therapy in Theory and Practice. In *Cultural Conceptions of Mental Health and Therapy*, ed. A. Marsella. Dordrecht: Reidel.

Connor, Linda, Patsy Asch, and Timothy Asch. 1986. *Jero Tapakan: Balinese Healer.* Cambridge: Cambridge University Press.

Crane, Jacquelyn, Jesen Fagerness, Lisa Osiecki, Gunnell Boyd, S. Evelyn Stewart, David L. Pauls, and Jeremiah M. Scharf. 2011. Family-Based Genetic Association Study of Dlgap3 in Tourette Syndrome. *American Journal of Medical Genetics Part B: Neuropsychiatric Genetics* 156 (1): 108–114.

Csordas, Thomas J., and Elizabeth Lewton. 1998. Practice, Performance and Experience in Ritual Healing. *Transcultural Psychiatric Research Review* 35 (4): 435–512.

Desjarlais, Robert, Leon Eisenberg, Byron Good, and Arthur Kleinman. 1995. *World Mental Health: Problems and Priorities in Low-Income Countries.* Oxford: Oxford University Press.

Devereux, George. 1980. *Basic Problems of Ethnopsychiatry.* Chicago: University of Chicago Press.

Edgerton, Robert B. 1992. *Sick Societies: Challenging the Myth of Primitive Harmony.* New York: Free Press.

Ercan-Sencicek, A. Gulhan, Althea A. Stillman, Ananda K. Ghosh, Kaya Bilguvar, Brian J. O'Roak, Christopher E. Mason, et al. 2010. L-Histidine Decarboxylase and Tourette's Syndrome. *New England Journal of Medicine* 362 (20): 1901–1908. doi:10.1056/NEJMoa0907006

Felling, Ryan J., and Harvey S. Singer. 2011. Neurobiology of Tourette Syndrome: Current Status and Need for Further Investigation. *The Journal of Neuroscience* 31 (35): 12387–12395.

Fernandez, Hubert H., Andre G. Machado, and Mayur Pandya. 2015. *A Practical Approach to Movement Disorders: Diagnosis and Management.* Second ed. - New York: Demos Medical Publishing, LLC.

Ferzacca, Steve. 2001. *Healing the Modern in a Central Javanese City*. Durham: Carolina Academic Press.

Freeman, Roger. 2015. *Tics and Tourette Syndrome: Key Clinical Perspectives*. London: Mac Keith Press.

Ganos, Christos, Mark J. Edwards, and Kirsten Müller-Vahl. 2016. "I Swear It Is Tourette's!": On Functional Coprolalia and Other Tic-Like Vocalizations. *Psychiatry Research* 246 (30): 821–826. doi:10.1016/j.psychres.2016.10.021

Geertz, Clifford, and Hildred Geertz. 1975a. *Kinship in Bali*. Chicago: University of Chicago Press.

Geertz, Hildred, and Clifford Geertz. 1975b. *Kinship in Bali*. Chicago: University of Chicago Press.

Ghanizadeh, Ahmad. 2010. Methionine Sulfoximine as a Novel Hypothesized Treatment for Tourette's Syndrome. *Journal of the Neurological Sciences* 293 (1–2): 126.; author reply 126-7. doi:10.1016/j.jns.2010.03.017

Hawksley, Jack, E. Cavanna Andrea, and Nagai Yoko. 2015. The Role of the Autonomic Nervous System in Tourette Syndrome. *Frontiers in Neuroscience* 9: 117. doi:10.3389/fnins.2015.00117

Hay, M. Cameron. 2001. *Remembering to Live: Illness at the Intersection of Anxiety and Knowledge in Rural Indonesia*. Ann Arbor: University of Michigan Press.

Hobart, Angela, Urs Ramseyer, and Albert Leemann. 2001. *The People of Bali*. Hoboken: Wiley-Blackwell.

Hodes, Matthew, and Susan Shur-Fen Gau. 2016. Positive Mental Health, Fighting Stigma and Promoting Resiliency for Children and Adolescents. In *ScienceDirect*. Restricted to UCB, UCD, UCI, UCLA, UCM, UCR, UCSC, UCSD, and UCSF. London: Academic Press is an imprint of Elsevier, http://uclibs.org/PID/283721

Hollenbeck, Peter J. 2003. A Jangling Journey: Life with Tourette Syndrome. *Cerebrum* 5 (3): 47–60.

Horowitz, Mardi J., and Steven P. Reidbord. 2014. Memory, Emotion, and Response to Trauma. In *The Handbook of Emotion and Memory: Research and Theory*, ed. Sven-Åke Christianson, 343–356. New York: Lawrence Erlbaum Associates.

Jenkins, Janis H., and Marvin Karno. 1992. The Meaning of Expressed Emotion: Theoretical Issues Raised by Cross-Cultural Research. *American Journal of Psychiatry* 149: 9–21.

Jennaway, Megan. 2002. *Sisters and Lovers: Women and Desire in Bali*. Lanham: Rowman & Littlefield Publishers.

Jilek, Wolfgang G. 1993. *Traditional Medicine Relevant to Psychiatry*. In *Treatment of Mental Disorders: A Review of Effectiveness*, ed. Giovanni de Girolamo, Norman Sartorius, Gavin Andrews, G. Allen German, and Leon Eisenberg. Washington, DC: American Psychiatric Press.

————. 1995. Emil Kraepelin and Comparative Sociocultural Psychiatry. Special Issue: Emil Kraepelin and 20th Century Psychiatry. *European Archives of Psychiatry and Clinical Neuroscience* 245 (4–5): 231–238. doi:10.1007/BF02191802

Keeney, Bradford, and I. Wayan Budi Asa Mekel. 2004. *Balians : Traditional Healers of Bali, Profiles of Healing*. Philadelphia: Ringing Rocks Press.

Kleinman, Arthur. 1991. *Rethinking Psychiatry: From Cultural Category to Personal Experience*. New York: Free Press.

Kobierska, Magdalena, Martyna Sitek, Katarzyna Gocyla, and Piotr Janik. 2014. Coprolalia and Copropraxia in Patients with Gilles De La Tourette Syndrome. *Neurologia i Neurochirurgia Polska Pol* 48 (1): 1–7. doi:10.1016/j.pjnns.2013.03.001

Lan, Chen-Chia, Chia-Chien Liu, and Ying-Sheue S. Chen. 2015. Quetiapine and Clozapine Combination Treatment for Tourette's Syndrome in an Adolescent Boy: Potential Role of Dopamine Supersensitivity in Loss of Treatment Response. *Journal of Child Adolescent Psychopharmacology* 25 (2): 188–190. doi:10.1089/cap.2014.0118

Lansing, John Stephen. 1995. *The Balinese, Case Studies in Cultural Anthropology*. Fort Worth: Harcourt Brace College Publishers.

Lemelson, Robert. 2003a. Obsessive-Compulsive Disorder in Bali: The Cultural Shaping of a Neuropsychiatric Disorder. *Transcultural Psychiatry* 3: 377–408.

————. 2003b. Traditional Healing and It's Discontents: Efficacy and Traditional Therapies of Neuropsychiatric Disorders in Bali. *Medical Anthropology Quarterly* 18 (1): 48–76.

————. 2014. *Bitter Honey*. 81 min. Watertown: Documentary Research Resources. http://www.der.org/films/bitter-honey.html

Lewis, Kendra, Lewis Rappa, Devon A. Sherwood-Jachimowicz, and Margareth Larose-Pierre. 2010. Aripiprazole for the Treatment of Adolescent Tourette's Syndrome: A Case Report. *Journal of Pharmacy Practice* 23 (3): 239–244. doi:10.1177/0897190009358771

Lin, Haiqun, Liliya Katsovich, Musie Ghebremichael, Diane B. Findley, Heidi Grantz, Paul J. Lombroso, et al. 2007. Psychosocial Stress Predicts Future Symptom Severities in Children and Adolescents with Tourette Syndrome and/or Obsessive-Compulsive Disorder. *Journal of Child Psychology and Psychiatry* 48 (2): 157–166.

Lizano, Paulo, Ami Popat-Jain, Jeremiah M. Scharf, Noah C. Berman, Alik Widge, Darin D. Dougherty, and Emad Eskandar. 2016. Challenges in Managing Treatment-Refractory Obsessive-Compulsive Disorder and Tourette's Syndrome. *Harvard Review of Psychiatry* 24 (4): 294–301. doi:10.1097/HRP.0000000000000121

Marsh, Rachel, Andrew J. Gerber, and Bradley S. Peterson. 2008. Neuroimaging Studies of Normal Brain Development and Their Relevance for Understanding

Childhood Neuropsychiatric Disorders. *Journal of the American Academy of Child and Adolescent Psychiatry* 47 (11): 1233–1251.

McKay, Dean, and Eric A. Storch. 2009. *Cognitive-Behavior Therapy for Children: Treating Complex and Refractory Cases.* New York: Springer Pub.

McMahon, William M., Alice S. Carter, Nancy Fredine, and David L. Pauls. 2003. Children at Familial Risk for Tourette's Disorder: Child and Parent Diagnoses. *American Journal of Medical Genetics Part B: Neuropsychiatric Genetics* 121 (1): 105–111.

McNaught, Kevin S.P., and Jonathan W. Mink. 2011. Advances in Understanding and Treatment of Tourette Syndrome. *Nature Reviews Neurology* 7 (12): 667–676. doi:10.1038/nrneurol.2011.167

McNay, Lois. 1999. Gender, Habitus and the Field Pierre Bourdieu and the Limits of Reflexivity. *Theory, Culture and Society* 16 (1): 95–117. doi:10.1177/026327699016001007

McPhee, Colin. 1956. *A House in Bali.* New York: Day and Co.

Mustar, Lukman. 1985. Pengaruh Faktor-Faktor Psiko-Sosio-Kultural Dalam Interaksi Antara Pengobatan Tradisional Dan Kliennya Di Palembang, Semarang, Bali (the Effect of Psycho-Socio-Cultural Factors in the Interaction between Traditional Therapy and Its Patients in Palembang, Semarang, Bali). Bali, Indonesia.

Nagai, Yoko, Andrea Cavanna, and Hugo D. Critchley. 2009. Influence of Sympathetic Autonomic Arousal on Tics: Implications for a Therapeutic Behavioral Intervention for Tourette Syndrome. *Journal of Psychosomatic Research* 67 (6): 599–605. doi: 10.1016/j.jpsychores.2009.06.004

Nagai, Yoko, Andrea E. Cavanna, Hugo D. Critchley, Jeremy J. Stern, Mary M. Robertson, and Eileen M. Joyce. 2014. Biofeedback Treatment for Tourette Syndrome: A Preliminary Randomized Controlled Trial. *Cognitive and Behavioral Neurology* 27 (1): 17–24. doi:10.1097/wnn.0000000000000019

O'Connor, Kieron P., Anick Laverdure, Annie Taillon, Emmanuel Stip, François Borgeat, and Marc Lavoie. 2009. Cognitive Behavioral Management of Tourette's Syndrome and Chronic Tic Disorder in Medicated and Unmedicated Samples. *Behaviour Research and Therapy* 47 (12): 1090–1095.

O'Rourke, Julia A., Jeremiah M. Scharf, Platko Jill, S. Evelyn Stewart, Cornelia Illmann, David A. Geller, et al. 2011. The Familial Association of Tourette's Disorder and Adhd: The Impact of OCD Symptoms. *American Journal of Medical Genetics Part B: Neuropsychiatriatric Genetics* 156B (5): 553–560. doi:10.1002/ajmg.b.31195

Parker, Lynette. 1997. Engendering School Children in Bali. *Journal of the Royal Anthropological Institute* 3 (3): 497–516.

Pringle, Robert. 2004. *A Short History of Bali: Indonesia's Hindu Realm.* Crows Nest: Allen & Unwin.

Rice, Timothy, and Barbara Coffey. 2015. Pharmacotherapeutic Challenges in Treatment of a Child with "the Triad" of Obsessive Compulsive Disorder, Attention-Deficit/Hyperactivity Disorder and Tourette's Disorder. *Journal of Child and Adolescent Psychopharmacology* 25 (2): 176–179. doi:10.1089/cap.2015.2522

Robertson, Mary M. 2006. Mood Disorders and Gilles De La Tourette's Syndrome: An Update on Prevalence, Etiology, Comorbidity, Clinical Associations, and Implications. *Journal of Psychosomatic Research* 61 (3): 349–358. doi:10.1016/j.jpsychores.2006.07.019

Saka, Esen, and Ann M. Graybiel. 2003. Pathophysiology of Tourette's Syndrome: Striatal Pathways Revisited. *Brain and Development* 25: S15–S19. doi:10.1016/S0387-7604(03)90002-7

Scahill, Lawrence, Gerald Erenberg, Cheston M. Berlin, Cathy Budman, Barbara J. Coffey, Joseph Jankovic, et al. 2006. Contemporary Assessment and Pharmacotherapy of Tourette Syndrome. *NeuroRx* 3 (2): 192–206.

Seligman, Rebecca, and Laurence J. Kirmayer. 2008. Dissociative Experience and Cultural Neuroscience: Narrative, Metaphor and Mechanism. *Culture, Medicine and Psychiatry* 32 (1): 31–64.

Serajee, Fatema J., and A.H.M. Mahbubul Huq. 2015. Advances in Tourette Syndrome: Diagnoses and Treatment. *Pediatric Clinics North America* 62 (3): 687–701. doi:10.1016/j.pcl.2015.03.007

Simons, R. 1996. *Boo! Culture, Experience and the Startle Reflex.* New York/Oxford: Oxford University Press.

Singer, Harvey S., and John T. Walkup. 1991. Tourette Syndrome and Other Tic Disorders Diagnosis, Pathophysiology, and Treatment. *Medicine* 70 (1): 15–32.

Staley, Douglas, Roxburgh Wand, and Gary Shady. 1997. Tourette Disorder: A Cross-Cultural Review. *Comprehensive Psychiatry* 38 (1): 6–16. doi:10.1016/S0010-440X(97)90047-X

Suryani, Luh K. 1984. Culture and Mental Disorder: The Case of Bebainan in Bali. *Culture, Medicine and Psychiatry* 8 (1): 95–113.

Swain, James E., Lawrence Scahill, Paul J. Lombroso, Robert A. King, and James F. Leckman. 2007. Tourette Syndrome and Tic Disorders: A Decade of Progress. *Journal of the American Academy of Child and Adolescent Psychiatry* 46 (8): 947–968. doi:10.1097/chi.0b013e318068fbcc

Thong, Denny, Bruce Carpenter, and Stanley Krippner. 1993. *A Psychiatrist in Paradise: Treating Mental Illness in Bali.* In *Bangkok.* Cheney Wash: White Lotus.

Weller, Elizabeth B., and Ronald A. Weller. 2009. Olanzapine as Treatment for Children and Adolescents with Tourette's Syndrome. *Current Psychiatry Reports* 11 (2): 95–96. https://www.ncbi.nlm.nih.gov/pubmed/19302761

Whyte, Susan Reynolds, and Benedicte Ingstad. 1995. Disability and Culture: An Overview. In *Disability and Culture*, ed. S.R. Whyte and B. Ingstad, 3–32. Berkeley: University of California Press.

Wicaksana, Inu. 2008. *Mereka Bilang Aku Sakit Jiwa: Refleksi Kasus-Kasus Psikiatri Dan Problematika Kesehatan Jiwa Di Indonesia*. Yogyakarta: Kanisius.

Wikan, U. 1990. *Managing Turbulent Hearts: A Balinese Formula for Living*. Chicago: University of Chicago Press.

Wilson, John P., and Beverley Raphael. 2013. *International Handbook of Traumatic Stress Syndromes*. Berlin/Heidelberg: Springer Science & Business Media.

Yamamuro, Kazuhiko, Manabu Makinodan, Toyosaku Ota, Junzo Iida, and Toshifumi Kishimoto. 2014. Paliperidone Extended Release for the Treatment of Pediatric and Adolescent Patients with Tourette's Disorder. *Annals of General Psychiatry* 13: 13. doi:10.1186/1744-859X-13-13

Yang, Lawrence H., Fang-Pei Chen, Kathleen Janel Sia, Jonathan Lam, Katherine Lam, Hong Ngo, et al. 2014. "What Matters Most:" a Cultural Mechanism Moderating Structural Vulnerability and Moral Experience of Mental Illness Stigma. *Social Science and Medicine* 103: 84–93.

Yoon, Dustin Y., Christopher A. Rippel, Andrew J. Kobets, Christina M. Morris, Jennifer E. Lee, Phillip N. Williams, et al. 2007. Dopaminergic Polymorphisms in Tourette Syndrome: Association with the Dat Gene (Slc6a3). *American Journal of Medical Genetics Part B: Neuropsychiatric Genetics* 144 (5): 605–610.

Yu, Dongmei, Carol A. Mathews, Jeremiah M. Scharf, Benjamin M. Neale, Lea K. Davis, Eric R. Gamazon, et al. 2015. Cross-Disorder Genome-Wide Analyses Suggest a Complex Genetic Relationship between Tourette's Syndrome and Ocd. *American Journal of Psychiatry* 172 (1): 82–93. doi:10.1176/appi.ajp. 2014.13101306

CHAPTER 5

Shadows and Illuminations: Interpreting and Framing Extraordinary Experience

Photo 5.1   Nyoman Kereta

5.1   STORY SUMMARY

Kereta was born in 1944 in a small rural village in Central Bali. He was a farmer his whole life and lives in the same extended family compound in which he was born. He remembers a pleasant childhood shaped by the

© The Author(s) 2017

R. Lemelson, A. Tucker, *Afflictions*, Culture, Mind, and Society,
DOI 10.1007/978-3-319-59984-7_5

rhythms of rice agriculture and the Balinese ritual calendar. Then in 1965, when Kereta was twenty-one, his village was caught in the wave of violence that swept the nation following a purported coup by the Indonesian Communist Party (PKI), and then a countercoup by General (later President) Suharto. Military and paramilitary forces purportedly belonging to the Indonesian Nationalist Party (PNI) entered his village looking for suspected members of the communist party. Kereta witnessed the roundup and massacre of several villagers in which both killers and victims were personal acquaintances. The troops singled out a number of villagers and had them march to a local cemetery. Although he was not targeted for violence, Kereta was extremely distressed by what he saw, and he felt he was in mortal danger. He sought refuge in the high branches of a tree so that no one could see him, and from there he bore witness to brutal killings, including individuals being hacked to death with machetes. Not long afterward, he witnessed his cousin take part in the brutal assassination of his own father outside of the family compound. Paramilitary members stabbed him with a sword and hit his head until his "brains splattered." Kereta also witnessed his father's eyes being gouged out with a pick. Some of the perpetrators were his neighbors. His father's body was eventually buried in a local cemetery, but never given the proper Balinese cremation ceremony.

Soon after these horrifically traumatic events, Kereta's long-standing problems with social withdrawal and fear began. He believed the constant terror he experienced in the wake of these killings weakened his life force. He had problems with his heart beating too rapidly and an "inner pressure" weighing down his body. For months after the massacre, he had difficulty eating and became very thin and withdrawn. He was jumpy, easily startled, and had periods when he felt his mind go blank. He was awakened by nightmares of being chased or people being butchered. In the years following the violence, Kereta became increasingly afraid of social gatherings and avoided public places and events. He withdrew from the social activities of his *banjar*, or village organization, and stopped participating in community work projects.

Then in 1974, he ate some eels that he had caught in an irrigated rice field, not knowing that they had been sprayed earlier that day with a powerful insecticide called Endrin. He became very ill, with symptoms of vomiting and dizziness that lasted for months before he recovered. After some reluctance due to his commonly known vulnerable condition, Kereta had an arranged marriage with a younger woman. It was a difficult transition for the couple, although Kereta cared deeply for his wife. Overwhelmed by his difficulties, she ran away from him and returned to her family, but she eventually came back to Kereta. They had a son, and then in 1984, a daughter. Unfortunately, there were complications with the delivery and the baby girl died. Kereta describes this as the most difficult time in his life. In his grief he cried continuously.

Kereta began seeing small, black figures, which he believed to be spirits known as the *wong samar*, or "the invisible people," a form of spirit being commonly recognized in Bali. He first saw the *wong samar* while cutting the grass in the rice field, describing them as wandering over the fields and hiding in stagnant water. The spirits made noises that gradually coalesced into words: "Why don't you take care of yourself? Will you take care of us?" He felt the figures were competing with one another to enter his head and take possession of his body.

> I wanted to hide in a quiet place, but there were always creatures and sounds. There were voices coming from the grass. There was an image of a black creature. The rice fields were full of voices.

When occupied by these spirits, Kereta would stay inside the family compound to avoid social contact. At other times, he would leave home for days, hiding in solitary places such as remote rice fields or the deeply cut canyons that crisscross the Balinese landscape. One *wong samar* being became his wife. When Kereta's social withdrawal grew so severe that it prevented him from participating in family and community events, and from leaving his bedroom, his family brought him to a *balian*, or traditional healer. According to the *balian*, his illness was caused by witchcraft. Kereta stayed at the healer's compound for a month to receive treatment but his problems persisted, and the healer brought Kereta to both the state mental hospital and to a local government hospital in Denpasar, which had a small inpatient psychiatric unit. The family believed that Kereta's illness was in part caused by weak nerves (B.I. *lemah syaraf*), and he would recover more quickly at the hospital.

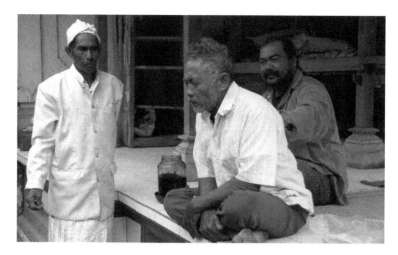

Photo 5.2 Kereta receiving treatment by a *balian usada* or literate healer

According to the initial intake notes, Kereta seemed dazed (B.I. *melamun,* B.B. *bengong*), confused (B.I. *bingung,* B.B. *paling*), and disturbed (B.I. *pikiran terganggu,* B.B.*inguh-inguhan*). He reported that he was dizzy (B.I. *pusing,* B.B. *pengeng*) and having difficulty breathing (B.I. *sesak napas,* B.B. *sesek*). He was diagnosed on the basis of the PPDGJ (*Pedoman Penggolongan dan Diagnosis Gangguan Jiwa*), the Indonesian diagnostic manual, which is based on the International Classification of Diseases (ICD) and the *Diagnostic and Statistical Manual of Mental Disorders* (*DSM*) systems. The initial diagnosis was Paranoid Acute Problem (298.30). A subsequent diagnosis, which was made at the one-year evaluation, was Schizophrenia Paranoid type (295.3) on the basis of the following *DSM-IV-TR* (2000) criteria: delusions resembling thought insertion, auditory and visual hallucinations, and delusions of a persecutory nature. Kereta was given chlorpromazine and another antipsychotic. The voices of the *wong samar* gradually subsided, until after about one week when the voices became "hazy and unclear." He was hospitalized for two more weeks and then discharged.

Kereta's experiences with spirit beings gradually waned. When he experienced a relapse in symptoms, he sought treatments, including traditional healing and pharmacological interventions prescribed by psychiatrists at the local and state mental hospitals in Bali. Certain social and political stressors continued to trouble him in his daily life, including enduring contact with neighbors and family members who took part in the violence against his loved ones during the events of 1965. This residual fear occasionally exacerbated his condition; for example, during the national election campaigns in 2002–2003, when Indonesia democratically elected its president for the first time, the spirits returned, asking Kereta to rejoin the Communist Party. In response to these lingering attacks, he wore a camouflage jacket and military helmet and slept outside in his family temple courtyard. He believed this prevented the spirits from entering his body and forcing him to return to the PKI.

After his discharge, Kereta returned to work as a farmer. He only took his medication briefly and intermittently because it was expensive and hard to procure form local pharmacies or community health centers. Occasionally, he engaged in community activities, but he continued to have difficulty socializing and sleeping, and he still experienced visitation by the spirits.

Kereta has come to terms with the fact that the spirit beings will be with him indefinitely. He seems to have gained a degree of peace with the shadows and illuminations that visit him, yet he also describes long periods where he does not see or hear any spirits at all. He contributes to the family livelihood through farming and making offerings to sell in the market, and is treated fondly by his wife, sons, and brother.

5.2   Multiple Ways to Frame and Interpret Psychotic Experience

Having complex relationships with spiritual beings, including seeing them, hearing them, or becoming a bodily host for them, would be prima facie evidence of a "'bizarre delusion" as diagnosed by most psychiatrists in Western countries. But in Indonesia, there is a strong cultural context for the normalization of spirit possession and interaction with the spirit world. Balinese people have elaborate beliefs about, experiences of, and frameworks for understanding and communicating with spirit beings, and on the whole retain a comparatively intimate acquaintance with the spiritual world or invisible realm (Geertz 1994). Kereta's experiences aligned with the normative sensory and behavioral repertoires of the cultural milieu.

The content of Kereta's visions is deeply grounded in a culturally specific and commonly shared cosmology. *Wong samar*, the spirits Kereta regularly engages with, are a potent class of spirit beings that have links to Balinese mythology and culture stretching back at least 700 years. People could avoid illness and death by paying tribute to the *wong samar* (Santikarma 1995). While it may seem bizarre that Kereta mentions being married to a *wong samar*, in Bali people can take such spirits—thought to have flattened upper lips, float an inch above the ground, and live in canyons or remote rice fields—as wives. They are reputed to be affectionate and loyal spouses if treated with respect, but vengeful if neglected (Wayan Sadha—personal communication). They remain ambivalent figures in folk belief; mystical or mysterious occurrences continue to be attributed to them, and even today some villages boast regular visits by *wong samar* at night, saying if you encounter one you might receive a special blessing (Lemelson 2014). Not every Balinese will see the *wong samar*, yet clearly Kereta's beliefs about the *wong samar* and his propitious relationship with them have a deep cultural basis.

Kereta did not have many of the characteristic features of subtypes of schizophrenia previously operant in *DSM-IV* (1994): His speech production was normal, and while his range of activities was restricted when he was actively "delusional" and appearing shy and anxious, Kereta had a range of volitional activities adequate for his roles in his *banjar*. Given his personal history of trauma and ongoing surveillance by both paramilitary and political informants, Kereta's other negative symptoms, such as his social isolation and loss of interest in the social world, should not be considered outright as a symptom of schizophrenia. These symptoms could be considered as adaptive because an openness of expression under these circumstances could have led to his imprisonment, or worse.

5.3   TRAUMA, HISTORY, AND SUBJECTIVITY IN *SHADOWS AND ILLUMINATIONS*

The lingering effects of the violence and upheaval of the mass killings of 1965 is a significant theme in *Shadows and Illuminations*. The supposed communist coup and the swift and bloody military response left many Indonesians physically injured, traumatized, and stigmatized. Kereta's experiencing, witnessing, and remembering these episodes of violence and hardship were formative moments with long-lasting repercussions in his personal schema of worry, anxiety, and distress. Even after Suharto's fall in 1998 the atmosphere around public discussion of the events of 1965–66 and beyond had become less tense and increasingly more open; many people still felt uncomfortable discussing the events and could face repercussions and trouble on neighborhood, village, and state levels for speaking out against the New Order government, speaking freely about past violence, or acknowledging past association with the Communist Party, no matter how minimal.

The events of 1965 penetrated deeply into Kereta's intrapsychic life, but also affected his social support network. At the time of the 1965 violence, Kereta was the only male in the house responsible for defending the family home (B.B. *nindihan natah*) when it was attacked by the *tameng*. Even after the violence, Kereta could do nothing but look on as his older sister was forced to marry one of the most vicious officers of the paramilitaries; this man is now his brother-in-law. Family members linked this relationship to the continuing pressures (B.I. *tekanan*) of his fears. Another neighbor believed that Kereta had been so troubled by the events because it was his second cousin (B.B. *mindon*) who encouraged the militia members (*tameng*) to attack Kereta's home. Violence over land reform (Robinson 1998) and anger toward relatives over their role as informants (Dwyer and Santikarma 2004) are common themes related to the events of the September 30th movement and mass killings in Bali (Cribb 2004; Dwyer 2009; Dwyer and Santikarma 2004; Retsikas 2006; Zurbuchen 2005). It is significant that Kereta had never narrated these events to his wife, sons, or extended family and certainly not to any of his *banjar* neighbors, some of whom participated in the mass killings. He had never even discussed this with those neighbors who had similar experiences.

A Western psychiatric perspective might hypothesize that Kereta is in part suffering from post-traumatic stress disorder (PTSD), an anxiety disorder that can occur after a traumatic or life-threatening event. Common symptoms of PTSD are re-experiencing events (flashbacks); hyper-arousal (feeling jittery or keyed up); and insomnia, depression, or numbness. In some cases, symptoms may not emerge for a long time following exposure to traumatic events (Briere and Scott 2015; Boehnlein et al. 2004; Kinzie 2016).

A diagnosis of PTSD with psychotic features encompasses some of Kereta's illness experience and his subsequent relationships with spirits. By comparison, among Cambodian refugees who experienced the traumas associated with the Khmer Rouge regime, a prominent cultural shaping of PTSD symptomatology is visitations by ghosts and other spirit beings (Boehnlein et al. 2004). There may be some connection among Kereta's initial traumas in 1965, the reactivation of loss, fear, and sadness as a result of losing his child in 1984, and his subsequent experience of the spirit beings. However, most Balinese people who witnessed the mass killings in 1965 (and they number in the hundreds of thousands) did not develop close relationships with spirit beings.

The neurobiological processes underlying an acute post-traumatic stress response have universal components, but their temporal configuration and interaction are powerfully shaped by how developmental, social, historical, and cultural contexts intersect with psychobiology (Kirmayer et al. 2007; Hinton and Good 2015; Hinton and Hinton 2014). For example, the complexity of remembering and forgetting painful past events in the Indonesian context is affected by prevalent cultural ideas about emotional expression. Javanese and Balinese cultures value interpersonal harmony (Browne 2001; Wikan 1989; Heider 1991) and therefore call for the management and regulation of strong or negative feelings. Ignoring these cultural norms for containment challenges the cosmological order and so risks exposing the community to natural disasters and other catastrophic retribution (Santikarma 1995).

Psychological processes, whether they are healthy or distressed, are not solely located in the individual, but also constructed through discursive processes of narrative, labeling, attribution, interpretation, and interaction that are fundamentally social. From this perspective, a psychiatric diagnosis can be considered at once a potentially useful tool and yet at the same time a "reducing valve" (Huxley 2009) that excludes many areas of relevance to Kereta's story, treatment, and subjectivity. In studying and attempting to ameliorate mental distress, cultural differences and individual subjectivity must be understood, contextualized, and respected (Kirmayer et al. 2015).

In local terms, rather than globalized psychiatric terms, Kereta described his illness as a Balinese illness category, *ngeb*, an illness caused by witnessing something horrific or bizarre. As a result, sufferers put themselves in a self-imposed exile characterized by muteness and a lack of participation in the social world. Kereta believes his *ngeb* began with the witnessing of the massacre in 1965. This initial *ngeb* was compounded by visual and auditory hallucinations of the *wong samar* world. The shock of these events weakened his *bayu*, or life force. Throughout insular Southeast Asia, *bayu* is seen as present in all matter, both living and dead (Laderman 1991). However, it is a force that is sensitive to disturbance and can be depleted through startle, fear, or other disturbance of balance (Wikan 1989). *Bayu* needs to be strong or large (B.B. *gede*) to maintain health. Kereta felt that his continually weakened *bayu* accounted for the predilection of his spirit beings to visit him. *Bayu* can be affected by emotional states such as sadness, and a cluster of symptoms—such as weakness, heaviness, and feeling empty—indicate that the *bayu* is weak or gone.

Kereta chose to disclose his painful and terrifying experiences only in the last meeting with the lead author, in 1997, which was significant. After ongoing interviews, which perhaps comprised the most intimate and in-depth conversations he had had about the events of 1965, he felt safe enough to disclose a personally difficult and politically charged story. As he was aware that the lead author was returning to the United States, he confidently disclosed his story, and thus helped begin the *Affliction* series.

While Kereta used the opportunity to share his harrowing episode of political violence for the first time, he did not seem to be re-experiencing unbearable distress during the retelling, and did not ask to stop filming. In subsequent interviews, from 2000 to the present, Kereta has always seemed to appreciate the visits and discussions, taking very active part in both reviewing old material and offering new aspects of his life experiences. He also participated in several trips to different healers, including Dewa Gde Alit, the healer he had lived with during his extended *ngeb* episode following the death of his daughter.

5.4   LAST ENCOUNTERS

Kereta's symptoms have waxed and waned over the succeeding years, and at the last visit, in late 2013, Kereta had been hospitalized with meningitis for several months. As a result he was quite frail and had lost his hearing. He was, as always, seemingly pleased to renew the friendship and continue the discussion of his life and experiences. He attended a screening of *40 Years of Silence* (Lemelson 2009), another film in which he features prominently, and seemed to very much enjoy his status as local cinema star.

The last interview with Kereta was rather difficult. As a result of his becoming deaf, all the questions had to be written out on large white paper for him to slowly read. As he would read each one, he would laugh and give his loud responses.

His wife stated that he still sees and hears the spirits, but when asked, Kereta reported:

> The black magic spirits? They are invisible, unseen. I cannot see the black magic spirits . . . But I still see the barong.[1]

Later:

> There are still many spirits that came into the body, the black magic from the head of the PKI wants to enter the body through my back. They get into my memories. There's a lot of them.

His wife noted that he frequently laughs and talks to himself. About his wife:

> I still love my wife. I do, I have to . . . but my wife is scared of me. She is scared to sleep together with me. Because she is scared of my sacrificed body, I am the sacrificed body.

And at last, he speaks of his relation with his troubled history and by extension, the troubled and unresolved history of Indonesia:

> Oh no, I am not scared of the Communist Party leader (spirit). I'm not now, he's my friend. But we don't dare spread communism, we're both scared. The leader of the PKI is scared to spread the lessons about communism. But we are both at peace.

NOTE

1. The protective dragon- like spirit, immortalized in Mead's *"Trance and Dance in Bali"*.

REFERENCES

American Psychiatric Association. 1994. *Diagnostic and Statistical Manual of Mental Disorders.* 4th ed. Washington, DC: Author.

———. 2000. *Diagnostic and Statistical Manual of Mental Disorders.* 4th ed., text rev. Washington, DC: Author.

Boehnlein, James K., J. David Kinzie, Utako Sekiya, Crystal Riley, Kanya Pou, and Bethany Rosborough. 2004. A Ten-Year Treatment Outcome Study of Traumatized Cambodian Refugees. *The Journal of Nervous and Mental Disease* 192 (10): 658–663.

Briere, John, and Catherine Scott. 2015. Complex Trauma in Adolescents and Adults: Effects and Treatment. *Psychiatric Clinics of North America* 38 (3): 515–527. doi:10.1016/j.psc.2015.05.004

Browne, Kevin O. 2001. (Ng)Amuk Revisited: Emotional Expression and Mental Illnes in Central Java, Indonesia. *Transcultural Psychiatry* 38: 147–165.

Cribb, Robert. 2004. The Indonesian Genocide of 1965–66. In *Teaching About Genocide: Issues, Approaches and Resources*, ed. S. Totten. Fayetteville: University of Arkansas Press.

Dwyer, Leslie. 2009. A Politics of Silences: Violence, Memory and Treacherous Speech in Post-1965 Bali. In *Genocide: Truth, Memory, and Representation*, ed. Alexander L. Hinton and Kevin L. O'Neill, 113–146. Durham: Duke University Press.

Dwyer, Leslie, and Degung Santikarma. 2004. When the World Turned to Chaos': 1965 and Its Aftermath. In *The Specter of Genocide Mass Murder in Historical Perspective*, ed. Robert Gellately and Ben Kiernan. New York: Cambridge University Press.

Geertz, Hildred. 1994. *Images of Power: Balinese Paintings Made for Gregory Bateson and Margaret Mead*. Honolulu: University of Hawaii Press.

Heider, Karl G. 1991. *Landscapes of Emotion: Mapping Three Cultures of Emotion in Indonesia*. Cambridge: Cambridge University Press.

Hinton, Devon E., and Byron J. Good. 2015. *Culture and PTSD: Trauma in Global and Historical Perspective*. Philadelphia: University of Pennsylvania Press.

Hinton, Devon E., and Alexander L. Hinton. 2014. *Genocide and Mass Violence: Memory, Symptom, and Recovery*. New York: Cambridge University Press.

Huxley, Aldous. 2009. *The Doors of Perception: Includes Heaven and Hell*. 1st Harper Perennial Modern Classics ed. New York: Harper Perennial.

Kinzie, J. David. 2016. Medical Approach to the Management of Traumatized Refugees. *Journal of Psychiatric Practice* 22 (2): 76–83. doi:10.1097/PRA. 0000000000000135

Kirmayer, Laurence J., Robert Lemelson, and Mark Barad, eds. 2007. *Understanding Trauma: Integrating Biological, Clinical, and Cultural Perspectives*. New York: Cambridge University Press.

Kirmayer, Laurence J., Robert Lemelson, and Constance A. Cummings, eds. 2015. *Re-Visioning Psychiatry: Cultural Phenomenology, Critical Neuroscience, and Global Mental Health*. New York: Cambridge University Press.

Laderman, Carol. 1991. *Taming the Wind of Desire: Psychology, Medicine, and Aesthetics in Malay Shamanistic Performance*. Berkeley: University of California Press.

Lemelson, Robert. 2009. *40 Years of Silence: An Indonesian Tragedy*. 86 min. Watertown: Documentary Educational Resources. http://www.der.org/films/forty-years-of-silence.html

———. 2014. 'The Spirits Enter Me to Force Me to Be a Communist': Political Embodiment, Idioms of Distress, Spirit Possession, and Thought Disorder in Bali. In *Genocide and Mass Violence: Memory, Symptom, and Recovery*, ed. Devon E. Hinton and Alexander L. Hinton, 175–189. New York: Cambridge University Press.

Retsikas, Konstantinos. 2006. The Semiotics of Violence: Ninja, Sorcerers, and State Terror in Post-Soeharto Indonesia. *Bijdragen tot de taal-, land-en volkenkunde/ Journal of the Humanities and Social Sciences of Southeast Asia* 162 (1): 56–94. doi:10.1163/22134379-90003674

Robinson, Geoffrey. 1998. *The Dark Side of Paradise. Political Violence in Bali.* Ithaca: Cornell University Press.

Santikarma, Degung. 1995. *Koh Ngomong, the Balinese Tactic and the Spirit of Resistance.* Fourth International Bali Studies Conference, Sydney University.

Wikan, Unni. 1989. Illness from Fright or Soul Loss: A North Balinese Culture-Bound Syndrome? *Culture, Medicine & Psychiatry* 13 (1): 25–50.

Zurbuchen, Mary Sabina. 2005. *Beginning to Remember: The Past in the Indonesian Present.* Singapore: NUS Press.

CHAPTER 6

Family Victim: Encountering Deviance and Representing Intersubjectivity

Photo 6.1 Estu Wardhani

6.1 STORY SUMMARY

Estu Wardhani is a Javanese man in his early thirties living in Gunung Kidul, a rural area on the outskirts of Yogyakarta. Intelligent and charismatic, Estu is married with two young daughters and runs a small business selling mobile phones. But there is another side to Estu, who calls himself the "bad coconut" of his Central Javanese family, and feels he is the victim of all of his family's karmic debt. His family and community have seen that his disruptive and aggressive patterns of conduct have stressed his interpersonal relationships and threatened his marriage.

Estu has been "different" ever since he was a young boy. Over the course of his life, this difference has manifested through behaviors that range from the mildly unusual to the deeply distressing. These behaviors include physical tics; chronic restlessness and an inability or unwillingness to carry out daily tasks; failure to complete his expected educational trajectory or hold a steady job; participation in underworld activities such as gambling, stealing, and theft; and aggressive and at times outright violent behavior toward friends and family. Estu describes himself simply as a "caged bird who longs to fly free," but his disruptive patterns of conduct deeply distress others and interfere with his ability to follow the path of normative Javanese development. Family members and healers struggle to determine exactly what is ailing him: Is he possessed by an evil spirit, is he a psychopath, or is he simply not yet willing or able to "be Javanese"? Relatives and healers carry out a search to find the root of Estu's problems and the corresponding treatment. This mobilizes culturally salient models of deviance, culpability, and rehabilitation informed by Javanese beliefs about development and maturity, family roles, spiritual practice and power, personal initiative, and collective responsibility. Estu's case questions the boundaries of what can be considered normative experience and documents how troubled or troubling behavior can be understood or interpreted in multiple ways outside the confines of Western psychiatric diagnostics.

Estu was born in 1975, the seventh of eight children, to one of the most well-respected families living in Gunung Kidul, a mostly impoverished rural region of southern Central Java. His father was a well-educated local schoolteacher. Since he was about eight or nine years old, Estu exhibited a series of odd physical tics and occasionally fainted, a disorder locally labeled as *saradan*. Despite his evident intellect, he seemed unable to complete even basic chores and rarely helped around the house. Because his mother felt sorry for him, she refrained from disciplining his misbehavior. As he got older, however, this misbehavior became more marked. When he was ten, he engaged in petty theft. In middle school his best friends were street kids (B.I. *anak jalanan*), and by high school Estu was skipping class, engaging in minor crime, and getting drunk, all practices very negatively sanctioned in rural Java. These experiments with deviance stood out in stark contrast to the rest of his siblings who were all driven and focused academic achievers. One by one these siblings went on to college, moved away from Gunung Kidul, got married, and launched successful professional careers, but Estu still seemed lost.

At the same time he was possibly making forays into the world of criminality, Estu became interested in the spiritual world. Like many young Javanese men he strove to improve his personal power by studying with various healers (B.I. *dukun*), traditional healers revered for their mystical prowess. He developed a particularly close relationship with Irah, a female *dukun* who ritually adopted Estu as her spiritual "son." While friends and family distrusted Irah and suspected her of practicing black magic, Estu felt she was a protective force in his life and was deeply upset when she passed away a number of years into their relationship.

Photo 6.2   Estu consults with one of his traditional healers

Estu attended college in Yogyakarta and there he fell in love with Ana, the younger sister of a friend. Despite frequent squabbles and different religious backgrounds (Ana is Muslim and Estu is Christian, and such intermarriage is still very uncommon in Indonesia), they decided to marry. When Estu consulted with another trusted *dukun*, Arjo, on the matter, the man predicted hardship because they were "not a good match."

Until a certain point of time your life will always be full of quarrels [...] If you can't endure it, it'll be like hell. But if you can endure your married life, the time will come for you to live happily.

This grim prediction proved accurate. Estu and Ana had frequent violent domestic disputes, usually triggered by Estu's unpredictable behavior and the couple's ongoing economic challenges. One of their main struggles was Estu's gambling; his parents and siblings frequently loaned the couple money to start their own business, but Estu gambled it away. In order to support his habit, Estu forged fake lottery tickets to collect rewards, feigned illness to collect charity, and on more than one occasion stole and pawned off other people's motorbikes. He sometimes resorted to direct coercion or threats. The birth of his daughter, Mega, while bringing joy, did little to calm Estu or unite him with his wife. Ana became so depressed and desperate that she would bang her head against the wall while fantasizing about leaving Estu. She even contemplated suicide.

When reflecting on his fraught marriage and his other problems, Estu thinks that he is spoiled and gets bored too easily. He also thinks there might be a malevolent being who takes possession of him. When he was around twenty, about the time he met Ana, he started hearing voices that would get angry, insult him, and encourage him to do bad things. Certain family members and *dukun* feel that this other being is actually Irah, working her black magic through him from the afterlife. Estu hates these voices and the things they make him do. He has considered committing suicide if he cannot rid himself of them and free his life from its frustrating cycle of deviant behavior, low self-regard, emotional outbursts, and attempts at rehabilitation. He describes at times feeling so worthless or so directionless that he does not even want to get out of bed in the morning, saying, "Sometimes when I wake up in the morning, [I think] 'Why should I get up? There is nothing I must do.' It's better for me to go to sleep again; I can have a dream, to be this, to be that." Yet, these periods of low motivation and low self-regard alternate with feelings of potency and possibility, fantasy, and grandiosity. This is expressed in his belief that he has achieved mystical powers to predict the future or read people's minds, that if he keeps playing he will win at gambling, or in his extended revenge fantasies.

Estu was subject to a range of frequent spiritual, behavioral, and pharmaceutical interventions in the face of his actions. On more than one occasion, he was temporarily imprisoned in a local jail, a known recourse for Javanese parents who want to discipline their disruptive children. Additionally, different *dukun* tried to entice or enable Estu to live a better life; some prescribed various religious rituals to right past spiritual errors, while others counseled Estu on practical matters such as financial management. In one memorable event, Puji, a *dukun* and one of Estu's closest advisors, took Estu to a cemetery at night and knocked him unconscious. When Estu awoke he was prompted to write a letter pledging to live a better life and was forced to sign this pledge in his own blood.

In addition to traditional Javanese healing practices, Estu was medically evaluated for his troubling condition. He was diagnosed with psychiatric disorders including attention deficit disorder, dysthymia, TS, and most troubling, anti-social personality disorder, and psychopathy. He was prescribed Haloperidol, a potent antipsychotic, and Fluoxetine (Prozac), a selective serotonin reuptake inhibitor. These medications reportedly made him feel better and more in control, but after a short while he stopped taking them.

Despite all these efforts, by 2003 Estu's situation completely deteriorated. He had scrawled angry graffiti on the walls of his house and business, threatened the lives of his family members, and was no longer welcome at the houses of any of his siblings. His parents had moved out of their home along with all of their belongings to avoid his destructive wrath.

Photo 6.3 Estu, his wife, Ana, and their daughter, Mega, under graffiti in his stall which reads "Life without hope"

Then in 2004, when it seemed like things could not get much worse, something changed. Estu's second daughter was born, and he adjusted to the rhythms of fatherhood in a way he had not when Mega was young. At around the same time, his father fell ill with cancer. Estu became his prime caretaker, nursing him and staying at his bedside. The two talked about everything that had happened, expressed their love for each other, and found resolution before his father succumbed to his illness and passed away. This experience was profoundly important to Estu, who felt proud that he could ease his father's suffering and gratified that this labor was acknowledged and valued.

By 2006, Estu retained the sense of calm and purpose that caring for his father had given him. While he still wrestles with feelings of restlessness and low self-worth, he holds down a steady job as a driver, saves money, and started his own cell phone business. This financial stability has positively affected his relationship with Ana, and their marriage has blossomed. Estu no longer hears voices or has suicidal thoughts. He also claims to have noble aspirations, saying he wants to use his life for the good of others. Locals now greet him on the street with calls of "Hello, Boss!" and he is among those neighborhood family men invited to participate in village meetings and contribute to ritual celebrations. This stability and social position is a new chapter in Estu's biography, a hard-won if still tenuous success for himself and his family that follows a decade of confusion, false starts, and personal strife.

However, as Estu seems to be settling in and settling down, his family is hesitantly beginning to consider that he has truly changed; however, they also warily acknowledge that this might be just another temporary reprieve.

6.2   Deviance, Social Control, and Intersubjective Experience

The issues that emerge as central to subjects' lives in the *Afflictions* films (Lemelson 2010–2011) are, perhaps surprisingly, rarely their symptoms per se. For Gusti, the social stigma and ensuing low self-concept she suffered were much more upsetting than her tics. For Kereta, the culturally inflected personal and social outcomes of traumatic experience were more upsetting than the phenomena of visual and auditory hallucinations. For Estu, the core issue was ultimately the interpretation of and response to deviance.

Deviance is a slippery term—socially constructed and to a significant extent relative. In other words, deviant behavior is basically what a majority of a group believes constitutes deviant behavior (Becker 1963; Goffman 1963). Often a matter of degree or intensity, deviance is contingent on factors such as the size and organization of the society, the social identity of the person engaging in deviant behavior, the intent or capacity of the deviant person to understand and uphold rules and norms, the circumstances under which the deviant act occurs, the visibility of the act, etc. All of these determine who or what will be labeled as deviant and if so labeled, what degree of deviance is viewed as immoral or pathological, and how this will be sanctioned. There are multiple, at times competing, accounts of how this concept should be theorized, from the classic conceptions of structuralism/functionalism (Durkheim 2014; Merton 1964) to anthropological concepts of deviance (Edgerton 1976) to contemporary notions such as the "subaltern" (Said 1979; Spivak 1999; Gramsci 1988). Deviance—including criminality, sexual abnormality, and mental illness—was of inherent interest to sociologists and anthropologists of the 1950s—1960s (Freilich et al. 1991; Edgerton 1976; Becker 1963), and a number of ethnographers have used participant observation fieldwork to study criminals and addressed some of the "experiential tangles" and issues that arose therein (Ferrell and Hamm 1998; Bourgois 1995).

Both milder forms of social deviance and more extreme episodes of reported violence occurred on multiple occasions during the shoot for *Family Victim*. A detailed retelling of this fieldwork provides an opportunity to discuss not just local understandings of deviance or the representation of deviant behavior on film, but also to explore how deviance is constructed dialogically and how shifting intersubjectivity can impact an ethnographer's understanding of what counts as deviant.

Estu says of himself that he has some form of "invisible disease," an ineffable problem whose source cannot be located and yet whose symptoms seem to manifest in his thoughts, personality, and behavior. One of the first explanatory models that could be applied to these "troubles" is a psychiatric one. Estu's brother-in-law, Mahar Agusno, is a well-respected Javanese psychiatrist and long-term collaborator on *Afflictions* and related projects. A number of competing psychiatric diagnoses and frames were discussed with Mahar. Following is a psychiatric exegesis, based in part on Mahar's evaluation, and a further analysis of "The Troubles with Estu" (which was the working title of *Family Victim* [Lemelson 2010]).

Because of his repeated anti-social behaviors and seeming lack of remorse, viewed through the lens of both a doctor and a family member who has experienced the repercussions of his actions firsthand, his psychiatrist considered whether Estu might be a psychopath or a sociopath. While both these terms are used in "folk" parlance and mental health discourse, neither are in the *DSM* system, which provides a related diagnosis, "Anti-social Personality Disorder."

Estu's symptoms of hearing voices might suggest psychiatric disturbance. Estu reports "inner voices" which appear when he is angry; they give him orders, criticize him, and encourage him to engage in problematic behavior.

> It seems that there's something alive, which can't accept it if it's treated rudely. They can't accept mean treatment, they rebel, [saying], "Don't accept it. Take revenge, when possible." If in fact inside here [points to heart] there is another being that is separate from myself, maybe it is that being who is working.

On another occasion, Estu reiterated:

> There are voices that speak in my heart… they are so soft, sometimes with feelings and sometimes with voices, which repeat inside myself which protest and tell me, "you have to do this… this… this… "

Estu sometimes talks back to these voices, asking what they want with him, yet he cannot make them go away. He says, "I ask the voice to shut up, but it keeps talking." Sometimes the voice seems like an alter; Estu says, "I feel there's another 'me.' Now I hate him so much. The one who is bad. Who is coward. If only he was in the form of a human being, I'd fight him. He makes me unsuccessful, a failure. Not like what I want."

It is difficult to tell whether these voices are auditory hallucinations secondary to a formal diagnosis of thought disorder (Tschoeke et al. 2014), a function of a "personality disorder," a depersonalization of Estu's anger, a part of himself from which he disassociates, an aspect of his personality that is split off and not integrated into his ego, or even a form of malingering. Estu is very bright and would understand how a diagnosis and the "sick role" (Parsons 1951) could deflect responsibility for his behaviors away from the purely volitional.

Estu's cycles of low motivation, low self-esteem and self-regard, and occasional suicidal ideation might indicate dysthymia, depression, or a related mood disorder. His apparent cycling between low mood and at times agitation appeared to point toward a further psychiatric diagnosis of bipolar disorder. Given his history, his dreams, and insistence that he is going to be a "big man" might be an indication of a distorted perception of the world, or what he is capable of in it.

Finally, Estu exhibited symptoms of TS, which can be co-morbid with ADHD, and is associated with poor impulse control and difficulty focusing for extended periods of time. An argument could be made that the effect of these disorders plays a role in Estu's problematic behavior and compulsions.

Each of these potential diagnoses seemed a plausible psychiatric explanation for Estu's troubling behavior. Yet, a textured understanding of local Javanese spiritual beliefs and models of human development and social interaction complicates the apparent simplicity of a psychiatric categorical model and gives a nuanced analysis to the expression and interpretation of Estu's non-normative behaviors and perceptions, accounting for the layers of culture that infuse and shape his experience.

Estu and his family think he might be possessed by the spirit of a deceased black magic practitioner or perhaps some other evil spirit. He has a long-sustained interest in black magic and communicating with the spirit world, and has developed relationships with various *dukun* to help him do so. Estu's family believes that his contact with dark or destructive forces has negatively impacted his behavior and by extension endangered his family. Some of this may have been accidental, caused by the residue of powerful forces contained in some of the accessories of Estu's studies in magic. For example, Estu had a *susuk*, or charm, implanted in his body by a *dukun* intended to protect him and give him strength, but the family believes it might actually be harming him. Estu's sister remembers when he brought other powerful magical implements, such as a *keris*, a ceremonial dagger that has magical and mystical powers and has deep symbolic meaning for Indonesians (Frey 2010; Mrázek 2011), into the family home, disturbing their peace and safety.

> ...when he lived with us a couple of years ago, he brought home some *keris*. And at that time [my son] was still a baby, and he cried all night and day, so we asked, "What is going on with him?" And weeks after that my younger brother admitted that he brought some *keris* and that the *dukun* that he went to already told him that because they might have bad impacts on babies and other people in the house who did not have protection, but he brought

them anyway to the house. And we just knew that [my son] could not stand their influence.

The family believes that beyond the powerful or possessed charms (B.I. *susuk*) and daggers, Estu may become possessed by the spirit of his beloved *dukun*, Mak Irah, and Estu concurs. Spiritual possession is a plausible interpretation for Estu's behavior according to Javanese logics of deviant or disturbed behavior; some family members have even consulted *dukun* to counter the powers acting through Estu with black magic of their own. However, his breaching of social norms is much more disturbing than his interactions with spirit beings or invisible realms. Despite these frameworks of interpretation available in a Javanese cultural context that to a certain extent normalize such interaction, Estu's family feels that his experiences go beyond the norm and threaten not only their own sense of moral order and expected behavior of a family member, but even their physical safety. What is most upsetting to them is his social aggression, which goes far beyond what is culturally normative. It is not, in *DSM* nomenclature, "culturally sanctioned."

For Estu, a historical and cultural analysis of idioms of distress contributes to an understanding of whether his behavior is meaningless pathology or meaningful, albeit upsetting, communication. There is a local idiom of distress that friends and family members use to describe Estu's behavior: *ngamuk* (Browne 2001a, b), which blurs the boundaries between mental illness and meaningful social communication.

Ana says that when Estu demands her jewelry or other things she knows he will use to gamble, "If I insist on not giving it to him, we will just fight. Well, I'd better give it to him rather than seeing him go *ngamuk*." She describes his "*ngamuk*" behavior as explosive lashing out physically at the people and things surrounding him, saying, "He becomes irritated. And when he gets irritated he may curse, ruin things [...] I'd better avoid him. I'm afraid that I'll get punched or something."

Ngamuk, or the more familiar term to Western audiences, "amok," is a much-discussed and fabled phenomenon in Indonesia and wider Southeast Asia (Williamson 2007; Ugarte 1999; Spores 1988; Burton-Bradley 1985; Westermeyer 1972); it has historically been understood by scholars as an episode of intense rage and violence, denoting an altered state where the individual at first appears to be brooding, and then suddenly loses all control. In the most severe cases, the *ngamuk* person may go on a murderous rampage, followed by an amnesiac lack of awareness of this violent event (Browne 2001a).

Historically, in Indonesia an understanding of amok was imbricated in a colonialist perspective on the Indonesian psychology: episodes of sudden violence against colonial powers was framed as mental disorder rather than protest, interpreted as an unstable individual going mad rather than acknowledging maddening structural inequalities that might push people to their limits. This tautological idea of an "unstable native" was used as justification for further surveillance and control (Good et al. 2008). Contemporary reinterpretations have rehabilitated amok to suggest that it may be a form of social commentary and protest rather than a sign of insanity (Larasati 2013). However, the idea of amok or *ngamuk* as a psychological problem and an expression of mental distress has persisted both in folk idiom and in psychiatric diagnostic criteria. The *DSM-IV-TR* categorized amok as a culture-bound dissociative disorder most prevalent among Southeast Asian males (APA 2000). Other mental health researchers have considered *ngamuk* to be an impulse control disorder that may have a relationship to manic states.

Some psychological anthropologists suggest that rather than a discrete episode of mental disturbance, *ngamuk* is an idiom of distress that refers to a wide range of anger reactions and represents various ambiguous categories of threatening behavior. From this perspective, *ngamuk* is a particularly Javanese mechanism that gives structure and meaning to a spectrum of deviant behaviors existing within a cultural environment that prizes self-control and a smooth presentation of self as a hallmark of psychological health and social appropriateness. Conditions which are commonly understood to cause vulnerability to *ngamuk* include depression, disappointment or unfulfilled desires, economic stress, jealousy, disturbance by spirits, and disputes with family members (Browne 2001a). These terms thus become referents for a constellation of pressures and affective disturbances that link the physical body, personal or subjective experience and the sociocultural demands upon individual and community (White 1994). Significantly, though, when read this way, *ngamuk* is not just a symptom of individual distress but an accusation toward the collective that has put the individual in a distressing position. While Javanese symptoms of *ngamuk* are displayed by an individual, its causes are deeply situated within a cultural and communal context. By labeling Estu's behavior as *ngamuk*, his wife and family situate his difficulties within a web of socioeconomic relationships.

However, Estu seems to be suffering from an unusual variant of *ngamuk*. *Ngamuk* is usually understood to be a comparatively self-limited and episodic experience; a person might have one episode of *ngamuk* in his or her lifetime and then never again. But Estu's problem is disturbingly chronic. As one *dukun*, Puji, explained:

> Estu's case can be classified into very rare. Why? Usually, if someone recovers, he will recover forever. But not him. He recovers, and gets worse again, recovers, gets worse.

Here, Puji's diagnosis appears to be widely agreed upon; such a chronic and recurrent variant of *ngamuk* is a local category of disturbance in Indonesia that is considered rare, severe, and disturbing enough to require hospitalization (Browne 2001a).

Estu's difficulties seem to have stemmed from an almost overwhelmingly complex tangle of conditions. In contemporary Java, there are multiple available explanations for deviance that incorporate Javanist spirituality (Smith 2008; Endraswara 2003), animist beliefs, and karmic retribution, both globalized pop psychology (Hoesterey 2012; Hoesterey and Clark 2012) and localized folk psychology and ethno-theories of balance and self-control (Geertz 1969), brain-based understandings of personhood and illness, and more. Rather than providing any clarity, however, these multiple potential explanations provided by his healers, elders, family, and localized agents of governmental authority and control seem to lead to further questions and complications while *not* providing effective mood or behavior change for Estu or a more harmonious or satisfactory relationship with his family. Ultimately, more important to all involved than finding the specific term or exact etiology of disturbance would be finding a way for Estu and his family to cope and get along on a day-to-day basis, being able to adapt, respond to, and manage his fluctuations in sensory experience, affect, and behavior.

6.3   The Intersubjective Reality of the Ethnographic Film

How does a filmmaker engaged in long-term, person-centered, and one might argue dialogical anthropology represent the intersubjective reality created by participants, and perhaps even more importantly, represent these shifts and conceptualize their finished films in relationship to these shifts? These intersubjective shifts certainly occur during the making of any film or research project but will be especially important when making films about deviance and mental illness, since the intersubjective work is already such a central part of that experience.

The intersubjective construction of Estu's deviance—a result of evaluations, interpretations, and exchanges between Estu, the lead author, and his family—can be tracked through a detailed case history of the research process, from recruitment to finished film.

After meeting and filming a number of subjects with rather clear-cut symptoms of TS, Ninik mentioned that several members of her family had significant tics, and introduced us to her brother Estu, who was then in his early twenties. During the intake interview, Mahar ensured that the multiple facets of Estu's "troubled and troublesome" personality and behavior were discussed, making it clear that the family found these to be quite distressing; at the same time, he continuously translated Estu's laments into symptoms of TS. It was apparent that Estu did have moderate tics, but his other troubles seemed much more pressing.

During this first interview, Estu seemed honest and direct in talking about his struggles, unlike the Central Javanese "modal personality" (Inkeles and Levinson 1969); he openly addressed things that most other people in this community would be extremely reluctant to discuss. He had a quick and sharp wit. When his "idiosyncrasies" were addressed, the problems that he and other family members described as extremely problematic did not seem all that problematic to me. In fact, many of these problems—such as shifting work interests, difficulty focusing, and a sense of boredom after dating a woman for more than two or three months—would be well within the norm of a young American man.

In American psychology, sociology, and cultural studies, the process of "finding one's identity" throughout adolescence and early adulthood, and the paradoxically normatively deviant adolescent period is a well-established idea (Erickson 1950; see review by Bucholtz 2002; Judd 1967). Feelings of restlessness and periods of "storm and stress" are expected by-products of normative adolescent development (Arnett 1999); even experimentation with substance use, misconduct, and transgressive behavior is to a certain extent expected and even somewhat indulged (Chen et al. 1998; Tisak et al. 2001), although it is acknowledged that this period of freedom may lead to crisis if adolescents don't plan for the subsequent stage of their lives and ultimately "settle down" (Schlegel 1995).

Of course, Estu lived in rural Java, not America. Initially it appeared that Estu's deviance was perhaps a case of a poor cultural fit between Estu and his Javanese surrounds. Goffman (1963) well illustrated the constructed and contingent nature of stigma and deviance; an individual can be stigmatized and thought of as deviant in relation to one group of people yet accepted or normative in relation to another; one could even say that there was a genetic component or neurobiological basis for deviance insofar as certain aspects of temperament might be genetically influenced and present since birth and certain kinds of temperament might be considered "good" and others "bad" or "deviant" by certain cultures (Edgerton 1976).

This bears upon some very fundamental and classic distinctions in psychological anthropology between culture and personality (Sapir and Mandelbaum 1985; Linton 1936; Wallace and Wallace 1970; Hsu 1972). Some aspects of Estu's behavior would not be at all in opposition to Western cultural values. But Java is a place where equanimity, the smoothing over of emotional highs and lows, self-control and containment, and the emotional work involved in the non-expression of negatively balanced emotional states are valued. All these made it difficult for Estu to "fit" in his particular cultural place; yet, his family clearly expected him to "buckle down" and contain himself and follow a path of normative Javanese masculinity and progression, in his family life, his relationships, and his career—none of which he seemed capable of.

In addition to ambivalence about the extent to which Estu could be considered deviant, after this initial interview and at this stage in the process of filmmaking, Estu's relevance to the TS research remained unclear—his tics seemed too mild to provide meaningful information about how they might be culturally shaped. It was only in follow-up interviews with Mahar and Ninik that understandings of the relevance of Estu's case to the research in culture and mental illness shifted.

After spending several weeks in Central Java for research, the team moved back to the original field site in Bali. In an extensive and wide-ranging interview there, Ninik began opening up about her true motivation for proposing Estu as a subject in the collaborative research; she had been looking for some input, advice, and guidance regarding how to deal with him. As it turns out, Estu's "troubles" were considerably more disturbing than anyone had let on in that initial interview in Gunung Kidul. Estu had made explicit threats against the lives of his family members, including his young nieces and nephews. In this interview, the depths of Ninik's despair over her brother became startlingly evident. This interview became a turning point in the research orientation toward Estu; the conflict within his family quickly took precedence over his Tourette's symptoms and, in fact, became the focus of the research. As with all the other *Afflictions* cases, interpersonal and social contexts of putative mental illness were central concerns. As Estu was positioned as a film participant, some tricky but fascinating intersubjective territory was brought into focus.

From 2000 to 2006, over the course of multiple interviews, the lead author grew increasingly close with the entire family, moving away from what was at first a fairly formal research relationship. The progression in the film, which shifts from focusing on Estu's answers to clinically oriented questions in the first interview to progressively more personal and frankly existential questions about his life, place in his world, relationship with his family members, and the moral quandaries raised by his actions, mirrored the deepening relationship between the lead author, Estu, and his family. Ninik was pinning her hopes on an external counselor or "agent of change," who could give authoritative advice, yet much skepticism remained about how bad Estu's behavior "really" was. Ninik repeatedly sought feedback and assessment of how the family should understand Estu and what they should do. Remaining neutral and reframing different aspects of Estu's behavior, so as not to isolate and further stigmatize him in the eyes of his family, was possible but the situation created an involvement and intimacy far beyond the typical role of a "participant observer."

In the middle of this growing intimacy and familiarity, however, the family conflict also seemed to be escalating, and was perhaps exacerbated by the presence of a foreign researcher, or at least, an outsider. By the shoot in 2003, Estu owed a large amount of money in gambling debts and was searching for a way to raise these funds to stave off his bookies. He requested money, or at least access to other family resources, and was denied. Estu then proceeded to his natal village on the rural plateau of Gunung Kidul, where his family still had land, planning to cut down a grove of valuable teak trees, which his father had planted several decades earlier, and sell the wood. Anticipating these plans, his father preemptively cut down the trees himself and hauled them away. When Estu arrived and discovered this, he became furious, and according to neighbors pulled out a knife and vowed to kill his father. The film crew arrived approximately a half hour after this outburst, and filmed Ninik and her elderly neighbors consoling one another after witnessing Estu's threats of violence and believing he was on a mission of attempted murder.

The lead author never personally witnessed these threats or acts of violence nor filmed them. However, respondents did report on these violent episodes almost as they unfolded, and their repercussions were witnessed and filmed. We went searching for Estu in the hopes we could discuss the issue, calm him down, and determine how much of a danger he was to others, considering the possibility that this outburst was primarily a performance aimed at the local community as a way for Estu to assert that he was still a man to be reckoned with. The police were contacted and they were quite familiar with Estu by this point; they picked him up, detained him briefly, and counseled him about his rash behavior.

When a subject threatens the lives of your colleagues' family and engages in activities that could result in extreme violence, this of course changes the way to understand, interpret, and perhaps represent him. At this point, Mahar's suggestion that Estu might be seriously disturbed, or even a psychopath, seemed more plausible. Estu frequently blamed others for problems that were a result of his own conduct. The episodes of violence against his family were troubling and alien to me, and ultimately called into question whether an empathetic connection to the other aspects of his experience was misplaced. Was Estu purposefully emphasizing those aspects of himself most likely to evoke sympathy, and setting them against the much more socially destructive, or even pathological, aspects of his narrative? Was he consciously playing on empathy to convince the anthropologist of what he perceived to be his family's unfair and unjust treatment of him, so that his desire for revenge and his acts of retribution against them might be overlooked or downplayed? The literature on psychopathy, going back at least to Cleckley's groundbreaking study (Cleckley 1941), frequently notes the ability of the psychopath to feign responses that he or she thinks are expected, in a socially normative sense, that is, to instrumentally "put on an act" in order to gain some desired outcome.

My personal and intellectual quest to understand Estu's deviance that emerged during research mirrored a process that Ninik had been undergoing for years. Aside from her research interests and investment in the film project, Ninik admits that the underlying reason she allowed her family to be filmed and interviewed was the hope that somehow, someday, along with the process, she could gain new insights into what her family should do with Estu. However, over the course of the film, Ninik also experienced a shift, from thinking the problem lay solely in Estu himself to thinking that her family played a role in his behavior, and hence, could be empowered to influence it.

As a member of the research team, and as a family member, participating in the film project led Ninik to rethink her options in terms of how to respond to Estu. In this way, the "clinical" research and film objectives became intertwined with her personal goals. She explains:

> I had expected that [through our participation in the research and film project] I would understand my brother better, really understand why he was like that, why he had so many troubles with his own life . . . . it might be because of the symptoms that he had, the Tourette that he had.
>
> In my family, we protected each other very well, so anything wrong that he did, we tried to make [amends]. But then it just happened too often. Eventually, along with the process of making the film, I came to the certain understanding that, "oh, maybe I should change this." I should not protect my family's dignity the way we had done before, by giving these people money to [make up] for the damage that my brother had caused them . . . But then I came to a certain understanding that we needed to do a different strategy. And so I started to tell my mom, my siblings, 'I think the only thing that will teach him lessons is to contain him. We can support his family, but not him. And if he does certain things that are wrong to other people, let him be responsible for what he has done.'
>
> We set limits. [. . .] And, things got much better . . .

Ninik's perspective seems to have undergone a shift in relation to the film production, incorporating an element of cultural relativism that underpinned the work.

While Ninik began fieldwork thinking that the problem lay solely in Estu's disturbing behavior, but after engaging in fieldwork, filmmaking, and the conversations around it, she also began to think that part of the problem might lie in the culturally conditioned responses she and her family were using to cope with it; perhaps if they used less "Javanese" means of reacting to Estu, they might get different results. Meanwhile, when the extent of Estu's violent and unpredictable behavior continued to emerge, there came the realization that the problem was more than just poor cultural fit.

The original evaluation was that Estu and his behaviors were at odds with normative rural Javanese culture—or at least, in local parlance he was not yet "fully Javanese," meaning he had not crossed the cultural barrier to becoming an adult in contemporary Javanese society—and this was compounded by a combination of personality characteristics, aspects of "mental illness," and specifics of family structure and processing which led to Estu being isolated and stigmatized by his own relatives. As the interviews with Estu and his family members began to lengthen and deepen, there were subtle shifts in how he should be viewed. This was turning into a somewhat more serious situation than just a young man at odds with his family and local community. The family felt deeply threatened and disturbed by this possibility; their perception of him seemed validated by numerous negative actions on his part.

As the researchers' and family members' estimations of Estu were changing, Estu simultaneously contributed to the shared understanding of his self and his predicament. While he has been a somewhat unreliable respondent, he has consistently traced his problems back to his family. His sense of himself was not that he was troubled and troublesome but that he was wronged and misunderstood. Early schools of sociological deviance theory provide evidence for the dynamic Estu may have been experiencing. Lemert (1967) suggests an escalating pattern of "primary" and "secondary" deviance, where being labeled as deviant and suffering the associated social penalties and stigma after a "primary deviation" leads to an internalized self-image as deviant and snowballs into growing resentment and hostility on the part of the deviant, and rejection and criminalization of the deviant by his surrounding community. This increases the chances of "secondary" deviance, which leads to stronger penalties against the labeled deviant and a growing resentment and hostility, and ultimately the solidification of self-identifying as deviant or criminal. In Estu's case, this was apparent over the course of his development as his behavior escalated from poor school performance to petty thievery and recreational drug use to domestic violence and threatened murder as he felt his family continually refused to listen to his attempts to change and get help, and his identity as a "bad" person solidified.

There were clearly significant differences between how Estu was clinically framed for research purposes, his own personal motivations for participation in the research project, his family's motivations, perceptions of him as a person, and professional interest in the family situation as an ethnographic filmmaker. Yet, each of these contributed to a shared—and sometimes contested—intersubjective understanding of Estu and the representation of his person and his narrative development on film.

There are explicit parallels to other cases. For example, Gusti's problems were clinically framed for research (TS symptoms), her own personal motivations for participation in the project (a cure, but more importantly a sympathetic witness), her family's motivation (a cure to ease their burden), the researchers' understanding of her as a person (a miserable and victimized woman who was bravely trying to better her situation), and professional interest in her as a film participant. Similarly, throughout the process of making both films, there were shifting senses of our selves and the work together; yet these dynamics took a particularly troubling turn in response to Estu's situation. The intersubjective reality that participants shared and contested impacted approval and consent about what was an "accurate" depiction of the family's life acceptable to be included in the film, as access to the film footage grew more immediate and widespread.

Deviance elicits labor and negotiation as people try to minimize its impact. "Trouble" is the sign that the limits of acceptable variation have been exceeded, and an "account" of that trouble, which explains why the deviant behavior occurred and the motives behind it, will determine what needs to be done about the trouble. Such "accounts" can exacerbate, justify, or excuse the deviant behavior, and the ensuing interpretations are dialectical and transactional. In the case of mental illness, for example, deciding whether someone is "mentally ill" or not, and therefore whether they should be held fully responsible for their actions "is always a social transaction with moral and jural features, and the outcome of this transaction is essentially negotiable" (Edgerton 1978, 463).

Estu's case seems to invite a return to thinking about deviance in a way that bridges multiple categories of unusual or disruptive behavior. Because the motivation for his troubling actions is so nebulous, his control over them debatable, and the cultural components of their interpretation so significant, his case hearkens back to earlier theories and proves them to still be useful for analysis. For example, there are multiple and sometimes conflicting accounts of his deviant behavior that are weighed and negotiated, leading to extensive interpretive, emotional, and attempted reparative work on behalf of Estu's immediate family, community, and healers. These different accounts of Estu's troubles lead to very different responses, and enable different outcomes. Accounts that suggest Estu has been unduly influenced by dark spiritual forces require rituals and a concerted effort on behalf of the entire family unit to purify their relationships and re-establish balance with the help of traditional healers and wise men, for example, while accounts that suggest he has a brain-based neuropsychiatric disorder call for medication and professional psychiatric help and behavioral, and developmental accounts require he grow up and take responsibility for his life and his actions or else face sanctions.

The finished film ultimately explores the multiple ways one can evaluate and attempt to understand a complex story like Estu's. In this way, the film demonstrates the forms of analytic consciousness an anthropologist goes through in attempting to make sense of a very complex situation, in this case a situation made more difficult by the ethical, moral, and legal implications of the actions of the protagonist. In effect, the film replicates the anthropologist's stance toward his subject and the subject matter: striving for some degree of neutrality and giving similar but at times differential weight, in a contextualized manner, to different explanatory models and modes of understanding. The film attempts to balance these different models, interpreting Estu's case using a psychiatric explanatory model, a traditional Javanese model of maturity and development, a criminological or even forensic analytic model, and finally a model based on interpersonal and personal insight and understanding. In this way the film attempts clearly to render a process that may not be particularly evident or familiar to those who have not yet engaged in extended fieldwork, where such conundrums and complexities abound.

6.4   Last Encounters

With Estu, unfortunately, there were no last encounters, no summing up. Estu withdrew from the film and research project, much as he ultimately withdrew from his family and community. He left Ana, his devoted but wounded spouse, and their three children. He married another woman, had two more children and moved to Bali as an itinerant laborer. He rarely speaks with his family, nor comes home. In 2015, the lead author, in conjunction with Ninik, reached out to Estu to do a final closing interview, to tie together the complex threads of the story that became *Family Victim*. Estu wanted $1000 to do the interview, so he would have "capital for his new business." That was not proffered, and the meeting never took place.

References

American Psychiatric Association. 2000. *Diagnostic and Statistical Manual of Mental Disorders*. 4th ed., text rev. Washington, DC: Author.

Arnett, Jeffrey J. 1999. Adolescent Storm and Stress, Reconsidered. *American Psychology* 54 (5): 317–326.

Becker, Howard S. 1963. *Outsiders: Studies in Social Deviance*. New York: Free Press.

Bourgois, Philippe. 1995. *In Search of Respect: Selling Crack in El Barrio*. Cambridge: Cambridge University Press.

Browne, Kevin O. 2001a. (Ng)Amuk Revisited: Emotional Expression and Mental Illnes in Central Java, Indonesia. *Transcultural Psychiatry* 38: 147–165.

———. 2001b. Cultural Formulation of Psychiatric Diagnoses. *Culture, Medicine and Psychiatry* 25 (4): 411–425.

Bucholtz, Mary. 2002. Youth and Cultural Practice. *Annual Review of Anthropology* 31 (1): 525–552. doi:10.1146/annurev.anthro.31.040402.085443

Burton-Bradley, B. G. 1985. The Amok Syndrome in Papua and New Guinea. *The Culture-Bound Syndromes*. http://link.springer.com/chapter/10.1007/978-94-009-5251-5_22

Chen, Chuansheng, Ellen Greenberger, Julia Lester, Qi Dong, and Miaw-Sheue Guo. 1998. A Cross-Cultural Study of Family and Peer Correlates of Adolescent Misconduct. *Developmental Psychology* 34 (4): 770–781. doi:10.1037/0012-1649.34.4.770

Cleckley, Hervey M. 1941. *The Mask of Sanity: An Attempt to Clarify Some Issues About the So-Called Psychopathic Personality*. Revised ed. New York: Plume.

Durkheim, Emile. 2014. *The Rules of Sociological Method: And Selected Texts on Sociology and Its Method*. New York: Simon and Schuster.

Edgerton, Robert B. 1976. *Deviance, a Cross-Cultural Perspective*. Menlo Park: Cummings Publishing Company.

———. 1978. The Study of Deviance: Moral Man or Everyman? In *The Making of Psychological Anthropology*, ed. George Spindler. Berkeley: University of California Press.

Endraswara, Suwardi. 2003. *Mistik Kejawen: Sinkretisme, Simbolisme, Dan Sufisme Dalam Budaya Spiritual Jawa*. Yogyakarta: Penerbit Narasi.

Erickson, Erik H. 1950. *Childhood and Society*. New York: Norton.

Ferrell, Jeff, and Mark Hamm. 1998. *Ethnography at the Edge: Crime, Deviance and, Field Research*. Chicago: University of Chicago Press.

Freilich, Morris, Douglas Raybeck, and Joel Savishinsky, eds. 1991. *Deviance: Anthropological Perspectives*. New York: Bergin & Garvey.

Frey, Edward. 2010. *The Kris Mystic Weapon of the Malay World*. Kuala Lumpur: ITBM.

Geertz, Clifford. 1969. *The Religion of Java*. New York: Free Press.

Goffman, Erving. 1963. *Stigma: Notes on the Management of Spoiled Identity*. Englewood Cliffs: Prentice-Hall.

Good, Byron J., Mary-Jo DelVecchio Good, Sandra Teresa Hyde, and Sarah Pinto. 2008. Postcolonial Disorders: Reflections on Subjectivity in the Contemporary World. In *Postcolonial Disorders*, ed. Mary-Jo DelVecchio Good, Sandra Teresa Hude, Sarah Pinto, and Byron J. Good, 1–40. Berkeley: University of California Press.

Gramsci, Antonio. 1988. *An Antonio Gramsci Reader: Selected Writings, 1916–1935*. New York: Schocken Books.

Hoesterey, James B. 2012. *Prophetic Cosmopolitanism: Islam, Pop Psychology, and Civic Virtue in Indonesia*. City & Society. http://onlinelibrary.wiley.com/doi/10.1111/j.1548-744X.2012.01067.x/full

Hoesterey, James B., and Marshall Clark. 2012. Film Islami: Gender, Piety and Pop Culture in Post-Authoritarian Indonesia. *Asian Studies Review* 36 (2): 207–226. http://www.tandfonline.com/doi/abs/10.1080/10357823.2012.685925

Hsu, Francis L. 1972. Psychological Anthropology in the Behavioral Sciences. In *Psychological Anthropology*, ed. Francis L. Hsu. Cambridge, MA: Schenkman.

Inkeles, Alex, and Daniel J. Levinson. 1969. National Character: The Study of Modal Personality and Sociocultural Systems. *The Handbook of Social Psychology* 4: 418–506.

Judd, Lewis L. 1967. The Normal Psychological Development of the American Adolescent: A Review. *California Medicine* 107 (6): 465–470.

Larasati, Rachmi D. 2013. *The Dance That Makes You Vanish: Cultural Reconstruction in Postgenocide Indonesia*. Minneapolis: University of Minnesota Press.

Lemelson, Robert, 2010. *Family Victim*. 38 min. Watertown: Documentary Educational Resources. http://www.der.org/films/family-victim.html

———. 2010–2011. *Afflictions: Culture and Mental Illness in Indonesia Series*. 182 min. Watertown: Documentary Educational Resources. http://www.der.org/films/afflictions.html

Lemert, Edwin M. 1967. *Human Deviance, Social Problems, and Social Control*. Englewood Cliffs: Prentice-Hall.

Linton, Ralph. 1936. *The Study of Man: An Introduction*. New York: Appleton-Century-Crofts.

Merton, Robert K. 1964. Anomie, Anomia, and Social Interaction: Contexts of Deviant Behavior. In *Anomie and Deviant Behavior*, ed. Marshall B. Clinard, 213–242. New York: Free Press.

Mrázek, Jan. 2011. The Visible and the Invisible in a Southeast Asian World. In *A Companion to Asian Art and Architecture*, ed. Rebeccca M. Brown and Deborah S. Hutto, 97–120. Chichester: Wiley-Blackwell.

Parsons, Talcott. 1951. Illness and the Role of the Physician: A Sociological Perspective. *American Journal of Orthopsychiatry* 21 (3): 452–460.

Said, Edward W. 1979. *Orientalism*. New York: Vintage.

Sapir, Edward, and David Goodman Mandelbaum. 1985. *Selected Writings of Edward Sapir in Language, Culture and Personality*. Vol. 342. Berkeley: University of California Press.

Schlegel, Alice. 1995. A Cross-Cultural Approach to Adolescence. *Ethos* 23 (1): 15–32.

Smith, Bianca. 2008. Kejawen Islam as Gendered Praxis in Javanese Village Religiosity. In *Indonesian Islam in a New Era*. Clayton: Monash University Press.

Spivak, Gayatri C. 1999. *A Critique of Postcolonial Reason*. Cambridge, MA: Harvard University Press.

Spores, John C. 1988. *Running Amok: An Historical Enquiry*. Athens: Ohio University Press.

Tisak, Marie S., John Tisak, and Sara E. Goldstein. 2001. How Do Young Children Misbehave in the Grocery Store and in the School? The Preschoolers' Perspective. *Early Education and Development* 12: 487–498. doi:10.1207/s15566935eed1204_1

Tschoeke, Stefan, Tilman Steinert, Erich Flammer, and Carmen Uhlmann. 2014. Similarities and Differences in Borderline Personality Disorder and Schizophrenia with Voice Hearing. *Journal of Nervous and Mental Disease* 202 (7): 544–549. doi:10.1097/nmd.0000000000000159

Ugarte, Eduardo F. 1999. *The Demoniacal Impulse: The Construction of Amok in the Philippines*. PhD Dissertation, University of Western Sydney. Retrieved from http://researchdirect.westernsydney.edu.au/islandora/object/uws:6395

Wallace, Anthony F.C. 1970. *Culture and Personality*. New York: Random House.

Westermeyer, Joseph. 1972. A Comparison of Amok and Other Homicide in Laos. *American Journal of Psychiatry* 129 (6): 703–709. doi:10.1176/ajp.129.6.703

White, Geoffrey M. 1994. Affecting Culture: Emotion and Morality in Everyday Life. In *Emotion and Culture*, ed. S. Kitayama and H.R. Markus, 219–239. Washington, DC: American Psychological Press.

Williamson, Thomas. 2007. Communicating Amok in Malaysia. *Identities: Global Studies in Culture and Power* 14 (3). doi:10.1080/10702890601163144

CHAPTER 7

Memory of My Face: Globalization, Madness, and Identity On-screen

Photo 7.1   Bambang Rujito

7.1   STORY SUMMARY

Bambang Rujito is an intelligent and educated man living in the outskirts of Jakarta, Indonesia's largest metropolis. He attended the prestigious University of Indonesia and has worked a variety of high-status jobs, including in the Indonesian stock market and for the Unilever Corporation. He is a soft-spoken but humorous conversationalist; his earnest reflections are often

© The Author(s) 2017
R. Lemelson, A. Tucker, *Afflictions*, Culture, Mind, and Society,
DOI 10.1007/978-3-319-59984-7_7

punctuated with a joke and a gentle self-deprecating laugh. He works part-time teaching English to neighborhood children and spends the rest of his days caring for his young son, doing household chores, and attending neighborhood prayer groups.

Bambang is in his mid-thirties, but he has had episodes of what local psychiatrists have diagnosed as schizoaffective disorder since he was a sophomore in high school, primarily characterized by the euphoria and excessive energy of mania. This mania is often combined with delusions and hallucinations inspired by current events: Wars in distant nations seem to be enacted before Bambang's eyes on the streets of his city. He believes himself to have befriended celebrities, declares his own political parties, and feels he has assumed the identities of esteemed religious leaders. Concern for Bambang's well-being during these bouts has led friends and family to hospitalize him numerous times throughout his adult life.

The globalized features of Bambang's experience are quite influential to his illness and recovery narrative. Western psychiatric diagnostics, institutionalized care and pharmaceuticals, work opportunities in a rapidly changing urban environment, participation in an interfaith religious community, and his family's understanding and acceptance of what Bambang describes as a "mental disability" all effect the trajectory of his illness. Meanwhile, the complex historically and politically shaded layers of his manic verbal expression give a deeper substance to Bambang's disorder. Through puns, word play influenced by Javanese vernacular joking style, and swift unexpected associations, Bambang vibrantly weaves together various threads such as lyrics from 1980s pop songs, Qur'anic verse, and allusions to Dutch colonial rule, into a lexical fabric of sometimes absurdist and sometimes strikingly insightful commentary.

The content and course of Bambang's schizoaffective disorder suggest that globalized popular culture does indeed pervade people's consciousness and the ways they understand and interpret their worlds. Meanwhile, it illustrates how the residues of colonialism, experienced as the lingering effects of subjugation or subjection, remain a significant part of those worlds.

Bambang was born in 1969 and grew up near Borobudur, a rural area in Central Java home to the world-famous temple of the same name. He lived surrounded by his sisters and a warm extended family with relatives living close together in neighboring villages. His grandfather worked for the prestigious national railway, his mother sold traditional health tonics known throughout Indonesia as *jamu*, and his father was a sailor often leaving home to travel the trade route from Jakarta to Japan.

When Bambang was only four, his father got in a violent fight in a distant port and died from his injuries. Bambang's mother moved to Jakarta to make her living selling coconut rice from a food stall while Bambang stayed behind with his aunt until he finished elementary school. He was a funny and clever child, and doted on by the community because of his unfortunate family circumstances. For middle school, Bambang went to live with his mother in a suburb of Jakarta. He worked hard, earned a reputation for being a perfectionist, rose to the top of his class, and was accepted into a prestigious local high school.

When he was a sophomore in 1986, Bambang began to struggle. He was dedicated to his studies in addition to participating in sports, and was often tired. Religion fascinated him but also led to disturbing thoughts, as he vividly imagined characters from Islamic cosmology and worried that theological doctrine did not always match up with everyday reality. Then his girlfriend broke up with him and he was devastated. The pop wisdom that "first love never dies" echoed in his mind, and he feared that since it had died he too was truly finished. One night, in the midst of his sadness, exhaustion, and frustration, he decided to pray. He lost consciousness and awoke into a world of hallucinations, feeling that his sins had come to life to pursue him. He was taken to the doctor, who first diagnosed him with a fever and thyroid problems. However, as the psychiatric elements of his illness became more apparent, his school suggested he take a year off to rest. He was hospitalized in a psychiatric facility in Bogor for a month, and after the prescribed period, he resumed his academic life.

Bambang began his studies at the University of Indonesia in Jakarta, but relapsed frequently. His friends often knew when he was becoming unwell because they would notice he was not sleeping. When encouraged to sleep, Bambang would reply that God does not sleep. He would feel smart and strong and perfectly devout, like he could become the next president or the next Great Imam. These feelings of power were sometimes countered by splitting headaches and bouts of weeping. Bambang would board a train for a long-distance trip only to impulsively get off before he reached his intended destination. He frequently got in trouble for shoplifting or bothering strangers, and was occasionally beaten by passersby angered by his misbehavior. He was again hospitalized in Bogor, but feeling unhappy there, he escaped. After about a month, he returned to a stable condition.

Bambang did not complete his university education but became an English teacher with plans for starting up his own school. He met a young woman named Yatmi, who was impressed by his language skills. They married in 1996 and were soon expecting a child. With his attentions turned to his work duties, Bambang's university registration expired, and then the school he started failed. When Yatmi was in her late pregnancy, Bambang relapsed again. This was Yatmi's first introduction to her husband's history of mental illness. Again, Bambang was taken to Bogor, but filled with loneliness, he left and then returned to a stable condition.

Bambang took a higher paying job working in the stock market to support his family. He often worked nights, reading the news feed from Reuters. He developed the habit of taking energy supplements and drinking cups of coffee to stay awake. In 1999, the mounting stress of his work caused him to resign. He went home, and hallucinating that it was Independence Day, he took his young toddler on a marathon walk to join in the celebration. The two wandered the malls and streets of South Jakarta for twenty-four hours, until Bambang decided to visit his sister. Because of these events, his child was taken away from him, and his mother decided to bring Bambang back to Central Java with her for treatment.

This period became Bambang's longest and most severe episode of mental illness. His family first tried to care for him at home, but they were unable to handle his behavior and committed him to psychiatric ward in Magelang in 2000. Bambang was briefly released to tend to his ailing mother. She ultimately passed away and he was re-hospitalized in 2002, at which point he met the film crew.

Bambang returned home in 2003 and did not experience any major relapses until 2011, although he has continued to struggle with erratic moods. He maintains his religious and official social life, attending neighborhood events and Qur'an recitation, but he has withdrawn from more casual friendships. Bambang feels that his wife and family do not view him any differently because of his illness, yet they have moved five or six times to avoid neighbors who have witnessed his relapses. Yatmi continues to support the family by working at a garment factory, where she has risen to a management position.

Bambang is ambivalent about his current situation. He wants to be an advocate for those with mental illness, asserting that it is just like any other illness and should not be stigmatized. He believes that with continued support he will continue to get better, yet he is often frustrated and feels that he is "mentally handicapped." He is alternately grateful for his family's financial assistance and emotional support and resentful that he is rarely consulted on major household decisions. He wants to re-enter the work force, but he has low self-confidence and is worried about future relapses. Although he once felt bright and filled with promise, on his bad days Bambang fears his life has been reduced to a boring routine of meaningless chores. However, he is also quite proud of the English lessons he has begun to teach part-time to neighborhood children, remains dedicated to developing his son's intellect and planning for his future education, and derives sustenance and encouragement from his Islamic faith and his religious community.

7.2 Post-coloniality, Globalization, and the Subjective Experience of Mental Illness

Within the field of psychiatry, the understanding of manic delusions and hallucinations associated with schizophrenic disorders has changed. Early twentieth-century psychoanalytic approaches stressed individual personality dysfunction or reactivity, offering various explanations as to the way delusions or voices might serve to shore up a vulnerable or damaged psyche (Berrios 1996; Berrios and Hauser 1988).

The 1960s–1970s saw increases in attempts to medicalize psychiatry, which led to the "decade of the brain," beginning in 1990. This era focused on genetic and/or synaptic causes for mental illness and sought cure in pharmaceuticals. Within this perspective of biological psychiatry, it is the fact that certain symptoms are present—like voice-hearing or manic delusions—that is important to diagnosis, rather than the content of what the voices are saying or what the delusions are about (Luhrmann et al. 2015). Rather than exploring their cultural or personal context, a purely biological psychiatry considers complex verbal productions a form of "irrationality" due to a disordered neurobiology, neurochemistry, and neurophysiology—a type of "form vs. content" distinction in psychiatry (Larkin 1979; Fabrega Jr. 1989, 1992).

Contemporary work in psychological anthropology and cross-cultural psychiatry has called for a return to an earlier understanding of how the content of delusions (or other symptoms of mental illness) might be personally meaningful, while additionally considering how culture might influence these. This newer approach seeks to account for a more refined understanding of brain function in mental illness, with the fundamental understanding that the brain "is inherently social dynamic, plastic, adaptable, and locally and globally integrated" while never forgetting that self-awareness, interpersonal interactions, and larger social processes give meaning to, and influence the trajectory and outcome of, mental health problems, necessitating an "ecosystemic approach" that accounts for these multiple factors (Kirmayer et al. 2015). A key example of what ethnography can offer in this area is Tanya Luhrmann's recent comparative work in auditory hallucinations experienced by people with schizophrenia in different cultures. Luhrmann suggests that "social kindling" or "culturally shaped patterns of attention" determine the kind of auditory phenomena the person with psychosis pays attention to and shares, and this attention may in turn shape the actual experience of psychosis (Luhrmann et al. 2015, see above). While Luhrmann's research addresses voice-hearing in schizophrenic patients, her conclusions are applicable to other symptoms of mental illness, including manic speech and delusion, in that the local social world will give it significance and meaning, either by shaping content or influencing the interpretations of that content.

If contemporary ethnography on major mental illness is taken into consideration, there is an opportunity for a rich analysis of Bambang's discourse; such an analysis must include an understanding of the content of manic speech, delusions, and even auditory hallucinations as having some meaning. By extension, this creates an opportunity for a deeper understanding of the way Bambang's episodes of illness expressed his frustrations at the conditions of middle-class Indonesian life during the transition to the new millennium. In other words, making meaning out of Bambang's ravings, rather than dismissing these as merely the effluvia of a man who is deeply disturbed, can lead to insight into his personal situation and provide national and cultural context.

When Bambang is having a schizoaffective episode, the flamboyant genius of his mania often manifests in free associations and verbal play that incorporate and interweave complex gestures, jests, innuendo, interpersonal communications, historical references and analogies, and plaintive lamentations. When taken together, these all artfully rearrange aspects of local histories and globalized popular culture. In one extended episode included in the film, Bambang quotes both Sukarno's nationalist maxims and the movie *Ghost* (Zucker 1990), rapturously sings a song from the 1980s progressive rock band Genesis, retells tragic events culled from the local news, postulates on the ancient Mataram kingdom and the value of the Australian dollar, and all in one breath mentions Indonesian soccer, Islamic prayer, and the tobacco trade. He also evokes Indonesia's colonial past, calling Indonesia "the Dutch territory," referencing the history of plantation agriculture and export, ironically claiming "the Dutch occupied us in order to teach us," and criticizing ex-president Suharto's development plans and mottos. So, are these loquacious interludes merely the incoherent speech typical of schizoaffective disorder, or are they related to the overwhelming information stream of globalization that seems to offer infinite possibilities for both meaning and absurdity? Can Bambang's commentary on Indonesian nationalism and geopolitical history, performed in the voice of an unhinged Javanese linguistic virtuoso, be heard as a poetic critique on the lingering madness of subjection and the maddening promises and premises, centripetal and centrifugal (Anderson-Fye 2003) forces of globalization?

Numerous post-colonial scholars have articulated the idea that colonialist and imperialist policies have a detrimental effect on the psyches of those subjugated. Famously, Franz Fanon, a Martinique-born and French-educated psychiatrist stationed in French-colonized Algeria, provided illustrative case studies from his patients to argue that a "constant and considerable stream of mental symptoms are direct sequels of this oppression" (Fanon 1963). Some of the symptoms he identified were hypervigilance, a painful inferiority complex and self-consciousness with regard to image and position, and the sense of an unstable identity, concluding that because colonialism systematically negates the colonized, they are forced to constantly question the very essence of their being (Fanon 1963).

The Dutch colonized what is now Indonesia for over three hundred years, although their influence was felt in varying degrees in different areas. Some territories, such as Aceh and Bali, resisted for decades, locals fought back bravely, and in the end were conquered by a brutal suppression campaign. Where they did have solid control, the Dutch instituted apartheid, deplorable plantation conditions, and the exploitation and extraction of resources that kept many Indonesians impoverished while supporting the industrialization and development of the Netherlands. The Dutch were forced out of Indonesia during World War II during the Japanese occupation and lost the war for independence, which was fought after Indonesia's declaration in 1945. Indonesia as a self-governing country is not even a century old (Vickers 2013).

Bambang directly references this history of Dutch colonialism in the speech of his manic episodes. Yet, he simultaneously references a history of resistance. He calls himself a "crazy Dutchman" in Javanese (*londo edan*) and claims, "I am the Commander and Prince of Jayakarta which was known as Batavia. I am the thirteenth grandson of Prince Diponegoro," assuming the identity of a Mataram prince who fought against Dutch colonization from 1825 to 1830, was arrested, and put in exile. When Bambang met the film's director—an anthropologist and a Caucasian American—Bambang teased, "You want to invade my country!"

Through these discourses of imprisonment, invasion, and insanity, Bambang makes explicit the connection between mental illness and subjugation that has been theorized by contemporary psychological anthropologists and post-colonial scholars who insist that investigation into the subjective experience of mental disorder must take into account the political histories of the construction of ideas about both "subjects" and "disorder" (Good et al. 2008a). The colonial view positions disorder within the person of the native, who, as Fanon stated, was seen as part of a landscape of a "hostile, ungovernable, and fundamentally rebellious Nature" (Fanon 1963). According to colonialist rhetoric, it was up to the occupying powers to impose "order"; and yet of course this pretext of "order" was used to carry out all kinds of violence. Those who protested this order—such as domestic servants who rebelled against their masters or plantation workers who organized—were at times labeled as violently or madly "running amok." In this milieu of oppression, some registered their discontent through passive resistance and verbal rebellion. In listening to Bambang, Indonesian historians might be reminded of the Samins, nineteenth-century Indonesian plantation workers who wore down the resolve of their Dutch overseers through implicitly disrespectful or evasive double entendres, cryptic puns, and confounding responses to orders. For example, if ordered to work, a Samin might not outright refuse but rather reply, "Sorry, I am already in service, my work is to sleep with my wife" (Vickers 2013).

These references to colonial domination and Indonesian resistance in Bambang's manic monologues indicate that colonial histories continue to shape post-colonial realities and affect the subjective worlds of citizens who did not directly experience colonial rule (Banerjee and Linstead 2001; Kiong and Fee 2003; Reuter 2009). While the residues of colonialism might not be immediately apparent in contemporary Indonesia, they linger through what anthropologist Byron Good calls the "haunting presence of the colonial" (Good et al. 2008a). These hauntings are multiple and encompass even the kinds of treatment Bambang is receiving. The presence of the mental institution within which Bambang finds himself can be traced to histories of Dutch health intervention, encompassing both genuine efforts to reduce infectious diseases and self-serving framings of the local mind as primitive or childlike (Pols 2006, 2007) There is also the oblique inheritance of "generational trauma," as children register the effects of being raised by parents who themselves still struggle with experiences of war or violence, which has been theorized to have not only psychological/familiar transmission processes but distinct epigenetic components (Yehuda and Bierer 2009; Yehuda et al. 2001). For Indonesians of Bambang's age, these generational traumas include not only Dutch colonial rule, but also the Japanese occupation, the difficult transition to independence, the killings of 1965 that occurred during the nationwide purge of suspected communists, and the autocratic rule of Suharto, which many critics have compared to colonialism due to the way his regime exploited and sometimes terrorized his subjects.

These traumas are woven into Bambang's story, albeit sometimes implicitly; while Yatmi did not know that Bambang had a history of mental illness when she married him, she was not exceedingly troubled by it because she believes her father had a similar condition. As she tells it, Yatmi's father's illness consisted mainly of discomfort around strangers, reluctance to leave the house, and a persistent fear that he was going to be taken away or imprisoned. Yatmi suggests that this illness may have stemmed from the violence and upheaval of the 1965 purge of communists that happened in Indonesia, where many of her father's friends were in fact imprisoned or killed (see Chap. 5 for a Balinese parallel). Bambang also thinks his father, of the same age as Yatmi's father, may have suffered from a similar mental illness, perhaps even schizoaffective disorder. Bambang believes the fight that cost his father his life was perhaps typical of recurring manic outbursts, although Bambang does not explicitly cite the events of 1965 as a possible cause of his father's instability.

In twenty-first-century urban Indonesia, these persistent haunting colonial presences and generational traumas, perhaps in themselves overwhelming, collide with the manic excesses of globalized culture, including reference and access to alternate narratives of development, possibility, and self-expression. Especially since the fall of Suharto in the late 1990s when censorship loosened and a sense of liberatory, international, and cosmopolitan polyvocality bloomed, Indonesian citizens have enthusiastically participated in global media and global discourses of identity politics, religious expression, and popular culture (Boellstorff 2004; Luvaas 2006, 2010; Mansurnoor 2004). Yet increased media access and far-reaching global networks also implicate everyday citizens in global struggles, stoking fear and worry with unrelenting representations of the new forms of enduring violence and inequality. As Homi Babha, another influential post-colonial scholar, puts it, the "colonial shadow falls across the successes of globalization" as economic policies create (or perpetuate) divided worlds; even accelerated and comparatively successful development cannot mask underlying problems such as enduring poverty, class and racial injustice, exploitation, and victimization.

The consumer of global media reads, sees, and hears about all this with increasing immediacy and detail, but may have limited tools to make sense of it or feel helpless to intervene. During his lucid moments, Bambang tells how many of his hallucinations were based on what he heard and read, as he projected global struggles onto his immediate surroundings, or introjected and internalized the characters of influential public figures. Traditional healers initially named Bambang's illness as being the result of "too many thoughts"; indeed his voracious reading worried the boundaries of his own personal experience and blurred distinctions between media and autobiography.

In thinking through the subjective experience of mental illness or mental distress, Byron Good suggests, "whether read as pathologies, modes of suffering, the domain of the imaginary, or as forms of repression, disordered subjectivity provides entrée to exploring dimensions of contemporary social life as lived experience" (Good et al. 2008b). Or as anthropologist Douglas Hollan states more plainly, explorations of mental illness can illustrate "how directly and deeply an organization of self and identity can be affected by differentials in social, economic, and political resources" (Hollan 2005). Ambivalence about colonialism, globalization, and his own subject position seems to trigger interpenetrating affects that cycle quickly for Bambang when he is unwell. As captured onscreen and included in the film, on the one hand he enacts a fascinating metonymic transfer of mental illness, saying "bye-bye Schizophrenia," symbolically relocating pathology onto the sur-rogate colonizing body in order to banish it. Yet, at the same time, Bambang gleefully welcomes the opportunity to practice his English and engage in the exchange, performing his broad cosmopolitan knowledge that just might have the power to change him from being "schizoaffective" to being "effective." In his rapidly shifting thoughts that dart from memory to media story and back again, Bambang negotiates the euphoria and grief of a globalized subjectivity, diagnosing this condition with yet another poignant pun: "The most disturbed patient, his name is 'The World.'"

Throughout the course of his illness, Bambang received different kinds of therapeutic interventions, including being cared for in the home by his family, undergoing inpatient institutional treatment, and managing his illness through ongoing outpatient pharmacological therapy and occasional counseling, and boarding at religious facilities. These alternatives speak to both changing and enduring approaches to how mental illness or disturbance is treated in Indonesia, and each has implications for how Bambang experiences his illness, and hence, shapes his sense of self.

It is a common assumption in the field of "global mental health" that infrastructure of therapeutic services similar to those provided in the West is needed to provide adequate care. However, institutional treatment in Indonesia can be unreliable, somewhat clouded by histories of colonial hierarchies, and in many ways runs counter to Javanese constructions of the healthy self.

Bambang was hospitalized at a psychiatric facility in Central Java that provides integrated treatment, including pharmaceutical medications, individual and group psychotherapy, ECT, and recreational, work, and art therapies. Despite being comprehensive, this milieu was not always positive for Bambang, in part because it was not congruent with cultural understandings of health and recovery. Institutionalization still carries a significant amount of stigma for Indonesian families; while the family and community may be comparatively accepting and forgiving of minor episodes of disturbance (Subandi 2015, 2011), institutionalization suggests more disturbing severity and chronicity of illness (Connor 1982). It is also quite expensive and risks putting the extended family into debt. For these reasons, some patients and families might find that institutional care exacerbates the stress of illness. Even temporary hospitalization, which separates the individual from his or her family or community, may lead to feelings of isolation and loneliness intolerable to a communally oriented Javanese person. Bambang abandoned institutional care numerous times because he was so miserable there, which is not unusual in Java.

Home care and family treatment harmonize with Indonesian folk models of well-being and communal approaches to recovery. Bambang's mother-in-law explained, "I guess when he gets ill, as Indonesians, we can't let him suffer by himself." Home care allows for a sense of continuity, contribution, and inclusive community. If this home care is in a small town where people know a patient's history and therefore might be more tolerant, it might prove more supportive or safe for someone with mental illness than an anonymous urban center. Bambang's aunt explained,

He was taken back to the family community in Central Java because he was ill, suffering from stress. How could he live in Jakarta, if he suffered from stress it would be hard to live there. He wandered around a lot, his family was afraid that people would beat him up, the poor guy But in Java, in this region, Magelang, most people still have pity on a person who suffers from stress, that's the point.

As Bambang's primary caretaker for a number of months, his uncle provided individualized and comprehensive attention; he frequently chatted with Bambang and tried to lighten his mood and minister to his needs. He tried to keep his nephew's self-esteem high and life balanced by providing him with basic chores that he could handle and bringing him on excursions. This has turned into a long-term solution: The family has successfully adjusted to Bambang's difficulties by allowing him to stay at home and care for his son while his wife works in a factory to financially support them.

However, there are significant challenges to this kind of home care, which is illustrated by Bambang's case. When Bambang was in the throes of mania, which he described as feeling "euphoric," he would stay awake for days at a time. He wandered away from the house and disrupted neighbors with trickster-like behavior, for example, switching off neighbors' electricity in a scheme to save them from the rising energy costs. Sometimes his behavior was deeply disturbing to others—once, he urinated inside a mosque and once he made an obscene gesture at schoolchildren, for which he was beaten harshly and had his teeth knocked out. When Bambang became too disruptive, his family would resort to locking him up in a room of their house.

Another significant area in relation to the issue of outcome is daily routines and particular work routines. While perhaps statistically contributing to better long-term outcomes, the process of adapting to flexible, low-pressure work at home, does not in and of itself guarantee a sense of self-esteem or efficacy in the world. Bambang was deeply depressed by the way his recurring illness prevented him from consistently and adequately performing his role as a contemporary middle-class husband, specifically as a breadwinner working a white-collar job outside the home. According to Bambang,

Bill Gates himself started in his garage, but he's been able to take over the world... What makes me feel a bit negative is that I just stay at home, my income is just a fraction of what my wife makes. That sometimes becomes a problem. Why, as a husband, can I not meet the needs of my family?

Interestingly, wage economies have been associated with poorer prognoses among those with major mental illness. This may partly be due to the more stringent requirements and definitions of successful employment and family contribution, which may in turn lead to more intense feelings of stress or failure. Due to Bambang's history of mental illness, it is challenging for him to perform fitting jobs that might be more lucrative. His manic behavior, when it surfaces, is unacceptable in an office environment. Furthermore, the tasks required to fulfill the role obligations of an educated upper-middle-class Indonesian man, such as working long hours in an office, working in high-pressure situations, or following current events, are often a trigger for his illness episodes.

However, while the tasks that Bambang engages in at home—cooking, laundry, childcare—are certainly integral to the functioning of the family, they make him feel "useless" because they are not the normative tasks for a married Javanese man. For Bambang, doing "women's work" feels ill-fitting, demeaning, and boring.

Bambang's Uncle Mugo sees a real economic basis for Bambang's mental health issues:

> In my opinion, I can say that if Bambang can get a job, a routine one, with God's blessing he will recover. The problem is, what he always has in his mind is (he) wants, really wants to be responsible for his family. 'What should I do so that I can feed my wife and child?' That's the only thing Bambang has in his mind.

Due to earning disparity with his wife and his lack of participation in activities befitting his role, Bambang feels like he is no longer treated as the man of the house should be treated, as a decision maker and "head of the household." Therefore, beyond a sense of economic failure, Bambang also laments the fact that his wife's opinion toward him has changed.

> She used to think I was smart … Now, she doesn't include me in making decisions… she thinks that it's useless even if she tries, I won't understand her anyway. … I keep silent. I realize that I have handicaps. I'm mentally handicapped.

Bambang's return in 2006 to English teaching seems to have eased some of these tensions. While this job is not full-time nor particularly lucrative, because it is prestigious work (and perhaps because it reminds Yatmi of what first attracted her to Bambang), it allows Bambang to feel like his wife "has a husband" again. While not "curing" Bambang's illness, this part-time work is therapeutic to Bambang in addressing his major worries about gender and role performance; it allows him to feel like "a man," both actively as a provider for his family, and as a recipient of the respect and consideration he feels he deserves.

While Bambang's economic struggles are compounded by his episodes of mental illness, he is not the only man struggling with lack of work opportunities and the corollary ambivalence about proper role performance. Many other men in Bambang's neighborhood are also helping out at home due to chronic unemployment or temporary joblessness due to the fluctuations of contract work.

Bambang's episode of mental illness in 1999 corresponded with a time of pan-Asian economic crisis and national political transition. Yet, as Indonesia has regained its footing over the last decade, the urban upper middle class in Indonesia has grown exponentially. The ideal of the married man as breadwinner and consumer with a car, new house, and television is now heavily promoted in the media and popular culture, but this ideal may not be equally accessible to all. While Bambang was from an average background, due to his hard work he succeeded at school and got accepted into a prestigious college. At the University of Indonesia, however, Bambang's Uncle Mugo says that many of his other friends were much more affluent, which may have led Bambang to feel inferior. After graduation, many of them were offered prestigious jobs at Indonesian organizations, like the national television station, but Bambang was not.

7.3   FROM STRANGENESS TO EMPATHY

The filmmaking team met Bambang, the subject of the film *Memory of My Face*, while shooting exploratory footage at *Rumah Sakit Jiwa Magelang* (RSJM), the state mental hospital in Magelang, Central Java. The visit happened to fall several days before Independence Day, and the hospital had organized a patient performance of *jathilan*, a locally popular folk possession dance, as a form of group therapy. It may seem odd that the hospital would have the patients perform *jathilan*, which in its more extreme versions has performers eating light bulbs, rolling on thorns, or even pressing their skin with a hot iron—ostensibly quite disturbing, painful, and even "crazy" behaviors. Yet the patients were engaged in these wild behaviors in order to be seen as normal, by participating in an accepted theatrical activity that has ancient animist roots across Indonesia and is interpreted by contemporary practitioners as both a strategy of community building and empirical proof of communication with the ancestors and other spiritual beings (Foley 1985; Browne 2003; Lemelson 2011b). Bambang was the most expressive dancer of the group and the cinematographer was drawn to film his performance.

Photo 7.2 Bambang participating in a *jathilan* dance performance at a mental hospital in central Java

After a walkthrough of the hospital grounds with Bambang as the guide, he gave an interview on one of the locked wards, talking fast and peppering the conversation with expressive Jakarta slang. The research team, fluent in the local language Bahasa Indonesia, could lexically understand him, but the deeper semantics of his words were almost entirely unintelligible, not surprising given his pressured speech, flight of ideas, lability and loosening associations that are common linguistic features of a heightened or manic state. So first attempts to relate to Bambang, at least in terms of understanding who he was and what he was trying to express, left the crew almost entirely lost. It was only after returning to the United States and analyzing the footage that Bambang's complex layers of allusion, symbolism, and emotion could be untangled.

An understudied and poorly conceptualized area in the psychology of long-term fieldwork is the issue of initial "astonishment" over what one finds, and the sense of cultural "strangeness" of the people one is working with (Shweder 1990), which may gradually diminish over time, as a familiarity with once different norms and practices develops. There is a lovely quotation from *A Kalahari Family* where Lorna Marshall says,

> My diary records my first impressions: I was frightened, a measurement of lack of understanding. The healers went into trance to cure the sick. I did not know what hysteria might develop. In another month, the dances were not frightening, but were romantically strange to me. I no longer can capture that pleasant tingle of strangeness. (Marshall and Ritchie 1951–2002)

Once one has spent a certain amount of time in a culturally different place, as an anthropologist, and has a degree of language fluency, the strange and at times wondrous, fantastic, or bizarre quality of what one is seeing, hearing, and in general experiencing slowly diminishes until it becomes "ordinary."

There may be a similar trajectory in clinical encounters with patients, even of similar cultural backgrounds (Shweder 1990). Since the dawn of psychiatry and the birth of comprehensive clinical analysis and case notes, psychiatrists have wondered about the sense of "difference" and strangeness in their encounters with their mentally ill patients. This is most pronounced when their patients are in the throes of a psychotic episode, but can occur in encounters with patients who are not obviously psychotic, but present with strange or unusual symptoms, or with personality disturbances or disorders. More difficult to describe is the sense of difference or strangeness that arises in therapeutic encounters that are more based on the subtle complexities of intersubjective experience—at times it may be difficult to develop an empathetic response to patients, wherein the psychiatrist or therapist does not feel a disjuncture in his or her understanding of what the patient is actually experiencing. Out of all the therapeutic modalities, psychoanalysis has perhaps the best models in language for interpreting, understanding, and expressing the subtle complexities of these intersubjective states.

When these two forms of initial "strangeness" intersect—in other words, when cultural "astonishment" is compounded by the strangeness of the clinical encounter—the initial sense of exotic otherness may be quite significant, meaning that a considerable amount of time is required before a psychological anthropologist working on mental illness can actually see beyond cultural differences and symptom expression to get to the more humanistic concerns about a subject and address more basic personal material.

At first, while taking in the stunning *jathilan* scene and wading through Bambang's multiple linguistic references, it was difficult to get a sense of the "real" Bambang. However, during follow-up interviews after he was released from the hospital and returned to his neighborhood in Jakarta, the lead author was able to engage in extended person-centered interviews and establish an ongoing relationship with him. It was then that attention could be given to the issues that mattered most for him, including his sense of disappointment and failure in the loss of career opportunities due to his illness; his contentious relationship with his wife who supported him economically and psychologically but also was herself deeply disappointed with his loss of status; his profound love for his son; and his involvement in a religious community that sustained him through his intermittent periods of illness. Yet, in retrospect it was this understanding of Bambang that allowed for interpretation of the content of his verbal play, going beyond exegesis to understand how his multiple historical and cultural references gave voice to a young man wrestling with the burden of stigma and contending with what seemed to be at times a hopeless life course of illness and disability, where he felt that he was constantly falling dishearteningly behind.

The structure of the film was designed to recreate this process for the viewer. The film opens in a large public psychiatric hospital in rural Central Java, with the initial footage of Bambang that the team shot; Bambang is a patient, manically psychotic, and performing for hospital Independence Day festivities, his face streaked with performance makeup, eating the Indonesian flag, as trance dancers might eat glass or live chickens. At this early stage, it is unclear what the viewer is seeing. The "strangeness" of what is clearly a performance is evident. It is only as the performance ends and the camera pans to the hospital entrance and the title card informs the viewer that this is a mental hospital, does the viewer begin to understand that the "strangeness" was present because they were seeing a performance, at a mental hospital, by patients. A bit later, after some further shots of patients resting and being contained on a lock ward, does the view see Bambang, in his hospital uniform—slightly more coherent but still bearing visual markers of "disorder" or "insanity." For both of these takes, Bambang is eager to be interviewed and "hamming it up" in a way that is simultaneously entertaining and quite sad. In these shots, the anthropological team almost seems to be modeling "order" or "sanity" in contrast—asking Bambang measured questions and trying to understand and make sense of his answers, but appearing slightly bemused. At this point in the film, the viewer is certain also to feel at a distance from Bambang.

The film transitions out of these opening sequences with a cross-fade from the florid patient—wearing the hospital gown, his head shaved to avoid the spread of lice—to a to a more hirsute but somber Bambang in his small family house in a poor neighborhood in urban Jakarta. The film unfolds over a number of years, but repeatedly returns to the scene of Bambang in the mental hospital. It was an editorial decision to return repeatedly to that original scene in the mental hospital to create contrast between his manic state and his "normal" self, at least in relation to his cognition and self-presentation. This more calm, self-reflective, somber (B.I. *lebih tenang*), and even perhaps somewhat depressed or melancholic state he is in in most of the rest of the film highlights his "disordered" state in the hospital.

This transition highlights the dramatic transformation Bambang has been through and also elicits a striking moment of self-reflection in the viewer, who must reconfigure their understanding of Bambang. If before he was "a crazy person," now he is clearly recognized as "a normal person." This demands some self-awareness on the part of the viewer, who must question their own assumptions, categorizations, and reactions to people with mental illness. In doing so, the film also calls attention to Bambang's own perspective on his illness, offering insight into his fears of being seen as noticeably handicapped by his wife, his peers, and the larger community, with an obvious illness being the defining factor in his life. On a visceral level, the viewer knows that Bambang's fears are founded, because the viewer felt startled by and distanced from Bambang in the opening shots. This transition also underscores the radical disorientation of a schizoaffective episode and introduces a significant theme of the film, which is how Bambang is struggling to understand, reconcile, and perhaps reluctantly accept the way mental illness has affected his life. Interestingly, participation in the film project impacted Bambang during this process of reconciliation and acceptance.

7.4   LAST ENCOUNTERS

During filming, and before the film was finalized, Bambang and his family were given opportunities to watch the footage. As a thoughtful and reflective man, Bambang has been thinking about his life throughout the course of research, but interacting with his own image has influenced him deeply. Bambang noted:

> When I was watching the documentary, a true film, I was so sad and I cried. I prayed "God please give a way out, a way I can get normal, and support my child."

Later in the interview, he said:

> This is more than just a soap opera. By seeing with what is disclosed, with all sorts of backgrounds, this is more than just a toothpaste advertisement. I feel that [way]. I am encouraged that this movie can help many people for healing.

After the film was made, Bambang and Yatmi interacted with the filmic depiction of Bambang by participating in screenings of the film at educational and social service organizations where they were interviewed by journalists and sat on panels with other participants in the *Afflictions* (Lemelson 2010–2011) series (Ronny 2013). At a screening for *Memory of My Face* (Lemelson 2011a) at Magelang Mental Hospital, in 2015, fifteen years after the original interview that opened the film, Bambang noted how difficult the last number of years had been,

> I feel touched watching the film, but also sad as well as ashamed every time while watching the film, seeing how out of control I was. I am happy that through the film I can share with other people about my recovery, especially the families who have member suffering from mental illness.

Later in the interview, he stated:

> I avoid people who are negative about mental illness or about meeting with people with mental illness. But I believe this film can open many eyes so people like me can be accepted by society.

Bambang and his wife Yatmi are now frequently called upon to present and discuss their story whenever the film is screened and have made themselves available as spokespeople for increased understanding, tolerance, and human rights in the care and advocacy for people living with severe mental illness. In this way, the film process has actually been rather significant in *reducing* the shame and stigma that he so deeply feared, by allowing Bambang to embrace his own history and have his story compassionately told in the film and in the popular media, contributing to a changing popular discourse on mental illness in Indonesia.

REFERENCES

Anderson-Fye, Eileen. 2003. Never Leave Yourself: Ethnopsychology as Mediator of Psychological Globalization Among Belizean Schoolgirls. *Ethos* 31 (1): 59–94.

Banerjee, Subhabrata B., and Stephen A. Linstead. 2001. Globalization, Multiculturalism and Other Fictions: Colonialism for the New Millennium? *Organization* 8 (4): 683–722.

Berrios, German E. 1996. *The History of Mental Symptoms: Descriptive Psychopathology Since the Nineteenth Century.* Cambridge: Cambridge University Press.

Berrios, German E., and Renate Hauser. 1988. The Early Development of Kraepelin's Ideas on Classification: A Conceptual History. *Psychological Medicine* 18 (4): 813–821.

Boellstorff, Tom. 2004. Authentic, of Course': Gay Language in Indonesia and Cultures of Belonging. In *Speaking in Queer Tongues: Globalization and Gay Language,* ed. William L. Leap and Tom Boellstorff, 181–201. Champaign: University of Illinois Press.

Browne, Kevin O. 2003. Awareness, Emptiness, and Javanese Selves: Jatilan Performance in Yogyakarta, Indonesia. *The Asia Pacific Journal of Anthropology* 4 (1, 2): 54–71.

Connor, Linda. 1982. Ships of Fools and Vessels of the Divine: Mental Hospitals and Madness: A Case Study. *Social Science & Medicine* 16 (7): 783–794. doi:10. 1016/0277-9536(82)90231-3

Fabrega, Horacio Jr. 1989. Cultural Relativism and Psychiatric Illness. *The Journal of Nervous and Mental Disease* 177 (7): 415–425. doi:10.1097/00005053-198907000-00005

———. 1992. The Role of Culture in a Theory of Psychiatric Illness. *Social Science & Medicine* 35 (1): 91–103.

Fanon, Frantz. 1963. *The Wretched of the Earth:* Preface by Jean-Paul Sartre (trans: Constance Farrington). New York: Grove Press.

Foley, Kathy. 1985. The Dancer and the Danced: Trance Dance and Theatrical Performance in West Java. *Asian Theatre Journal* 2 (1): 28–49. doi:10.2307/ 1124505

Good, Byron J, Mary-Jo DelVecchio Good, Sandra Teresa Hyde, and Sarah Pinto. 2008a. Postcolonial Disorders: Reflections on Subjectivity in the Contemporary World. In *Postcolonial Disorders*, ed. Mary-Jo DelVecchio Good, Sandra T. Hyde, Sarah Pinto, and Byron J. Good, 1–40. Berkeley: University of California Press.

Good, Mary-Jo DelVecchio, Sandra T. Hyde, Sarah Pinto, and Byron J. Good, eds. 2008b. *Postcolonial Disorders: Reflections on Subjectivity in the Contemporary World*. Berkeley: University of California Press.

Hollan, Douglas. 2005. Dreaming of a Global World. In *A Companion to Psychological Anthropology: Modernity and Psychocultural Change*, ed. Conerly Casey and Robert B. Edgerton, 90–102. Malden: Blackwell.

Kiong, Tong C., and Lian K. Fee. 2003. Cultural Knowledge, Nation-States, and the Limits of Globalization in Southeast Asia. In *Globalization in Southeast Asia: Local, National, and Transnational Perspectives*, 42–64. New York: Berghahn.

Kirmayer, Laurence J., Robert Lemelson, and Constance A. Cummings, eds. 2015. *Re-Visioning Psychiatry: Cultural Phenomenology, Critical Neuroscience, and Global Mental Health*. New York: Cambridge University Press.

Larkin, Anne R. 1979. The Form and Content of Schizophrenic Hallucinations. *The American Journal of Psychiatry* 136 (7): 940–942.

Lemelson, Robert, 2010–2011. *Afflictions: Culture and Mental Illness in Indonesia Series*. 182 min. Watertown: Documentary Educational Resources. http://www.der.org/films/afflictions.html

———. 2011a. *Memory of My Face*. 22 min. Watertown: Documentary Education Resources. http://www.der.org/films/memory-of-my-face.html

———. 2011b. *Jathilan: Trance and Possession in Java*. Watertown: Documentary Educational Resources. http://www.der.org/films/jathilan.html

Luhrmann, Tanya M., R. Padmavati, Hema Tharoor, and Akwasi Osei. 2015. Hearing Voices in Different Cultures: A Social Kindling Hypothesis. *Topics in Cognitive Science* 7 (4): 646–663. doi:10.1111/tops.12158

Luvaas, Brent. 2006. Re-Producing Pop the Aesthetics of Ambivalence in a Contemporary Dance Music. *International Journal of Cultural Studies* 9 (2): 167–187. doi:10.1177/1367877906064029

———. 2010. Designer Vandalism: Indonesian Indie Fashion and the Cultural Practice of Cut 'n' Paste. *Visual Anthropology Review* 26 (1): 1–16. doi:10.1111/j.1548-7458.2010.01043.x

Mansurnoor, Iik A. 2004. Response of Southeast Asian Muslims to the Increasingly Globalized World: Discourse and Action. *Historia Actual Online* 5. Retrieved from https://dialnet.unirioja.es/servlet/articulo?codigo=996060

Marshall, John, and Claire Ritchie, 1951–2002. *A Kalahari Family*. 360 min. Watertown: Kalfam Productions and Documentary Educational Resources. http://www.der.org/films/a-kalahari-family.html

Pols, Hans. 2006. The Development of Psychiatry in Indonesia: From Colonial to Modern Times. *International Review of Psychiatry* 18 (4): 363–370. doi:10.1080/09540260600775421

———. 2007. Psychological Knowledge in a Colonial Context: Theories on the Nature of the "Native Mind" in the Former Dutch East Indies. *History of Psychology* 10 (2): 111–131.

Reuter, Thomas. 2009. Globalisation and Local Identities: The Rise of New Ethnic and Religious Movements in Post-Suharto Indonesia. *Asian Journal of Social Science* 37 (6): 857–871.

Ronny. 2013. Kisah Para Penderita Skizofrenia Dalam Film. *Antara Kalteng.* Retrieved from http://kalteng.antaranews.com/berita/222941/kisah-para-penderita-skizofrenia-dalam-film

Subandi, M.A. 2011. Family Expressed Emotion in a Javanese Cultural Context. *Culture, Medicine, and Psychiatry* 35 (3): 331–346. doi:10.1007/s11013-011-9220-4

———. 2015. Bangkit: The Processes of Recovery from First Episode Psychosis in Java. *Culture, Medicine, and Psychiatry* 39 (4): 597–613. doi:10.1007/s11013-015-9427-x

Vickers, Adrian. 2013. *A History of Modern Indonesia.* 2nd ed. New York: Cambridge University Press.

Yehuda, Rachel, and Linda M. Bierer. 2009. The Relevance of Epigenetics to PTSD: Implications for the DSM-V. *Journal of Traumatic Stress* 22 (5): 427–434.

Yehuda, Rachel, Sarah L. Halligan, and Linda M. Bierer. 2001. Relationship of Parental Trauma Exposure and Ptsd to Ptsd, Depressive and Anxiety Disorders in Offspring. *Journal of Psychiatric Research* 35 (5): 261–270.

Zucker, Jerry, 1990. *Ghost.* 2 hr, 7 min. Paramount Pictures.

Ritual Burdens: Culturally Defined Stressors and Developmental Progressions

Photo 8.1 Ni Ketut Kasih

8.1 STORY SUMMARY

Ni Ketut Kasih is an elderly widow with a kind face who lives in a small village in Central Bali. She is the proud mother of four children, and the beloved grandmother of twelve grandchildren. When she is not helping her family around the house with chores such as sweeping and cooking, she may be socializing with other women down by the river, meditating, or reading.

© The Author(s) 2017
R. Lemelson, A. Tucker, *Afflictions*, Culture, Mind, and Society,
DOI 10.1007/978-3-319-59984-7_8

Ketut has lived her whole life surrounded by the complex rhythms and requirements of the Balinese ritual calendar, with temple observances, holy days, and village and regional festivals occurring on a weekly or, at times even daily, basis. Tourists flock from all over the world to witness these Balinese ceremonies lush with sensory delights—filled with the fragrant smoke of incense, the colorful offerings of fruit and flowers, often with artful gamelan music and temple dances performed amongst ornately carved architecture and a crowd dressed in their golden-threaded best. However, for the Balinese themselves, these rituals are much more than a spectacle; they are a spiritual mandate and social requirement, which demand a great amount of labor and sacrifice on the part of those who practice them. A large portion of ritual duties and responsibilities falls particularly heavily upon Balinese women who not only often contribute financially, but also must spend countless hours crafting offerings by hand.

For many decades now, Ketut has had particular difficulty with the stress surrounding ritual obligations. She anticipates ceremonies far in advance of their coming, repeatedly questioning family members about the state of their preparations. Ketut has been renowned in her village for the speed and mastery with which she can prepare offerings, and this has contributed to her status as a ritual specialist and ceremonial leader. However, in her worry that her family will not be able to fulfill their ritual obligations, Ketut will be unable to sleep. She finds her mind crowded with thoughts as she remembers the stresses of her childhood, when her father was taken as a prisoner of war and she was forced to abandon school to help support her family. Sometimes the worries get to be too much and Ketut will have a "fit." She might disappear, leaving her family to wander to distant places, or act out in strange and disturbing ways such as disrobing in the market or challenging others to a fight. When her family feels that Ketut requires assistance beyond what they can provide, they take her to the state mental hospital or they provide her with medications prescribed for these episodes of behavior and emotional disturbance. Ketut usually recovers quickly and experiences long stretches of peace before another ritual or financial obligation evokes more worry and another episode of illness.

Ketut's reaction to family obligation stressors and ritual requirements raises questions about the purpose ritual serves and the cost that it carries for the individuals that prepare for and perform them. Her case provides an example of one unique schema of stress wherein cultural obligations, traumatic historical events, biography, and neurobiology overlap to trigger cyclical episodes of mental illness. In doing so, it illuminates personal constructs of distress and the binding associations that make certain burdens unbearable.

Ni Ketut Kasih was born the eighth child in a family of twelve. Her father was a weapons specialist who had fought the Japanese during World War II. Then in 1947, when Ketut was still a little girl, he defended his people against the Dutch in Indonesia's struggle for independence. He was captured during a mission and interred in a camp for prisoners of war, apart from the family for months until he was finally able to escape. Ketut's mother was sick at the time, and there was no money for school fees. Ketut was forced to postpone her hopes for education in order to care and provide for her family. She worked as a seamstress and a peddler, selling small items to help raise money for her family's food and ritual needs. After her father was reunited with the family, Ketut was able to attend elementary school. She happily remembers these carefree days when her only obligation was to study. However, because of ongoing financial difficulties, she was forced to abandon her education after completing the sixth grade.

Over the years, Ketut became a successful small businesswoman, selling fish that she herself would transport to market from coastal Jimbaran in a big battered Colt truck. In early 1965, there was a crisis in the fish market, portending the larger national crisis to come, and Ketut was left with significant debts. Her family could not help her because they themselves were struggling due to the violent upheavals of that time; a purported communist coup had led to a takeover by Suharto's New Order regime, and in Bali thousands of people were killed or imprisoned in the waves of violence, suppression, and surveillance. Ketut's uncle and cousin were killed, she witnessed massacres of fellow villagers, and hunger and stress led many of her family members to fall ill. After this difficult era, Ketut's family arranged a marriage for her with a distant relative. Ketut felt upset that she did not get to pick her own husband, but she did not dare resist; soon after, the feelings of anger diminished and she settled into a companionable and loving relationship with her husband, Pak Mangku.

Ketut gave birth to the couple's first child, Wayan, in 1969 three days after a ritual ceremony. This precipitated the first of many episodes of "inner sickness" that Ketut would experience over her life. She did not want to claim her son, refused to breastfeed, and exhibited episodes of disassociation and disorientation, acting as if she could not remember who she was. She was ill for about three and a half months, during which time her family sought a variety of treatments. Her father searched all over south Bali for a traditional healer who could provide relief. He found one who said that the problem stemmed from a crack Ketut suffered to her skull as a child, and prescribed a mix of sticky rice and betel leaves to be applied to the damaged areas. The family also sought treatment from their spiritual advisor who conducted religious purification healing ceremonies. He recited a prayer, and gave Ketut oil to drink after which mucous came pouring out of her mouth and nose, a commonly recognized sign of recovery in Indonesia. Ketut returned to her normal self within a month of this treatment. Ketut lived her life fairly free of incident after this episode for over fifteen years. She gave birth to three more children and took care of the household while selling staples at a small food stall in the nearby market.

Then in 1986, Ni Ketut Kasih attended a large-scale family ritual marking both the wedding of her brother-in-law and a tooth filing ceremony, a Balinese rite of passage. She arrived at the ritual and suddenly began to weep, felt weak, and was unable to greet her relatives until she finally collapsed. She was taken to see psychiatrist Dr. I Gusti Putu Panteri, was prescribed Thorazine, and recovered within eleven days. She soon relapsed again, however, at which point her family brought her to the psychiatric ward at the regency public hospital.

Photo 8.2   Ni Ketut Kasih evaluated by her psychiatrist, Dr. Panteri

Over the following decades, Ketut would relapse and be hospitalized more than 35 times, sometimes briefly, sometimes for a month or more. When she recovers she can be without incident for months, but her relapses can be severe. She and her family both believe that in every case the triggers for her episodes are the emotional burdens posed by ritual events and family obligations. Ketut says their onset is marked by a feeling that her family is facing a challenge or event that they will not be able to handle. Her husband says that at these times, especially when the family is in fact unable to contribute financially to village or temple rituals and therefore unable to fulfill their ritual obligations, Ketut feels greatly disappointed.

Ketut says she can often tell when a relapse is coming. She is often unable to sleep a day or two before she gets sick and will be sensitive to the sound of the wind or the rain falling on leaves. She may be bothered by physical symptoms, feeling like there is a hole in her head that is filled with rice and sand or that she has been stabbed in the chest with a bamboo stake. Alternatively, she may feel empty, as if she has already lost consciousness. She will become unable to see her own shadow or imagine her own face when she was young, unable to remember a time when she was happy. She feels afraid of her husband and worries about making mistakes, and at the same time, she feels suspicious of friends and neighbors, thinking that they may secretly want to do her harm.

Once her "fit" is in full effect, Ketut has a lot of energy. She wakes up very early in the morning or in the middle of the night and may disappear, wandering far from the house. Sometimes her energy takes the form of industrious spiritual labor where she makes many offerings for the Gods— even more than usual—and talks a lot about the invisible world. At times she may disrobe in public, evoking the Balinese style from a previous era where women wore only a sarong with their breasts exposed. Ketut may also express feelings of anger or aggression, occasionally throwing things, striking out at family members or challenging them to a physical fight. There have been a number of occasions where Ketut has experienced epileptic seizures during these periods of extra energy and unusual behavior.

Ketut and her family find pharmaceuticals to be effective in responding to her symptoms and restoring her usual calm demeanor. She has been prescribed chlorpromazine in the past, and up until the present takes two antipsychotic medications including other phenothiazines (such as trifluoperazine) tablets or if she is hospitalized, a monthly intramuscular fluphenazine injection. She also has prescription for Haloperidol, which her family administers if her symptoms start to flare up, and takes a daily routine of an antispasmodic such as trihexyphenidyl to manage the stiffness, tremors, spasms, and extrapyramidal effects of the antipsychotics.

In accordance with the Balinese conceptualization of health, Ketut and her family also continue to attend to the spiritual as well as the biological aspects of her well-being. After years of struggle tending to her responsibilities as a village ritual specialist (B.B. *pemangku*), which she assumed after the death of her husband, Ketut's family has relieved her of the burden of this activity as well as the responsibility for preparing offerings, unless she so chose to participate. Her children and grandchildren assume the responsibility for the family's other ritual requirements, sometimes even receiving help from other villagers, in an attempt to protect Ketut's peace of mind. From time to time Ketut will still experience an episode of disordered behavior, emotion, and thought, but taking the empathetic view that anyone can become overly stressed, the family actively rejects any stigmatization of her symptoms, instead calmly taking each episode as it comes.

8.2   THE BEAUTY AND BURDEN OF BALINESE RITUAL IN NI KETUT KASIH'S CYCLES OF ILLNESS

Ritual plays a large role in Ketut's illness experience by acting as a powerful trigger for anxious, manic, and disordered states. While ritual can serve various positive functions in a society, such as providing a regulated symbolic system to express shared emotional states and maintain societal equilibrium, it may have a collective and personal darker side; Freud once called religious ritual a "universal neurosis" used to repress and displace a given society's antisocial impulses and taboo desires (Freud 1934). In any case, ritual—in the Balinese case in particular, the preparation of voluminous offerings to be used during ritual—serves as a meeting point where familial and community relationships, the schedules and customs of preparation that influence day-to-day routines, and personal feelings and associations come together.

Bali is known as one of the most "ritually dense" cultures in the world. The Balinese ritual calendar is two hundred and ten days long and full of cyclical events. The ritual year is marked by the twin rituals of *Galungan*, when departed souls are invited back to earth to be honored, and *Kuningan* ten days later, when they return to heaven. There are temple ceremonies every full moon (B.I. *bulan purnama*) and every fifteen days (B.B. *kajeng kliwon*), as well as annual temple anniversaries known as *odalan*, which must be held both for village temples and private family temples. In addition, every thirty-five days there are honor days, such as *Tumpek Landep*, the day where all metal goods are blessed and offerings are made for kitchen implements, garden tools, metallic parts of machinery, and vehicles. There are also other holy days, such as *Nyepi*, the day of silence, and *Hari Raya Saraswati*, honoring the goddess of knowledge. Of course, there are also large-scale rituals to mark important life cycle events, which in Bali include a series of ceremonies for newborns, including the forty-two-day ceremony to ensure safe development, the three-month ceremony where the baby touches ground for the first time, and the hair-cutting ceremony; puberty rituals; the tooth filing ceremony at adolescence to extinguish "animalistic" tendencies such as lust and greed; the wedding ceremony; and a series of funerary rituals including the *Ngaben*, or a Balinese cremation.

An integral element of Balinese ritual is the offerings (B.B. *banten*). In the film, Ketut and her family refer to the practice of *ngayah*, "committing oneself to God through making ritual offerings." This concept suggests that the emphasis in preparing offerings is not solely the tangible end result, but the devotional process manifested in the finished product. This devotion is expressed and displayed not only through offerings made at special occasions, which include towers of arranged fruit and baskets of flowers, but also through *canang*, the daily offerings that women craft and leave at important areas in the house and local environment, such as at doorways or intersections. These offerings made from leaves, flowers, sliced fruit or pieces of rice, coins, and incense are rich with symbolic meaning referencing Hindu deities, the life cycle, and philosophical theories of value and balance.

Beyond the purely aesthetic, offerings can be seen as result-oriented, "pragmatic interventions which aim to change the state of affairs in this world, to bring about material well-being and prevent suffering" (Geertz 1991). This pragmatic approach to ritual offerings is supported by local beliefs about the high cost of making a ritual mistake. In traditional Balinese logics of illness and healing, a wide variety of personal and family ills—from a headache to a slowly healing broken leg to an argumentative husband to a meager harvest—are frequently interpreted as having their source or etiology in forgotten or improperly performed rituals. Those suffering will often consult with *balian*, traditional healers and ritual experts, to determine what has gone wrong and which corrective rituals are required to effect cure. Many families go into to debt to ensure a ceremony is performed in a timely and appropriately appointed manner in order to prevent such ill effects.

Therefore, in making offerings and performing rituals properly, individual Balinese women take responsibility for the well-being of themselves, their families, and their communities. The extensive female networks of labor and communication and the female leadership in organizing sometimes hundreds of family members involved in ritual preparations—plaiting leaves, cutting fruit, and molding rice—may speak to the valued and important role women play in Balinese spiritual life. However, knowing that the Herculean task of making offerings is always and only relegated to women, it may also be interpreted negatively as some Balinese choose to call it, "ritual slavery" (Lemelson 2011).

While this may seem extreme, understanding the required physical labor, time, spiritual and emotional investment, and monetary resources required to make offerings and fulfill family obligations combined with the overdetermined significance of ritual in Balinese family and community life, makes it clearer how ceremonies may become not just culturally elaborated festivities, but also culturally marked stressors that might strain pre-existing vulnerabilities or precipitate an illness episode.

Indeed, it has been ethnographically demonstrated that ritual obligations are a common stressor in Bali and throughout Indonesia. Hollan and Wellenkamp, working on Sulawesi (Hollan and Wellenkamp 1994, 1996), singled out ritual as "one of the most significant and emotionally charged" aspects of adult life because there is often so much at stake personally and communally. The many things that need to be taken into consideration to make a ritual run smoothly, combined with the many feelings and memories and associations rituals evoke, is commonly understood throughout the archipelago to lead to "too many thoughts." It is also commonly understood that if these thoughts become too overwhelming or the stress of them goes unmanaged, mental illness may result. Ketut notes:

> If there is a ritual that is coming ... two days before I already have those symptoms again ...When there is a ritual, two days before I already can't sleep... because I'm thinking about problems that are going to come in another two days.

8.3   CHRONOLOGIES OF TRAUMA, CULTURALLY INFLECTED EMOTIONS, AND SOCIAL SUPPORT

It becomes a complicated and ironic fact of Balinese life that ritual activity, which is intended to promote and protect the purity and balance of the community, can also cause significant psychological pressure for an individual. In Ketut's illness narrative, they become causal stressors for episodes of mental illness particularly because they also evoke a formative episode in Ketut's childhood wherein she was dealing with a combination of pressures that were truly overwhelming. This originary experience was shaped by cultural, historical, and personal circumstances.

Ketut remembers being forced into a role of premature responsibility because her father was absent from the household and her mother was sick. Ketut suggests that the help she was expected to provide was too advanced for her age, saying, "At home, I shouldered the burdens. The burdens of my parents, I took them on."

This childhood experience differs from the cultural ideal: for the Balinese, as perhaps in most societies, childhood is supposed to be a relatively carefree time. In Bali, children are considered vulnerable to spirit attack, and therefore must be protected and indulged. Children may make demands on their parents and are humored by their older siblings. Furthermore, because they are not yet "aware" the way adults are, children are not held to the same strict rules of conduct (Bateson and Mead 1942; Jensen and Suryani 1992; John 1953). Ketut still identifies with and longs for this carefree time, when she remembers having a "happy" face, telling herself, "That's your face from when you were young, that's what you were like when you were young, because in Bali when you're young you're happy."

The loss of her father put an end to this culturally designated period of relative ease. This was a time of personal difficulty for Ketut, where she was certainly experiencing a cluster of emotions including confusion, feelings of sadness and pity for her suffering father, and anxiety to know that he was gone and not knowing when he was going to come back.

Given that Ketut's father was imprisoned and taken from the family in the process of fighting for Indonesian independence, Ketut's story cannot be separated from Indonesia's history of colonialism and national development. When Ketut was a child, the Dutch had colonized parts of Indonesia for centuries, although the Balinese had successfully resisted Dutch rule until 1908. As a revolutionary Indonesian nationalist movement was growing, the country was swept into World War II. The Japanese invaded and defeated the Dutch in 1942. They were at first welcomed as liberators who would unite Indonesia with the rest of Asia. Indonesia officially declared independence in 1945, but the country remained under Japanese rule and conditions rapidly deteriorated. Many people died of starvation due to extreme shortages of food and many Indonesians were mistreated as laborers and comfort women. When Allied Forces defeated the Japanese, they agreed to return Indonesia to Dutch rule. In 1946, the Dutch took Bali and other outer islands and the war for independence lasted until 1949. The entire nation was affected by these political struggles; Ketut's immediate and extended family network of support were among the hundreds of thousands strained under these conditions.

Research in the neurobiology of stress has provided insight into the seemingly atypical chronology of trauma, where past and present distresses are folded into one another and certain memories repeat with a perpetual sense of urgency. Culturally, personally, and historically determined frameworks of interpretation intertwine and interact with emerging sensations, thoughts, or emotions in a complex loop that creates meaning for the person experiencing them (Hacking 1995). Various sensations, emotions, and interpretations are linked together through conscious or unconscious association and through neurophysiologic pathways. Embodied memories, cultural metaphors, historical trauma coalesce into personal schemas or scripts of stress that frame and interpret current sensation and experience. Past experience, which may re-emerge as flashbacks, re-experiencing events, or traumatic memory, may link physical sensations with distressing emotions. For example, for a survivor, a fleeting sensation of dizziness may recall the dizziness of malnutrition she experienced during wartime, and thus simultaneously evoke emotions of terror or grief. In a correlative process known as "kindling," if a physical sensation is repeatedly experienced in the context of distress, then future distress will become likely to evoke these sensations as a stress response. So if this same survivor feels sad, she may also soon start to feel dizzy (Hinton et al. 2008).

In Ketut's case, present family obligation stressors are amplified by Ketut's personal history of trauma and responsibility. Each newly emerging stressor recalls her past formative experiences of stress, confounding present anxiety with the past anxieties of worrying about her father and having to assume responsibility for her family. Furthermore, the ritual and economic burdens Ketut was forced to take on in the household were folded into the emotional and physical stressors of war: both the socio-historical milieu of anxiety and violence, and the physiological responses to hunger and starvation may have amplified her stress at that time.

Other associational processes may shape emotion and sensation as they occur. These processes can amplify, mute, or generate new sensations. One is the loop of anxiety and attention; certain feelings or sensations are unpleasant and cause high alert, yet constantly scanning for, thinking about, or attending to such feelings may cause them to intensify. Significant factors determine what feelings or sensations deserve such close attention, including ethnopsychology, traumatic memory, and self-image. Different emotions and sensations have different saliency for different cultures, and cultural context will determine the comparative normativity or pathology of certain sensations or emotions. Feelings of shame or embarrassment are particularly laden feelings in Balinese culture; therefore, the presence or threat of shame is likely to lead to heightened attention. A self-image built from such cultural frameworks, past events, perceived innate qualities, and interpersonal relationships will further affect how an individual interprets his or her own sensations or emotions.

Many of the emotions that become disturbing to Ketut when she is having an episode are very common idioms of personal and interpersonal distress salient to Indonesian cultures in general and Balinese people in particular. In a psychocultural context that prizes harmonious interpersonal relations and a smooth personal demeanor, these emotions not only articulate distress, but also evoke distress. Particularly upsetting are feelings of shame or embarrassment, feelings of suspicion, and feelings of anger.

There is a large literature on the role of culture in shaping emotions, and many scholars have commented on the significance, depth, and nuance of shame, or *malu*, in Indonesian cultures (Heider 1991, 2011). *Malu* (B.B. *lek*) may in some contexts be similar to the Western understanding of shame, a sense of losing face when unable to uphold norms or requirements or unfavorably compared to others, and so on. So, in this way, shame is a result or a reaction, a negative state associated with embarrassment and guilt. But *malu* may also connote an active preventative process of managing emotions internally to prevent one from becoming ashamed. To know a sense of shame is to acknowledge the capacity of your behavior to offend or destabilize others, and therefore knowing and displaying proper "shame," which in this context may mean deference or a regulatory self-consciousness, may become a sign of maturity or a sense of pride. Indeed, children are complimented when they are mature enough to "know a sense of shame." Clifford Geertz (1991) interpreted the Balinese sense of shame as a kind of stage fright, an anxiety over the possibility of social awkwardness, insult, or poor role performance in the constant negotiation and renegotiation of status. While *malu* itself is clearly not a singular "cause" of her episodes, Ketut herself notes the power it has over her equanimity, and clearly associates feelings of shame as a significant stressor for her as when she says, "If I have too much shame I go crazy."

Another mental state associated with Ketut's episodes is that of suspicion. When she is starting to feel unwell, it is stated that Ketut starts to feel that "this world is a world of treachery," questions the seemingly innocuous motivations of guests who come to the house, and feels afraid that people outside of her immediate family plan to harm her. These feelings are somewhat corroborated by her family, who suggest Ketut may have fallen ill because other people were jealous of her.

Whether or not one can posit that Balinese culture is governed by a "paranoid ethos" (Schwartz 1973), there is a pervasive belief in black magic and a corollary sense of fear or suspicion that arises particularly in the contexts of illness or misfortune. It is often the onset of illness or otherwise abnormal behavior that indicates a person has been the victim of black magic or witchcraft. Black magic can come in many forms, sent through telepathy, poisoned food served by a family member, the touch of a witch (Wikan 1990), or in the form of projectile needles, bullets, pins, or other implements. Black magic, along with ritual error, may be one of the most commonly invoked explanatory models of illness in Bali. The reason for use of black magic is usually revenge against a direct offense or jealousy of others' good fortune, and extended kin are the most frequently accused (Wikan 1990). This vernacular understanding of black magic as a causal factor for symptoms of mental and other illness provides a clear explanation for why Ketut would feel suspicious when she starts to feel ill, and why rituals, involving meeting with the aunts, uncles, and in-laws, who might harbor secret mal intent against her, would be cause for fear or worry.

Finally, the expression of anger is also seen as being in direct relationship to mental illness. Ketut's family often feels she needs to be medicated at times when she expresses anger and aggression. Certainly while aggression can be upsetting in many cultures, it may be even more so in Bali. In the early ethnography of Bali, Margaret Mead, who had a particular interest in childhood, analyzed childrearing tactics that she felt specifically trained against the expression of anger (Bateson and Mead 1942). The prohibition against anger is active for all members of Balinese culture, but may particularly apply to women who are supposed to be decorous, graceful, and deferent. Because of these restrictions on behavior, if and when someone does reach the point of noticeably expressing anger, it signals that something has gone terribly wrong. While the correlation may not be as direct as equating being visibly angry and being crazy, the embodied loss of control and detachment from social norms that expressions of anger display may be a very powerful indicator for the Balinese that a person's emotional states are unmanageable or that he or she has lost touch with the Balinese reality.

Considering the interaction of experiencing, expressing, and interpreting negative feelings raises the interesting question: Do these negative feelings trigger the onset of mental illness because they are so upsetting to the person having them, are they interpreted as mental illness because they are so outside the idealized norm, or does the complex interplay of personal subjectivity and cultural context construct the phenomenology of mental illness? Or does the sociocultural demand for smooth demeanor during times of stress add additional pressure to an already high-pressure situation?

Variations on these core questions have been central to the project, the psychological anthropology, particularly between domains of culture and personality, and what the relationships between these two and how and in what ways does personality and its adaptive capacities function as a primary, intermediate, or intervening variable (Kardiner et al. 1945; Kardiner and Linton 1974). Ni Ketut Kasih's story provides an "experience near" and "thick" description through which these complex relationships can be explored.

Ni Ketut Kasih's decades-long experience of mental illness provides a longitudinal perspective on mental health within the family system. In a complex but compelling interaction, Ketut's family is both stressor and strength through her life course. It is clear that extended family relationships can act as a stressor in a sociocultural context like Ketut's. Contact with this extended family elicits feelings of responsibility to adequately represent and support family members and ancestors, shame if rituals are improperly carried out or cannot be afforded, and anger or jealousy over economic differences amongst the kin network that then must be suppressed.

However, perhaps more significantly, Ketut's immediate family provides a buffer of support. They do this primarily by actively resisting labeling Ketut or defining her by any stigmatizing diagnosis. While she at times describes herself as mentally ill (B.I. *sakit jiwa*), her family adamantly does not call her mad (B.I. *gila*, B.B. *buduh*). Despite the fact that she has been institutionalized many times, the family chooses to normalize Ketut's experiences of dysregulation. They say, "Crazy, in Indonesian it's 'crazy.' In Bali it's 'crazy.' But we don't make assumptions like that. We see our mother as having too many burdens on her thoughts, and anyone can experience that. Relatives of my mother still say, 'This woman is sick like this because she indeed has many burdens.' There isn't a problem."

The most important thing is that my mother is healthy.

Photo 8.3   Ni Ketut Kasih in the warm embrace of her family

In avoiding conflating Ketut's symptoms with her Self, her family emphasizes the temporary or transient quality to her illness, leaving plenty of room for her many periods of stability and lucidity and underscoring a sense of continuity to Ketut's daily life. While she does periodically spend time in psychiatric care, the family does not stigmatize the kind of illness she suffers from, instead treating her mental illness like any other illness. Therefore, she is not institutionalized indefinitely nor identified as ill when she is in fact feeling better. The family does not focus on their mother's diagnosis but rather her observable condition—if she is doing well she is treated as such, if she is not doing well they take her to the hospital for care, and the moment she seems recovered they bring her home.

Furthermore, the family shares responsibility for her care. In collectivist and interdependent societies, such as those found in Indonesia and Bali, the kin network and environment are considered profoundly significant in determining the behavior or outcome of any individual. Therefore, if one person's well-being is threatened, responsibility is shared in terms of both etiology and cure. Ketut's son says "we make efforts for her to recover," emphasizing the collective investment and effort of the family unit. This effort is visible in actions like staying awake to guard or monitor Ketut if she is having a spell of energetic sleeplessness during the night. The family also engages in a kind of collective prevention, protecting their mother from potential triggers and searching for ways to keep Ketut in a balanced state. Even extended family and non-kin villagers who know Ketut sometimes provide assistance. For example, if she has wandered away or gone to the market during an episode, they help bring her home.

The family also shares responsibility for Ketut's tasks when she is unable to carry them out. For example, when Ketut's first son was young and she was dealing with her illness, he lived with and was cared for by his grand-father. Kin and villagers adapt to Ketut's shifting needs and capabilities, affording her duties when she can handle them and easing such expectations when she cannot. Illustratively, Ketut was still given important ritual responsibilities, such as being a counselor for village religious issues and being a temple priest, even after episodes of illness. However, now her son has taken over these duties because he feels more capable. He explained, "I have a wife, there is already someone to help me, and I advised her so that my mother doesn't take on those burdens again. . . so that we young people take that responsibility, that it's now our burden. Mother should just be calm, like that. That's what I told her to do. The important thing is that my mother is healthy."

It may be that in the interdependent family structure that is prevalent in much of the developing world, this approach of communal responsibility and collective care may seem less out of the ordinary than for families in the West, who, for example, for reasons of increased mobility may live far away from their networks of support. In Ketut's case, shared care, and a separa-tion between symptoms and identity due to such things as spiritual attribu-tion, supports her periodic recovery and ongoing integration in the family. Further cause may be because such communities have more flexible or accommodating expectations for their members, and more opportunities for ill people to actively contribute and feel productive.

8.4   SEEING BEYOND A SPARKLING FACE

When Ketut is met at the community clinic in Central rural Bali in 1997, (a shot seen immediately after the title card, at the opening of the film) she seemed the epitome of an elegant, "sparkling" Balinese woman so well captured in Unni Wikan's classic account (Wikan 1990). However, the façade started showing some cracks upon the initial psychiatric interview with Dr. Panteri and her daughter that day. It became clear that underneath the laughing, polite banter there was a current of disturbance, something "off" in the culturally typical account one would expect of a Balinese woman in her position. Then, in the course of the interview, it emerged that she had been hospitalized for psychiatric problems a number of times in the previous two decades, a clear indicator that hers was not the "typical" life course of someone in her position. Ketut and her daughter agreed to be filmed further in their house compound.

This allowed for a more extensive interview to be conducted with Ketut, her husband, and several of her children. At this point, the focus was both getting to know Ketut through gathering her life history and understanding her challenges and experiences by doing basic clinically oriented interviews as to her psychiatric diagnoses, and hearing her family's accounts of her history, summarized above.

One thing that was evident was the warm and open attitude in Ketut's family about her condition, and their willingness to share it with a foreigner and associated film crew. At no time was there reluctance or hesitation about them narrating and interpreting her story, and the story of the family. Indeed, both her husband and children seemed extraordinarily protective when they spoke for and about Ketut.

After these initial meetings in 1997, while local collaborators occasionally got updates from Ketut and her family, Ketut was not formally interviewed again until 2008. The long lapse of time was due to involvement in other projects, and in fact at that point, Ketut was not going to be included as a participant in the emerging *Afflictions* series. It was only as *Afflictions* evolved that a role for her began to emerge; however, in 2008 just what aspects of her story might be focused on or what role she might have in a film was only slightly theorized.

Ketut had quite visibly aged in the preceding years. In addition, she seemed quite withdrawn when the team showed up with a small camera crew, presenting a very different social face than when she was first shot in 1997. Her countenance was sad and frightened, and she did not want to come out of her darkened bedroom. Given this, Ketut was not asked to make an entrance or participate in the film project. Instead, extensive interviews were conducted with her grown children and family. In addition, remarkably, her father was still alive, well into his late eighties or early nineties, and seemed *compos mentis*. A fascinating interview unfolded about not only his experience in World War II and Indonesia's war of independence from the Dutch (1945–1949), but also how both the wars and the intense privation and suffering experienced all through Bali played an influential role in Ketut's childhood. The confluence of his story and the obviously warm and supportive environment that the family had created to support Ketut in her illness became touchstones for the emerging story of *Ritual Burdens* (Lemelson 2011).

It was interesting to see how Ketut's attitudes and ideas about the film project changed over time. The original interview took place in 1997. The family was visited intermittently to film over the following decade, between 1997 and 2008, and renewed a more in-depth relationship and filming schedule with the family from 2008 to 2010. This long research period had been punctuated by rather severe episodes of mental illness that had often required Ketut to be hospitalized. At various points she had clearly decompensated, and during one visit was not even able to leave her room to participate in an interview. On other occasions she was able to more actively participate, even though her physical appearance and social presentation were markedly affected by her illness, and over more than a decade of filming increasingly displayed the ravages of time.

Some of these ravages are due to the natural course of aging, and having lived through traumas that have left their mark on Ketut's countenance, but some of these ravages are specific to the course of the treatment of her mental illness. Ketut is being treated with long-term antipsychotic/neuroleptic medication, which is most useful in treating schizophrenia. Ketut does have some symptoms that overlap with schizophrenia, in particular feelings of paranoia; however, as explained above these feelings may be culturally more normative rather than a clinical symptom. Furthermore, schizophrenia is usually characterized by many symptoms Ketut does *not* exhibit, such as the positive Schneiderian first rank symptoms of delusions and hallucinations. While it may seem that she has some of the negative symptoms of schizophrenia, such as affective flattening and social withdrawal, these seem more reactive in nature and related to a sense of fear and paranoia rather than a primary illness marker of schizophrenia or related thought disorder.

The diagnosis of bipolar disorder, raised in initial meetings by her Balinese psychiatrist but not reflected in much or her treatment, may more accurately reflect Ketut's condition. Bipolar causes unusual shifts in mood, energy, sleep patterns, and the inability to carry out day-to-day tasks. Those with bipolar disorder will experience unusually intense emotional states that occur in distinct periods called "mood episodes," euphoric or overexcited manic episodes, or extremely sad or inactive depressive episodes. Sometimes, a mood episode includes symptoms of both, hence known as a mixed state. People with bipolar disorder also may be explosive and irritable during a mood episode.

Bipolar illness is usually treated with a mood stabilizer, such as lithium (Martin 2007). However, lithium treatment is more difficult to implement than an antipsychotic because its dosage and prescription require the monitoring of lithium carbonate blood levels. Currently, the only laboratory in Indonesia available for these blood tests is in Jakarta, making such monitoring expensive and inconvenient. Antipsychotic medication is effective in its behaviorally inhibiting effect, but does not necessarily ameliorate the core causes or symptoms of bipolar disorder. Meanwhile, antipsychotics, due to their effects of dopaminergic production and uptake physiology that leads to low levels in the central nervous system, causes side effects that lithium does not, including that of tardive dyskinesia, which leads to uncontrollable twitching of the mouth and eyebrows. Tardive dyskinesia, after its initial onset, can be irreversible. These side effects are visible throughout the film, and unfortunately as visible and continuous markers of difference are deeply stigmatizing in her community, they have also led to long-term physical effects of stiffness and pain in her jaw, causing her much distress.

8.5   Last Encounters

In 2010, a polished rough cut of what would become *Ritual Burdens* was completed. Ketut and her family were shown the film to get their reactions and feedback. Her family clearly and enthusiastically gave their permission for the film to be screened in a variety of different contexts. They were very supportive of the larger mission of the *Afflictions* project and valued the process of honestly documenting and representing their mother's experience living with ongoing mental illness (although, as discussed, they purposefully rejected the explanatory model of "mental illness" in favor of indigenous ideas about "burdens" and "stress").

But there was another burden on the film project. The final screening with Ni Ketut Kasih in 2013 came at a cost. In the early sequences, she seemed to enjoy seeing footage of her younger self and of her husband, who had passed away a number of years earlier. However, as the film went on, Ketut grew increasingly upset and requested that the screening computer be turned off, as watching herself age, struggle with episodes of illness, and exhibit the side effect of her tardive dyskinesia on-screen proved too painful for her to bear. It was overwhelming to see herself, younger and seemingly happier, and to think of all she had missed in life.

Ni Ketut   I'm confused, sir, I'm confused if I remember.

And then:

Son   Why are you crying? Hey.
Daughter   Mother, you shouldn't cry, Mother.
Ketut   I'm stressed. I'm stressed (continues weeping). Oh No! Stop!

At this point the film was stopped, but it was some time before Ketut stopped crying. Her family noted how sad she was, remembering the past and all she had lost. Ketut then asked for her medicine, so she could "forget and go to sleep." Her family got it for her, Ketut went to her bedroom, and the lead author and crew said goodbye one last time to Ketut and her family.

REFERENCES

Bateson, Gregory, and Margaret Mead. 1942. *Balinese Character: A Photographic Analysis*. Special Publications of the New York Academy of Sciences, ed. W. G. Valentine, vol II. New York: The New York Academy of Sciences.

Freud, Sigmund. 1934. *The Future of an Illusion*. London: Hogarth Press.

Geertz, Hildred. 1991. *State and Society in Bali: Historical, Textual, and Anthropological Approaches*. Leiden: Brill.

Hacking, Ian. 1995. The Looping Effects of Human Kinds. In *Causal Cognition: An Interdisciplinary Approach*, ed. Dan Sperber, David Premack, and Ann J. Premack, 351–383. Oxford: Oxford University Press.

Heider, Karl. 1991. *Landscapes of Emotion: Mapping Three Cultures of Emotion in Indonesia*. Cambridge: Cambridge University Press.

Heider, Karl G. 2011. *The Cultural Context of Emotion: Folk Psychology in West Sumatra*. New York: Palgrave Macmillan.

Hinton, Devon E., David Howes, and Laurence J. Kirmayer. 2008. Toward a Medical Anthropology of Sensations: Definitions and Research Agenda. *Transcultural Psychiatry* 45 (2): 142–162. doi:10.1177/1363461508089763

Hollan, Douglas, and Jane C. Wellankamp. 1994. *Contentment and Suffering: Culture and Experience in Toraja*. New York: Columbia University Press.

Hollan, Douglas, and Jane C. Wellenkamp. 1996. *The Thread of Life: Toraja Reflections on the Life Cycle*. Honolulu: University of Hawaii Press.

Jensen, Gordon D., and Luh K. Suryani. 1992. *The Balinese People: A Reinvestigation of Character*. New York: Oxford University Press.

Kardiner, Abram, and Ralph Linton. 1974. *The Individual and His Society: The Psychodynamics of Primitive Social Organization*. Westport: Greenwood Press.

Kardiner, Abram, Ralph Linton, Cora A. Du Bois, and Carl Withers. 1945. *The Psychological Frontiers of Society*. New York: Columbia University Press.

Lemelson, Robert. 2011. *Ritual Burdens*. 25 min. Watertown: Documentary Educational Resources. http://www.der.org/films/ritual-burdens.html

Martin, Emily. 2007. *Bipolar Expeditions: Mania and Depression in American Culture*. Princeton: Princeton University Press.

Schwartz, Theodore. 1973. Cult and Context: The Paranoid Ethos in Melanesia. *Ethos* 1 (2): 153–174.

Whiting, John W.M. 1953. Review of Growth and Culture, a Photographic Study of Balinese Childhood, Margaret Mead and Frances Cooke MacGregor. *American Anthropologist* 55 (2): 262–263.

Wikan, Unni. 1990. *Managing Turbulent Hearts: A Balinese Formula for Living*. Chicago: University of Chicago Press.

CHAPTER 9

Kites and Monsters: Continuity in Cultural Practices

Photo 9.1 Wayan Adi Yoga Suwarduana

9.1 STORY SUMMARY

Wayan Yoga is a young Balinese man in his early twenties. He is pleasant, energetic, and unself-conscious, with many hobbies and interests including cooking, drawing, and the traditional Balinese arts of music and dance. He lives in the same patrilineal family compound where he was born, maintains

© The Author(s) 2017
R. Lemelson, A. Tucker, *Afflictions*, Culture, Mind, and Society,
DOI 10.1007/978-3-319-59984-7_9

a bustling social life, and is actively dating while planning his career as chef on a cruise ship or at a hotel. Wayan has TS, but he seems to barely notice it; both he and his family de-emphasize its role in his overwhelmingly positive and normative young adulthood, instead demonstrating how the stability and continuity of loving family support has bolstered him through his childhood and adolescence.

Wayan Yoga was born in urban South Bali, the elder of two boys living in a warm and lively extended family compound. From a very early age, Wayan Yoga exhibited an interest in the arts. As a young child he was captivated by the monsters of Balinese mythology brought to life onstage in village theaters and folk storytelling practices and enjoyed drawing pictures of these creatures and dancing out the action of these dynamic tales. If not drawing or dancing, he could be found fishing or flying kites with the other boys from the neighborhood.

When Wayan was about four and a half years old, his family noticed he was blinking frequently and severely, and repetitively yelling out "dirty" words and phrases such as "bitch," "fuck," "cunt of the dog," and so on. He would also flex and release his stomach muscles in an exaggerated manner, and he seemed to have difficulty focusing his attention. He had become deeply interested, in a way not shared by his young friends, with the monsters, giants, and other terrifying creatures from Balinese mythology, talking about them all the time and describing bloody battles between them and humankind. The family was concerned and uncomfortable with his behavior, in particular with his shouting of inappropriate words, so his father took him to see the doctor on staff at the hotel where he worked. The doctor prescribed some medication, which did not have a marked effect. The family then took Wayan to a traditional healer, but Wayan's condition did not improve after this visit either. His father called a family meeting and after consulting with the group, decided to pursue further medical treatment with a specialist. In doing so, he found Dr. I Gusti Putu Panteri who did an initial evaluation. He diagnosed Wayan with TS and ADHD and prescribed a low dose of Haloperidol, an antipsychotic medication that is a front line treatment for TS in Bali.

Dr. Panteri presented the neurobiological model of TS to the family, explaining to them that Wayan's behaviors were to a great extent out of his control, but that he was otherwise perfectly normal and healthy. Dr. Panteri explained that there were other Balinese people with TS, and he counseled the family not to get angry or upset at Wayan, not to think of him as "naughty" and not to worry about him too much, but to support him and to become an advocate for him when necessary, encouraging them to educate others about TS. Once Wayan entered elementary school, the family did in fact explain his condition to his teachers and peers so that he would not be stigmatized or punished in school. They also adhered to the pharmacological regimen prescribed by Dr. Panteri, monitoring Wayans intake of Haldol.

As he grew, Wayan continued to experience symptoms as the disorder progressed, in parallel to brain development and maturation. When he was eight, he was regularly taking his medication but continued to display occasional bizarre movements and still had difficulty focusing for long periods of time. However, his parents remained convinced that his encounter and treatment with the psychiatrist had been a turning point in Wayan's behavior, after which he more or less continued to do well. His relationships with his peers were normal and he still enjoyed flying kites and drawing. The family took every effort to include Wayan in family activities, and if it seemed that he was isolating himself or seemed to be in a dissociated state of consciousness, they would try to engage him.

By his middle adolescence, Wayan was still occasionally experiencing new symptoms—he no longer moved his stomach or shouted out inappropriate words but would flap his arms and jiggle his hands, especially when he was relaxing watching television in the evenings. Due to changes in the family's economic situation, they could not afford the prescription medication for Wayan but were using Chinese herbal medicine and felt that it had a positive effect. Wayan seemed not to have internalized any negative feelings about himself due to his movements, maintaining an active social life; indeed, because his peers and family members were so used to his movements, they didn't pay much attention to them. Wayan, confident in his emerging manhood, said that if anyone dared tease him about these movements that were out of his control he would knock them about a bit to teach them a lesson. He seemed to naturally grow out of his childhood over-involvement with demons and monsters, although his affinity for kites had deepened, and he was now making his own, which were quite beautiful.

After he graduated from high school, Wayan attended culinary school in order to get a job on a cruise ship as his cousin had done, a job that can be quite prestigious in Indonesia because of the relatively high salary. If that did not work out, he planned to work in a hotel like his father. After initial nerves about attending school, Wayan reminded himself that if he put his mind to it, he could achieve anything, and now he feels confident preparing various meals. His family currently describes his symptoms as in almost total remission, only emerging when he feels stressed, despite the fact that he is no longer taking any medicine. He is actively and optimistically planning for his future as a husband, father, and family man, still passing his free time building kites, drawing, playing music, dancing, and hanging out with his neighbors playing computer games.

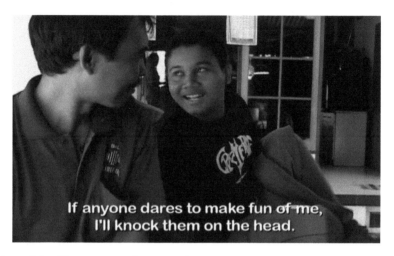

If anyone dares to make fun of me, I'll knock them on the head.

Photo 9.2   Wayan Yoga refuses to be bullied because of his disorder

Wayan's TS has been relatively insignificant to his evolving sense of self when compared to the saturation of symbols, images, and narratives of his culture. Wayan had to learn to negotiate the kinds of movements caused by TS, his levels of interest in morbid matters, and he had to develop goals that were culturally appropriate. The protective buffer of his family guided him successfully into normative Balinese adulthood.

9.2   Normalizing Unusual Movements

Wayan and his family fairly quickly embraced a psychiatric model of TS. At first glance, this model might not seem "continuous" with Balinese culture because it offers a very different etiological view of tic symptoms than is consistent with Balinese explanatory models around etiology. However, in the case of a neuropsychiatric disorder such as TS, a psychiatric perspective may have provided a sense of stability or continuity, rather than disruption, for Wayan and his family.

In some cases, a psychiatric model of neuropsychiatric disorders might free people from the quest for meaning in their illness experience which, while perhaps counterintuitive, in the case of TS and other disorders such as OCD may in and of itself bring great relief. From an insider's perspective, the movements and behaviors of TS are experienced as meaningless, albeit compulsory. However, the meanings ascribed to them in Balinese healing logic might add layers of distress to the experience, as patients contend with accusations of black magic, fears of having made ritual mistakes, or an internalized sense of being punished, in sum, indicating that something has gone significantly wrong in their social circle and/or spiritual lives. In Gusti's experience, this was clearly the case. Meanwhile, Wayan Yoga's experience attests to the potential benefits of a neurobiological explanation for illness or difference, which in effect suggests that the tic and other behaviors involved in TS are in fact "meaningless," indicating nothing more than a neurological disorder that is unrelated to cosmological order, interpersonal or community relations, or even personal intention or agency.

There also appeared to be some congruity between Wayan's symptoms and Balinese performance culture and gendered aesthetic. First, there were Wayan's obsessions when he was a little boy. His parents reported his obsession with fearsome characters from folklore and mythology, including *ogoh-ogoh*, or monsters, *buta kala*, or evil spirits, and *Rangda*, the Balinese witch. He relished retelling stories featuring these characters and the violence they do to human beings, and often recounted and re-enacted these for local collaborators. Given the previously described co-occurrence with OCD and ADHD, these thoughts should not be considered unusual; OCD often encompasses recurring thoughts of a morbid, sexual, or violent nature, such as hurting others, even though the person with these thoughts would never follow through on this (Bouvard et al. 2016; Wetterneck et al. 2015), while ADHD can be associated with impulsivity and aggression due to disinhibition (Ahmad and Hinshaw 2016). At the same time, folk tales filled with a kind of gleeful violence can be found throughout the world and are often greatly enjoyed by children and adults (and some might even argue these folk tales are cathartic or therapeutic) (Bascom 1954; Johnson and Price-Williams 1996). The content of Wayan's obsessions was to a certain extent both culturally and developmentally normative and appropriate, even though his level of engagement with them was not. As he matured, with the support of his family Wayan redirected his attention into other culturally available and appropriate activities, such as kite building and dancing.

Even the physical expression of Wayan's tics might have seemed culturally normative. While his family did perceive his physical movements as somewhat unusual and out of place, in and of themselves they also seemed familiar. As opposed to women, like Gusti, who are expected to be composed and decorous, men are allowed a wider range of dynamic physical expression, normatively "active" and "self-projecting" (Parker 1997), and "bolder, noisier, and more 'forward' in their socializing" (Parker 2004, p. 304). Therefore, while it is certainly not normative per se for young boys to shout out curses, it may be slightly less obtrusive, or more likely to be forgiven or overlooked in boys.

As in Gusti's case, performance genres may have also provided a framework of interpretation or intelligibility for Wayan's explosive movements. In contrast to the embodied and expected female habitus of smooth, contained, and gentle movement, both men and male dancers have a freer range of motion, with different permissible and even admirable movement qualities, some of which may be quite explosive and staccato. Like Gusti, some of Wayan's tics seemed to mimic the movements performed in traditional dances, particularly the repetitive inflating and constricting of his stomach muscles and the tensing of his arms bent at the elbow. Indeed when Wayan's father re-creates his son's tics, he could easily be thought to be referencing Balinese dance. In Wayan's case, however, these movements are congruent with the movements of revered male characters, including warriors in the Balinese *Baris* dance and kings in the *Topeng Tua* dance, movements Wayan in fact performs proudly for the camera near the end of the film. Therefore, while his tic movements are out of context, they are not inherently incongruous with a culturally constructed gender identity and hence not in and of themselves devaluing.

Like Gusti was, Wayan is surrounded by and embedded in a rich base of intricate artistic production and cultural forms. These interact with the symptoms of their neuropsychiatric disorder, acting as a central frame of reference for interpreting their physical comportment and expression, both directly and consciously and perhaps unconsciously lending positive or negative value to certain physical qualities or behaviors and embodied gender norms and ideals.

Photo 9.3 Wayan Yoga, now an adult, continues his artistic endeavors

An emphasis on Wayan's essential nature that remained unchanged, as a backdrop to what was framed as a comparatively insignificant disorder, may have set up Wayan and his family well to actually allow him to "grow out" of his TS. Research into TS increasingly suggests that it might be a developmental disorder, meaning that it occurs or arises during a particular stage in child development, retarding or interfering with typical development processes. Some developmental disorders lead to lifelong difficulties, but for others naturally occurring developmental processes ultimately mitigate the disorder, and symptoms fall away to a significant extent by the time an individual has reached adulthood. This hypothesis is supported by data gathered in two of the largest fMRI studies of TS conducted to date, which identified age-related abnormalities in frontostriatal networks and in frontoparietal connectivity, suggesting that TS patients are not undergoing typical maturational changes in the brain (Marsh et al. 2008; Church et al. 2009). However, tics and symptoms of TS can often fade once the person develops out of adolescence into young adulthood (Felling and Singer 2011).

In other words, even if an individual with TS receives little in the form of targeted treatment or therapy, over time his or her symptoms may subside on their own. Wayan's TS indeed seems to have followed this course; while initially the family believed that the prescribed medication was at most causing and at least supporting their son's improvement, after a number of years they were forced to stop giving him the medication due to financial hardship. His tics seemed to remain mostly in remission, and they believed he continued to improve.

Since the WHO's DOSMD study, much has been made of the protective aspects of culture outside the industrialized West; in the case of Wayan Yoga, family support and a meaningful social role in his community have promoted his positive long-term outcome. His life story embodies the "good" (Robbins 2013) of continuity, which is explored ethnographically within Yoga's family and the matrix of Balinese cultural practices that have buffered his normative development; the idea of "continuity" is also explored as a filmmaking strategy, returning to Wayan's home at regular intervals throughout his childhood and young adulthood, exploring similar topics, such as symptoms, treatment, social experience, and so on, and filming similar interactions, in order to capture the stability and positive growth Wayan enjoyed over the years despite living with a neuropsychiatric disorder.

9.3   LONGITUDINAL FIELDWORK AND A CHILD'S GROWTH

Wayan Yoga's case is unusual or even an outlier in the rest of the *Afflictions* series. For one, it is the only story that involves a young child, although through the course of the film the young child grows into a young adult. This raised some issues, particularly with regard to consent; a five year old is unable to give full consent and this could be ethically problematic. Because Wayan's parents understand that the lead author is a researcher affiliated with their psychiatrist (Dr. Panteri), they gave us permission to film. At that point, in 1997 the plan was that the footage would be solely used for research and teaching purposes, rather than be crafted into an ethnographic film per se. This was explained to Wayan's parents and they readily gave consent. As the project developed over the years and there was evolving use of the material, detailed discussions of this material were held with the family. Once there was a rough cut, Wayan was already nineteen, so consent was discussed with him directly.

With each session of shooting the film there was more supportive material of Wayan dancing, drawing, narrating traditional Balinese mythological and cosmological narratives, kite building and kite flying, and finally playing musical instruments and building his career as a Balinese chef. By shooting these continuously over the years, it was easy to construct an edited narrative that linked these continuities over time. In addition, the film constructed animated sequences that not only illustrated stories Wayan was telling but also mirrored his development and developmental abilities as a creative young artist.

Wayan's case was unusual in other ways. Despite what could be considered comparatively positive outcomes for many of the *Afflictions* participants, his was, honestly, really the only "happy" story in the series. As in the story laid out in the film, Wayan's development and progression was shaped by these Balinese cultural practices as well as a supportive family, in conjunction with the gender and attribution issues discussed earlier. The story was a counterpoint to the rest of the stories in the series, and pointed out how the right mix of temperament and personality, combined with a supportive family and cultural environment, and additionally supported by an attributional and labeling model that de-emphasized stigmatization, could lead to the overwhelmingly positive outcome shown in the film. It also illustrates that, at least in ethnographic film, one does not necessarily need conflict or great suffering to make a film interesting on its own terms. Interesting contexts, some character development and change, and a degree of emotional resolution can be enough to create a satisfactory and interesting film.

9.4   LAST ENCOUNTERS

In our last interview, as seen in the last scenes in *Kites and Monsters* (Lemelson 2011a), Wayan had grown into a self-confident young man, hopeful for his future. He was asked, "When you were little ... you liked drawing and thinking about evil spirits. . .do you still like them? Do you still think about them or. . .?" He replied:

> No, no, but when it comes to Seclusion Holiday month I still make *Ogoh-Ogoh* of spirits (large paper-mache models for display in the village). I make them with my friends. But no, I do not think much about them.

Asked about his daily routine, he said:

> Oh, I come home, and sometimes sleep. I then play video games with my friends, or visit my girlfriends. I have two!

When asked about his future:

> Oh, of course I want to have children. How many depends on my capacity (to support them).

And, finally, his TS:

> Oh, it doesn't bother me anymore. That was in the past.

As he spoke he was drawing a beautiful Balinese landscape, and at the end of the interview, he gave this to the lead author, much as he had done when he was five, and eight, and fourteen. He agreed to do a dance performance, and play a pleasant melody on the *rindik*, a bamboo gamelan. As we drove away, Wayan could be seen outside trying to get his beloved kites into the air.

9.5   The "Outcome Paradox" Revisited

In the preface, it was mentioned that the "Outcome Paradox," or the finding that people diagnosed with schizophrenia do better in the developing world than in the developed world, was one of the reasons that the research that would eventually result in the *Afflictions* (Lemelson 2010a–2011) series was begun.

The six films of part two have provided contextualized, experience-near accounts of some of the factors that are relevant to the differential outcome paradox. The WHO studies were focused on schizophrenia, and three of the films in *Afflictions* (*Shadows and Illuminations* [Lemelson 2010c], *Ritual Burdens* [Lemelson 2011b], and *Memory of My Face* [Lemelson 2011c]) were on disorders related to schizophrenia. The other three (*Kites and Monsters* [Lemelson 2011a], *The Bird Dancer* [Lemelson 2010a], and *Family Victim* [Lemelson 2010b]) focused on neuropsychiatric disorders. Even recognizing the multiple differences in psychotic illness and neuropsychiatric disorders, the factors below contributed to differential outcome for both sets of disorders.

As we can see using the case method approach in *Afflictions*, the question of what factors lead to better or worse outcome for serious mental illness is complex and individualized, and neither the individual variation of personality strengths that can buffer stressors and lead to greater resilience, nor the biological factors leading to predisposition to developing these complex illnesses can be diminished. But in these case studies, out of the recurring commonalities that contribute to better outcome, almost all are sociocultural, rather than biological or psychopathological.

One of these commonalities is clearly the importance of family environment. *The Bird Dancer* demonstrates a negative example, where the rejecting, critical, and even at times abusive behavior of certain family members clearly exacerbated—if not actually caused—Gusti Ayu's unhappy condition. The continual stress of these circumstances certainly contributed to the exacerbation of her symptoms, and it could be argued that the stress response system, which clearly was frequently activated, further exacerbated her overall poor outcome in the early years. Also in *The Bird Dancer*, the lack of any local cultural explanatory label that could encompass the symptoms of her disorder, combined with an attribution of witchcraft or sorcery, contributed to her poor outcome.

The comparison with Wayan Yoga in *Kites and Monsters* could not be more profound. Yoga's very positive outcome is clearly related to a warm and supportive family environment, and the low level of stress further led to a diminution of his overall symptoms. The labeling at the onset of his condition as one of a "nerve disorder" caused a subsequent depersonalizing of the symptoms and reframed the problematic behaviors for the community, leading to positive community reception and little if any social rejection.

The situation in the psychoses-related disorders is somewhat more complex. Again, family played an important role in outcome in all of the three films. It is significant that not only were all three participants—Kereta, Bambang, and Ketut—married with children, but their families were all quite emotionally supportive, accepting their conditions and providing attributional and labeling alternatives. In Kereta's case, labeling his experiences as "over-involvement with the spirits" rather than a local variant of "madness" allowed him to return to his life and family after he would suffer a negative episode of symptom exacerbation. In Ni Ketut Kasih's case, while the family and Ketut herself recognized she had a "mental disorder," their attribution that the illness was caused by "too many burdens" took away the stigma of an illness not only due to disordered biology, but particularly to her life history and life circumstances. This allowed the family to take positive actions to reduce her "burdens" and continue to supply loving, compassionate social support.

In Bambang's case, however, his internalization of psychiatric diagnoses and labels contributed to his lingering sense of self as damaged and impotent, and almost certainly contributed to negative view of his prospects for a productive and happy life. This points to the growing influence of global-ization in shaping not only the material conditions of the lives of people living with mental illness, but their internal views of themselves and their relation to their illness experience.

Flexible daily and work routines and roles also played a role. Each of the characters in these three films was able to work on their own schedules, or be released from work responsibilities by their families when their condition deteriorated. This clearly reduced the stress on all three and allowed a resumption of a positive work identity when their symptoms allowed for it.

Access to treatment in the *Afflictions* series pointed out the strengths and weakness of both psychiatric/biomedical treatment and locally available traditional therapeutics. In all of the cases, medication at times assisted in diminishing the more severe exacerbations of the illnesses, but always came at some cost. The side effects of the medications that Gusti Ayu took were always too severe for her, and she discontinued all the medication pre-scribed. Kereta appreciated that the antipsychotic medication made his spirits diminish, but he too chose to discontinue its use. Ni Ketut Kasih's continuous ingestion of antipsychotics has led to her tardive dyskinesia, which she and the family feel can be more stigmatizing than the symptoms of her illness.

Similarly, traditional therapeutics functioned in variable ways. In Gusti Ayu's case, her search for healing caused her to go through numerous healings, which were at times painful, scarring, and humiliating, but did not ever lead to a diminution of her symptoms. Kereta had a very positive experience of social support with a healer, with whom he lived for over a month, but at the end, his wife did not agree with the therapeutics, prefer-ring "the pill" of biomedically oriented psychiatry to the "oil" of traditional therapeutics.

As can be seen by the above examples drawn from the films, when it comes to better or worse recovery, multiple factors interplay in highly individualized ways to create variably textured and distinct forms of adap-tation. One conclusion here is that while identifying the broad factors linked to differential outcome is extremely important, at the end each of these will play a somewhat different and distinct role in the lives of patients and their families. It is these distinctions, as filtered through story, narrative, and experiential accounts, that films such as those in the *Afflictions* series have the opportunity to highlight and emphasize not only for the researchers exploring the relation of culture and mental illness, but for the families and communities of those afflicted with these disorders.

REFERENCES

Ahmad, Shaikh I., and Stephen P. Hinshaw. 2016. Attention-Deficit/Hyperactivity Disorder, Trait Impulsivity, and Externalizing Behavior in a Longitudinal Sample. *Journal of Abnormal Child Psychology.* doi:10.1007/s10802-016-0226-9

Bascom, William R. 1954. Four Functions of Folklore. *The Journal of American Folklore* 67 (266): 333–349. doi:10.2307/536411

Bouvard, Martine, Nathalie Fournet, Anne Denis, Adelaide Sixdenier, and David Clark. 2016. Intrusive Thoughts in Patients with Obsessive Compulsive Disorder and Non-clinical Participants: A Comparison Using the International Intrusive Thought Interview Schedule. *Cognitive Behaviour Therapy.* 1–13. 10.1080/16506073.2016.1262894

Church, Jessica A., Damien A. Fair, Nico U.F. Dosenbach, Alexander L. Cohen, Francis M. Miezin, Steven E. Petersen, and Bradley L. Schlaggar. 2009. Control Networks in Paediatric Tourette Syndrome Show Immature and Anomalous Patterns of Functional Connectivity. *Brain* 132 (Pt 1): 225–238. doi:10.1093/brain/awn223

Felling, Ryan J., and Harvey S. Singer. 2011. Neurobiology of Tourette Syndrome: Current Status and Need for Further Investigation. *Journal of Neuroscience* 31 (35): 12387–12395. doi:10.1523/JNEUROSCI.0150-11.2011

Johnson, Allen W., and Douglass R. Price-Williams. 1996. *Oedipus Ubiquitous: The Family Complex in World Folk Literature.* Redwood City: Stanford University Press.

Lemelson, Robert. 2010a–2011. *Afflictions: Culture and Mental Illness in Indonesia Series.* 182 min. Watertown: Documentary Educational Resources. http://www.der.org/films/afflictions.html

———. 2010b. *The Bird Dancer*, from the *Afflictions: Culture and Mental Illness in Indonesia Series.* 40 min. Watertown: Documentary Educational Resources. http://www.der.org/films/bird-dancer.html

———. 2010c. *Family Victim*, from the *Afflictions: Culture and Mental Illness in Indonesia Series.* 38 min. Watertown: Documentary Educational Resources. http://www.der.org/films/family-victim.html

———. 2011a. *Kites and Monsters*, from the *Afflictions: Culture and Mental Illness in Indonesia Series.* 22 min. Watertown: Documentary Educational Resources. http://www.der.org/films/kites-and-monsters.html

———. 2011b. *Memory of My Face*, from the *Afflictions: Culture and Mental Illness in Indonesia Series.* 22 min. Watertown: Documentary Educational Resources. http://www.der.org/films/ritual-burdens.html

———. 2011c. *Ritual Burdens*, from the *Afflictions: Culture and Mental Illness in Indonesia Series.* 25 min. Watertown: Documentary Educational Resources. http://www.der.org/films/memory-of-my-face.html

Marsh, Rachel, Andrew J. Gerber, and Bradley S. Peterson. 2008. Neuroimaging Studies of Normal Brain Development and Their Relevance for Understanding Childhood Neuropsychiatric Disorders. *Journal of the American Academy of Child & Adolescent Psychiatry* 47 (11): 1233–1251. doi:10.1097/CHI. 0b013e318185e703

Parker, Lynette. 1997. Engendering School Children in Bali. *Journal of the Royal Anthropological Institute* 3 (3): 497–516. doi:10.2307/3034764

———. 2004. Balinese. *Encyclopedia of Sex and Gender* 1: 303–313.

Robbins, Joel M. 2013. Beyond the Suffering Subject: Toward an Anthropology of the Good. *Journal of the Royal Anthropological Institute* 19 (3): 447–462. doi:10.1111/1467-9655.12044

Wetterneck, Chad T., Jedidiah Siev, Thomas G. Adams, Joseph C. Slimowicz, and Angela H. Smith. 2015. Assessing Sexually Intrusive Thoughts: Parsing Unacceptable Thoughts on the Dimensional Obsessive-Compulsive Scale. *Behavior Therapy* 46 (4): 544–556. doi:10.1016/j.beth.2015.05.006

PART III

The Practice of Visual Psychological Anthropology

Photo 1   The story of the False Pedanda (From the Mead Bateson collection)

CHAPTER 10

The Process of Visual Psychological Anthropology

10.1 THEORY AND PRACTICE IN THE MAKING OF THE *AFFLICTIONS* SERIES: OUTLINE OF PART 3

How do films like the *Afflictions* (Lemelson 2010–2011) series get made? How might filmmakers work with subjects so that they choose to narrate the emotionally powerful stories of their lives? What are some of the technical issues involved? These are all essentially questions about "how to" make similar films. This final section of the book will answer these types of questions, from a personal, theoretical, and practical perspective.[1] It will diverge into the first person to the extent that some of the lessons learned are drawn from the personal experience of making the *Afflictions* series.

The first chapter in the section (Chap. 10) is organized around foundational film concepts not necessarily familiar to those in psychological anthropology, such as pre-production, production, and post-production. This is the longest chapter in the book, with the production process being described in some detail. This is to help prevent the novice filmmaker from foundering on the many shoals of the production process. If the reader is not interested in the specific technical details, she is encouraged to move on to the next chapter.

Chapter 11 addresses the more intangible but even more important issues one must grapple with when making the kinds of films described in this book, such as incorporating self-reflexivity; navigating the complexity of relationships that develop through filmmaking; and unpacking the ethics of filming, fieldwork, and representation. At the end of this section, the reader

© The Author(s) 2017
R. Lemelson, A. Tucker, *Afflictions*, Culture, Mind, and Society,
DOI 10.1007/978-3-319-59984-7_10

should have a good grasp of the many interlocking practical and theoretical aspects of a visual psychological anthropology.

The final chapter discusses the dissemination of edited films in teaching, public presentations, and the wider digital public sphere as an integral part of the work of visual psychological anthropology. The chapter concludes with some potential directions and prospects for visual psychological anthropology.

10.2   PRE-PRODUCTION: THEORETICAL POSITIONS AND PRACTICAL REALITIES

From the moment they are first conceptualized, the production of ethnographic films is both similar to, and different from, that of documentary or commercial films. Perhaps one of the most significant differences stems from the "bottom-up" and emergent approach of ethnography versus a "top-down" approach of these other types of films. All commercial films, and many documentaries, have a script and storyline in place before the shoot, which determines plans and schedules in the field. For example, a Hollywood commercial production can shoot two pages of script per day. One script page equals roughly one screen minute, so scripts are usually 120 pages for a two-hour film and shooting lasts for about three months. The total filming environment is controlled and to a great extent nothing is accidental (even if there are improvisational elements to the production), in a large part to meet budget restrictions.

This detailed pre-planning is less possible in ethnographic filmmaking, which seeks to capture "life as lived" and follows the natural unfolding of events. David MacDougall has called this "exploratory" documentary filmmaking (2003) and has argued for how exciting it can be; what is sacrificed in ease of planning and preparation is made up for in the investigative process as the film ends up reflecting what the anthropologist/filmmaker has learned during filming, some of which is bound to be unexpected, rather than reflecting an original unswerving idea. Instead of the shoot progressing according to a preconceived theme, the themes are emergent through shooting and editing.

One goal for the *Afflictions* films was to build on this exploratory nature of ethnographic film in the field to innovate forms of storytelling about ethnographic material that are more character- and emotion-driven than typical ethnographic film. Ethnographic methodologies were used to capture emergent events, and the work was inductive from these rather than from a script. The footage was then shaped into narratives that focused on those elements more than some other ethnographic films, which has traditionally emphasized the ethnographic content to the exclusion of a focus on character, emotion, aesthetics, or production values. As discussed throughout this book, visual psychological anthropology focuses as much on emotion, character, and narrative as on the didactic explication of cultural material. To do this requires skills beyond the psychological, anthropological, and linguistic; film production skills, too, are crucial to ending up with footage suitable for such a film.

There is also the need, as is the case in any creative process, to articulate a clear idea and vision for the project; to allow for the aforementioned emergence, this should be a delineation of the overall scope of the research, rather than a specific direction or structure for the film itself. For most, this will be based on the research that the anthropologist is already engaged in. Of course the resulting film may diverge in significant ways from the original research and its objectives, but the linkage will still be there (at least in the mind of the anthropologist, if not fully on-screen). For example, the Elemental Productions' film *40 Years of Silence* (Lemelson 2009) was intended to be an exploration of the role of childhood trauma and its variable outcomes in relation to historical events, specifically the mass killings of 1965 in Indonesia. As such, there was a much more clearly defined vision as to what the final film would look like from the very beginning of the project as compared to the *Afflictions* films. Although the narrative changed over the six years of the project, the basic idea and vision remained the same; from initial conception to final film release, *40 Years* was a factual documentary integrating historical accounts with personal narrative biographies of four families, to illustrate the effects of the violence and trauma on these families and by extension on broader Indonesian society. Elemental Productions' projects made after *Afflictions* (such as *Jathilan* [Lemelson 2011], *Ngaben* [Lemelson 2012], *Bitter Honey* [Lemelson 2015], and *Tajen* [Lemelson 2017]) went further to flesh out the general terms of what the finished film's story and aesthetic would be prior to shooting in the field, which to a significant degree made for a faster and more focused process. However, even with this method, much of the storyline and film trajectory comes from the research foci and the changes in the participants' lives, and therefore is by its very nature unknowable at the outset, and so still fundamentally emergent.

10.2.1   The Practicalities of Planning a Shoot

Once a film project is underway, several practical issues arise. The first is simply fundraising. Many anthropologists shoot their original material during their fieldwork, so funding brought to the table for original research can cover initial filming. Yet while this initial material may be crucial to begin many ethnographic film projects, it is rarely sufficient to finish them. Typically, one reviews raw footage, works it over in the editing process, and then discovers themes that need to be followed up on and content that needs to be shot, which requires returning to the field—but raising the funds to do so can be quite difficult. For a discussion on raising and managing funds for ethnographic filmmaking, see the website supplement that accompanies this book (see www.afflictionsbook.com).

That is not to say that films cannot be made entirely on one shoot. For example, to make the Elemental film *Ngaben*, which documented a Balinese funerary practice from the perspective of a grieving son, raw footage was shot over the course of three days in the field and then edited to completion upon return. No other material was needed and the short film that resulted was successful, in that it made its way into numerous film festivals and won some awards. But in terms of the amount of time necessary to make an ethnographic film, it is an outlier.

A second major planning task for any film shoot is discussing which images and scenes should ideally be shot. Such preparation aids in developing a tentative itinerary and gathering equipment. If particular projects are ongoing, then before heading to the field it is helpful to have preliminary discussions about ongoing projects, in consultation with local collaborators on the ground who can provide updates about the subjects' lives. By reviewing the narrative that is evolving in the editing process, the questions that have emerged through these edits, the gaps that have been found in previously gathered footage, any new information that has become apparent, and real-time developments in characters' lives, the needs for the filming can be assessed and a tentative shot list drawn up. This shot list can include anything from topics to be covered in interviews to descriptive or elaborative B-roll needs. From the shot list, a preliminary shooting schedule and trip itinerary can be determined as to where one will go to shoot, how long one will stay in a particular site, and what shots can be gotten at each site.

This schedule of course depends on the available time frame. If one plans on being in the field for one to two years, as is common with dissertation fieldwork, there is the luxury of shooting more or less continuously for long periods of time, documenting subjects' lived experiences as they naturally occur and recording the numerous unfolding aspects of the research and cultural setting. In many ways, this way of filmmaking is preferable. An extended stay in the field with a regular shooting schedule allows a filmmaker to capture daily life, in all its depth and complexity—but even more importantly, it allows for the capture of events as they spontaneously occur, be these life cycle events such as births, deaths, and weddings; political and historical events; changes in the onset, course, and outcome of illness; and idiosyncratic developments in subjects' lives, to name but a few. The ensuing footage will have the look and feel of "life as lived" rather than "life as told" (Bruner 1984), and one can get, in Heider's framework, more "whole sequences" of events (1976), particularly ones that depend on a longer span of time to unfold. This allows for less reliance on the artificialities of "interviews, cutting away to B-roll" standard to journalism, but problematic for ethnographic film, which strives for realism and authenticity.

In addition to these real-time developments, another benefit of ongoing filming is that subjects may become more inured to the camera's presence, sometimes to the extent that it even ceases to be consciously noticed, thus arguably resulting in material less influenced by the camera's presence.

For a variety of logistical reasons, however, the *Afflictions* shooting schedule has not allowed for a long period in the field. Although still benefitting from a longitudinal approach, the series was predominantly shot during two- to five-week-long "summer shoots." This temporal limitation, which is common to most anthropologists with university teaching schedules, certainly shapes filmmaking methods, particularly in gathering the stories and narratives from which to build plot lines and character development arcs. However, if one is committed to longer-term film projects, rather than a singular shoot, there can be benefits to "going and returning." Relationships with participants can be strengthened, as participants begin to expect or even anticipate the anthropologist's return and over time a relationship develops. One can see changes over time in a wide range of domains, which can lead to a deeper understanding of one's material—some changes might be more apparent due to temporary distance from the subjects. Finally, one can follow up on themes that arise in the edit, and fill in missing shots or material on these subsequent shoots.

When returning to the field on the second, third, or fourth shoot, with somewhat more limited time, it is important to develop a solid production schedule in pre-production. Typically, at this stage one creates interview schedules and domains that need to be covered for the film as well as specific shot lists of the B-roll or "insertion" shots. Of course, all these are flexible in the exigencies of a specific shoot, but these lists do need to be thought through and compiled.

Before departure there are the practical aspects of arranging accommodations, communicating with local colleagues and collaborators, and acquiring any necessary filming visas (the complexity of which should not be underestimated!). It takes at least three to six months before the shoot to get the appropriate filming visas, which are often not included under a more general research visa. This is made all the more important if one is documenting sensitive subjects of a political nature; telling a governmental agency that one is going to do a documentary on a politically sensitive topic often raises red flags and could potentially cause the visa to be denied, shutting down the film project.[2]

Photo 10.1   Lemelson discusses the shoot with Kereta

10.2.1.1 Equipment Choices

Another practical preproduction issue is what equipment to bring, and how much. The discussion below uses the history of the *Afflictions* production (and other films) in relation to changes in technology and subsequently to the nature of what can be filmed.

If one has limited resources and is planning to shoot solo, the discussion is straightforward, as equipment will necessarily be limited to a single camera, an onboard mic, the best possible tripod one can afford, an external audio recording device and microphone, and perhaps one or two lights or flexfolds. A more complex shoot requires careful thought about what equipment, in particular camera equipment, to bring. Before leaving on a production shoot, equipment must be organized based on shooting needs. Depending on the staffing and how many shooters are available, two cameras can be dedicated to shooting interview footage, one of which can also be used for additional B-roll, and the other one reserved as a general backup camera. This may seem an obvious point, but in gathering equipment one should always prepare for contingencies, bringing not just extra cameras in case one breaks but backups of crucial equipment.

Technological changes affect shooting and production to the extent that the camera used influences the kinds of shots that can be gathered. Elemental Productions has used different cameras over the last fifteen years, following these technological developments. The first camera was the VX 1000, a Sony camera that was really the first "prosumer" camera. It shot onto mini DV tapes; it was small, durable, and unobtrusive; it was easy to use; and had a good lens. This camera was used through the early 2000s, and then replaced with other, more professional but also larger cameras (the Sony PD 150 and the Sony PD 170); these had greater flexibility in terms of aperture and f-stop settings and thus a better ability to create different depths of field and shoot in lower light settings than the VX 1000 but was still much less bulky and intrusive than tape cameras of that era, which were often large, shoulder mounted, and heavy.

From 2000 to 2006, a 16-mm camera (the Arriflex S) was in frequent use. The Arriflex yielded much more lush, vibrant images than the standard definition video cameras and was configured to shoot time-lapse; these visuals can be seen sprinkled through the *Afflictions* series. A small 8-mm camera was also occasionally used. Its images had a "home movie" feel—quite granular and lacking the clarity of a 16-mm camera—but was still useful to create an atmosphere of intimacy in some *Afflictions* scenes.

With the new availability of powerful high-definition cameras in the mid-2000s, 8 and 16-mm cameras were substituted with modern high-definition cameras, which provided the same look and feel without the expense and hassle of developing film, transferring this film to a video format (telecine), and then digitizing that tape so it could be read by an editing system. Another transition was the introduction of digital single lens reflex (DSLR) cameras with interchangeable lenses. These cameras are small and unobtrusive, looking no different than the cameras that many tourists in Bali and Java use on a daily basis, and thus tended to feel less intrusive to the participants than larger film cameras. With the advent of cameras such as the Sony CX 100 and CX 300, which combined the power of a traditional video camera with the ease and size of a DSLR, shot quality improved and the ability to shoot in many different light settings increased. All of these cameras are available for rent, so a great quality camera can still be accessible without the expense of purchase.

Recently, Elemental has increased its use of GoPro cameras, which are tiny cameras initially developed for extreme sports now being adapted for use in feature and documentary films. These cameras can be placed or affixed in many different ways and allow the filmmaker access to visual perspectives that were previously unobtainable. We have not yet shot with smart phones, though it would certainly be possible to do so with the latest generation with 12 megapixel or above resolutions and 4 K sizes. Many new options are on the horizon, such as the possibility of using virtual reality cameras that shoot in 360 degrees, which could have profound implications for shooting the "gestalt" of a fieldwork setting.

10.2.1.2 Managing Footage

Once in the field, each crewmember should have an "objectives list" of shots to be gathered. If there is more than one cameraperson, they may split up and travel to different locations. The organization of footage should start in the field as soon as it is gathered. Each cameraperson should have a logbook which, in addition to containing itineraries, schedules, and so on, should have pages for reporting information about all shots filmed, including date, location, affiliated project, camera used, shot location, and a brief synopsis of the shoot including characters filmed and what happened during the filming, and finally the drives and the folder number to which the footage has been or will be uploaded.

These drives or folders refer to the location to which the footage is then transferred. Every evening in the field, footage should be transferred, or "dumped" off of each individual camera into computers. "Prep folders" should be prepared for each camera, which are pre-made file folders based on the previously established dates and itineraries, and the footage should be offloaded into the folder pre-designated for each specific camera and date. The footage should be offloaded from the cameras onto two "mirror" external hard drives, each containing an exact replica of the totality of footage gathered, to decrease chances of losing material in the case of equipment loss or damage. All of the file structure, folders, and so on should be created on the computer before one goes to the field to ensure consistency in the process of transferring the footage each day to a hard disk.

With the advent of digital media, it is easier than ever for material to be transferred, which means that it is also easier for data to get mixed up, misplaced, or lost; so these prep folders are an important first step in keeping everything accessible and organized. It cannot be stressed enough how important it is to have a disciplined naming convention and offloading practice in the field. Without these, upon return it will be difficult to manage footage, leading to much wasted time and effort.

In addition, it helps to remember that shooting rarely goes exactly according to plan—sometimes schedules change and desired footage cannot be acquired, and sometimes opportunities arise that lead to excellent but unanticipated footage shot on the spot. Cross-checking with the logbooks, which function as supplements to the digital folders, enables clear record keeping of every shot recorded, even unexpected or serendipitous ones.

10.3   PRODUCTION: MULTIPLE ISSUES AND SOLUTIONS

After all the extensive theorizing, planning, organizing, and gathering resources, both financial and technological, one can begin the production stage, which is the heart of any film. In one sense, the production process is very technical—getting the right types and amounts of shots, having them well composed and clean, and gathering usable and compelling audio (all of these will be discussed below).

10.3.1   Gaining Multiple Visual Perspectives Through a Range of Shots

A first goal for any productive shoot is to acquire usable and aesthetic visual material. A number of different types of shots should be considered. "Establishing shots" of any shooting locale are good for initially contextualizing the participant's experience and providing aspects of the surrounding environment that the audience will be able to identify, from rice paddies to city landmarks. Great landscape and other aesthetic images can lend a film visual appeal when used as establishing shots, but care must be taken not to exoticize or otherwise misrepresent the lived environment of the main subject(s).

Sometimes searching for establishing shots results in extraordinary footage. For example, during one shoot in 2010 in Yogyakarta gathering footage for *Family Victim* (Lemelson 2010b), the famous volcano Mt. Merapi erupted. Mt. Merapi is a visually distinctive feature of the Yogyakarta landscape and a mystical and spiritual landmark believed to be linked to the local Sultan and the well-being of the region. Shots of the volcano's foreboding dark plumes of smoke pouring out into the air were ultimately used to introduce themes of uncontrollable forces and volatility in another Elemental Productions' film about trance possession performance, *Jathilan* (Lemelson 2011b).

In addition to establishing shots, other supporting visual material is necessary to visual psychological anthropology. Some time in the field is always dedicated to shooting "B-roll" in addition to interview and action footage. B-roll is secondary footage that can be edited in to add meaning, texture, elaboration, and a sense of place to the primary interviews and action. This footage can also be intercut into longer interviews to preserve a sense of visual dynamism, illustrate important themes or concepts in the subjects' lives, and it can provide background and insight into those lives by providing an embodied, sensory, and subjective sense of their daily lives and routine. In *Afflictions*, different kinds of B-roll were needed: uniquely Indonesian, Javanese, or Balinese images that would help viewers contextualize or place the characters; footage supporting the narrative development of an ongoing project; and new or emergent footage. Additional B-roll is gathered as new interviews unfold, new participants are brought into a narrative, and subjects and crew enter new situations.

This "non-edit-specific B-roll" develops organically from what interviewees do and say. Even so, the anthropologist's background knowledge is useful. For example, over the course of filming *The Bird Dancer*, two different aspects of Gusti's experience crystallized; first, her isolation from her family and community, and later, her emerging sense of connectedness as a result of both internal changes in her self-concept and external changes in her work circumstances that gave her a sense of belonging and purpose. Sequences illustrating both these aspects of her story were actually filmed in the same shoot. Knowing that there was a bustling and colorful marketplace in Denpasar, about an hour south from Gusti's natal compound, and that the light in late afternoon (i.e. "golden hour") was generally quite good as compared to the frequent overcast skies in the region where Gusti lived, the crew took Gusti there. First she was filmed interacting with Balinese merchants and shoppers to illustrate the latter theme of connectedness, but then shots were also taken of her standing on a busy street, looking forlornly toward the camera as waves of traffic passed her by, to illustrate her isolation in the midst of a dense social world (perhaps an at the time unconscious visual homage to Edgerton's 1979 *Alone Together* ethnography about Venice beach in Los Angeles). Thus, in the same shoot B-roll was taken that illustrated very different psychological themes explored at different points in the film.

10.3.2 Creative Re-enactments

Gusti Ayu's role in participating in these "set" shots, where a subject is specifically asked to do something as opposed to more "naturalistic" ones where the subject is simply being documented going about their daily activities, points to a degree of artifice in some ethnographic film shoots. The decision to engage in this artifice has been contested through the history of ethnographic film and visual anthropology. Early anthropologists, such as Malinowski and Evans-Pritchard, emphasized the "normal and spontaneous" nature of their visual documentation and hence the "disciplinary truth" of their images (Banks and Ruby 2011). Other early anthropologists were sure to note whether or not an image was posed, captured during the natural unfolding of events, or recorded in slightly atypical or staged circumstances, for technical reasons such as lighting, for example, or when capturing events of a more delicate or personal nature (Edwards 2011).

Mainstream documentary filmmaking has not been so strict; re-creations have been commonplace and are evident in recent films such as the Oscar-winning *Man on a Wire* (Marsh 2008) about tightrope walker Phillip Petit; Oscar-nominated *The Imposter* (Layton 2012); and *Burma VJ* (Østergaard 2009), an extraordinary film about the 2007–2008 Saffron Revolution where much of the observational material in the film was gathered surreptitiously and at great risk to the shooters, many of whom were later arrested and imprisoned. Other popular documentaries by esteemed contemporary filmmakers, such as Errol Morris, use re-created material extensively. Morris has been criticized because some of the scenes he re-created in his popular films such as *Thin Blue Line* (1988) and *Fog of War* (2003) were done with such professional expertise that they were indistinguishable from actual archival footage (Morris 2008); however, Morris, fascinated with the elusive and contested nature of truth, defends his use of re-enactment to highlight his interest in the interrogation of character's subjectivities (Jaffe 2005; Morris 2008).

An earlier example of the problematics of re-creations can be seen in the Lois Buñuel satirical and surrealistic film *Las Hurdes* ([Land Without Bread] 1933). During its time, this surrealist masterpiece was considered a model of documentary filmmaking, but some now consider it the first "mocku-mentary," in some ways presaging the Sasha Baron Cohen film *Borat* (2006) in its ironic underscoring of the "wretchedness" of the people it claims to be dispassionately observing. Much has been made of the staging of events in *Las Hurdes*—from an image of a dead donkey covered in bees (the donkey was smeared with honey to attract them), to staged shots of people to make them look wretched, to a(n) (in)famous shot of a mountain goat falling off a cliff.

In the first image, at the moment the goat slips in the distance, a puff of smoke appears in the lower right-hand side of the frame. A reverse angle match-on-action shot then shows the animal falling from above. From one image to the next, the camera shifts from one side of the mountain to the other. To fabricate an illusion of continuity, the film crew shot the goat, hauled its carcass up the side of the mountain, and threw it off again. By leaving the traces of this process in the film, however, the director under-mines the illusion and exposes the artifice of montage (Ruoff 1998).

When this clip is shown to students, a certain percentage of them take it as an observational shot of a naturally occurring and spontaneously observed event. It is always surprising that, absorbed in the cinematic world, these "digital natives" forget that it would be impossible for the cameras to be so precisely positioned without some setup. Given that Buñuel was almost certainly creating this film in a satirical tone, it is further surprising that eighty years later people are still taken in by this cinematic trickery. Due to expectations of ethnographic film's observational veracity and use as scientific "evidence," such re-enactment techniques remain uncommon.

Re-enactments/re-creations were used sparingly in *Afflictions*, avoided unless necessary due to the lack of directly observed ethnographic material or to illustrate the more ineffable aspects of subjects' experiences, such as hallucinations or visions. For example, in *Shadows and Illuminations*, Kereta's spirit visitations were represented by shots of several wooden masks of demonic spirits (B.B. *Buta Kala*), which were hung on strings and sticks in a rice paddy, their reflections flickering in the water.

Other sequences that similarly represented perceptions, ideas, or images that did not occur in real life were used in other films; such sequences are only restricted by the production team's creativity. For example, in *Family Victim*, Estu recalls a prescient dream wherein he saw a cocoon floating in a river from which a cricket emerged, became a butterfly, and flew away as his parents looked on. Estu claimed that this dream helped him overcome some of his negative inclinations and started a new chapter in his life. As this was a dream—and therefore entirely internal, and already by its very nature symbolic—it was theoretically and ethically unproblematic to re-create it.

The footage was shot at a rushing stream in Los Angeles using a pod from a wild cucumber plant that stood in for the cocoon; in the film, the pod floats down the stream, then there is a caterpillar crawling across a rock under two shadowy figures standing in for Estu's parents. Building on this naturalistic animal imagery used to underscore Estu's transformation, a subsequent slow motion shot of a bird harks back to an earlier image in the film; while previously the lone bird in the sky had represented his isolation, his desire for freedom, and his longing to overcome his problems, now it represented his success at achieving a life free from strife that the dream seemed to indicate was possible for him. A blue filter was added in the edit to give these shots a more dreamlike appearance.

While certainly venturing outside strict observational ethnography, and to a certain extent "re-creating" the experience of a visual hallucination or a dream, such artistic shots did not involve re-creating entire events from a participant's life.

Should re-enacting a more complex scene seem necessary for a film, there are number of theoretical and related production points to consider. From a theoretical perspective, it is crucial to create a visual distinction between a creative re-enactment and ethnographic footage. It would be intellectually dishonest and ethically problematic if the re-enactment were not easily distinguishable from observed footage. Perhaps counterintuitively, then, a mistake to avoid in shooting re-enactments is trying to make them "true to life." In other words, and in practical terms, the videographer should use techniques that call attention to the act of filming, such as extreme angles, fragmentary close-ups that obscure the protagonist's identity, or blurred focus. Creating this visually stylized difference between the "constructed" and "observational" footage can alert the viewer that a theatrical re-creation, rather than a direct recording of actual events, is being shown.

A rare example of an *Afflictions* re-enactment comes in an episode that falls about two-thirds of the way through the film *Family Victim*, when Estu attempts to kill his father. In real life, the research and film team arrived at Estu's house about a half hour after he ran "amok," and heard about the incident from horrified neighbors, Estu's sister Ninik, and his wife Anna. Much time was spent in the edit bay theorizing about how to represent this part of the story, which was a key incident in Estu's life and a key element in the overarching thematic development of the film. After numerous cuts, in which different versions of the story were tried out, a sequence was settled on. It worked well, except it lacked a visual component, since the team had not been physically present for Estu's outburst. This gap was filled in on a later shoot, in a series of re-creations.

In the scene depicting Estu's attempt to attack his father, a number of different visual strategies were employed. This resulted in a series of shots: first, a blurry shot of an actor banging angrily on the door from behind, followed by fragmented close-ups of feet walking out of a Javanese-style house, a shot of a hand holding a knife, and a distance shot of a departing motorcycle. These created a sense of continuity with the story narrated by Ninik and Anna, filled in the missing visuals to this dramatic section of the story, and yet were obviously visually distinct from the rest of the film to purposefully signal that these scenes were re-enacted.

Earlier in the film, a re-enactment was also used to illustrate the dramatic treatment one *dukun* described of bringing Estu to a graveyard; in this scene, a younger, thinner man pleads with an older, larger man, who then strikes him. This scene was shot with actors, seen only in silhouette, and the footage was altered by using a "day for night" effect (which transforms footage shot during the day so that it appears to be shot at night). Each of these techniques (day for night; silhouette) is a visual cue for the viewer that what they are watching is a re-creation.

Perhaps some viewers may still be confused about whether any of these shots were observational footage—much as some viewers are still confused as to whether Buñuel's footage of the goat falling off the cliff from different perspectives at once is directly observational. But unfortunately, one cannot account for all misperceptions raised by the medium of film. Such persistent misunderstanding has occurred when screening *Ritual Burdens*. In this film, the elderly main participant, Ketut Kasih, reflects on her childhood. To bring her memories to life, the film included evocative shots of a child playing and running, manipulated with a filter that made these appear hazy and in slow motion. At one screening, a member of the audience was very impressed that footage of the main participant was obtained from seventy years previously, not realizing that this was new B-roll shot for the research project. Despite these occasional misunderstandings, with the use of techniques intended to draw attention to the re-enacted shots, such instances of confusion are few and far between.

In summary, if and when re-enactment is used—even those simply depicting dreams, fantasies, and so on that never actually "happened"—it must be cued for the viewer as such by using a visual style distinct from the rest of the film. Creativity is welcome in developing this distinct style beyond the standard techniques discussed above—shooting from extreme angles, shooting partial parts of the body, not shooting the face directly, shooting in profile or from a sufficient distance to obscure the identity of the actor, using silhouette, colored filters, blurry focus, slow motion, and so on. If it is necessary to have actors playing the roles of subjects in the film, as is commonly done in historical re-enactments, the viewer must know that these are re-creations. This signaling is preferably explicitly included in the scene itself, with a title card, voice-over, or distinct filming technique, rather than in the end credits, where viewers might miss it.

Re-enactment is just one of many available storytelling strategies to represent and highlight certain elements of a film subject's experience. But the heart of a visual psychological anthropology is emotionally meaningful and culturally contextualized first-person testimony—which can most often be achieved by conducting compelling and insightful interviews.

10.3.3   *Technical Aspects of Shooting Interviews*

First, there are a few practical aspects of recording interviews. The decisions made about how to shoot an interview—how many cameras to use; at what angles and distances the camera(s) are placed; handheld vs. tripod shooting; and who to focus on—are all extremely important considerations. The discussion below, of course, is not intended to argue for a uniform approach to interviews in visual psychological anthropology. Many shooting and editing decisions will be determined by the ethnographic intentions of the filmmaker—specifically, the kinds of narration, depictions of the interview process, and representations of the anthropologist/subject relationship desired in the final film. How these considerations affected the *Afflictions* shoot can be instructive.

Afflictions was originally shot so that all the interviews included participants, either in a single "two shot" (where two or more people are within the frame) or in a pan back and forth between the interviewer and the interviewee. While this was useful for certain types of storytelling, it made it very difficult to edit the footage to allow for the subjects alone to narrate their own experience on-screen—its very structure meant the anthropologist and local collaborators were included in many of the shots. This problem was more than just technical; it indicated a theoretical frame for the entire film project, making it difficult to privilege the participant's own narration of their subjective experience. As a result of these difficulties that became apparent in the editing process, this two-shot style was later supplemented with a "one shot," with just the main subject in the frame. This provided an image uninterrupted by camera pans, and also allowed for clearer sound, as in this setup the main subject's voice could be recorded with a wired clip mic (lavalier) rather than a boom.

When filming interviews, multiple cameras are desirable if possible. One camera should be focused on the face of the interviewee, with the eye line directed toward the interviewer. One can hypothetically have the interviewee look directly into the camera, but without the use of technology such as Errol Morris' Interrotron (a device where the interviewee is talking to an image of the interviewer on a monitor, and the camera is shooting head on) (Leimbacher 2009), this can make for an awkward interview because the interviewee is not talking directly to a person, but to the camera.

Another camera could be dedicated to focusing on the interviewee's body language: how they are sitting, what they are doing with their hands, and so on. This lends an element of visual and sensory interest for the viewer, contains significant information, and allows for cutaways in the edit that capture aspects of the interview beyond simply what is being said. Using multiple cameras also helps because the more angles and distances shot, the more potentially usable footage there is to select from during the editing process.

Some may be surprised to realize that most of the footage shot will not be useful or usable for a particular project. Indeed, before the digital era the ratio of film shot to film used in final film was three to one hundred hours shot per hour of final film. In the digital age, the ratios can go up radically, from hundreds to even thousands of hours shot per hour of edited film, because with digital video there is no processing and associated costs as there were in traditional film, so filmmakers tend to be more liberal about what they shoot. This is one of the downsides of digital technologies—the pull to "shoot everything, all the time." This can generate an enormous amount of wasted footage. One should still maintain a careful perspective and shoot only what is needed, rather than shooting continuously. The ability to be thoughtfully selective comes with time and practice, as one moves form the shoot to the edit, and back to additional shoots.

In conducting interviews and gathering other types of shots, ethnographic filmmakers can be at a disadvantage when compared to commercial and even some documentary filmmakers. Part of this comes from the fact that the team is shooting on the locations of subjects' everyday lives and "on the fly" in locations as they emerge. As such, the environment of production is unpredictable with regard to lighting and sound. Furthermore, in the case of *Afflictions*, many interiors of Indonesian homes are dimly lit with fluorescent bulbs; but outdoor locations, which are often well lit and aesthetically pleasing, can also be quite noisy due to local fauna, traffic, and the like, and there is no guarantee as to how well lit any particular location will be. To minimize these issues, *Afflictions* was largely shot with available light and used cameras that handle low light well. Later film projects (such as *Bitter Honey* and *Standing on the Edge of a Thorn*) used additional direct and diffused lighting in the form of flat panels, soft boxes, flexfolds, and so on. Poorly lit subjects and settings are generally considered the work of amateur filmmakers, so lighting considerations are truly important.

In addition to these shooting and lighting considerations, getting good audio is crucial. Many documentary professionals state that sound is in fact the *key* technical aspect of filmmaking, overriding even the visual. When starting out, a novice visual ethnographer may accidentally record poor sound. It will help to use a good microphone, as cheap microphones tend to pick up more unwanted ambient sound. However, even with the best equipment, there are often ambient sounds to contend with such as rain, traffic, chickens, or cicadas. Some of this can be manipulated in editing, but a quality-focused recording on location, with a well-rated "shotgun," lavalier, or wireless mic, is key to getting usable audio. A second digital audio recorder is also useful in recording interviews or location sounds, and can provide additional audio sources for sound design. These secondary audio sources can be synched with the video in the edit.

10.3.4 Interviewing Considerations

While a strictly "talking heads" type of film should be avoided, interviews are key components in visual psychological anthropology. The hallmark method of psychological anthropology is PCE, which involves lengthy interviews on subjects of a personal nature, inquiring into aspects of family life, personal desires, and aspirations. Participants in PCE address sensitive topics and often put themselves out on a limb and stakes can be high—if they feel their confidence has been betrayed, it can lead to great hurt and controversy (see Scheper-Hughes 2000).

Person-centered interviews have been infrequently filmed in psychological anthropology; this is not only because of available technologies, but because of the very nature of content collected. There is no anonymity—or veneer of anonymity—when being recorded on camera, the way there might be on audiotape or written ethnography. Within a written ethnography, pseudonyms can be used, identifying details removed, composite biographical case studies created, and so on. On camera, the respondent's actual face, voice, and surroundings are immediately apparent. The issues of lack of anonymity in relation to informed consent will be discussed in Chap. 11. But once film participants do provide their informed consent to be filmed, one can move on to the interview process.

Some *Afflictions* participants (Kereta in *Shadows and Illuminations*, Gusti Ayu in *The Bird Dancer*, and Ni Ketut Kasih in *Ritual Burdens*) engaged in PCE to varying degrees with the lead author during his extended initial fieldwork prior to the film project. Others had been research subjects, but not PCE participants. Follow-up PCE with all participants, which was conducted during annual shoots over a number of years, followed a similar process. First, a local collaborator contacted the participants before the crew arrived in the field to discuss how they were doing and to plan the upcoming filming schedule. The local collaborator made an appointment with the participant for an upcoming interview, or, if the plan was to film the person over an extended period, initiated a more detailed discussion about how the days would unfold.

When the film crew arrived in country and at the house or family compound, after greeting the participant and (usually) their families, some time was devoted to the exchange of pleasantries and a renewal of friendship. In general, at this stage in a film project, any in-depth discussion of personal lives and the events therein is to be avoided, as that would cut the feet out from under the interview to come. It is important to refrain from going in depth into material that will likely emerge from the interview itself, as it is better if the filmed narrative is more spontaneous and less rehearsed.

Meanwhile, the small film crew prepared for the interview; from a technical standpoint, they checked the lighting, determined the best background and composition for the shots, and set up equipment. From a more interpersonal standpoint they also strategized about who should be in the interview, who should be on- or off-camera, and who it might be better to keep from being directly involved. In many cases, it was acceptable to have family present, either actively participating in the interview or simply listening in to facilitate their own greater understanding, empathy, or compassion regarding the participant's experience. However, there were times where material was of such a sensitive nature that it was preferable for certain family or community members to be out of earshot.

As previously discussed in the case study chapters in Part 2 of this book, the specific content of this sensitive material varied. Gusti Ayu's discussion of her brother's abusive treatment would have been practically impossible with her brother present. Estu also wanted to discuss his anger and resentment toward his family. In Bambang's case, caution was necessary because he was initially afraid his neighbors would discover he was a former psychiatric patient and stigmatize him or even fire him from his job as a private English tutor. In this latter case, a cover was created to explain the arrival of a foreign camera crew; inquisitive neighbors were told a documentary on English language instruction in Indonesia was being shot. As the filming progressed, and Bambang became more comfortable in his role as an advocate for people living with mental illness, this need for a cover fell away. Happily, the community responded in kind, supporting Bambang in various ways and embracing him as someone who was mentally ill, but also a valued advocate and teacher. Whatever the particulars, the need for privacy can create particular challenges in cultural context; in Indonesia, most spaces in the home and community are considered public social spaces.

Once all these matters had been attended to, the interview commenced. Person-centered interviewing in general proceeds with an open-ended, semi-structured, participant-led format. This means that while the interviewer generally has specific topics and domains in mind that she wants to explore, the questions are non-directive, at least in the beginning, and the interviewer invites the participant to narrate their own concerns and the issues that are at stake with them in the present, allowing this material to unfold at a natural pace.

Classical person-centered interviewing methodology provides a checklist of open interview topics (Hollan and Wellankamp 1994), useful guideposts for subjects that can be explored. However, because of the *Afflictions* project's main concerns, the person-centered interviewing went beyond these to delve deeply into specific domains about living with mental illness, including topics such as family relations, stigma, phenomenology of illness experience, culturally informed ideas about illness attribution, significant events or stressors related to the onset or course of their affliction, and so on. Interviews varied according to participants and occasionally strayed from a strictly person-centered format when the participant brought up topics related to the understanding and care of their illness, such as diagnosis and treatment options.

While conducting an interview, it is very important to be as thoughtful a listener as possible, never talking over or interrupting the participant's narration of their experience. This helps build mutual trust and rapport, but pragmatically also ensures material is usable for the film edit. If the interviewer interrupts, talks over, or has a back-and-forth with the participant in such a way that the interviewer cannot be artfully edited out, important material can been rendered unusable for film purposes.

10.3.5   Theorizing, Evoking, and Capturing Emotional Material

While honest, coherent, and relevant personal narratives are a goal of visual psychological anthropology, without an emotional force to them, they may not be compelling, or even usable, in a film. The great film editor Walter Murch has a "rule of six" in prioritizing an edit. In this list of priorities he says, "If you have to give up something, don't ever give up emotion before story. Don't give up story before rhythm" (Jarrett and Murch 2000). The fact that the editor of feature films such as *The Godfather* (1972) and *Apocalypse Now* (1979), so very different in many ways from ethnographic film, makes emotion the number one concern in narrative film construction should signal its importance in making compelling films.

In psychological anthropology there has been an explicit focus on differences in cross-cultural models of emotion (Lutz 1988), personhood, identity, and self (White and Marsella 1984; Kitayama and Markus 1994; Spiro 1993), or in current parlance, subjectivity and phenomenology (Willen and Seeman 2012). There have been similar changes in the approach toward visual or filmic depictions of the emotional self. In the early experiments in ethnographic film, such as *Nanook of the North* (Flaherty 1922) and the Mead and Bateson films (1950, 1952, 1954), there was little room for, or interest in, generating or even documenting emotional display and experience. Certainly the fact that these were silent films made it a bit more difficult to explore the nuances of emotional topics in depth. If emotional topics were explored, they would have to be displayed in exaggerated gestures and facial expressions (think of Charlie Chaplin in *The Gold Rush* [1925]). It was also due to the nature of what these kinds of films were attempting to accomplish—*Nanook* was made in a popular genre of descriptive documentary, while Mead and Bateson's films were intended to be "scientific documentation."[3]

There were undercurrents of emotion in earlier explorations in ethnographic film, but typically for the time, these were de-emphasized in favor of more descriptive approaches, such as in *Bitter Melons* (Marshall 1971), with its subtle and restrained tragedy, or analytical ones, as in *The Ax Fight* (Asch and Chagnon 1975). Even *Dead Birds* (Gardner 1963), which involves the death of a young child, arguably one of the most devastating experiences there can be, displays a curious lack of emotional engagement because of the dispassionate manner in which Gardner shot, edited, and narrated the film. Similarly, Marshall's early Ju'Hoansi films, such as *The Hunters* (1957), which involves an ongoing struggle to hunt and forage in the harsh environs of the Kalahari Desert, and *Bitter Melons* (1971), which actually ends with a foreshadowing of death by starvation and privation, maintain a dispassionate emotional climate, again due to the use of voice-over narration.

This is not to say that there wasn't emotion expressed in some of these earlier films, such as the depiction of rage and conflict in Timothy Asch's *The Ax Fight*, or the muted sadness that pervades John Marshall's *Bitter Melons*. But what is missing in these earlier films is emotion occurring in personal everyday life, or as evoked in the intersubjective interplay between interviewer and interviewee. Interestingly, Marshall returns to some of these same scenes in his six-hour magnum opus *A Kalahari Family* (Marshall and Ritchie 1951–2002) and, skillfully using the first-person voices and narrations of his participants and a simple but recurring musical *leitmotif*, he evokes a much greater degree of emotional response on the part of the audience with some of the same visual material. Marshall also incorporated footage used in *The Hunters* and the later classic *N!ai* (1980) (as well as a number of his smaller and shorter films); he intercut footage from these earlier films with more journalistic interviews, where Marshall questions his participants directly. This is an effective approach where the filmmaker can combine observational footage gathered over the course of a number of years with a more person-centered, subjectivity-oriented interview material that allows for direct emotional expression. But in large part, ethnographic film has studiously avoided an evocation or even representation of emotion in favor of "objective," dispassionate depiction of whatever aspect of culture the film is focusing on.

Another issue involved in the hesitation or reluctance of anthropologists to cinematically depict topics that may have an emotional component relates to the field's broader disengagement and studied avoidance of depicting experience-near understandings of subjectivity and emotion in the period of "normative" anthropology (1940–1970s) where the study of "Culture" writ large was of paramount importance in a variety of subfields and sub-disciplines such as British social anthropology, French structuralism, American interpretivism, and symbolic anthropology. Ethnographic films generally followed suit, with few having overt emotional content. This neutral edifice began to fracture with the rise of the anthropology of the 1970s and 1980s, and engagement with "anthropology that will break your heart" (Behar 1997) and the compelling, individualized, and phenomeno-logically oriented narratives of the 1990s and beyond. These values were also reflected in how ethnographic films were structured, and the material gathered by filmmakers and anthropologists therein was organized with an increasing emphasis on stories that had emotional content (in addition to the sampling of films previously mentioned throughout earlier chapters, see Vannini [2015] for a review of trends in ethnographic films being made in and outside the academy in the past decade or so). The parallels here between theory and practice in anthropology and ethnographic and visual anthropology are not surprising.

Given these shifting norms and values, many people who watch *Afflictions* note how personal some of the discussions are and ask how the interviews were able to achieve such intimacy. The only way to obtain such material is by building long-term relationships between the anthropologist and participants based on trust, understanding, empathy, and mutual respect. These do not develop overnight, and compelling interview material will most likely not emerge during a single shoot or fieldwork excursion, but over an extended period. This is one reason why the *Afflictions* series only coalesced into its final form after over a decade of material gathered in multiple shoots and fieldwork experiences. Also, given the *Afflictions* series' focus on culture and mental illness, many of the domains addressed explicitly explore phenomenology and subjectivity, which are intricately and continuously interwoven with emotion. By necessity, then, all the films frame, explain, and reference the participant's emotional lives and much of this emotion came out during interviews.

For example, in *The Bird Dancer* (Lemelson 2010a), the emotional climax comes when Gusti Ayu, who has suffered so greatly from her family and community's reaction to her TS, meets Dayu, a woman who also has TS but has not been subjected to stigma or exclusion. During a group interview, in a moment of empathy for a stranger, Dayu weeps to witness Gusti's anguish. In *Memory of My Face* (Lemelson 2011a), the climactic moment occurs when Bambang admits to feeling isolated and defeated by his illness and social estrangement, while his wife Yatmi says that she copes with her disappointment through surrendering to God's will (B.I. *pasrah*). But the complexities of capturing and evoking emotion in an interview, and the complex ethical and contextual considerations therein, can be seen most clearly in a scene from *Shadows and Illuminations* (Lemelson 2010c).

Photo 10.2   Bambang's wife Yatmi's strategy for dealing with her husband's illness

10.3.5.1 Afflictions *Example: Participant Subjectivity and the Evocation of Emotional Narratives*

By the time the cut of *Shadows and Illuminations* was shaping up and final interviews planned, the film was rich with biographical information and character development, but rather thin on emotional impact. A key piece of material was still missing, namely, Kereta's emotional response to the difficulties and tragedies in his life. This absence was due in part to the Balinese cultural presentation of self, where displays of sad or troubled emotions are de-emphasized. Balinese people generally seek to manage their emotional expression and maintain a pleasant and bright appearance, even in situations where they may be internally experiencing sadness, strife, or pain. This attempt to remain positive embodies balance and self-control, which are hallmark cultural values in personal demeanor and interpersonal relationships (Bateson and Mead 1942; Geertz 1966) and yet by no means preclude the internal experience of such negatively valenced emotions and the occasional need to express them (Connor 1995; Wikan 1990; Lemelson 2012).

It might also be argued that Kereta, having some form of psychotic illness, had further difficulty processing and expressing these emotions (Gur et al. 2006; Girard et al. 2016; Lee et al. 2016). For the purpose of accurately depicting Kereta's compelling life concerns, however, it was necessary to show the emotional impact of Kereta's multiple traumas and his isolation and sense of estrangement from the social world.

Long-term PCE with Kereta made it clear that two events had deeply affected him: the death of his second child shortly after her birth, and the temporary separation from his wife, Made Ada, who left him for a year and a half in the early years of their marriage. If questions were posed about these periods of loss and grief, it was likely that an emotional response, which could be crucial in communicating Kereta's experience to viewers, would be forthcoming. But to do this for the film would mean to purposely go against norms of Indonesian etiquette; it was decided that if uncomfortable topics or long awkward silences arose, this discomfort should not be diffused by jokes or idle chatter, as would happen in a typical Balinese social context, but rather allowed to build and, hopefully, elicit more revealing responses. This tactic could be considered a cross-cultural fieldwork application of the "abstinence rule" used in the psychoanalytic process (Killingmo 1997), where the therapist avoids social pleasantries with the idea that minimal interaction allows suppressed emotional material to surface more freely. By engaging in a form of cultural abstinence—by not adopting the Indonesian norm of diffusing strong emotions in polite conversation—the hope was that deeper emotions could be accessed.

Indeed, there were extended silences in the raw interview footage, as Kereta and Made Ada hesitated and struggled to provide their account of grief. But they ultimately shared frank and illuminating recollections of their life together, where they acknowledge separations, compromises, and yet an abiding affection for one another (for transcript of this excerpt, see Lemelson and Tucker 2015). In the edit, portions of the interview were cut to accelerate and smooth out its pace and flow, but the poignant nature of their relationship and life together comes through very clearly, illustrating how the complementary tools of PCE and film editing can communicate the power of more common losses and grief in the life of someone who is mentally ill to create a powerful narrative that illustrates key aspects of his biography and subjectivity. In this interview, PCE was able to make latent (or at least, undiscussed) emotional content manifest and present. It was film editing, however, that allowed this now manifest content to be emotionally accessible to viewers across cultural norms of affect expression and cinematic timing. Notably, this interview was shot toward the end of a multi-year film process—it was only with longitudinal ethnography that the ethnographer and filmmaker had the sufficient background knowledge of film participants to make this judgment call. Clearly there are benefits to a longitudinal project, but numerous complexities as well.

I love him too, but just a little.

Photo 10.3   Kereta and his wife, Made Ada, reflect back on their marriage

10.3.6 Longitudinality and *Afflictions* Filming

The longitudinal approach of *Afflictions* was not without precedent. There are notable longitudinal documentary film projects, such as the *Up* series (Apted 1964–present), which follows a cohort of fourteen British citizens, beginning in 1964 when they were all seven years old, and checking in with them every seven years to film and interview them over the course of two days in order to make an additional film about their lives (the most recent being shot when the subjects were all 56). The project was conceived to function in part as commentary on Britain's class system, but includes much content relevant to psychological anthropology. The participants were interviewed about topics such as their psychological state, including degree of happiness with their lives and their worries, and thoughts about the future. Of course, it is also a portrait of life-course development, testing the hypothesis that a person's personality and hence to a certain extent, their fate, is determined by the age of seven according to the Jesuit quotation, "Show me the child up to the age of seven and I will show you the man." The film also captures deepening friendships between the project participants and with the filmmaker, Michael Apted. This approach has since been used for films in other societies, such as Russia, Japan, South Africa, and many others (https://en.wikipedia.org/wiki/Up_Series).

Other well-known longitudinal documentaries are driven by similar concerns, such as *Following Sean* (Arlyck 2005), which traces the life course of a young boy raised in countercultural communities in San Francisco from the age of four, when he was a smart boy allowed to roam wild and smoke marijuana, through his unexpectedly staid and responsible adulthood. *The Children of Golzow* (Junge 1961–2007) follows members of a small German town, addressing the subjects' personal lives and the implications of German reunification. More recently, *American Promise* (Brewster and Stephenson 2013) explores issues of class and race by following two young African-American boys for thirteen years over the course of their private education at the predominantly white New York prep school, Dalton.

There are relatively few projects that have attempted to do longitudinal visual ethnography. The first and most compelling is John Marshall's work in the Kalahari, discussed previously. Sarah Elder's (Elder and Kamerling 1974) longitudinal work with indigenous peoples of Alaska (since the 1970s) employs a collaborative approach where she and her film subjects determined the themes and events to be recorded, making films on whaling and walrus hunting, ritual and performance, and modernization and the lifestyle and psychological changes it brings. While Elder collaborated with the same communities over time, she has taken a topical approach rather than a psychological one in her films, addressing areas of importance and concern to the community without focusing on biographical or psychological development of individual subjects over time.

The *Afflictions* films were shot over a time frame of six to fourteen years, depending on the individual film in the series, making it one of the longer projects in the annals of ethnographic film. All of the *Afflictions* films incorporate footage shot over the course of multiple years.

A common goal longitudinal projects share with other genres of film is to avoid confusing the viewer. This can be potentially more difficult when doing longitudinal visual ethnography as compared to making a dramatic film or even a documentary shot over a short period, due to the visual changes that come with passing time. In a written ethnography, such visual and physical changes are invisible by default, and the commonly understood conventions of writing make it easy to combine different scenes or periods from a participant's life, or jump from one interview or observation session to another. A year or more of fieldwork can be compressed into a single volume, with evocative incidents selected to make critical points. With a film, however, one needs to ensure that the viewer will understand that a particular participant is the same person visible in the last shot, even though he or she may have changed their appearance.

In some cases people's appearance change is not much of an issue. For example, in *The Bird Dancer* (Lemelson 2010a), Gusti Ayu's appearance shifts over time: in the earliest shots, she has medium-length hair, and then few years later, on the advice of a healer, she cut her hair extremely short. Her hairstyle and weight continued to vary from year to year, yet she was always recognizably the same person so no adjustments needed to be made in the edit. In other cases, artful visual transitions may be needed to help the viewer recognize a film participant despite changes in appearance or the passage of time. In *Ritual Burdens*, Ketut's appearance changed markedly over eleven years of filming. The film incorporated a visual morph between shots of Ketut in 1997 and in 2008 to clarify that these were of the same person.

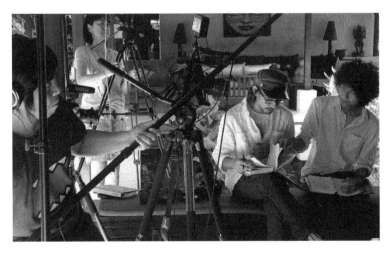

Photo 10.4 Local crew taking notes during a production shoot

10.3.6.1 Afflictions *Example: Visual Strategies in Longitudinal Filming*

The visual challenges that come with a longitudinal approach can also yield visual approaches that make strong theoretical points, as illustrated by the visual depiction of Wayan Yoga in *Kites and Monsters*. Wayan and his father were shot in exactly the same configuration during every shoot, over the course of fourteen years. The first interview was conducted with Dr. Panteri, Wayan Sadha, the lead author, and Wayan's entire extended family. Wayan and his father were arranged in a semi-circular configuration on their pavilion (B.B. *bale'*), as seen in the first segment of the film. Upon returning three years later, there was an opportunity to create continuity between the first shoot and the second; and in subsequent shoots when Wayan was aged fourteen and nineteen, he and his father were again placed in the same manner. Adopting an almost theatrical staging, this allowed the various "characters"—the anthropologist, field assistant, subject and father, and various other family members—to be in the same position each time, thus creating a sense of familiarity and continuity over the years. This shot composition mirrored the main theme of the film—that the continuities in Balinese cultural practices provide a supportive scaffolding[4] for Wayan's continued growth in the face of managing a neuropsychiatric disorder.

In addition, on each shoot similar supportive B-roll was gathered—of Wayan dancing, drawing, narrating traditional Balinese mythological and cosmological narratives, kite building and kite flying, playing musical instruments, and cooking. Again, shooting these similar activities over the years made it easy to compose an edit that linked them as continuities over time. Further animated sequences illustrated the stories Wayan was telling and enacted his developmental progression as a creative young artist, as the images progressed from a childlike to more mature drawing style.

Ultimately, no matter the particular visual strategies used, returning year after year builds a rapport, a sense of collaboration and cooperation, and an expectation of enduring relationship that would be difficult to obtain with single shoots, even extended ones. It also yielded multiple storylines, and the range and diversity of subjects can lead to significant insights. Finally, the strengthening of personal bonds between anthropologist and participants yielded progressively deeper and more authentic material.

A number of questions arise when attempting a longitudinal visual ethnography. How long does one have to be in the field and be shooting for it to be truly longitudinal, and does one have to be continuously there? What is the impact of "leaving and returning"? What is gained by a longitudinal approach and what, if anything, is lost? Or, to put it another way, are there "decreasing returns" in coming back repeatedly to the same material? How does one know when one has "completed" or at least sufficiently explored the possibilities of the domain or subject, leaving little left to uncover in terms of an educational or theory-building perspective? These are questions that should be in the mind and incorporated into the planning of those wanting to do projects in a visual psychological anthropology; each will find their own answers along the way. Other issues that arise in the post-production or editing phase will be discussed below.

10.4 Post-production: A Stylistic Approach to Editing and Storytelling

The post-production stage is the stage when the film footage is edited and a narrative is constructed. Scenes build upon scenes to create a complete story, the crafting of which is one of the most creative parts of visual psychological anthropology. This is where theory, creativity, artistry, and even imagination can play major roles. There are both practical and conceptual elements to this process.

10.4.1 Some Practical Post-production Steps

After returning with a range of footage from the field, including interviews, B-roll, and re-enactments, a number of steps need to be taken to ensure the material is workable in an edit.

If the footage is in a foreign language, one of the first tasks is to have the material transcribed and translated. In *Afflictions*, up to four languages (Balinese, Javanese, Indonesian, and/or English) may be used in the footage, so this task is usually given to local Indonesian transcribers or translators. The translations typically consist of one line of transcribed material, with the English translation underneath. Both of these are linked to a time code that notates its position in the recorded material. There are also short descriptors that capture the main idea or focus of the material at hand. An example of an interview with Gusti Ayu is below:

Feels sad when seeing others with illness:

01:05:54	Gusti Ayu	Iya. Saya juga sedih juga ngeliat orang itu seperti ya.
		Right. I'm also sad to see people like that, you know?
01:06:01:	Pak Rob	Oh, Gusti merasa sedih waktu melihat itu?
		Oh, you feel sad when you see that?
01:06:03:	Gusti Ayu	Iya sedih. Malahan saya sendiri tu kadang berdoa, mendoakan dia biar dia bisa diberi, begini mukzizatlah sama Tuhan, diberi kesembuhan. (Pak Rob: Iya. Ehm.)
		Yes, sad. You know, sometimes I even pray for those people that God give them miracles, that they can recover. (Rob: Okay)

Having a disciplined workflow around transcribing and translation is very helpful in moving a production forward, as editors are not usually fluent in the language they are editing in and rely on timely and accurate transcriptions and translations.

In addition, when returning from the field, all the footage should be offloaded from the cameras and drives. At this point, the footage is still in various formats based on the camera used to record it (e.g. Canon and Panasonic.) since the file types are different from camera to camera (e.g. AVI and DVC-PRO). While each camera uses its own formats, all footage must be converted into the desired format. Editing systems use different "codecs," which are data compression programs that allow multiple cameras' outputs to be read by the same editing program.

It is important to note that each editing program uses a specific video format. For example, Final Cut Pro works best with certain file types, while Avid and Premier require other formats. Regardless of which format the preferred editing software uses, all footage must be in the same format. Many beginning filmmakers are not thinking about post-production at the time of shoot, but these technical aspects of filmmaking may in fact determine whether or not a final film can even be edited together from the footage that was shot. Before shooting begins, ideally filmmakers need to know which program they will be editing on, so that in the field they use a camera that records with suitable file types. They also need to be thinking about the final picture size and frame rate because different frame rates cannot be edited together.

After all of the footage is converted, it can be collected into an editing program project file consisting of all footage from a specific date and camera and then organized. In organizing clips at Elemental Productions, we assign a name or title to every clip in such a file using a specific naming convention designed to streamline archiving and facilitate easy searching within the archive. A sample title might be "INTV-Gusti-Ricefield_sunset_1." In this system, each file name begins with a specific four-letter code, which is an abbreviation for the content of the footage; in this case, INTV stands for a formal interview, but there are many other codes such as CHAR for footage of main characters that are not shot in a formal interview style, ARCH for archival footage, PORT for portrait shots, SCEN for scenic footage, and so on. The second word in the sequence, which in this example is Gusti, refers to either the character's name or a description of the shot. The third word or phrase further describes the shot or additional characters in the shot. The goal is to create a description of the shot so anyone can read the name and get a very good idea of what is in the shot without having to view the actual clip. If a longer shot sequence has been broken down into smaller sequences or segments, a number is added at the end of the title to indicate where it stands in the sequence, which in this example is designated by the number "1." Further descriptive identifiers can be added to clips when being digitally filed, including additional information about the location of the shot, the viewpoint, or angle of the camera used (e.g. from the main character's perspective, the interviewer's perspective, or general B-roll), the time of day of the footage, the language spoken, key words regarding content, and so on.

After being so named, the project files should be loaded into an editing program. The process of digitizing and organizing the footage this way is time consuming, but it makes searching for and accessing files much easier and hence makes the editing process much more efficient in the long run. One can find clips using many different identifiers, and can locate specific shots quickly. Furthermore, if certain technical problems were to arise, continuity in the naming, dating, and descriptions of footage means that data could be restored by referring back to the project files, one of the external hard drives, or the prep folders.

While an ethnographic filmmaker just starting out or initially working alone may not see the need for such a rigorous and somewhat time-consuming organizational system, if the research grows into a longitudinal project as it has in the case of the *Afflictions* series and other Elemental Productions projects, the visual data collected ultimately may span a decade or more, encompassing thousands of hours of raw footage, and a rotating crew of people may work with this data for film or other research purposes. At this level, having clear rules for filing and accessing data is crucial. A combination of easily searchable visual clips, organized into clear and understandable headers, streamlines the editing process. It also quickly becomes evident during the editing process what footage might be missing, pointing toward what should be included on shot lists for future field shoots.[5]

10.4.2 Editing: Thinking Ahead About Editing and Production Values

In the early years of ethnographic film, relatively simple editing was the standard, with heavy reliance on the "jump cut" (where one shot is cut back to back with another), such as in *Trance and Dance in Bali* (1952). In *Dead Birds* (1963), however, Gardner cut together several different battle scenes to create a composite. At the time, some critics felt this editing compromised the veracity of film as a medium of documentation. In the decades since, especially with the advent of digital non-linear editing systems, it has become generally accepted that many different types of editing are at the heart of the filmmaking process: Without editing there would be no film (see Vannini (2015) review and Henley (2000) for outline of trends in approaches to shooting and editing in contemporary ethnographic film).

One way to learn the basics of film editing conventions (without going to film school) is to self-educate. A familiarity with some of early pioneers of continuity editing (e.g. D.W. Griffith) or Soviet montage theory (e.g. Sergei Eisenstein), for example, will inform editing choices that make powerful visual statements. The surrealists and other early experimental filmmakers (such as the work of the aforementioned Lois Buñuel and Maya Deren) offer plenty of ideas to explore. But a good way to learn is to watch different ethnographic films that espouse a variety of storytelling techniques. There are ample examples of didactic and expository films in early ethnographic films such as *Dani Houses* (Heider 1974a), *Dani Sweet Potatoes* (Heider 1974b), *At the Time of Whaling* (Elder and Kamerling 1974), any of the Nesilik Eskimo series (1963–1965), and many others that take a descriptive look at the relationship between culture and practice or *habitus*, as seen through subsistence practices and technology. These films are well shot and edited, providing a visual and corporeal richness to the ethnographies.

At the dawn of the twenty-first century, which has been framed as the "golden age" of documentary film (Hornaday 2015), there are now also many examples of emotional and character-based narrative documentaries that illustrate a staggering range of editing styles. One of the first decisions to make in an edit is what sort of narrative voice(s) will be used to tell the story.

10.4.3   Narration and Narrative Voices

In making editing decisions, anthropologists need to take multiple perspectives: that of how the subject experiences their lives and might feel about their portrayal; that of the viewer and what they might think and feel when watching the film; and the analytical perspective of the anthropologist. These must all be integrated in the attempt to say something about culture and the human experience through a coherent and evocative film.

Historically, many ethnographic films have relied on voice-over to express these different perspectives. There are multiple voice-over styles. Many early ethnographic films relied on a continuous stream of narration (the so-called voice of God narrative style) that tells much, or even all, of the visual story—a good example of this is *Trance and Dance in Bali* (Mead and Bateson 1952). An alternative to this is the sporadic voice-over—*Family Victim*, for example, includes only two voice-over segments. An even more restrained use of voice-over is to pose an initial opening question; this option is used in *Ritual Burdens*. These examples assume the voice-over is coming from the perspective of the anthropologist; there is also the participant voice-over, where the narration is given by the film's main participant. Of course, voice-over can also be eschewed completely, letting the story unfold through observational footage and dialogue, interviews, narratives, and so on from a number of different participants' perspectives—and in contemporary sensory ethnography, even such narration or dialogue is limited.

Voice-over has its benefits. It can manage the flow of visual information for the viewer, lending clarity, and reference different bodies of information not immediately apparent to the viewer or not captured on film. In fact, early versions of *Afflictions* films that used more voice-over than the existing versions received positive feedback from colleagues. They felt that the expository voice-over addressing the chronological course of fieldwork, biographical developments over time, and theoretical issues in psychological and medical anthropology was useful for teaching.

However, criticisms of all the different voice-over styles are myriad. At its worst, continuous voice-over can result in a pedantic and plodding film, giving a predigested engagement with the subject matter, as the narrator overloads information where it is neither needed nor appropriate, in effect subjugating the visual or sensory elements of the film to linear narration. Furthermore, in a continuous voice-over the anthropologist and/or filmmaker's standpoint is privileged while the voice of the subject is diminished or, worse, misrepresented. An infamous example of the shortcomings of voice-over is *Dead Birds* (1985) where Robert Gardner, the anthropologist narrator, speaks in the voice of the subject. While the voice-over is engaging and even poetic, and was used in part as a response to the technical limitations of the time before synched audio, it has been criticized for inauthenticity and worse, making major assumptions about what the main subject is experiencing and feeling rather than including his voice directly.

10.4.3.1 Afflictions *Example: The Narrative Development of* The Bird Dancer

The limitations and theoretical problems with voice-over became significant in the first film to emerge from the *Afflictions* visual research, a film about Gusti Ayu predating *The Bird Dancer*. This film, entitled *Movements and Madness* (Lemelson and Yngvesson 2006), was edited with several different foci in mind. One was a transcultural psychiatric research framework that privileged issues such as cultural models of mental illness, cultural shaping of symptoms, and differential diagnosis. The other was a narrative arc charting the conflicted personal journey of the anthropologist in relation to Gusti, questioning whether he should help Gusti Ayu or intervene in her life, and if so, how. Since this first set of issues is theoretical and abstract, and the second involves a self-reflexive understanding of internal processes, almost constant voice-over narration was relied upon.

One of the influences on *Movements and Madness* was the personal journey film, quite popular in mainstream documentaries of the time (McElwee 1986; Mosso et al. 2013). There are certainly circumstances where a film narrative can be based on how the filmmaker or anthropologist understands, interprets, and reacts to a situation. One is if the anthropologist or filmmaker's story has its own innate drama—films like Greg MacGillivray's *The Alps* (Judson 2007) or *Everest* (MacGillivray et al. 1998), both about mountaineering and the potential life and death struggles therein, or Dennis O'Rourke's *The Good Woman of Bangkok* (O'Rourke 1991), where the documentarian is simultaneously the customer of his sex-worker subject. Another is if the filmmaker is an interesting "character," such as Ross McElwee in *Sherman's March* (McElwee 1986).

However, for this project, the self-conscious voice-over narration was theoretically problematic. Contemporary psychological anthropology ascribes to the tenet that one works inductively from the material and closely follows those issues that have salience for subjects' "lived experience" (Nordstrom 1995). In addition, contemporary psychological anthropologists are taught to value an "experience near" (Wikan 1991) understanding the world of subjects from an "emic" perspective, that is, "from the natives' point of view," which means valuing the ethos, embodied (Csordas 1990) worldview, and personality of one's subjects. This also includes analyzing and providing a "thick description" (Geertz 1973) of the issues important to them, at least for the purposes of attempting to come to understandings about what motivated them to behave as they did and to make the choices or decisions they made.

It became clear that continuous voice-over focusing on thematic concerns that largely privileged transcultural psychiatry theory and the anthropologist's experience—to the *exclusion* of the participant's subjectivity and lived worlds—contributed to neither good filmmaking nor compelling ethnography. As a result, when *Movements and Madness* was reworked into *The Bird Dancer*, most of the voice-over was dropped and the story focused largely on Gusti's experience, replacing voice-over with Gusti's voice drawn from person-centered interviews, leaving only a few interspersed segments of voice-over and a guiding question to open the film, a style then applied to all the *Afflictions* films.

What emerged was a shorter but better film, from both ethnographic and cinematic perspectives. This improvement can be somewhat objectively assessed; Documentary Educational Resources (DER), the well-known ethnographic film distributor, rejected *Movements and Madness* for distribution, citing among other things the use of voice-over and the subsequent diminishment of Gusti Ayu's "voice" and the focus on the anthropologist at the expense of the subject. When the footage was reworked into *The Bird Dancer*, DER picked it up for distribution and the film was nominated (as part of the *Afflictions* series) for a "Best Limited Series" award by the International Documentary Association (IDA).

10.4.4 Utilizing Diverse Stylistic Devices to Evoke Internal and Cultural Worlds

Once the type of narrative device is chosen, the types of shots and stylistic devices that will be used to give substance, depth, and emphasis to a film must be considered. Editing often involves a variation of the classic Freudian "condensation" (Freud and Strachey 1954) where symbolic images with multi-layered meanings are packed into a brief but dense audio-visual frame. Thanks to this condensation, camera shots can "speak a thousand words" to quickly illustrate or underscore broader themes in the films, making theoretical concepts more concrete. For example, a quick shot of Javanese women carrying their goods to market with baskets on their heads passing under a promotional billboard for *Eat Pray Love* (Murphy 2010), such as used in *Memory of My Face*, or of a tattooed Balinese youth in punk bracelets and a spiked Mohawk haircut reverently preparing a ritual offering at a street-corner shrine, such as used in *The Bird Dancer*, may directly capture the daily realities of globalization with a tangibility that academic exegesis can only talk around.

However, when making films about the experience of mental illness, one must go beyond what is externally observable because so much of the experience cannot be seen. The effort to represent the lived realities of mental illness visually—to make subjective states "filmable"—while simultaneously thinking ethnographically has led us to experiment with several strategies, drawn from or suggested by the participant's own experience, that can successfully represent the more interior, psychological, or autonomous aspects of their experience and illustrate how these are embedded in a cultural context.

10.4.4.1 Afflictions *Examples: Using Distinct Visual Styles to Reflect Individual Subjectivity*

In *Kites and Monsters*, Wayan's developing sense of self was illustrated both in relation to his TS and to Balinese mythology, as well as symbols and tropes as he grew from a child into a confident young man. The lead author had worked as psychotherapist and was trained in clinical psychology, and in therapeutic sessions frequently encouraged children to draw, both to help relieve the boredom and anxiety of the clinical encounter and to provide interpretative and projective content. Wayan loved to draw, and the themes and interests reflected in his drawings indeed mirrored both common topics in Balinese iconography and the morbid obsessions experienced by some children with certain forms of TS (Grad et al. 1987). His quite skilled original artwork was used in the edit as an organizing device, taking his original drawings and then creating animated representations of the stories he told, drawn in a similar style. Similarly, Wayan loved to improvise Balinese dance for the film team. Capturing his evident joy and pride in these traditional movement forms and his increasing mastery of them as he aged provided another opportunity to represent how culture acted as a stabilizing buffer throughout the course of his development.

A different approach was taken in *Family Victim*. It became clear through the film and research process that one of Estu's most persistent concerns was a pervasive feeling of loneliness and alienation. The film visually established these themes with shots of solitary objects, such as trains and kites, alone in a wide visual field. Visual comparisons juxtaposed Estu, alone in his small shop plaintively describing his attempts at reconciliation with his family, with shots of solitary farmers in rice fields and solitary bike riders on deserted roads in rural Java, emphasizing the isolating impact of his behavior.

Another overarching theme in the film was Estu's attempts to free himself from his psychological troubles and the toxic effect they had on his family relationships, to shake off the difficulties of his past and find a new, more satisfying, personal identity. Various evocations of flight were used to evoke this desire, from the opening shot of his graffiti reading "Wild Hearts Fly Free" to symbolic shots of birds.

The visual metaphors and symbols chosen in visual psychological anthropology can and should reflect not just personal imagery but also the multiple cultural and environmental contexts that suffuse any experience of mental illness, leading to some significant contrasts from film to film. For example, the elderly subject of *Ritual Burdens*, Ketut Kasih, lives in rural Bali and her daily life is spent in a traditional agrarian community surrounded by rice fields. She uses this natural imagery to describe her heightening sensations, becoming acutely sensitive to the sound of the wind blowing through trees or sunlight reflected on water, or ominously feeling like her head is filling up with pouring rice; this was mirrored with the natural imagery used in the film.

However, Bambang lives in the sprawling metropolis of Jakarta surrounded by local culture and globalized media, which affected him powerfully during his episodes of mania. In *Memory of My Face*, the way this vertiginous media saturation interacted with his increasingly energetic, grandiose, and agitated internal state was depicted with an animated sequence. This sequence adapted the style of Indonesian shadow puppet theater (*wayang kulit*); with flickering lantern light in the background, images of neurons, mosques, political figures, conflicts in the Middle East, Islamic iconography such as the star and crescent, and more all appear to swirl around at a quickening pace.

Shadows and Illuminations presented one of the most complex representational challenges because Kereta's experiences were absorbed in Balinese iconography and cosmology not commonly referenced nor understood outside Bali. His experience was represented with a series of images derived from an extraordinary collection of paintings gathered by

Mead and Bateson during their groundbreaking fieldwork in Bali in the mid-1930s (Geertz 1994, 2016), which depicts many different areas of Balinese cultural life. These were drawn during the same decade Kereta was a child and served as a rich visual reference for the cultural symbols he frequently mentioned in his interviews. Many of the images chosen also seem to directly depict elements of Kereta's biography, such as the evocative images of demons and the narrative painting of difficult labor and stillbirth.

These examples from the *Afflictions* series illustrate a move away from "thin depictions" toward "thick descriptions" (Taylor 1996, 86) and visual "poetry" (Taylor 1996, 88). This approach allows the films to communicate the tone and content of individuals' hallucinations, fantasies, and personal symbolic imagery, while providing a dynamic sensory experience for the viewer, complementing more visually bland interviews and taking the viewer deeper into another's reality by borrowing from cultural iconography and contextualizing individual experience within a particular cultural place with its own visual and auditory landscapes, textures, and styles. These strategies can allow filmmakers to explore their own creativity and innovate original ways of conveying multiple layers of personal, cultural, and clinical information.

10.4.5   *The Contested Use of Sound and Music in Ethnographic Films*

While ethnographic film is often also referred to as "visual" anthropology, of course other senses are involved and recruited for meaning-making within the filmmaking and film viewing experience, including hearing. Sound was a significant issue for all early documentary filmmakers because synch sound was not widespread until the early 1960s. Before that, documentarians in the field either worked with a sound recordist or shot footage without sound, forced to re-create most or all sound in post-production. With the advent of high-quality standard definition video recording in the early 1990s, filmmakers enjoyed the ability to capture sound directly, even with portable and lightweight cameras. Quality sound is now commonplace, but the question of how to craft meaningful and effective sound design remains. The discrete soundscape of each *Afflictions* film uses ambient sound, originally composed music, and a curated soundtrack to meet representational needs; each of these elements will be discussed below.

The *Afflictions* films have made ample use of ambient sounds taken from the local environment to enrich, enhance, or ground what is on-screen. Sometimes this requires finessing in post-production if certain ambient sounds that were present on the scene (and might be expected by a viewer) were not captured in the recording. For example, sounds such as children laughing at a performance, or even something as simple as a creaky door closing, have been easily added to the final sound editing; while manipulated to a certain extent, this play with sound does not significantly detract from the film's veracity but does contribute to a viewer's sense of "reality."

This use of ambient sound, as well as other basic principles of sound design commonplace to trained documentarians, might seem new to ethnographic filmmakers; for example, recording a minute of "room tone," or the sound of the shooting environment when no one is speaking and nothing else is going on, can later be quite helpful in editing scenes to smooth out transitions and fill in spaces where nothing was being said. While in everyday life it may be imagined that one is sitting in "silence," there is in fact constant noise, and the total absence of sound—or the inclusion of the almost subconscious background noises from another locale—is jarring to a viewer if suddenly juxtaposed against natural sound. This is particularly true in Indonesia, where it is rare indeed to find a setting not suffused with a complex ambient soundscape.

Using a musical soundtrack is another way in which psychologically oriented ethnographic films can be distinguished from traditional visual presentations of fieldwork. Of course music will play an integral role in films of live dramatic, ritual, musical, or otherwise artistic performances. But even when not depicting such events, an additive musical soundtrack can convey emotional and cultural information and contribute to an intersubjective engagement with viewers, although this is perhaps more controversial.

Some anthropologists roundly oppose the use of music. Karl Heider, in his seminal book *Ethnographic Film* (1976), holds the opinion that music is a "distraction" best avoided in ethnographic film unless it was recorded as part of a live event being recorded, and hence "appropriate" to the situation. Even folk songs or local music is out of place in Heider's estimation, if these were not co-occurring with and "complementary to" what was happening visually on-screen (Heider 1976). In her defense of immersive observational cinema (Grimshaw 2011; Grimshaw and Ravetz 2009), Anna Grimshaw also opposes the use of soundtracks in favor of a deep sensory awareness of the character's environment and of the acutely attentive relationship between filmmaker and subject.

This resistance is understandable; certainly ethnographic films aim for a veracity in observation, and there are no obvious soundtracks to people's lives, thus one could argue that the use of soundtracks becomes manipulative and outside of subjects' lived reality. There is something to be said for this argument, and certainly the use of a soundtrack would be anathema to cinéma vérité or direct cinema. However, as psychological anthropologists know, individual experience, subjectivity, and phenomenology are difficult to represent only visually, and music may evoke or express many of the more ephemeral aspects of emotional experience. Music is extraordinarily important to people's lives, and to ignore its expressive potential would be to ignore the ongoing (although sometimes subconscious) sensory-emotional dialogue that music provides. Since psychological anthropology is trying to understand, explain, represent, and interrelate the multiple subjective and phenomenological contexts in which people are embedded, it makes sense that one think about the role that music plays in constructing subjective and intersubjective emotional reality.

In this case, eliciting emotion is not manipulative, but rather crucially important in understanding the dilemmas and contexts of participants' lives. Because, as Suzanne Langer has suggested, "the tonal structures we call 'music' bear a close logical similarity to the forms of human feeling [...] music is a tonal analogue of emotive life" (Barbash and Taylor 1997, 418); a musical soundtrack can be a powerful way to emphasize and convey emotion in film that might not be immediately apparent or forceful in the images alone. As such, Elemental Productions' film catalog has made an extensive use of soundtrack, moderate use of soundtrack, and no soundtrack at all, all depending on the exigencies of each project, and arguably, the emotional impact of the *Afflictions* films is enhanced by their musical soundtracks.[6]

10.4.5.1 Afflictions *Example: Using Soundtracks and Original Scores to Convey Biographical, Emotional, and Cultural Information*

Within any soundtrack, the judicious and appropriate use of originally composed music can support, highlight, and strengthen the key points of a film, and there are a number of options for sourcing the music for a film soundtrack. One choice is to include pieces of music that the film subjects are listening to or playing during production, or otherwise to use specific pieces or genres of music that may be important to their personal history or symbolic of their mental state. For example, in *Kites and Monsters* Wayan had an active interest in Balinese performing arts. He was recorded playing the Balinese bamboo xylophone, or *rindik*, and this music was placed over a montage of Wayan growing up over the years, serving an aesthetic purpose of filling in the silence over the still images, but also signifying the protective role local culture had played in guiding him to successful adulthood.

Two different sound sources for the soundtrack of *Memory of My Face* similarly multitasked to enhance the aesthetic, ethnographic, and idiosyncratic themes of the film. First was the inclusion of *dangdut* music. *Dangdut* is a complex and syncretic musical genre, drawing influences from Bollywood, the Middle East, and indigenous musical traditions of Indonesia, while staying in step with changes in Western pop music. It has grown wildly popular over the last several decades in Javanese urban and suburban neighborhoods. The *Afflictions* composer created an original *dangdut* selection to open the film as a nod to the multiple local and globalized influences on Bambang's life and ultimately, his mental illness experience.

Second was the use of musical references and development of a soundtrack score based on a moment of spontaneous song; during an episode of manic disturbance, Bambang, who is deeply interested in and familiar with a variety of Western musical pop modalities, spontaneously sang Phil Collins' *Against All Odds* (1983). This scene was surprisingly poignant; as he interpreted the song's plaintive call to a lover who has gone, seemingly erasing the protagonist's sense of his own identity in the process, Bambang mistakenly sang that he has nothing left but a "memory of my face."[7] This could be taken as a metaphoric commentary on the destabilizing and disruptive force of his illness on Bambang's life. It also could function as a more literal commentary on the radical changes in appearance Bambang experienced over the course of fieldwork due to episodes of mental illness—in particular, when his head was shaved in the hospital and when he lost teeth after getting beaten up by villagers angered by his inappropriate manic behavior. Because of its startling prescience, this variation on the lyric was chosen as the title for the film. In addition, much of the music for the film was based on a 1980s' soft rock genre, as it seemed in synch with Bambang's globalized world and interests.

In contrast, *Ritual Burdens* used a well-known Balinese lullaby, *Putri Cening Ayu*, to underscore Ketut Kasih's perspective on her childhood, which she viewed as carefree and happy, before the onslaught of poverty, illness, and various forms of structural violence. The chord progression of the song was slightly altered to fit within a major Western tonal structure, rather than following a specifically Balinese scalar modality. The result was a beautiful and poignant song that any Balinese viewer would recognize and perhaps feel a deep affinity toward, but was approachable for Western ears.

These uses of music may seem more recognizably ethnographic, in that the pieces selected emerge directly from the participant's lived experience, than the use of an original musical soundtrack designed specifically to enhance the emotional impact of particular testimony or information, which some might interpret as manipulative.

The scores developed for the *Afflictions* series reflect each film's distinct participants and settings; the soundtrack for each film ends up sounding different because the inspiration for it, and the mood and environment it conveys, is drawn directly from the participant's experiences. In composing a soundtrack, there is usually a solo "lead" instrument association with each main participant—Kereta's instrument in *Shadows and Illuminations* is a violin, Gusti's is a flute in *The Bird Dancer*, and so forth. The ethos and perspective of the participant are represented by the genre of music used for the soundtrack score and instrumentation; Kereta and Ketut Kasih espouse more enduring, traditional values, which are reflected in the choice of traditional gamelan in *Shadows and Illuminations* and *Ritual Burdens.* Estu in *Family Victim* and Bambang in *Memory of My Face* come from a younger generation infused with Westernized and globalized values and media, which is reflected in the modern and syncretic scores for those films.

In addition to character perspective and environment, the musical score can also reflect interpersonal dynamics and narrative arcs. For example, a simple melodic string piece parallels the sweetness—and at times *bitter*sweetness—of Kereta and Ada's long marriage in *Shadows and Illuminations.* The opening of *The Bird Dancer* establishes a sense of childhood and innocence, but with an undertone of foreboding and perhaps anxiety, by taking a simple, haunting melodic piano (here, the opening of the film *To Kill a Mockingbird* (Mulligan 1962) was an inspiration) and once again shaping instrumentation, tonal progression, and rhythm to fit a Balinese idiom.

With the advice, consultation, and collaboration of composers,[8] musicians, and music lovers, a process for creating such syncretic soundtracks for the films was developed for the *Afflictions* series, both composing original music and seeking out previously composed pieces that call upon musical traditions of Indonesia and the West. For example, a number of contemporary composers that have attempted to integrate Indonesian tonalities, harmonies, scalar progressions, instrumentation, and so on were explored to provide inspiration for the soundtracks. Lou Harrison, a late twentieth-century minimalist composer, created a number of experimental compositions, combining gamelan and Indonesian instrumentation with Western strings, choral works, and piano that influenced the compositions for

Afflictions. British composer Colin Bass, who goes by the stage name Sabah Habas Mustapha, works in Bandung and has released a number of syncretic CDs that successfully navigate the complexities of Indonesian instrumentation and tuning with Western tonalities and musical styles. His work was inspirational on how to meld modern, popular music of Indonesia with Western modalities. *Afflictions* drew upon both of these composers for inspiration for the final score. Another piece that provided inspiration was the soundtrack to the film *Legong, Dance of the Virgins* (De la Falaise 1935), played by San Francisco-based Clubfoot Orchestra and Gamelan Sekar Jaya.

Indonesia is one of the most musically diverse societies on the planet.[9] But even within single societies, such as Bali, there are complex musical traditions. Picking specific songs, or even genres, from within these traditions for use in a soundtrack was initially a daunting task, which required the help of a music editor with an encyclopedic knowledge of musical styles and genres. In addition, the score for *Afflictions* was greatly enhanced by the collaboration and contribution of prominent Balinese performers and ethnomusicologists.

When determining the soundtrack for a film, it is useful to remember the role that music might play in facilitating cross-cultural identification. Different pieces and even genres of music are familiar in the United States and Indonesia, and musical conventions will, to a certain extent, determine viewers' interpretation of the emotion or mood expressed. In developing a soundtrack, a filmmaker must strike a balance between including local music that will help layer cultural information and ground the viewer in a cultural place and perhaps more familiar-sounding music that will be able to communicate the intended meaning to a Western or American audience through familiar Western tonalities and melodic structures.

Whether sound or music is an inherent aspect of the context or environment in which filming takes place, is used by participants themselves for specific purposes, or is selected and included after fieldwork during post-production in order to underscore specific subjective and experiential aspects of the stories being told, psychologically oriented ethnographic film provides an opportunity to use sound to make meaning. Sound should therefore be considered an important part of ethnographic filmmaking, and filmmakers should think about having a music and sound approach, concept, or style for each film.

Taking into account the way ethnographic film invites us to think with multiple senses, it certainly can be a creative, aesthetic, and sensory enterprise. What is wonderful about this process is that one has the chance to be creative with others, collaborating with a film team that brings different skill sets and aesthetic sensibilities to the project. Another aspect of building a powerful film is gaining feedback, in various forms, from one's audiences.

10.4.6   Using Audience and Film Subject Feedback to Inform Film's Final Version

The *Afflictions* series has benefitted from holding test screenings of "rough cuts" with an assortment of target audiences. Each film in *Afflictions* was extensively screened for academic audiences. These test screenings were generally attended by faculty, graduate students, and other interested parties. Their feedback was invaluable in ensuring the film's message was clear and intent was realized. If two or more reviewers in these test audiences did not understand a major point, were confused about the characters, or did not understand the progression of the story, then more work remained to be done in the editing room. Such a process of using feedback to improve the clarity of work is not so different from anthropologists presenting their monographs, articles, or book chapters at conferences and seminars, or workshopping them with working groups at various stages of development.

The other key audience to screen for is the participants themselves, and secondarily their communities. Rough cuts are always screened for the main participants in the films and their families. They watch initial raw footage and then versions of the film during the editing process and provide feedback, determine what they feel comfortable sharing, or specify any sections they would like changed or withdrawn; the latter has very rarely occurred, however. After extensive and repeated viewings, most subjects feel satisfied with their representation.

Some participants have been invited to attend public screenings of finished films with their local communities and elsewhere in Indonesia, and engage with audience members through Q&A sessions (Andarningtyas 2012). Some of the participants—Gusti Ayu and Bambang in particular— have come to see this participation as advocacy work.

This process of screening also has been incorporated into the final versions of the films, so audiences would understand the intimate collaborative nature of the filmmaking. In *The Bird Dancer*, a scene is included of a public screening of a rough cut of the film, with several of the main participants in the film, notably Gusti Ayu and Dayu, at the front of the audience taking questions and answers. Beyond the events included in the films, there have been many screenings over the years, where the participants themselves come and answer questions and are interviewed by the press, and so on. If one looks in the audience in the screening scene of *The Bird Dancer*, one will see the characters of several other *Afflictions* or related films in the audience.

10.4.7 Filming, Editing, Writing: Ongoing and Interactive Methods of Analysis

Finally, in addition to these reflexive processes as reflected in the film, it is crucial to integrate the film with written ethnography. The interesting thing about film and video as a medium of *academic* expression, particularly of important social, political, or historical issues, is that films, by their very nature, must express and emphasize fewer ideas; one does not have the luxury, even in feature-length films, of elaborating upon a larger amount of background information, covering all details, addressing all asides, and so on. The medium renders that impossible. As previously described, visual psychological anthropology uses visual methods of "condensation," but there is not much room for analysis or exegesis within the film; so in some ways, film is more like poetry. However, perhaps paradoxically, because psychological anthropologists making films do not have the luxury of providing detailed citations or nuanced argumentation within the visual work, participants' perspectives may come across in a somewhat more pointed way on-screen than via the written word, despite attempts to express these with a degree of subtlety and artistry. The medium determines the message to a certain extent, and there are pros and cons to using film. In some ways, film allows for a more direct exploration of core issues at the heart of complicated issues and for the deployment of polyvalent symbolic imagery, but this may come at the expense of contextualization and explanation. By providing an accompanying written ethnography, some of the risks of projection and simplification to the detriment of academic nuance and precision can be minimized, even as new modalities of knowing and understanding are accessed.

Having described, in some detail, the technical, practical, and theoretical considerations involved in producing visual psychological anthropology films, we can move to another set of key issues: the importance of collaboration, the question of intervention, and additional ethical issues that arise throughout the filming process.

NOTES

1. We have reserved much of the technical information, however, for the supplementary website. See www.afflictionsbook.com

2. After *40 Years of Silence* was released, several ministries in Indonesia retracted the lead author's filming visa and imposed a non-official blacklist or ban for several years. During this time, local colleagues were able to approach the relevant ministries and the visa was restored, under the condition that there would be no further exploration of the 1965 issue.

3. The ethnic "dramas" of this earlier period, such as *Legong: Dance of the Virgins*, did explore and display emotional scenes in a quite melodramatic way; a young girl, Poutou, falls in love with a handsome gamelan player, Nyoman, in the marketplace. But Nyoman falls in love with Poutu's half-sister when he catches sight of her bathing in a public bath. When Poutou learns of this, she dances her final sacred *Legong* dance, and then commits suicide by throwing herself down a ravine. While obviously simplistic and melodramatic, the film does illustrate a range of emotions on the faces of its characters, thus belying not only contemporary representations of the Balinese as a "simple and carefree people," but also anthropological descriptions, most typically those of Mead and Bateson's "Balinese Character," where the final sentence sums up the overarching view of the relationship between Balinese culture, personality, and emotions: "...life is a rhythmic, patterned unreality of pleasant, significant movements centered in one's own body to which all emotion long ago withdrew." It is interesting, particularly in light of the research in Baliology over the ensuing decades, that this early film exploration of a young Balinese woman's deep emotion would really be the only representation of the deeper currents of emotion that underlie experience, particularly women's experience, in Bali until the publication of Unni Wikan's work.

4. Scaffolding is usually used in development psychology to mean the process whereby parents or caregivers provide forms of encouragement, help, and assistance to children and allow them to achieve tasks and make progress in the development of goals in a way that would have not been possible through the children's actions themselves (Wood et al. 1976). This concept could also be utilized in a more general cultural way to illustrate how culture, in this case the musical, artistic, and even mythological and cosmological components embedded in Balinese storytelling and fables, supported and encouraged Wayan's growth even though this growth could have been impacted seriously by his neuropsychiatric disorder.

5. While footage organization is a standard aspect of industry documentary and non-fiction television post-production, and all editors organize their clips and reels according to an easily articulated set of organizing features, the naming and archival system Elemental Productions has developed is in fact quite

unique. Due to the longitudinal nature of the projects, and the shifting focus of different films where similar characters may be used to tell different stories (for example, Kereta being included in both the films *40 Years of Silence* and *Shadows and Illuminations*), the whole body of the archive must remain accessible to different editors working on different films. This is different from industry non-fiction documentaries, where only one project is tackled at a time.

6. Interestingly, a soundtrack can be a useful emotional landmark not just for film viewers but also film editors. During preliminary editing, some editors prefer to edit to "temp," or "scratch" music—music that will not be in the final soundtrack but matches the general feel of the film or scene one hopes to create. This can be helpful because as one cuts a sequence to music, a natural rhythm and movement develops that makes the assembly flow more organically; it also becomes easier to synch specific elements in the film, particularly points of emphasis such as emotional or high or low points in the film.

7. The original lyrics are "All I can do is watch you leave [...] You're the only one who really knew me at all/ Take a look at me now/ There's just an empty space/ And there's nothing left here to remind me/ Just the memory of your face."

8. Original music in the films was composed by long-time collaborator and composer Malcolm Cross. Despite the challenges of working with both Western and Indonesian musical instruments—such as differently tuned instruments and different rhythmic structures, to name only two—Malcolm has been able to adapt traditional Javanese and Balinese melodies to powerful effect. There are two CDs of original music from the *Afflictions* series, and other films, entitled *Indonesian Post-Modern* Volumes 1 and 2, available on www.elementalproductions.org

9. In a wide-ranging project in the 1990s, ethnomusicologist Phillip Yampolsky traveled across the archipelago recording and documenting musical traditions. His resulting twenty-volume CD set, *The Music of Indonesia* (Yampolksy 1991–1999), provides a sample of this diversity.

References

Andarningtyas, Natisha. 2012. Kisah Para Penderita Skizofrenia dalam Film. *Antara News*. Retrieved via http://www.antaranews.com/berita/396063/kisah-para-penderita-skizofrenia-dalam-film

Apted, Michael. 1964–Present. *Up Series*. Manchester: Granada Television.

Arlyck, Ralph. 2005. *Following Sean*. 1 hr, 27 min. Poughkeepsie: Timed Exposures.

Asch, Timothy, and Napoleon Chagnon. 1975. *The Ax Fight*. 30 min. Watertown: Documentary Educational Resources. http://www.der.org/films/ax-fight.html

Balikci, Asen. 1963–1965. *Series, Nesilik Eskimo.* Watertown: Documentary Educational Resources. http://www.der.org/films/netsilik.html

Banks, Marcus, and Jay Ruby, eds. 2011. *Made to Be Seen: Perspectives on the History of Visual Anthropology.* Chicago: University of Chicago Press.

Barbash, Ilisa, and Lucien Taylor. 1997. *Cross-Cultural Filmmaking: A Handbook for Making Documentary and Ethnographic Films and Videos.* Berkeley: University of California Press.

Baron-Cohen, Sasha. 2006. *Borat: Cultural Learnings of America for Make Benefit Glorious Nation of Kazakhstan.* 1 hr, 24 min. Twentieth Century Fox.

Bateson, Gregory, and Margaret Mead. 1942. In *Balinese Character: A Photographic Analysis,* Special Publications of the New York Academy of Sciences, ed. W.G. Valentine, vol. II. New York: The New York Academy of Sciences.

———. 1950. *Karba's First Years.* 20 min. New York: New York University Film Library.

———. 1954. *Bathing Babies in Three Cultures.* 11 min. University Park: Pennsylvania State University.

Behar, Ruth. 1997. *The Vulnerable Observer: Anthropology That Breaks Your Heart.* Boston: Beacon Press.

Brewster, Joe, and Michele Stephenson. 2013. *American Promise.* 2 hr, 15 min. PBS.

Bruner, Jerome. 1984. Interaction, Communication, and Self. *Journal of the American Academy of Child Psychiatry* 23 (1): 1–7.

Buñuel, Luis. 1933. *Las Hurdes [Land Without Bread].* 27 min. Paris: Les Films du Panthéon.

Chaplin, Charlie. 1925. *The Gold Rush.* 95 min. United Artists.

Collins, Phil. 1983. Against All Odds (Take a Look at Me Now) [Song lyrics]. Atlantic Records.

Connor, Linda. 1995. The Action of the Body on Society: Washing a Corpse in Bali. *Journal of the Royal Anthropological Institute* 1 (3): 537–559. doi:10.2307/3034574

Coppola, Francis Ford. 1972. *The Godfather.* 2 hr, 55 min. Paramount Pictures.

———. 1979. *Apocalypse Now.* 2 hr, 33 min. Zoetrope Studios.

Csordas, Thomas J. 1990. Embodiment as a Paradigm for Anthropology. *Ethos* 18 (1): 5–47. doi:10.1525/eth.1990.18.1.02a00010

De la Falaise, Henry. 1935. *Legong, Dance of the Virgins.* 65 min. DuWorld Pictures (US) and Paramount International.

Edwards, Elizabeth. 2011. Tracing Photography. In *Made to Be Seen: Perspectives on the History of Visual Anthropology,* ed. Marcus Banks and Jay Ruby, 159–189. Chicago: University of Chicago Press.

Elder, Sarah, and Leonard Kamerling. 1974. *At the Time of Whaling.* 38 min. Watertown: Documentary Educational Resources. http://www.der.org/films/at-the-time-of-whaling.html

Flaherty, Robert J. 1922. *Nanook of the North*. 1 hr, 19 min. Pathé Exchange.

Freud, Sigmund, and J. Strachey. 1954. *The Interpretation of Dreams*. Trans J. Strachey. London: Hogarth Press.

Gardner, Robert. 1963. *Dead Birds*. 83 min. Watertown: Documentary Educational Resources. http://www.der.org/films/dead-birds.html

Geertz, Clifford. 1966. Religion as a Cultural System. In *Anthropological Approaches to the Study of Religion*, ed. Michael Banton, 1–46. London: Tavistock.

———. 1973. *The Interpretation of Cultures: Selected Essays*. New York: Basic Books.

Geertz, Hildred. 1994. *Images of Power: Balinese Paintings Made for Gregory Bateson and Margaret Mead*. Honolulu: University of Hawaii Press.

———. 2016. *Storytelling in Bali*. Leiden: Brill.

Girard, Todd A., Louis Lakatos, and Mahesh Menon. 2016. Aberrant Modulation of Brain Activation by Emotional Valence During Self-Referential Processing Among Patients with Delusions of Reference. *Journal of Behavior Therapy and Experimental Psychiatry*. doi:10.1016/j.jbtep.2016.11.007

Grad, Linda R., David Pelcovitz, Madelyn Olson, Michael Matthews, and Gary J. Grad. 1987. Obsessive-Compulsive Symptomatology in Children with Tourette's Syndrome. *Journal of the American Academy of Child and Adolescent Psychiatry* 26 (1): 69–73.

Grimshaw, Anna. 2011. The Bellwether Ewe: Recent Developments in Ethnographic Filmmaking and the Aesthetics of Anthropological Inquiry. *Cultural Anthropology* 26 (2): 247–262.

Grimshaw, Anna, and Amanda Ravetz. 2009. Rethinking Observational Cinema. *Journal of the Royal Anthropological Institute* 15 (3): 538–556. doi:10.1111/j.1467-9655.2009.01573.x

Gur, Raquel E., Christian G. Kohler, J. Daniel Ragland, Steven J. Siegel, Kathleen Lesko, Warren B. Bilker, and Ruben C. Gur. 2006. Flat Affect in Schizophrenia: Relation to Emotion Processing and Neurocognitive Measures. *Schizophrenia Bulletin* 32 (2): 279–287.

Heider, Karl. 1974a. *Dani Houses*. 35 min. Watertown: Documentary Educational Resources. http://www.der.org/films/karl-heider-dani-films.html

———. 1974b. *Dani Sweet Potatoes*. 35 min. Watertown: Documentary Educational Resources. http://www.der.org/films/karl-heider-dani-films.html

———. 1976. *Ethnographic Film*. Austin: University of Texas Press.

Henley, Paul. 2000. Filmmaking and Ethnographic Research. In *Image-based Research: A Sourcebook for Qualitative Researchers*, ed. Jon Prosser, 42–59. London: Routledgefalmer.

Hollan, Douglas, and Jane C. Wellankamp. 1994. *Contentment and Suffering: Culture and Experience in Toraja*. New York: Columbia University Press.

Hornaday, Anne. 2015. In the Golden Age of Documentaries, the Medium Could Use More Artistry. *The Washington Post Online*. Retrieved via https://www.washingtonpost.com/lifestyle/style/in-the-golden-age-of-documentaries-the-medium-could-use-more-artistry/2015/06/11/da59033a-0edf-11e5-adec-e82f8395c032_story.html?utm_term=.90fda5496321

Jaffe, Ira. 2005. Errol Morris's Forms of Control. In *Three Documentary Filmmakers: Errol Morris, Ross McElwee, Jean Rouch*, ed. William Rothman, 19–42. Albany: SUNY Press.

Jarrett, Michael, and Walter Murch. 2000. Sound Doctrine: An Interview with Walter Murch. *Film Quarterly* 53 (3): 2–11. doi:10.2307/1213731

Judson, Stephen. 2007. *The Alps*. 45 min. Laguna Beach: MacGillivray Freeman Films.

Junge, Winfried. 1961–2007. *Der Kinder von Golzow [The children of Golzow]*. 42 hr, 50 min.

Killingmo, Bjørn. 1997. The So-called Rule of Abstinence Revisited. *The Scandinavian Psychoanalytic Review* 20 (2): 144–159. doi:10.1080/01062301.1997.10592567

Kitayama, Shinobu, and Hazel R. Markus. 1994. *Emotion and Culture: Empirical Studies of Mutual Influence*. Washington, DC: American Psychological Association.

Layton, Bart. 2012. *The Imposter*. 95 min. Picturehouse Entertainment.

Lee, Junghee, William P. Horan, Jonathan K. Wynn, and Michael F. Green. 2016. Neural Correlates of Belief and Emotion Attribution in Schizophrenia. *PLOS One* 11 (11): e0165546. doi:10.1371/journal.pone.0165546

Leimbacher, Irina. 2009. Facetime. *Film Comment* 45 (1): 52–57.

Lemelson, Robert. 2009. *40 Years of Silence: An Indonesian Tragedy*. 86 min. Watertown: Documentary Educational Resources. http://www.der.org/films/forty-years-of-silence.html

———. 2010–2011. *Afflictions: Culture and Mental Illness in Indonesia Series*. 182 min. Watertown: Documentary Educational Resources. http://www.der.org/films/afflictions.html

———. 2010a. *The Bird Dancer*. 40 min. Watertown: Documentary Educational Resources. http://www.der.org/films/bird-dancer.html

———. 2010b. *Family Victim*. 38 min. Watertown: Documentary Educational Resources. http://www.der.org/films/family-victim.html

———. 2010c. *Shadows and Illuminations*. 35 min. Watertown: Documentary Educational Resources. http://www.der.org/films/shadows-and-illuminations.html

———. 2011. *Jathilan: Trance and Possession in Java*. 27 min. Watertown: Documentary Educational Resources. http://www.der.org/films/jathilan.html

———. 2011a. *Memory of My Face*. 22 min. Watertown: Documentary Education Resources. http://www.der.org/films/memory-of-my-face.html

———. 2011b. *Ritual Burdens*. 25 min. Watertown: Documentary Educational Resources. http://www.der.org/films/ritual-burdens.html

———. 2012. *Ngaben: Emotion and Restraint in a Balinese Heart*. 16 min. Watertown: Documentary Educational Resources. http://www.der.org/films/ngaben.html

———. 2015. *Bitter Honey*. 81 min. Watertown: Documentary Educational Resources. http://www.der.org/films/bitter-honey.html

———. 2017. *Tajen*. Elemental Productions.

Lemelson, Robert, and Anne Tucker. 2015. Steps Toward an Integration of Psychological and Visual Anthropology: Issues Raised in the Production of the Film Series *Afflictions: Culture and Mental Illness in Indonesia*. *Ethos* 43 (1): 6–39.

Lemelson, Robert, and Dag Yngvesson. 2006. *Movements and Madness: Gusti Ayu*. 71 min.

Lutz, Catherine. 1988. *Unnatural Emotions: Everyday Sentiments on a Micronesian Atoll and Their Challenge to Western Theory*. Chicago: University of Chicago Press.

MacDougall, David. 2003. Beyond Observational Cinema. In *Principles of Visual Anthropology*, ed. Paul Hockings. Berlin: Mouton de Gruyter.

MacGillivray, Greg, David Breashears, and Stephen Judson. 1998. *Everest*. 40 min. Laguna Beach: MacGillivray Freeman Films.

Marsh, James. 2008. *Man on a Wire*. 1 hr, 34 min. Magnolia Pictures.

Marshall, John. 1957. *The Hunters*. 1 hr, 12 min. Watertown: Documentary Educational Resources. http://www.der.org/films/hunters.html

———. 1971. *Bitter Melons*. 30 min. Watertown: Documentary Educational Resources. http://www.der.org/films/bitter-melons.html

———. 1980. *N!ai, Story of a !Kung Woman*. 59 min. Watertown: Documentary Educational Resources. http://www.der.org/films/nai-kung-woman.html

Marshall, John, and Claire Ritchie. 1951–2002. *A Kalahari Family*. 360 min. Watertown: Kalfam Productions and Documentary Educational Resources. http://www.der.org/films/a-kalahari-family.html

McElwee, Ross. 1986. *Sherman's March*. New York: First Run Features.

Mead, Margaret, and Gregory Bateson. 1952. *Trance and Dance in Bali*. 22 min. New York: New York University Film Library.

Morris, Errol. 1988. *The Thin Blue Line*. 103 min. Miramax Films.

———. 2003. *The Fog of War*. 107 min. Sony Pictures Classics.

———. 2008. *Standard Operating Procedure*. 118 min. Los Angeles: Sony Picture Classics.

Mosso, Luca, Daniela Persico, Alessandro Stellino, and Ross McElwee. 2013. *News from Home: Il Cinema di Ross McElwee*. Milano: Agenzia X.

Mulligan, Robert. 1962. *To Kill a Mockingbird*. 2 hr, 9 min. Columbia Pictures.

Murphy, Ryan. 2010. *Eat, Pray, Love*. 2 hr, 13 min. Columbia Pictures.

Nordstrom, Carolyn. 1995. War on the Front Lines. In *Fieldwork Under Fire: Contemporary Studies of Violence and Survival*, ed. Carolyn Nordstrom and Antonius C.G.M. Robben, 129–155. Berkeley: University of California Press.

O'Rourke, Dennis. 1991. *The Good Woman of Bangkok*. 82 min. Linfield, New South Wales. Film Australia.

Østergaard, Anders. 2009. *Burma VJ: Reporting from a Closed Country*. Dogwoof Pictures (UK) and Oscilloscope Laboratories (US).

Ruoff, Jeffrey. 1998. An Ethnographic Surrealist Film: Luis Buñuel's Land Without Bread. *Visual Anthropology Review* 14 (1): 45–57.

Scheper-Hughes, Nancy. 2000. Ire in Ireland. *Ethnography* 1 (1): 117–140. doi:10.1177/14661380022230660

Spiro, Melford E. 1993. Is the Western Conception of the Self "Peculiar" within the Context of the World Cultures? *Ethos* 21 (2): 107–153.

Taylor, Lucien. 1996. Iconophobia; How Anthropology Lost it in the Movies. *Transition* 69: 64–88.

Vannini, Phillip. 2015. Ethnographic Film and Video on Hybrid Television: Learning from the Content, Style, and Distribution of Popular Ethnographic Documentaries. *Journal of Contemporary Ethnography* 44 (4): 391–416.

White, Geoffrey M., and Anthony J. Marsella, eds. 1984. *Cultural Conceptions of Mental Health and Therapy*. Dordrecht: D. Reidel.

Wikan, Unni. 1990. *Managing Turbulent Hearts: A Balinese Formula for Living*. Chicago: University of Chicago Press.

———. 1991. Toward an Experience-Near Anthropology. *Cultural Anthropology* 6 (3): 285–305. doi:10.1525/can.1991.6.3.02a00020

Willen, Sarah S., and Don Seeman. 2012. Introduction: Experience and inquiétude. *Ethos* 40 (1): 1–23. doi:10.1111/j.1548-1352.2011.01228.x

Wood, David, Jerome S. Bruner, and Gail Ross. 1976. The Role of Tutoring in Problem Solving. *Journal of Child Psychiatry and Psychology* 17 (2): 89–100.

Yampolksy, Phillip. 1991–1999. *The Music of Indonesia [20-volume CD set]*. Washington, DC: Smithsonian Folkways.

Collaboration, Intervention, Compensation, and Ethics

Ethnographic film production is social and collaborative as compared to the mostly solitary act of writing a dissertation or a book. Throughout the process, there are opportunities to work with camera people, editors, musicians, producers, and other production assistants, not to mention collaborate and interact with film participants. These latter collaborations and interactions can give rise to some unique ethical issues, in particular because film participants sacrifice their anonymity more pointedly than participants in or subjects of written ethnography. Without an understanding of the key roles these domains play in the creation of visual psychological anthropology, the filmmaker risks both harming participants and creating thematically and ethically problematic films. Through a series of reflexive and retrospective accounts, this section addresses issues of relationships, collaborations, and ethical and other considerations that arise at the intersection of fieldwork, personal experience, and the relationships between filmmaker/anthropologist, research collaborators, and film subjects/participants.

11.1 HISTORY OF COLLABORATION IN ETHNOGRAPHIC FILM: PRECEDENTS AND MODELS

In thinking through models of collaboration, it is worth returning to the roots of ethnographic film and the way the pioneers of the genre approached working together on visual research. During the early years of ethnographic film, there were multiple models for collaboration between

© The Author(s) 2017   245
R. Lemelson, A. Tucker, *Afflictions*, Culture, Mind, and Society,
DOI 10.1007/978-3-319-59984-7_11

filmmakers and anthropologists. In one model, both were members of a larger research team. For example, Robert Gardner's *Dead Birds* (1963) was shot over the course of six months in the highlands of New Guinea as part of a larger research expedition, in part sponsored by the Film Study Center of Harvard's Peabody Museum, to make a comprehensive anthropological study of Dani tribal life in the Baliem Valley. The team included still photographer Eliot Elisofon, photographer and soundman Michael Rockefeller, anthropologist Jan Broekhuyse, anthropology graduate student Karl Heider, and writer Peter Matthiessen. This collaboration led to the production of written and visual documentation of the social and cultural fabric of the warrior-farmer community, which included two anthropological monographs, Matthiessen's *Under the Mountain Wall: A Chronicle of Two Seasons in the Stone Age* (1962) and *Gardens of War* (1968), a book of still photographs by Gardner and Heider, and of course Gardner's film.

Similarly, John Marshall began his career in visual anthropology as an eighteen-year-old, when he was the photographer on the expedition his father, Laurence K. Marshall, initiated in collaboration with Harvard University. Over a series of visits with the Ju/'Hoansi of Namibia, the entire family—including Marshall's father, his mother Lorna, and his sister Elizabeth—collected ethnographic data. Elizabeth produced her written ethnography *The Harmless People* (1959) and later *The Old Ways* (Thomas 2006), and Marshall shot his early films including *The Hunters* (1957), *Bitter Melons* (1971), parts of *N!ai, the Story of a !Kung Woman* (1980), and other shorts.

These early iconic films were products of the golden age of collaborative research projects in the social sciences in the 1950s and 1960s. There was much excitement about the possibility of uncovering the "deep" rules and structures governing human life. Due to the interest in collaboration, and an atmosphere conducive to the study of the social sciences, it was feasible to request funding for a filmmaker to accompany an interdisciplinary research expedition.

In these cases, the filmmaker gained access to film subjects through an anthropologist already well established in the area; the anthropologist provided contacts, relationships, and domains of exploration for the filmmaker and in return got to participate, either substantively or nominally, in the film production. The roles of anthropologist and filmmaker remained clearly delineated. This was the standard for decades.

Timothy Asch was a pioneer in this model of collaborative filmmaking. He viewed himself strictly and solely as the filmmaker. As such he had little theoretical anthropological points of his own to make; rather, he was guided by the needs of the anthropologists' projects. This resulted in some of the classics of ethnographic film, including *The Feast* (1970) and *The Ax Fight* (1975), which Asch made with anthropologist Napoleon Chagnon among the Yanomami, the series of films about the Balinese healer Jero Tapakan, made in collaboration with the anthropologist Linda Connor et al. (1979–1983), and other films in Indonesia.

This kind of collaboration had its strengths. Being comparatively unfamiliar with the local language and people, for example, meant that Asch could film more unobtrusively, unlike Connor who had lived in the community and remembers being frequently interrupted by old friends wanting to talk or onlookers asking questions. He was also able to offer a fresh and visually oriented perspective on data already familiar to her that she found to be enriching and illuminating (Connor 1988), suggesting that such a setup has the potential to add complexity, depth, and additional perspectives that complement whatever structural, linguistic, or other approaches the anthropologist herself may be using.

This model of collaboration can also bring a whole set of problems, which arose most notably in Asch's work with Chagnon (Borofsky 2005). Asch and Chagnon's collaboration was challenged by what Asch classified as Chagnon's gradually dissipating interest and dedication to the film project, and what Chagnon has recounted as Asch's behavior creating difficulty for him in the field (Ruby 1995). Perhaps ironically, the unfamiliarity that allows the filmmaker to work undisturbed also means he lacks the local knowledge that the anthropologist has, which can lead to misunderstanding or even offense and puts a heavier burden on the anthropologist, who then has to do extra work translating, brokering, organizing logistics, and doing damage control. Unfortunately, as Peter Biella and others note, many collaborations between ethnographers and filmmakers eventually end in contention and discord, as careers and talents develop, projects change or end, and working relationships become more complex and prone to conflict (Biella 1989; Biella, personal communication 2000). Along these lines, it is interesting to note that, unlike Asch who remained dedicated to working with anthropologists as part of a team despite such challenges, both Gardner and Marshall broke off to make films on their own, ultimately preferring this method. Gardner went on to Ethiopia and India and formulated his unique style of sensory filmmaking, informed by but not dependent on local knowledge. Marshall filmed in South Africa for eight years, and was then banned from the country in 1958 for advocating for the Ju/'Hoansi. He went on to a successful career as an independent documentary film cinematographer in the United States, shooting the classic *Titicut Follies* (1967) and other films, before being allowed to return to South Africa in 1978 to continue his work with the Ju/'Hoansi.

Jean Rouch, another profoundly influential innovator in the history of ethnographic film, preferred to shoot primarily on his own. Benefitting from technological advances that enabled synchronous sound and ever more lightweight camera equipment, advances that the previous filmmakers did not have access to at the start of their careers, Rouch disliked working with a team; he felt the ethnographer could be the only one with sufficient time in the field and understanding of the local language and culture to make educated, appropriate, and interesting choices behind the camera ([1973] 2003). While behind the camera, he preferred to work mostly alone, functioning as anthropologist, director, and cameraman all at once; he often worked in close collaboration with the characters in front of the camera to determine the content and narrative trajectory of his films. In his now-classic projects *The Human Pyramid* (1959) and *Jaguar* (1967), Rouch asked non-actors to play themselves in films with loosely scripted storylines. In these collaborations, participants—be they the white and black students of *The Human Pyramid* or the migrant workers of *Jaguar*—were asked to explore hypothetical situations based on real-life social, cultural, and political moments, calling upon their personal experiences to inform their acting.

Ultimately, with the advent of cheap digital technologies, the need for the anthropologist to work with a filmmaker is much lessened—she can film on her own. This is not necessarily all for the good; although there is certainly an increase in the number and diversity of digital projects, the quality has been variable, as the anthropologist is often a film autodidact with more, or less, experience making films. When a collaborative relationship can be formed, there are the previously described potential upsides to handing over filmmaking tasks to a professional, while the anthropologist steps in as an advisor, consultant, and cultural broker.

Despite various forms of collaboration between filmmakers and anthropologists, or filmmaker cum anthropologists and their film subjects during research and filming, it has often been taken for granted that when it comes to editing and polishing the film, the filmmakers, and not the subjects, make most content, aesthetic, and technological decisions. While screening rough cuts and final products with subjects to ensure that participants are comfortable with the material and feel that their experience is being accurately represented has become common practice (e.g. Gill 2014), "collaboration" tends to refer to that between anthropologists and filmmaker or the film production team (Coffman 2009). Other forms of collaboration between filmmakers, subjects, and community do exist; for example, "participatory visual ethnography" has received positive critical analysis in recent anthropological works for putting the needs, purposes, and perspectives of film subjects and their communities first, often when covering politically and emotionally charged topics (Coffman 2009; Gubrium and Harper 2013; Pink 2001, 2012) or being utilized for activist community work or "social interventions," (Collier and Collier 1986; also see Pink's introduction to the Applied Anthropology issue of *Visual Anthropology Review* and other case studies in this issue, 2004).

There are caveats in any working collaborative relationship. For example, when the anthropologist and filmmaker hold distinct positions, it is important discuss who "owns" any footage to be shot; a potential danger is that the filmmakers might believe that because they shot the footage they "own it," while the anthropologists might hold that because the "content" and access to subjects, settings, and so on are through their work, at a minimum the footage should be shared.

Furthermore, when delineating separate roles in this manner, collaborators should come to an understanding of how the material will be used early in the process; otherwise anthropologists may have little control over the material, its import, how subjects are portrayed, how research is portrayed, or indeed how they themselves are portrayed.[1] Unfortunately, this is often the case when anthropologists collaborate with television documentary outlets such as the Discovery Channel, National Geographic, and the History Channel. This style of "collaboration" is only partly collaborative, and should only be considered if the anthropologist is willing to take the risk that their work could be truncated, misunderstood, or even misrepresented.

Even if filmmaker and anthropologist come to some understanding that both will have a role in making a film, it can be challenging to determine final decision-making powers in any edit. Conflicts will naturally arise, as anthropologists and filmmakers have been trained to see many things differently, and priorities in academia and film communities can vary widely. Anthropologists may want specific information included, explained in particular ways to address important issues in their field. Filmmakers can oppose these on the grounds that they make uninteresting films.

Whether anthropologists/filmmakers are working with an entire team, one or two collaborators, or alone, the principle of professionalism and clear communication about the above issues will save a lot of pain and suffering, and allow projects to be swiftly ushered out into the world.

11.2   The Importance of Local Collaborators

While there still is a popular image of the solo anthropologist in the field, in general ethnographic films thrive on local collaboration. Collaboration can bring many benefits, including access to research participants, ideas for research concept development, a richer and more contextualized understanding of data gathered, and the sustainability of long-term fieldwork projects. As local collaborators can draw on their knowledge of local culture directly from their own experience rather than from academic or etic perspective, they can assist in orienting the anthropologist toward key aspects of practices, phenomenology, and experiential relevance. In addition, they may have established networks of information and support that they have better access to than foreign researchers. Local research collaborators share a common language, both literally and figuratively, with film subjects; this builds a crucial sense of trust (Chambers 1985; Coffey 1999; Fluehr-Lobban 2008a, b, 2013; Kulick and Wilson 1995; Marcus and Fischer 1999; Ruby 2000).

Photo 11.1   Local collaborators and crew shoot an interview

Local collaborators can assist gathering case material and provide updates that influence project development, production planning, and ongoing film editing. In addition, they can assist in shooting material during the rest of the year for fill-ins of shots, interview material for an edit in progress, or when something of significance is occurring (such as a life cycle ritual like a wedding or funeral, or when a subject is going through a personal time of transition and change, and the depiction of this is relevant for the emerging film).

But perhaps even more importantly, local researchers maintain ongoing relationships of trust and support for participants that extend well beyond the limited time of film shoots, to the benefit of both these individuals and the research project. Collaborators can play various roles in the film subjects' lives, from that of friend, to counselor, to practical strategist, and more. At the most basic level, local members of the research team can make regular social calls on film subjects in their homes to maintain friendships; at the most delicate and complex, they can provide emotional support for any issues that arise out of the film process or other life events.

In relation to the *Afflictions* (Lemelson 2010–2011) series, maintaining these relationships of trust was particularly critical with Javanese Indonesian subjects, who prefer to maintain smooth and harmonious relationships—or at least, the appearance of them—by avoiding discussion of difficult or sensitive issues. When asked how she was able to get emotionally sensitive materials with Javanese subjects, Ninik Supartini noted:

> I believe in anthropological research like this, we need to build trust between [ourselves] as researchers, and also with the subjects. And that's why I have tried so hard to maintain a relationship between the subjects and me ... I keep visiting the subjects, building the friendships with them, asking what is new in their life ... Really, as the local collaborator I don't think I limit myself for the work I have to prepare for when the team is in Indonesia. I go beyond that.

Ninik sees being with the research subjects "throughout the journey of the filming and the journey of their life struggles" as just as important a part of research as taking field notes or writing up case summaries. Accordingly, she maintains ongoing in-person friendships with the film participants as well as provides some practical support when necessary; for example, when it was time for Bambang's son to attend school but did not have the funds for the uniform and other necessities, she secured a financial sponsor for him.

In short, a combination of regular visits from the anthropologist and ongoing friendships with the local collaborating team allows research participants to feel increasingly comfortable in opening up about the details of their daily lives. This provides useful research data for those who want to understand the everyday experience and long-term trajectories of people living with mental illness. But it also serves as a support system for those vulnerable research subjects who may need assistance and friendship. As Tillman-Healy has described, part of using "friendship as method" means that in addition to the traditional forms of data gathering, the pace and procedures used are "those we use to build and sustain a friendship: conversation, everyday involvement, compassion, giving, and vulnerability" (Tillman-Healy 2003). Friendship and fieldwork are similar endeavors, as both involve interacting with others and moving through similar phases of gaining first entrée, learning new argot and codes of behavior, negotiating and reflecting on roles, and passing through stages of increasing intimacy from role-limited or instrumental interaction, to personal yet still role-bound relationships, to moments of true presence (Tillman-Healy 2003).

11.3   Intervention and Compensation

One of the first issues that will arise in working with film participants is how they will be compensated, if at all, for their participation and time. Directly paying informants is still a somewhat contested act that has been debated throughout the field's history. For example, while Margaret Mead (1969) believed in paying for work done, such as by interpreters or secretaries in the field, she proposed that ideally an anthropologist would not pay for information, such as interviews or demonstrations. The "benefit" gleaned by informants for those contributions would be more intangible, that is, the intellectual excitement of being part of the project, a new perspective on their own culture and information about the anthropologist's world, and exposure to fieldwork skills and techniques. Mead's ideal informant was a "systematic collaborator" who, like the anthropologist, sought a deeper understanding of their own culture and was motivated to discuss it at length simply for that reason. Seemingly, the intellectual rewards precluded the need for any additional monetary or tangible reimbursement for the collaborator's time.

Since Mead, "reflections on fieldwork" (Rabinow 1977) of many varieties (Fabian 2014; Madison 2011; Springwood and King 2001) have listed and often decried or bemoaned the ways in which goods have been exchanged for information as a standard part of fieldwork. Napoleon Chagnon and Tim Asch's extensive film work with the Yanomami of Venezuela (Asch and Chagnon 1974; Chagnon and Asch 1973) became one of the most hotly criticized ethnographic projects in the history of the field, in part because Chagnon compensated his informants with objects such as fish hooks, matches, steel tools, and machetes, which some alleged escalated violence between tribe members (Borofsky 2005), due to jealousy and access to new weapons. In a perhaps equally contested counterexample, Colin Turnbull was criticized for his *failure* to provide his Ik research subjects with any compensation, despite the fact that he had more than adequate provisions and they were literally starving (Grinker 2001).

Subjects in research on mental illness and disability may be suffering due to multiple factors, feeling pain in economic, familial, social, physical, even spiritual domains. In these circumstances, direct intervention on the part of the anthropologist may seem called for, but it is not always possible. Helping with the economics and daily routines of your subjects and friends, even in minor ways, can perhaps effect positive change in their lives more successfully—and perhaps counterintuitively, in a *less* problematic manner— than a direct intervention into the specifics of the violence or abuse they may be suffering, but the matters of intervention and payment are quite complicated.

11.4 *AFFLICTIONS* EXAMPLE: THE COMPLEXITIES OF PAYMENT AND INTERVENTION IN THE MAKING OF *THE BIRD DANCER*

Sometimes paying a subject for their time or participation is not a straight-forward process. In Gusti's case, the lead author and local collaborators debated how to pay her. One suggestion was to pay a doctor to provide Gusti with free medical care in thanks for her participation; another was to pay her directly. The latter avenue was chosen, however, it turned out that Gusti's older brother immediately took the money from her to use for family purposes. While certainly much of this went toward the ever-present ceremonial obligations that every Balinese bears, the fact that he took it without leaving any for Gusti to spend as she saw fit upset her further. While this setup at first appeared to be respecting and honoring Gusti's individual participation in the project, it actually overlooked the collectivist values and local patriarchal kinship networks in which resources are distributed in Bali.

So what at first appeared to be a straightforward payment transaction was in fact quite complicated, and potentially caused more harm than good.

Even more complicated than offering Gusti money was the question of whether to intervene into Gusti's family situation, and if so, how. Over the course of research, it became clear to us that much of Gusti's suffering was being caused by her family's (mis)treatment of her. Simultaneous to the family's sincere and ongoing search for a cure was a sense of frustration, shame, and anger about Gusti's illness and its socially embarrassing symptoms. As previously described, Gusti's condition stressed the entire family as their attempts to cure her weighed on their economic resources. Gusti's brother berated and mocked Gusti and, in extreme moments, lashed out physically. It was this violence, combined with the rejection, anger, criticism, ridicule, and contempt that her brother expressed toward her, that was most painful for Gusti and that she saw as a stressor that exacerbated her symptoms and worsened her condition.

Despite concern, there was little that could be done to ameliorate this situation. There was certainly little in either national or customary (B.I. *adat*) law that would realistically apply in her situation, and local authorities would most certainly have left the matter up to the family (Hakimi et al. 2001). Therefore, while the lead author had a long-term affiliation and relationship with this family, and could to a certain extent discuss their situation, he was still an outsider and realistically there was little he could do in way of intervention. Directly intervening in a family process, no matter how distressing for both the subject and the anthropologist, would have been problematic (see Chap. 6); if efforts had been made to directly intervene when Gusti described the abuse meted out to her at her brother's hands, it is quite likely he, and subsequently the family and Gusti herself, would have rejected any additional help or advice.

That said, Gusti was supported in her decision to leave the family compound and find employment as a maid in Denpasar. Unfortunately, after gathering up the courage and resources to do this, Gusti's relationship with her employer in many ways replicated her family dynamics—the woman was imperious and worked Gusti very hard, with long hours and few days off. In 2011, through a colleague who owned a fair-trade factory, Gusti was hired to make souvenirs for the globalized trade in Bali "*object d'art.*" The owner had progressive policies and had employed other Balinese people with disabilities. As of late 2016, Gusti has been working at the factory, lives nearby, and now is fully self-supporting. In addition, she is demonstrably happier with both her work and social situation, having made friends in this much-improved environment. She is even, at long last, being courted by a young man from a neighboring village.

This intervention into Gusti's work life arguably had a more powerful and lasting effect on her daily routine, relationships and economic status, than a direct confrontation with her family would have had, and did not require any pointed or implied critique of family dynamics. Through work Gusti left the house and her stressful situation, gained higher social status as a wage earner, and met new people, which along with her elevated social status could potentially increase her ability to gain a husband.

Ultimately, researchers or fieldworkers attempting to "help" a subject or informant, even with the best intentions and motivations, will probably encounter some difficulty. Even a relatively thorough understanding of the local culture does not necessarily confer the insight and wisdom to make truly helpful interventions in the participant's life. As in Gusti's case, any efforts are subject to the contextual and idiosyncratic aspects of the participant's life circumstances, personality, family, treatment course, and more. This is not to say that one should never attempt to aid long-term subjects, only that such aid is complicated, and unlikely to follow the expected course or have the expected outcomes.

11.5   ANTHROPOLOGICAL ETHICS AND THE *AFFLICTIONS* PROJECT

The AAA executive board recently published a position paper "Statement on Ethics: Principles of Professional Responsibility" (2002)[2] which outlined a number of key ethical domains anthropologists should be aware of and address in their research. Some of the domains that were and are relevant for the *Afflictions* project include:

- Do no harm
- Obtain informed consent and necessary permissions
- Make your results accessible
- Protect and preserve your records

These principles provide the structure for a discussion of ethical issues that arose during the making of *Afflictions* and, by extension, will certainly be relevant for other ethnographic filmmakers interested in visual psychological anthropology. Specific cases from the *Afflictions* series are explored in relation to a number of these categories—in some greater or lesser detail in relation to their relevance to the project—in order to provide context-specific and textured examples.

11.5.1   *"Do No Harm": Trauma and Visual Psychological Anthropology*

While the official ethical code of the AAA acknowledges that ethics are to a certain extent contextual and specific to particular situations, in general anthropologists are called to avoid harm or wrong, understanding that the development of knowledge can lead to change which may be positive or negative for the people involved, and to respect the well-being of all participants and preserve their safety and privacy.

One issue of great ethical importance to film projects that touch upon traumatic and violent histories is the risks for participants in disclosing aspects of personal experience that involve state and community violence, particularly when they may still be dealing with the underlying trauma associated with those experiences. First and foremost, the participants may be putting themselves or their families at risk simply by disclosing the facts of their traumatic history, and this risk is potentially heightened due to the public nature of video. The disclosure of experiences associated with state terror and community violence is often severely sanctioned, with the participant risking harassment, violence, imprisonment, or even death. It is necessary to have clear, extensive, and ongoing discussions about this risk with participants as the project progresses, and political contexts for potential violence and retribution shift—and particularly, before the release of any material—but such discussions do not eliminate the risks associated with disclosure. For *Afflictions*, local collaborators are in ongoing contact with the participants, and check in on them to see if there are any repercussions from their participation.

Alongside the dangers of potential outside retribution for disclosing traumatic histories on-screen, conducting long-term PCE raises subtle ethical quandaries with regard to the participant's psychological well-being. Is it right to deliberately re-expose a person to traumatic memories that have not been verbalized and/or have potentially been long repressed, and thus risk re-igniting the negative emotional states associated with them? This risk is both immediate to the interview and ongoing after the interview is over. In the short-term, retelling stories of past may cause the subject to re-experience the negative emotional and physical states associated with the trauma, which can be significantly distressing. There is also a risk that the retelling of long suppressed or buried memories can "kindle" (in the psychiatric sense) or catalyze a longer-term decompensation into psychopathological states such as psychosis (Kinzie and Boehnlein 1989). Of course, there are certain psychiatric treatment modalities, such as narrative exposure therapy, which argue for the potential benefits of having subjects repeatedly narrate or retell their stories of trauma; outcomes of such therapy for people of various cultural backgrounds and types of trauma are reported to be a decrease in trauma symptoms and depression (Foa et al. 1995; Neuner et al. 2004), and have been suggested, if not clinically proven, in experimental and interdisciplinary feminist folklore on narrative and trauma (Carver and Lawless 2010). But, even if present, such benefits would be diminished in ethnographic work as compared to a more formalized course of treatment.

There are number of standard procedures anthropologists can follow to mitigate the risks associated with asking subjects to recall and re-narrate past experiences of trauma, social violence, and loss. One obviously is to make the subjects aware of the risks, as part of an "informed consent" process where the interviewer and subject engage in conversation about the risks associated with retelling past traumas but the complexities here are numerous (see below and also Sankar 2004; Fluehr-Lobban 1994). If after this informed consent process the interviewer and subject decide to move forward despite the risks, there are other cautionary procedures that should be planned and implemented. One is telling the subjects that, if they so decide, they may stop their narration, the interview session, or their participation in the research entirely, at any point. This raises some challenges for a filmmaker, however, because some of the best material from a dramatic perspective can come from emotionally difficult retellings: A true commitment to ethical filmmaking may mean a willingness to forego what could potentially be the most powerful sequence in your film.

Take for example, the case of Abraham Bomba in the film *Shoah* (Lanzmann 1985). This example simultaneously highlights the ethical problem of pressuring a film subject to continue their trauma narrative when they clearly do not want to—and in fact have repeatedly requested to stop—and also the dramatic effect and utility of gaining such difficult narrative material. In this instance the filmmaker, Claude Lanzmann, is interviewing his subject, Mr. Bomba, in a barbershop where he is cutting someone's hair. (We later find in the films notes that this was a staged re-enactment, that Mr. Bomba was no longer a barber, and that the filmmaker had actually set this up in order to re-evoke or dramatically re-create the story Mr. Bomba is about to narrate). Mr. Bomba, a Jew who had been deported to Auschwitz, recounts how he was required to cut thousands of people's hair in the antechamber before the gas chambers. If he had refused, he would have been immediately executed. One day several months into his imprisonment, people from his own village were brought in to be murdered and Bomba was forced to cut the hair of his own family members. A more dramatic and horrific scene can hardly be imagined, and Mr. Bomba repeatedly asks the filmmaker for permission to stop the interview, while from off-camera, Lanzmann is heard repeatedly pressuring him to continue. This is one of the most poignant and difficult to watch scenes in the entire nine-hour film series; one can only imagine the anguish Mr. Bomba relived in the retelling of this narrative. Yet ultimately, his suffering plays an important role in the emotional force and power of the film series, and thus functions as an extraordinarily important addition to the historical recounting of the Holocaust.

More closely related to the subject matter here is Joshua Oppenheimer's documentary *The Act of Killing* (2012), which uses not just retelling, but re-enactment in a chillingly creative way. Oppenheimer films perpetrators who carried out some of the killings that took place in Medan, Indonesia, in 1965, as they willingly re-enact their past violent murders, indulging their fantasies of being Hollywood movie stars while drawing out the dark truths about the dynamics of these killings. This film was potentially dangerous for the filmmakers, in that many of those who orchestrated the killings of 1965 are still in power. Indonesian film crewmembers chose to remain anonymous in the credits for fear of retribution, and Oppenheimer claims he cannot return to Indonesia after exposing the perpetrators and other political actors. Participation at times seems transformative for some past perpetrators who seem to undergo a profound and perhaps remorseful realization about what they had done (while other seemed unaffected on-screen); while such transformation may seem like a positive moral development (is this the role of documentary film?) it could have potentially had dramatic and unpredictable repercussions. Those few scenes where victims participated in the filming were certainly potentially triggering, as in one scene where the son of a victim breaks down on-screen as he imagines what his father went through and voices his family's grief. Ultimately, the filming was troubling and upsetting to some degree for all involved, but if Oppenheimer had stopped he would have missed the opportunity to get psychological insight into the human scale of these mass killings, and the chance to bring this history to a wide global audience.[3]

11.5.2 Afflictions *Example: 1965 and the Risks of Disclosure in "Shadows and Illuminations"*

The lingering effects of the same violence and upheaval that Oppenheimer explores in his films were also significant for a number of *Afflictions* participants. The supposed communist coup and the swift and bloody military response left many Indonesians physically injured, traumatized, and stigmatized. Discussion of this event was forbidden and dangerous, unless grounded in the monolithic state narrative about the events and meaning of 1965. Meanwhile, cultural models of trauma response favored an avoidance of open discussion of these events and those in power manipulated a politics of memory wherein the victims of the events of 1965 were themselves framed as perpetrators in need of forgiveness and rehabilitation (Lemelson and Suryani 2006; Lemelson et al. 2010).

This history raised particular ethical issues in relation to harm and its avoidance when conducting visual psychological anthropology in Indonesia. While public discussions of the events of 1965–1966 have become increasingly more open since Suharto's fall in 1997, many people still feel uncomfortable discussing these events and can still face repercussions and trouble on neighborhood, village, and state levels for speaking out against the New Order government, speaking freely about past violence, or acknowledging past association with the communist party, no matter how minimal (Dwyer 2009; Dwyer and Santikarma 2003; Retsikas 2006; Zurbuchen 2005).

While the events of 1965 figure more prominently in certain characters' stories than others, in many of their narratives experienced, witnessed, and remembered episodes of violence and hardship echo as formative moments with long-lasting repercussions in personal schemas of worry, anxiety, and distress; Ni Ketut Kasih, Bambang's wife Yatmi, and other characters mention this. For Kereta of *Shadows and Illuminations*, it was a core element of his story and his experience of mental illness.

Over the course of multiple interviews with Kereta, the numerous causes for his lingering grief were explored, but it was only in the last meeting, right before returning to the United States from fieldwork in the Spring of 1997, that, in hushed tones, Kereta revealed his trauma narrative about 1965, in perhaps the most intimate and in-depth conversations Kereta had had about these events than he had ever had with anyone in his life. By his own admission, Kereta had never narrated these events to his wife, or sons, extended family, and certainly not to any of his *banjar* neighbors, some of whom participated in the mass killings. He had never even discussed this with those neighbors he knew had had similar experiences. A local clinician and researcher who had worked with Kereta said that he "is quiet, he doesn't talk things out and keeps everything to himself. It seems that this trait played a significant role in his experience of trauma. When he was terrified after witnessing the incident, he had no one to talk to, and he didn't dare talk about it. . . He never revealed this to me or others."

His choice to disclose such painful and terrifying experiences at this moment was significant. Perhaps he felt safe telling a trusted outsider his difficult and politically charged story. After ongoing interviews, he had developed a close relationship with the lead author, so he felt safe; at the same time, the lead author was soon returning to the United States, and therefore he could be confident knowing the information he divulged would not be used against him in his local Balinese communities.

While Kereta did use the research as an opportunity to share his harrowing episode of political violence for the first time, he did not seem to be re-experiencing unbearable distress during the retelling, and did not ask to stop filming; in fact, as described above, it may have been a (consciously or unconsciously) strategic move to reveal his past to a foreigner and relieve some of his long-pent-up feelings and memories about the event (indeed there is evidence for biological, in this case immunological change, in retelling narratives long psychologically hidden or repressed) (Pennebaker 2012; Pennebaker and Beall 1986; Smyth et al. 2012). However, even if the process had caused Kereta more distress than it did, the testimony is crucial not only to understanding Kereta's experience of mental disturbance but also to building a record of the long-term impacts of the 1965 genocide (Cribb 2004)—on the mental health of everyday Indonesians.

In order to mitigate the risk caused by re-exposing a subject to traumatic memories, it is helpful for an anthropologist to work with local psychiatric or medical treatment providers who are familiar with the case and the research, and are also familiar with treatment modalities for trauma. While in many instances it may be unreasonable to expect such expert resources will be available, for the *Shadows and Illuminations* production Indonesian research partners trained in psychiatry, psychology, and counseling were standing by and willing to provide aid, in the form of on-site or remote counseling and/or medication or consultation, if that became necessary.

Kereta does not appear to have experienced any long-term negative effects of recounting his trauma on-screen. In fact, it appears to be the opposite; he clearly enjoyed the attention and focus on his experience and condition that the filmmaking relationship fostered. He has become more easygoing and comfortable over the years, although it is difficult to say whether this was due to the relationship and the attention it brought to his life and experiences, or to the relaxation of the forms of surveillance of political beliefs and actions under the New Order period, or both.

11.5.3   "Obtaining Informed Consent": The Complexity of True Consent

Related to the "Do No Harm" precept is the ethics of visual representation and informed consent. Particularly in the current internet era, anthropologists must realize the ease of access to sensitive information in the YouTube digital age; even if this context of constantly available and constantly new media filming is "forever," in that the stories one tells about film subjects and the filmic representation of their lives may survive long after the circumstances of their lives might have changed. Films can still function to essentially "freeze" a subject in time. Given their subject matter, the *Afflictions* films have captured their subjects going through very difficult times in their lives, even experiencing crisis, such as hospitalization for active psychotic symptoms or depression. These moments are calcified in representational images that may create an enduring depiction of a subject that elides or excises the majority of their life experience, providing a one-dimensional view that does not accurately reflect the changes—either positive or negative—that have occurred in their life since. This is somewhat mitigated by shooting diachronically, capturing the subjects over many years throughout the many changes they experience over the course of their lives, and yet, what the world knows of the subject will be what they see on-screen.

Filmmakers need to think about the implications of this when constructing their film, understanding the multiple ways in which their subjects could be perceived—not just by students or other outsiders, but more importantly by members of their local communities. The growth of globalized digital media networks, comparatively new in the history of ethnographic film, means that these representations are more immediately accessible to a wider audience than ever before, often instantly available in subjects' local communities at the click of a button or with the typing of a simple search phrase on YouTube or Vimeo. Filmmakers working on mental illness and other issues in psychological anthropology such as family dynamics, personal development, and intimate relationships gain access to sensitive information and thus have an ethical imperative to consider the potentially beneficial but also potentially harmful impact their films might have on the changing landscape of ethnographic and non-fictional film and video. The ethics of representation become heightened because visual methods strip subjects of their anonymity and confidentiality by representing them visually, even as the research probes into areas where subjects may feel most vulnerable and leaves them open to criticism or stigma.

As stated earlier, in the *Afflictions* film production, rough cuts are shown to participants before a film is finalized and released in order to gain a fuller and more complete "formal consent." More than just signing a form, it is key the subject has a comprehensive understanding of the purposes of the project, the audiences who will see the film, the potential impact the film's release might have on their lives, and so on. Because this policy is implemented for all films, there is the opportunity to observe a range of possible subject responses about how they feel about their visual representation on-screen. Interestingly, perhaps the most common response participants have is that they feel the representation of their story is accurate. Now, this needs to be taken with a grain of salt as it could be interpreted as the subjects wanting to appear compliant and friendly, particularly in Java and Bali, where direct conflict is actively avoided and a veneer of social harmony is deeply prized (Geertz 1969), but perhaps it is the result of filmmaking methods in visual psychological anthropology that hold quite closely to subjects' "lived experience."

An example of the complexities of this process can be seen in *Memory of My Face*. At first, it was difficult if not impossible to gain informed consent from Bambang to film while he was manic in the mental hospital, so consent was given by the director of the hospital, who was also Bambang's psychiatrist. This footage was kept confidential and private until true informed consent was gained from Bambang. The team returned to film Bambang over the years from 2002 to 2011 and held numerous discussions with him about the purpose of the film, his participation in it, and issues of informed consent. Bambang was a well-educated man who understood the implications of his participation in the project, including the potential harm that could come to him in the form of the shame and stigma directed toward Indonesians living with severe mental illness. Indeed, in his daily life he was quite discreet and careful to not let his local community know that he was a former patient in the state mental hospital because he believed that it would impact his ability to find work as an elementary school tutor or instructor in the *kampung*. Despite all this, he supported the project and became an active advocate for mental health issues through his participation in screenings and Q&As.

It is rare for participants to ask that material be cut out of the film, but some notable strong exceptions have occurred, particularly in the portrayal of Estu and his family in *Family Victim.*

11.5.4   Afflictions Example: Negotiation and the Informed Consent Process in Family Victim

Throughout the process of shooting and editing the final cut of *Family Victim*, there were ongoing negotiations with Estu's family about the content of the film. In 2004, Estu and Ninik were shown an early cut of *Family Victim*, well before the planned release date. After this private screening there were extensive discussions about the film, the portrayal of Estu as the main participant, how the film would be used and where it might be screened, the implications of the film for Estu's relationship with his family, and what would happen if and when the film was screened in his local community.

Surprisingly, it was Ninik who initially objected to this early cut. She was especially concerned—frankly, even somewhat horrified—when viewing certain scenes, because she felt they exposed family secrets. For example, Ninik was adamant that the way Estu's relationship with his father had been positioned, interpreted, and explained needed to be reworked. Furthermore, in their desperation over Estu's misconduct, his family had taken recourse, in a disturbing but anthropologically fascinating turn, to their own violent intentions. It was common knowledge among Estu's family that he had studied various forms of "black" magic in order to enact revenge upon his family for what he perceived to be their slights and lack of support. While to a Western viewer without a belief in the supernatural this may not seem like significant violence and perhaps more like therapeutic venting, to a Javanese believer this is akin to plotting murder. It turned out his family was also seeking advice from *dukun* and *orang tua*, traditional figures with knowledge and power in supernatural realms, seeking to learn more about Estu or use this magical advice and power to change or stop him. It was only through an extended and at times quite painful process of discussion, evaluation, and modification that all agreed on a version that was palatable to Ninik, yet still met the lead author's standards for what the film was attempting to present.

In an interesting countertrajectory, upon viewing that early cut Estu gave his consent for the film to be released, saying, "It is an accurate picture of my life, and I'm okay with other people seeing it." Due to a number of other factors, the final film was not completed until 2010. At this point, the lead author had not seen Estu for a number of years but felt significant work on informed consent had been done with him on previous similar cuts—indeed the earlier cut Estu had approved was in some ways harsher and more direct in the way it depicted family criticisms of his behavior than the final version; as the film was edited, there was an attempt to portray him in as comprehensive and sympathetic a light as possible, given the multiple levels of moral complexity, dysfunction, and disruption that his family believed stemmed from his behavior.

In 2009, Elemental uploaded a two-minute trailer of the film to YouTube. YouTube had only been around for several years at this point, yet its distribution was already global. Within a week of the trailer being released, someone in rural Java—in fact, in Estu's local community—had seen it and had pointed it out to Estu. Although Estu did not contact me directly, Ninik informed me that he was apparently quite upset by the trailer, and his anger over his representation in the film had caused a further rift between himself and his family. The representation of his "problems" and socially deviant behavior (e.g. problems with theft, gambling, explosive temper, and violent threats to family members) were troubling and eventually enraging to Estu, as if he had been shown a dirty mirror of himself. Ultimately, it turned out the film was also quite difficult for other members of Ninik's and Estu's family to watch, not only because it depicted painful disputes in the family history, but also because it had captured the recent passing of the patriarch of the family, which was difficult to re-experience through film while their grief was still fresh. The lead author immediately took the YouTube trailer down.

Family conflict had been ongoing for a number of years, as depicted in the film, so this YouTube trailer was just one more step in a very long journey of Estu's estrangement from his family; however it was a significant concern for the lead author. It was agreed upon not to plan any further screenings of the film in Central Java, at the least to lessen any further exposure of the material to people who might know Estu or the family personally; in fact, at the time of this writing, the film has yet to be screened in Indonesia.

After this incident, the lead author invited Estu to watch the final cut of the film together on a number of occasions. However, it was only in 2013 that Estu said he would be willing to watch the film. This change of heart may perhaps have taken shape because of changes in his life or because the matriarch of the family also passed away, or hope there would be some sort of financial gain for Estu. According to conversations with Estu's siblings, as time has gone by and with the passing of the parental generation, the shame, sadness, and difficulties associated with problems depicted in the film have lessened significantly. The topics addressed in the film are no longer such powerful sources of ongoing friction in the family, and therefore the film itself no longer evokes such raw feelings. Despite this, Estu and the lead author have yet to screen the film together. This opportunity is greatly anticipated because the research team and lead author considered Estu a friend and very much valued his perspective on the film; however there is not much hope for this, given the recent changes in Estu's life as reflected at the end of Chap. 6.

11.5.4.1 Informed Consent: Some Final Thoughts

Ultimately, when it comes to consent, participants may at first feel comfortable with material that later angers and upsets them, or they may consent to material depicting them in a way they identify with, and once they no longer identify with the character on-screen, they may protest. What should be done if, in a case like Estu's, a subject has revoked previous consent once the film is in distribution? What happens if a film subject decides they no longer want their image to be shown on-screen or to be associated with the project? Is the filmmaker/anthropologist at that point obligated to pull copies from distribution (which is nearly impossible in today's digital age) and/or make other efforts to stop the film from being seen?

There is no one-size-fits-all answer to these questions, but some lessons can be derived from this difficult situation. One is that the degree to which the material one gathers is of a sensitive and personal nature is the degree to which it is imbued with possibilities for negatively valenced emotions such as shame, guilt, or embarrassment. Even if at the time of the initial interview or film shoot one's subjects or collaborators may have expressed a sense of relief or other similar positive emotions about disclosing a difficult or long-hidden personal matter, they may have very intense and powerful feelings about the later public disclosure of this sensitive information via film.

In these circumstances, particularly when decisions about film distribution are being made, the subjects always have some element of power over the material and in their relationship with the anthropologist. While ideally research consent would be standardized, and consent protocols and conditions would apply to all subjects in a particular project, in reality, during long-term fieldwork, relationships go far beyond the set parameters of typical ethnographic research, and the purposes and domains in which material is gathered in the course of these complex encounters become greatly problematized. In this case, because Ninik was a research collaborator, friend, cultural broker, and subject herself, on top of the fact that this became a visual project, not just fodder for an academic scholarly article in a journal, the sensitivity increased manyfold, as in visual research many aspects of anonymity and confidentiality are abridged. But in this case, Ninik did retain a significant amount of influence over the project in order to directly shape and in some cases erase significant parts of the complex story that became *Family Victim*. So, while very revealing, the film only included aspects of the story that were edited according to the parameters of this complex relationship. While this example may be more complicated than a typical encounter at the interface of psychological and visual anthropology, the fact that these multiple issues were raised and, over the course of more than fifteen years, eventually settled in a multilayered series of discussions, negotiations, emotional encounters, and compromises demonstrates the complexity of attempting to produce a psychologically oriented visual anthropology.

What also emerged during this process was an understanding that certain material and interpretations of that material were better left "out of bounds." One could ask, at this point, where the line of objectivity and subjectivity lies, if a significant aspect of a respondent's story could be excised just like that. But these are the conundrums that arise during the processes of fieldwork and filmmaking; one makes ethical promises to one's subjects and collaborators and one needs to abide by those, even if the resulting process is not as clear and complete as hoped for.

11.5.5 *"Making Your Results Accessible" in Visual Psychological Anthropology*

The "results" of one's visual research can be made readily available to a wide academic and general audience. A film can be shared with the public in multiple formats such as DVDs, either via a mainstream or educational distributor, multiple types of streaming, and public presentations to academic and film-oriented audiences, as well as to the community of origin. *Afflictions* films come with free study guides, oriented at an upper division undergraduate level, that outline a number of the themes and issues in each film. The films are also available to stream internationally in a wide variety of platforms, and with the exception of educational distribution, they are either free or available for a nominal price, which allows the larger interested public in Indonesia to watch and use them. Arguably, if made in a certain way, visual research has more of a chance to receive non-specialized coverage due to its translational appeal, and so has the possibility to play in movie theaters and/or receive journalistic coverage.

11.5.6 *"Protect and Preserve Your Records": Considerations for Better Practice*

Following this ethical guideline, one should have robust procedures in place for protecting and preserving records of visual psychological anthropology.

With video resources, one should immediately download footage each day after the shoot and log all clips. Elemental Productions stores footage on a password-protected hard disk, and only the film crew has access to them. When returning from the field, these assets are further loaded and digitally organized using a proprietary coding scheme, and then uploaded onto a secure, local server with a redundant array of inexpensive disk (e.g. a redundant array of independent disks, or RAID array) controlled by a local server. No one can access the server without a password. At this point, nothing is uploaded to the internet. They are also backed up to a separate RAID array, for preservation in case one of the originals has a total failure. The original hard disks are kept in a separate location.

Note that while the video footage is a primary concern, visual anthropology includes written records too, such as transcribed transcripts, field notes, production handbooks, interview schedules, materials gathered in the field such as subjects' drawings, and so on. All paper assets are stored in a locked, secure location.

11.6   CONCLUSION: ETHICS DISCUSSIONS NEED TO BE CONTINUOUSLY ADDRESSED

In visual psychological anthropology, as in other areas of anthropology, as projects continue, relationships with collaborators, subjects, and communities become increasingly complex; one's material grows and needs continuous safeguarding; films mature and near completion, raising new concerns about issues such as doing no harm and informed consent. Each of these areas has complex and interrelated ethical issues and brings new ethical challenges.

It is quite clear that, even with the best efforts to do one's complete due diligence, engage in informed consent, take proper care of the material, and balance complex, competing concerns, one must commit to multiple and continuous levels of ethical oversight of a film project. There will always be unseen and expected hurdles to surmount in order to finish and distribute a film based on longitudinal PCE in an ethical manner, but meeting this challenge appropriately will not only fulfill one's ethical obligations, but in general result in a better film.

NOTES

1. The lead author was once told by a collaborator that he should not expect to have any rights or access to material, using the analogy of an animal in a wildlife documentary that has no rights to the material that is being shot about it.

2. The AAA has a position paper on "Guidelines for the Evaluation of Ethnographic Visual Material," and the Society for Visual Anthropology (SVA) has had numerous forums on ethics in visual anthropology, but neither has released a position paper on ethics for visual anthropology separate from the more generalized AAA "Statement on Ethics."

3. His second film on the same topic, *The Look of Silence* (2014), illustrates the complex issues of memory, narration, and how, absent any formal legal and state process like a Truth and Reconciliation commission, an individual can seek some form of understanding by confronting perpetrators of genocide. Oppenheimer clearly set up the circumstances by which the main character remembers the killing (in part by watching footage from *The Act of Killing*) and himself helps to orchestrate the confrontation.

REFERENCES

American Anthropological Association. 2002. *Principles of Professional Responsibility*. AAA Ethics Blog [online]. Retrieved via http://ethics.americananthro.org/category/statement/

Asch, Timothy, and Napoleon Chagnon. 1970. *The Feast*. 29 min. Watertown: Documentary Educational Resources. http://www.der.org/films/feast.html

———. 1974. *A Father Washes His Children*. Watertown: Documentary Educational Resources. http://www.der.org/films/father-washes-his-children.html

———. 1975. *The Ax Fight*, from the *Yanomamo Series*. 30 min. Watertown: Documentary Educational Resources. http://www.der.org/films/ax-fight.html

Biella, Peter. 1989. Trouble Shooting: Overcoming Problems of Collaborations with Filmmakers. *New York Folklore* 15 (3–4): 47–67.

Borofsky, Rob. 2005. *Yanomami: The Fierce Controversy and What We Can Learn from It*. Berkeley: University of California Press.

Carver, M. Heather, and Elaine J. Lawless. 2010. *Troubling Violence: A Performance Project*. Jackson: University Press of Mississippi.

Chagnon, Napoleon, and Timothy Asch. 1973. *Magical Death*. 29 min. Watertown: Documentary Educational Resources.

Chambers, Erve. 1985. *Applied Anthropology: A Practical Guide*. Englewood Cliffs: Prentice-Hall.

Coffey, Amanda. 1999. *The Ethnographic Self: Fieldwork and the Representation of Identity*. London: Sage.

Coffman, Elizabeth. 2009. Documentary and Collaboration: Placing the Camera in the Community. *Journal of Film and Video* 61 (1): 62–78.

Collier, John, and Malcolm Collier. 1986. *Visual Anthropology: Photography as a Research Method*. Minneapolis: University of Minnesota Press.

Connor, Linda. 1988. Third Eye: Some Reflections on Collaboration on Ethnographic Film. In *Anthropological Filmmaking: Anthropological Perspectives on the Production of Film and Video for General Public Audiences*, ed. Jack R. Rollwagen. Newark: Harwood.

Connor, Linda, Timothy Asch, and Patsy Asch. 1979–1983. *Jero Tapakan Series*. Watertown: Documentary Educational Resources. http://der.org/films/jero-tapakan-series.html

Cribb, Robert. 2004. The Indonesian Genocide of 1965–66. In *Teaching about Genocide: Issues, Approaches and Resources*, ed. S. Totten. Fayetteville: University of Arkansas Press.

Dwyer, Leslie. 2009. A Politics of Silences: Violence, Memory and Treacherous Speech in Post-1965 Bali. In *Genocide: Truth, Memory, and Representation*, ed. Alexander L. Hinton and Kevin L. O'Neill, 113–146. Raleigh: Duke University Press. doi:10.1215/9780822392361-005

Dwyer, Leslie, and Degung Santikarma. 2003. When the World Turned to Chaos: 1965 and Its Aftermath in Bali. In *The Specter of Genocide: Mass Murder in Historical Perspective*, ed. Robert Gellately and Ben Kiernan. New York: Cambridge University Press. doi:10.1017/cbo9780511819674.013

Fabian, Johannes. 2014. *Time and the Other: How Anthropology Makes its Object*. New York: Columbia University Press.

Fluehr-Lobban, Carolyn. 1994. Informed Consent in Anthropological Research: We Are Not Exempt. *Human Organization* 53 (1): 1–10.

———. 2008a. Anthropology and Ethics in America's Declining Imperial Age. *Anthropology Today* 24 (4): 18–22.

———. 2008b. New Ethical Challenges for Anthropologists. *Chronicle Review* 55: B11–B12.

————. 2013. *Ethics and Anthropology: Ideas and Practice*. Lanham: Alta Mira Press.

Foa, Edna B., Chris Molnar, and Laurie Cashman. 1995. Change in Rape Narratives During Exposure Therapy for Posttraumatic Stress Disorder. *Journal of Traumatic Stress* 8 (4): 675–690.

Gardner, Robert. 1963. *Dead Birds*. 83 min. Watertown: Documentary Educational Resources. http://www.der.org/films/dead-birds.html

Gardner, Robert, and Karl G. Heider. 1968. Gardens of War. In *Life and Death in the New Guinea Stone Age*. New York: Random House.

Geertz, Clifford. 1969. *The Religion of Java*. New York: Free Press.

Gill, Harjant. 2014. Before Picking Up The Camera: My Process to Ethnographic Film. *Anthropology Now* 6 (1): 72–80.

Grinker, Roy R. 2001. *In the Arms of Africa: The Life of Colin Turnbull*. Chicago: University of Chicago Press.

Gubrium, Aline, and Krista Harper. 2013. *Participatory Visual and Digital Methods*. Walnut Creek: Left Coast Press.

Hakimi, Mohammad, Elli N. Hayati, V. Utari Marlinawati, Anna Winkvist, and Mary C. Ellsberg. 2001. *Silence for the Sake of Harmony: Domestic Violence and Women's Health in Central Java*. Yogyakarta: CHN-RL GMU.

Kinzie, J. David, and James J. Boehnlein. 1989. Post-Traumatic Psychosis Among Cambodian Refugees. *Journal of Traumatic Stress* 2 (2): 185–198.

Kulick, Don, and Margaret Wilson, eds. 1995. *Taboo: Sex, Identity and Erotic Subjectivity in Anthropological Fieldwork*. New York: Routledge.

Lanzmann, Claude. 1985. *Shoah*. 9 hr, 26 min. BBC.

Lemelson, Robert. 2010–2011. *Afflictions: Culture and Mental Illness in Indonesia Series*. 182 min. Watertown: Documentary Educational Resources. http://www.der.org/films/afflictions.html

Lemelson, Robert, Ninik Supartini, and Emily Ng. 2010. Ethnographic Case Study: Anak PKI: A Longitudinal Case Study of the Effects of Social Ostracism, Political Violence, and Bullying on an Adolescent Javanese Boy. In *Formative Experiences: The Interaction of Caregiving, Culture, and Developmental Psychobiology*, ed. Carol M. Worthman, Paul M. Plotsky, Daniel S. Schechter, and Constance A. Cummings, 378–389. New York: Cambridge University Press.

Lemelson, Robert, and Luh Ketut Suryani. 2006. The Spirits, Ngeb, and the Social Suppression of Memory: A Complex Clinical Case from Bali. *Culture, Medicine and Psychiatry* 30 (3): 389–413.

Madison, D. Soyini. 2011. *Critical Ethnography: Method, Ethics, and Performance*. London: Sage.

Marcus, George E., and Michael M.J. Fischer. 1999. *Anthropology as Cultural Critique: An Experimental Moment in the Human Sciences*. Chicago: University of Chicago Press.

Marshall, John. 1957. *The Hunters*. 1 hr, 12 min. Watertown: Documentary Educational Resources. http://www.der.org/films/hunters.html

————. 1971. *Bitter Melons*. 30 min. Watertown: Documentary Educational Resources. http://www.der.org/films/bitter-melons.html

————. 1980. *N!ai, Story of a !Kung Woman*. 59 min. Watertown: Documentary Educational Resources. http://www.der.org/films/nai-kung-woman.html

Mattheisien, Peter. 1962. *Under the Mountain Wall: A Chronicle of Two Seasons in the Stone Age*. New York: Viking.

Mead, Margaret. 1969. Research with Human Beings: A Model Derived from Anthropological Field Practice. *Daedalus* 98 (2): 361–386. http://www.jstor.org/stable/20023882

Neuner, Frank, Margarete Schauer, Christine Klaschik, Unni Karunakara, and Thomas Elbert. 2004. A Comparison of Narrative Exposure Therapy, Supportive Counseling, and Psychoeducation for Treating Posttraumatic Stress Disorder in an African Refugee Settlement. *Journal of Consulting and Clinical Psychology* 72 (4): 579. doi:10.1037/0022-006X.72.4.579

Oppenheimer, Joshua. 2012. *The Act of Killing*. 1 hr, 55 min. Final Cut for Real.

————. 2014. *The Look of Silence*. 1 hr, 43 min. Final Cut for Real.

Pennebaker, James W. 2012. *Opening Up: The Healing Power of Expressing Emotions*. New York: Guilford Press.

Pennebaker, James W., and Sandra K. Beall. 1986. Confronting a Traumatic event: Toward an Understanding of Inhibition and Disease. *Journal of Abnormal Psychology* 95 (3): 274.

Pink, Sarah. 2001. *Doing Visual Ethnography: Images, Media and Representation in Research*. London: Sage.

————. 2004. Guest Editor Introduction: Applied Visual Anthropology Social Intervention Visual Methodologies and Anthropology Theory. *Visual Anthropology Review* 20 (1): 3–16.

————. 2012. *Situating Everyday Life: Practices and Places*. London: Sage.

Rabinow, Paul. 1977. *Reflections on Fieldwork in Morocco*. Berkeley: University of California Press.

Retsikas, Konstantinos. 2006. The Semiotics of Violence: Ninja, Sorcerers, and State Terror in Post-Soeharto Indonesia. *Bijdragen tot de taal-, land-en volkenkunde/Journal of the Humanities and Social Sciences of Southeast Asia* 162 (1): 56–94. doi:10.1163/22134379-90003674

Rouch, Jean. 1959. *The Human Pyramid*. 1 hr, 30 min. Les Films de la Pléiade.

————. 1967. *Jaguar*. 88 min. Icarus Films.

————. 1973/2003. *Ciné-Ethnography*. Trans. S. Feld. Minneapolis: University of Minnesota Press.

Ruby, Jay. 1995. Out of Sync: The Cinema of Tim Asch. *Visual Anthropology Review* 11 (1): 19–37. doi:10.1525/var.1995.11.1.19

————. 2000. *Picturing Culture: Explorations of Film and Anthropology*. Chicago: University of Chicago Press.

Sankar, Pamela. 2004. Communication and Miscommunication in Informed Consent to Research. *Medical Anthropology Quarterly* 18 (4): 429–446. doi:10.1525/maq.2004.18.4.429

Smyth, Joshua M., James W. Pennebaker, and Danielle Arigo. 2012. What Are the Health Effects of Disclosure? In *Handbook of Health Psychology*, ed. Andrew Baum, Tracey A. Revenson, and Jerome Singer, 175–192. New York: Psychology Press.

Springwood, Charles Fruehling, and C. Richard King. 2001. Unsettling Engagements: On the Ends of Rapport in Critical Ethnography. *Qualitative Inquiry* 7 (4): 403–417.

Thomas, Elizabeth M. 1959. *The Harmless People*. New York: Alfred A. Knopf.

———. 2006. *The Old Ways: A Story of the First People*. New York: Farrar, Straus and Giroux.

Tillman-Healy, Lisa. 2003. Friendship as Method. *Qualitative Inquiry* 9 (5): 729–749.

Wiseman, Frederick. 1967. *Titicut Follies*. 84 min. Zipporah Films.

Zurbuchen, Mary Sabina. 2005. *Beginning to Remember: The Past in the Indonesian Present*. Singapore: NUS Press.

CHAPTER 12

Visual Psychological Anthropology: Implications for Teaching and the Future

There are both opportunities and challenges ahead for ethnographic film that is resonant and integrated with the methods and insights of contemporary psychological anthropology. The new ease and accessibility of digital technology means the filmmaking process is more affordable and flexible than early visual anthropologists could ever have imagined, allowing for new sorts of films that would have once been less feasible. Even with the exigencies of limited and circumscribed budgets, longitudinal filmmaking is now cheaper than it has ever been before. Thanks to these technological advancements, psychological anthropologists currently have an amazing opportunity to break new ground, to come up with new ways of knowing and new modes of representation, to educate a new generation of "digital native" students who are sophisticated visual communicators and consumers, to contribute to translational or applied psychological anthropology and cultural psychiatry, and to connect the research with a larger audience and to emotionally move them by showing the humanity of the participants, both their universal struggles and the cultural specificity of their lives. This book has offered both theoretical and practical considerations for a visual psychological anthropology. But what audiences could most benefit from this sort of work?

© The Author(s) 2017
R. Lemelson, A. Tucker, *Afflictions*, Culture, Mind, and Society,
DOI 10.1007/978-3-319-59984-7_12

12.1   The Use of Film in Psychological Anthropology Pedagogy

One of the primary audiences that visual psychological anthropology is directed toward is undergraduate and graduate students. There are multiple ways in which visual psychological anthropology can be used in pedagogical presentations. Certainly, many anthropologists include at least a nominal clip of fieldwork for teaching and scholarly presentations. This can be made to illustrate a point about fieldwork or to introduce the fieldwork setting. A slightly more involved demonstration would be to incorporate more extended clips that illustrate a point about fieldwork or theory. As anthropologists become more comfortable with editing the film footage of their fieldwork, an even more sophisticated presentation is possible, where anthropologists engage with some of the basics of filming to edit on their video data and then integrate it into their presentations using programs such as PowerPoint or Keynote.

In the classroom, most faculty use films to differing degrees. Most professors integrate some film into lectures and seminars, in the form of outtakes from research, film clips from other films, or complete films. For example, in basic survey courses in cultural anthropology, films are typically employed to illustrate specific aspects of technology, social structure, ritual, and so on. In this way, films give students a glimpse or illustration of what they are reading about in the accompanying ethnographies or articles. In psychological anthropology per se, films are frequently and similarly used in domain-specific sense (e.g. used as an investigation or illustration of a broader topic or theme or field of study, such as child development) rather than taking a biographical or character-based perspective, which might better allow for a focus on issues of phenomenology, subjectivity, emotion, and so on.

Psychological anthropologists who are teaching undergraduates impart certain frames of reference and approaches to understanding the world, specifically with regard to theories of human behavior and how culture shapes its particularities. In helping students understand the theoretical approaches to these issues, and how the components of a particular theory are related to each other and overlapping or competing theories, psychological anthropologists are also trying to cultivate in students a critical perspective on the development of these theories. At the minimum, they understand their historical context, progression, and development. Perhaps as important is relating these theoretical constructs to the intentional worlds our subjects live in. Film can help situate these debates in by depicting the themes in the lives of individuals who embody aspects of these theories.

But one of the most powerful uses of film is to emotionally engage the student in an immersive film experience.

12.2 Teaching Visual Psychological Anthropology Films: Some Examples and Caveats

Films can provide a visceral, immediate, and even emotionally powerful counterpoint to written material as seen through the following examples taken from the teaching experience of the lead author. In teaching an undergraduate course on cross-cultural human development in a psychology department, some of the early modules were on cross-cultural perspectives on childbirth. Different visual examples of childbirth were drawn from several different sources, such as the film *We Know How to Do These Things* (1997), about birth in Nepal and the *Childhood Series* produced by PBS, which had three short examples of childbirth in the United States, Russia, and Brazil. *We Know How to Do These Things* is an ethnographic film shot in the Direct Cinema style, filmed with cameras on tripods, which documents a difficult childbirth in a village in central Nepal, shot in real time. Before watching this film, the students were asked about if they planned to have children. Perhaps two-thirds of the class raised their hand. After some opening titters and giggles about aspects of the film, an increasingly stony silence settled over the class. The students had an obviously strong reaction, as evidenced by the frightened and pale looks of many of the women in the class. The class again was asked how many still want to have children—now, less than a third raised their hands.

Introducing students to a real-time, immersive, and visually raw and real approach to childbirth provides a different experience than reading an article or book chapter about the embodied and subjective experience of the relationship of childbirth, pain, risk, and the variety of cultural settings that this takes place in every day all over the world. Having the events displayed visually in the classroom also meant that the students were not able to "turn away" from the experience being played out on the screen. Bringing it back to the students by asking them what their experience of watching the filmed childbirth was like and how that would affect their own decisions at some point later in their lives made the material much more resonant for them on a deep emotional and psychological level.

During a graduate seminar in psychological anthropology, another instance arose wherein a film had an obvious deep emotional impact on a student. The class watched a film entitled *First Person Plural* (2000), an autobiographical journey through transnational adoption that takes place in the United States and Korea, specifically in Korean orphanages. After the film played, one of the students, a young man of Korean descent, was clearly devastated. He disclosed to the class that he had been raised in a Korean orphanage under very similar circumstances to those the film documents, and then was adopted by an American family quite similar to the family in the film. As a result of watching this film, he began an autobiographical project, documenting his journey from Korea to the United States as a child, which culminated in a thoughtful and self-reflexive paper on the subject. If one of the goals of anthropology is to teach students in an empathetic way about the lives of cultural "others," film offers a direct and immediate way to achieve this goal—in this case, even eliciting the spontaneous sharing of personal experience, which might contribute to such cross-cultural understanding.

There are some dangers to relying on film however. Not all responses from audiences are the ones expected or desired by the filmmaker anthropologist. In teaching material on the Yanamamo to undergraduates, through the lens of Tim Asch's films, certainly one of the most common responses is a sense of retreat or even revulsion. When watching the intense emotional aggressive displays as seen in *The Ax Fight* (1975), or in watching the Yanamamo men snorting hallucinogenic *yage*, with green mucus pouring out of their noses and mouths, students often respond very negatively. In some, it increases or calcifies the attitude that the people being depicted are "savages," and such a problematic response might be more likely to occur with a general audience. It is impossible to always know the reaction certain material will evoke in an audience—and the responses a viewer may have to film content will be colored by their own cultural conventions, and as such, screenings are therefore never uncomplicated, even when it comes to teaching.

In 2014, the lead author's production company, Elemental Productions, released a feature-length film on polygamy in Bali entitled *Bitter Honey*. Throughout the course of the seven-year project, it was explicit throughout the production that film was *not* in any way a critique or rejection of polygamy as a kinship form. Yet, when the film was reviewed in multiple mainstream media outlets, the message that reviewers took away was that polygamy was a barbaric or outdated or primitive or abusive kinship form, and the film was perceived as a clarion call to modify or even abolish polygamy (Olds 2014; Rich 2014). When these reviews started coming in, a director's statement (Lemelson 2014) was released to clarify the film's intention and belief about polygamy as a kinship form. This read, in part:

> I overcame some initial hesitance to start a project about polygamy because, trained as an anthropologist, I was reluctant to portray a kind of marriage that certain audiences might judge negatively. But I soon realized that the emotional stories these wives have to tell held a powerful message about the relationships between men and women and the ways social rules and structures can put women at a disadvantage—or even trap or subjugate them.
>
> For the families I got to know, ongoing male domination and control determine the course of women's domestic, intimate, and economic lives. Yet in this and other ways, polygamous unions are similar to typical marriages. The struggles of polygamous wives are simply an extension of the overall diminished sense of choice and agency that women still experience in many public and private spheres [...]
>
> I was lucky to work with a team of Balinese collaborators who advised me in making this film. We hope that it accurately portrays the complexities of the lives of these families.

In the end, however, these misinterpretations of both the ethnographic material in films and the anthropologist's intent are outliers. In general, as noted repeatedly in this volume, films have an important role to play in range of understandings, from didactic information, to theoretical issues, to biographical narratives and not the least of which, to an emphatic understanding of other cultural worlds, filtered through the lives of the individuals who inhabit these worlds. This, needless to say, is a central orientation of the discipline of anthropology.

12.3   Public Presentation and Visual Psychological Anthropology

The use of relevant and impactful film may help push anthropology to regain the public relevance it had in the first half of the twentieth century. Some anthropologists used to be public intellectuals whose ideas mattered to the public and to other fields of scholarship. In particular, Margaret Mead was a public figure who pronounced on a range of topics from childhood to parenting to adolescent sexuality to analyses of nation states in the Cold War

(Mead 1966). Similarly there are a number of anthropologists in the current generation who have assumed the mantle of a public figure (such as Melvin Konner, with his works on a wide range of topics (Konner 1993, 2009, 2015) and Tanya Luhrmann via her opinion pieces on religion, magic, mental illness, and voice hearing in *The New York Times* [https://www.nytimes.com/by/t-m-luhrmann]). These past and present anthropologists have discussed and disseminated both their research, and relevant research in the field, to a broad public audience.

While there are some in contemporary anthropology who have taken public dissemination as an important aspect of their practice, many anthropologists rarely engage in public discussion or display of their data and theories. Anthropology has become increasingly insular, where many of the debates and discussions of research take place within the field, rather than on the public stage. During the last several generations, anthropology has become increasingly professionalized, witnessing an expansion in the number of practicing anthropologists as reflected in the membership in the American Anthropological Association (AAA) and an associated growth in influence on campuses, yet there has been a sense of disengagement from the public sphere.[1]

The same professionalization effect applies to ethnographic film. Most (but not all—see the wider interest in sensory ethnographies such as *Sweetgrass* [2009] and *Leviathan* [2012]) ethnographic films are publically viewed at specialist film festivals, such as the Society for Visual Anthropology film festival (http://societyforvisualanthropology.org/film-video-and-multimedia-festival). Again, in the past this was not true for ethnographic film. In previous generations, an anthropologist making an ethnographic film would collaborate with an established filmmaker who was associated with a commercial production company, producing content distributed on television or other broadcast mediums. This was expensive and time consuming, but it guaranteed a wide audience. Series such as *Odyssey* (1980–1981) and *Millennium* (Maybury-Lewis 1992) aired on prime time and had audiences numbering in the millions. The way ethnographic films used to be made, and the way people used to consume media—that is, with a limited number of films and limited venues for airing and watching these—guaranteed it a wide audience, meaning the ethnographic filmmaker was also a public figure.

The savvy use of visual or multi-modal media might reintroduce anthropological research, and might return ethnographic film to a position of relevance in the broader public's eye. In written anthropology, there has been a rise of public or semi-public digital platforms in which to discuss one's research, findings, and more general thoughts and beliefs on specific topics, such as the Public Library of Science, or PLOS blogs (http://blogs.plos.org/) or the recently unveiled "Sapiens" website (http://www.sapiens.org/). Here anthropologists present, debate, and discuss their findings in a way that was not possible a generation ago, with the swirl, flow, and global reach of digital media. The widespread use and accessibility of the internet and social media means that it is easier for an ethnographic film or other visual or multimedia material to be made and immediately presented to viewers.

The digital realm has provided additional venues for the dissemination of ethnographic film. Currently, it is more common for anthropologists to distribute their films and other digital productions on the internet, either for a specific audience of fellow specialists or, less commonly, toward a more pragmatic end, such as raising awareness about an issue or advocating for a certain group (e.g. Dizard 2013).

The *Afflictions* (Lemelson 2010–2011) series demonstrates the possibilities for multiple forms of public engagement. It is available to anthropologists and institutional screenings at www.der.org. It has been screened widely to diverse audiences in the mental health field, at clinics, hospitals, conferences, and academic settings. It is widely disseminated to the general public on the internet, through venues like Amazon, Vimeo, YouTube, and other streaming venues. But perhaps most impactfully, it has increasingly been put to use for purposes of education, awareness, and advocacy by local organizations working on the ground in Indonesia. The *Afflictions* films have been shown at various venues and events in Indonesia and have been used as part of campaigns to familiarize and de-stigmatize mental illness by organizations such as the Schizophrenia Society of Indonesia (*Komunitas Peduli Skizofrenia Indonesia*, or KPSI) and the Department of Social Welfare. The films have also been screened at Indonesian universities for medical, psychology, and other students (Andarningtyas 2012; Erna Dinata, personal communication 2014). These screenings are used as part of efforts to promote a "person first" view of those with mental illness, which demystifies mental illness and neuropsychiatric disorders to promote greater understanding, acceptance, and better social supports.

The main subjects/participants in the film often attend these screenings and participate in Q&A sessions, discussing their role and depiction in the film, and speaking on the issues the films grapple with. In this way audiences can meet the participants in the flesh, engage with them as real people, discuss the changes they have experienced on- and off-screen, and ask them about their understanding of the film and its impact on their lives. The film participants can advocate for their own experiences and share the new narratives of their mental illness that they developed over the course of filming, shooting, talking to the research team, and meeting others affiliated with the project. The ability to act as a spokesperson for growing social acceptance for people with mental illness, and to be present at screenings to interact with specialist and general audiences has also been very fulfilling for Bambang, who said:

> In fact, this film can help many people get better. It serves as a motivation for me. As it turns out, I can take advantage of this disease. My suffering [h]as a silver lining.

This dialogue and interaction that is possible with a film can rival or exceed that of a book or journal article. The transformation from the beginning of the films, where Gusti is a self-loathing and miserable teenager and Bambang is confined to a psychiatric ward, to seeing them both confidently and eloquently testifying to and then answering questions about their lived experience makes for powerful viewing. The films have been well received by professionals, academics, and Indonesians with mental illness; some viewers with mental illness have expressed surprise and a sense of gratification at seeing experiences similar to theirs portrayed on-screen (Siregar 2013).

12.4   CHALLENGING ANTHROPOLOGY'S FOCUS AS "A DISCIPLINE OF WORDS": WHAT THE FUTURE PORTENDS?

A strong case in this book is that psychological anthropologists should seize the opportunity to integrate filming in the methodological toolkit they bring to the field. Why haven't they done so to date? There are three broad answers.

The first is a matter of finance. In the past, making a film was prohibitively expensive and by necessity anthropologists needed to collaborate with established filmmakers and production companies. That is clearly no longer the case as the cost of getting equipment that will meet the needs of many film projects becomes increasingly affordable.

The second is a matter of technical expertise and training. Again in the past gaining the necessary skills to operate film cameras and related equipment such as editing systems was usually an investment of time and expertise that most anthropologists could not afford.

The third regards the utilization of film material for academic advancement. Certainly departments of anthropology have grappled with how to evaluate visual materials, in this case ethnographic film, as a criterion for tenure. The first author received feedback from a tenure committee that, to paraphrase, "...he has completed eight films. That could be comparable to a monograph." This recognition, of course, does not take in the enormous amount of work that goes into a completed, multi-year film, as well as the potential a film can have on one's subfield, the broader public, and perhaps most significantly, the community where one has done one's fieldwork.

Criteria that can be used to evaluate an ethnographic film, or other visual material, for tenure purposes could be:

1. Distribution by a reputable educational distributor, such as Documentary Educational Resources.
2. Admission to one or more ethnographic film festivals.
3. Admission to an online, peer-reviewed video journal
4. *Review* in an anthropological scholarly journal.

If these criteria, or other similar formulations, are adopted by university anthropology departments, the tenure barrier can be lifted.

In order to make the best of the opportunities afforded by a visual psychological anthropology, a significant goal must be to achieve a balance between verbal and written material and visual representation, to recognize that good ethnographic film *is* scholarship, both part and product of high-quality ethnographic research. Indeed, the future of ethnography proper will be increasingly visual and multi-modal as researchers, educators, and learners evolve along with the media and technology used in social, expressive, research, and academic lives.

Visual anthropology, and in particular artfully edited, person-centered, and narrative driven films, should not be thought of merely as educational or entertaining content that supplements or complements written scholarship; rather it should count as scholarship in its own right, it should be acknowledged for the kinds of insights and access it can provide that the written word cannot provide, and it should be embraced, taught, and included in new forms of multi-modal anthropological scholarship.

If one of the goals of an increasingly engaged and activist anthropology is to think through the ways in which such work affects the individuals, communities, and societies in which anthropologists work, it is quite clear that a "journal only" approach to the dissemination of the knowledge and subsequent understanding it creates has limitations in effecting any sort of change or difference in the lives of the participants—or even, a response from them regarding the work. While the written word, in the form of journal articles, book chapters, and monographs, will remain the standard and perhaps most highly valued form of presentation in anthropology, those in the field need to clearly and carefully think through the limitations of this mode of expression. In particular, anthropologists need to consider how people are consuming information and knowledge, and what is lost and gained in these different and varied modes of consumption.

Given these considerations, an articulation for the next step to be taken in psychological anthropology is an investment in visual psychological anthropology. Since psychological anthropologists will need solid practical but also theoretical grounding in how to make films appropriate to and expressive of their field and genre, visual psychological anthropology is a way to push core psychological anthropology methods into a new era of visual research. The principles outlined below are a natural extension of the fieldwork and multi-modal ethnographic research described over the course of the book. The ethnographic findings about the lived experience of mental illness and neuropsychiatric disorder in Indonesia have related to a reflexive examination of filmmaking process, and both inform the proposal below.

First, one needs a firm grounding in both anthropological theory and a specific topical domain, before one sets out to film anything. For example, at the heart of the six *Afflictions* films were substantive research projects in both transcultural psychiatry and psychological anthropology. Underlying each of these broad subjects was an engagement not only with the central questions of the research, but also the multiple domains and frames needed to understand, expand upon, and contextualize the research. For example, the *Afflictions* series dealt with issues of gender and power, of stigma and isolation, of deviance and control, of developmental progressions and their vicissitudes, of kinship and family processes, of the shaping processes of history on subjective experience, of the many forms of social violence and trauma, of extraordinary experience and the complexities of interpretation, of multiple forms of healing, of reflexivity, ethics, and at their extremes, about the possibilities for redemption and overcoming. Each one of these has deep roots in anthropological history and practice, and without a continual engagement (and ongoing, reflexive forms of learning) with these theories and their articulation, the film process would have foundered on the shoals of misunderstanding and misinterpretation. It is this process that makes a film "ethnographic."

But a film is not just an explication of a research theory and project. It has to highlight elements of the research, but it is much more. At its heart is a story—a story of the research, certainly, but also a story of a time and place; a narrative of an individual; and can also be a story of the researcher or filmmaker and their relationship to all of these areas. It should also be, at some level, an aesthetic experience that engages (and possibly challenges) the senses, perceptions, internal schemas, and understandings of the viewer.

It is this last point that anthropologists who want to engage in a visual psychological anthropology need the most guidance and preparation. One assumes that their training in theory in anthropology and in the reading and understanding of ethnography will prepare and guide them to generate both interesting and important questions for their research, and give them a set of methodological tools to explore these. Where their preparation can fail them, however, is engaging similar tools, both theoretical and methodological, to explore their important research questions and scholarly interests in a visual and narrative way. One of the purposes of this book has been to provide a set of guidelines, and illustrative examples, on how to not only craft competent and engaging films, but how to connect these films to a more classical descriptive written ethnography, which formed the core six chapters of Part 2.

It is possible that conducting field research geared toward the ultimate product of an edited film—as opposed to, or in addition to, a written monograph—will engender a particular way of doing ethnography in the field. Technical and interpersonal methodologies for working with a visual research team have been discussed; could it be that a filmic eye for, or a collaborative approach to, ethnography may lead to new ways of knowing participants? Does it enable or invite certain kinds of insights that other forms of data collection do not? How is thinking filmically a new way of knowing?

One of the challenges in achieving this multi-modal integration and balance is mastering the technical expertise required to integrate psychological anthropology and film. Training is necessary for the development of the technical skill and filmmaking craft required to make high-quality psychologically oriented anthropological ethnographic film. It is not enough simply to have a camera available, since the footage appropriate for data collection and analysis, shot by an often unsteady hand, poorly lit, poorly composed, and with inadequate audio levels, will not necessarily be compelling, or even usable, when attempts are made to transform this material either into full-length films or even shorter compositions edited for lecture, conference, or translational presentations. Fortunately, even a basic understanding of filmmaking techniques (e.g. shot composition, lighting, and camera angles), editing skills (e.g. cutting and re-combining footage using a specific computer program, and basic sound mixing), and moving image storytelling can boost the production value of ethnographic film and video without significant additional expense. An increase in moving image fluency and professionalization within the field will lead to a wider recognition of psychological anthropology's scholarly contributions and translational appeal, which would encourage future collaborations between anthropologists and filmmakers to mutual benefit.

Therefore, increased training in the consumption and production of ethnographic film and related areas in visual anthropology should be an integral part of psychological anthropology education. However, as has been recently argued (Lemelson and Tucker 2015; Lemelson 2013; Ruby 2013), this opportunity has not been sufficiently explored by either seasoned or emerging visual and psychological anthropologists. The failure to seize this digital moment risks the field being left behind or having our material expropriated.

Psychological anthropologists wanting to make films to highlight their concerns and life work need a more masterful grasp not just of the technical skills required to craft good films, but also of the underlying theory and method of how audio-visual and film materials communicate. While it is expected that many, if not most, anthropologists from any sub-discipline who want to make films will most likely be working with a diverse team, to be a useful part of this team anthropologists need basic competencies in filmic and visual thinking. They also need to be afforded a degree of creative freedom to make unique stylistic choices that will result in films that are faithful to individual experience, communicative of cultural and psychological content, and just as importantly, exciting to watch.

The effort put in to learn the skills of filmmaking, and its integration into one's research, can lead to deeply satisfying work and, more importantly, expand upon what it means to have a vocation as a psychological anthropologist. It can involve one in engaging relations with film professionals, interactions with local colleagues who can become lifelong friends, and most importantly, can allow one to reach across boundaries of time and space, language, history, gender, and cultural difference, to engage, connect, and bond with others, as you tell their stories to the world.

NOTE

1. This disengagement with the public is common across different social science disciplines. The 2012 documentary *The Perverts Guide to Ideology*, narrated by the Slovene philosopher and psychoanalyst Slavoj Zizek, is one of the few popular explications of critical social theory in documentary film oriented toward the general public. The film has a continuous narrative by Zizek and ranges over psychoanalytic, Marxist, post-modern, and related theories to explore ideology as it is embodied in cinema.

REFERENCES

Ambrosino, Michael. 1980–1981. *Odyssey Series*. 16 hr, 42 min. Watertown. Documentary Educational Resources. http://www.der.org/films/odyssey-series. html

Andarningtyas, Natisha. 2012. Kisah Para Penderita Skizofrenia dalam Film. *Antara News*. Retrieved via http://www.antaranews.com/berita/396063/kisah-para-penderita-skizofrenia-dalam-film

Asch, Timothy, and Napoleon Chagnon. 1975. *The Ax Fight*. 30 min. Watertown: Documentary Educational Resources. http://www.der.org/films/ax-fight.html

Castaing-Taylor, Lucien [See also Taylor, Lucien], and Ilisa Barbash. 2009. *Sweetgrass*. 101 min. Cinema Guild.

Castaing-Taylor, Lucien [See also Taylor, Lucien], and Verena Paravel. 2012. *Leviathan*. 1 hr, 27 min. The Cinema Guild.

Dizard, Jesse. 2013. *Treading Water*. 26 min. Advanced Laboratory for Visual Anthropology. http://www.csuchico.edu/alva/projects/2013/treading-water. shtml

Johnson, Barbara. 1997. *We Know How to Do These Things: Birth in a Newar Village*. 40 min. Watertown: Documentary Educational Resources. http://www.der.org/films/we-know-how.html

Konner, Melvin. 1993. *Medicine at the Crossroads: The Crisis in Health Care*. New York: Pantheon Books.

———. 2009. *The Jewish Body*. New York: Penguin Random House.

———. 2015. *Women After All: Sex, Evolution, and the End of Male Supremacy*. New York: W. W. Norton.

Lemelson, Robert. 2010–2011. *Afflictions: Culture and Mental Illness in Indonesia Series*. 182 min. Watertown: Documentary Educational Resources. http://www.der.org/films/afflictions.html

———. 2013. Why I Make Ethnographic Films (Instead of Writing a Monograph...). Psychocultural Cinema. Retrieved via http://psychoculturalcinema.com/why-i-make-ethnographic-films-instead-of-writing-a-monograph/

———. 2014. Director's Statement. Bitter Honey Website. Retrieved via http://www.bitterhoneyfilm.com/

Lemelson, Robert, and Annie Tucker. 2015. Steps Toward an Integration of Psychological and Visual Anthropology: Issues Raised in the Production of the Film Series Afflictions – Culture and Mental Illness in Indonesia. *Ethos* 43 (1): 6–39.

Maybury-Lewis, David. 1992. *Millennium: Tribal Wisdom and the Modern World series.* 600 min. Los Angeles: KCET Los Angeles.

Mead, Margaret. 1966. *Soviet Attitudes Toward Authority: An Interdisciplinary Approach to Problems of Soviet Character.* New York: Schocken Books.

Olds, Dorri. 2014. 'Bitter Honey' Shows Ugly Side of Bali, Where Polygamy and Domestic Abuse Reign. *The Blot Magazine*, October 2.

Rich, Jamie S. 2014. Outmoded Marriage Customs in Bali are the Subject of Documentary 'Bitter Honey': Indie & Art House Films. *The Oregonian*, November 27.

Ruby, Jay. 2013. The Digital Revolution and Ethnographic Film. Psychocultural Cinema. Retrieved via http://psychoculturalcinema.com/thedigital-revolution-and-anthropological-film/

Siregar, Lisa. 2013. Working to Help Indonesians Understand Schizophrenia. *The Jakarta Globe* [online]. Retrieved via http://jakartaglobe.id/features/working-to-help-indonesians-understand-schizophrenia/

Appendix

Name	Year	Director	Running time	Production company/distributor
40 Years of Silence: An Indonesian Tragedy	2009	Robert Lemelson	86 min	Documentary Educational Resources
The Act of Killing	2012	Joshua Oppenheimer	122 min	Final Cut for Real
Afflictions: Culture and Mental Illness in Indonesia Series	2010–2011	Robert Lemelson	182 min	Documentary Educational Resources
The Alps	2007	Stephen Judson	45 min	MacGillivray Freeman Films
An American Family	1973	Craig P. Gilbert		PBS
American Promise	2013	Joe Brewster and Michele Stephenson	2 hr, 15 min	PBS
Apocalypse Now	1979	Francis Ford Coppola	2 hr, 33 min	Zoetrope Studios
Are the Kids Alright?	2004	Karen Bernstein and Ellen Spiro	56 min	Fanlight Productions
At the Time of Whaling	1974	Sarah Elder and Leonard Kamerling	38 min	Documentary Educational Resources

(*continued*)

R. Lemelson, A. Tucker, *Afflictions*, Culture, Mind, and Society,
DOI 10.1007/978-3-319-59984-7

Name	Year	Director	Running time	Production company/ distributor
The Ax Fight	1975	Timothy Asch and Napoleon Chagnon	30 min	Documentary Educational Resources
Bathing Babies in Three Cultures	1954	Gregory Bateson and Margaret Mead	11 min	Pennsylvania State University
Bethel: Community and Schizophrenia in Northern Japan	2007	Karen Nakamura	40 min	Manic Films
The Bird Dancer	2010	Robert Lemelson	40 min	Documentary Educational Resources
Bitter Honey	2015	Robert Lemelson	81 min	Documentary Educational Resources
Bitter Melons	1971	John Marshall	30 min	Documentary Educational Resources
Borat: Cultural Learnings of America for Make Benefit Glorious Nation of Kazakhstan	2006	Sasha Baron-Cohen	1 hr, 24 min	Twentieth Century Fox
Borneo [Martin and Osa Johnson]	1937	Truman H. Talley	76 min	Turner Classic Movies
Burma VJ: Reporting from a Closed Country	2009	Anders Ostergaard	1 hr, 24 min	Dogwoof Pictures (UK) and Oscilloscope Laboratories (USA)
Calcutta	1969	Louis Malle	105 min	Nouvelle Éditions de Films
A Celebration of Origins	1992	E. Douglas Lewis, Timothy Asch and Patsy Asch	45 min	Documentary Educational Resources
Chronique d'un été [Chronicle of a Summer]	1961	Jean Rouch and Edgar Morin	1 hr, 25 min	Argo Films
Crisis: Behind a Presidential Commitment	1963	Richard Drew	52 min	National Film Registry of the Library of Congress

(*continued*)

Name	Year	Director	Running time	Production company/ distributor
A Curing Ceremony	1969	John Marshall	9 min	Documentary Educational Resources
Da Feast!	2009	Artemis Willis	22 min	Documentary Educational Resources
Dani Houses	1974	Karl Heider	35 min, 9 min extras	Documentary Educational Resources
Dani Sweet Potatoes	1974	Karl Heider	35 min, 9 min extras	Documentary Educational Resources
Dead Birds	1963	Robert Gardner	83 min	Documentary Educational Resources
Death by Myth	1951–2001	John Marshall	90 min	Documentary Educational Resources
Der Kinder von Golzow [The Children of Golzow]	1961–2007	Winfried Junge	42 hr, 50 min	
The Devil and Daniel Johnston	2005	Jeff Feuerzeig	110 min	Sony Pictures Classics
The Divine Horseman: The Living Gods of Haiti	1953	Maya Deren	52 min	Howard Gottlieb Archival Research Center
Bob Dylan: Don't Look Back	1967	D. A. Pennebaker	1 hr, 36 min	Leacock-Pennebaker
Eat, Pray, Love	2010	Ryan Murphy	2 hr, 13 min	Columbia Pictures
The Emperor's Naked Army Marches On	1987	Kazuo Hara	122 min	Imamura Productions
The Epic of Everest	1927	John B. L. Noel	1 hr, 27 min	BFI
Everest	1998	Greg MacGillvray, David Breashears and Stephen Judson	40 min	MacGillivray Freeman Films
Extreme Private Eros: Love Song	1974	Kazuo Hara	98 min	Shisso Production

(continued)

Name	Year	Director	Running time	Production company/ distributor
Family Victim	2010	Robert Lemelson	38 min	Documentary Educational Resources
A Father Washes His Children	1974	Timothy Asch and Napoleon Chagnon	15 min	Documentary Educational Resources
The Feast	1970	Timothy Asch and Napoleon Chagnon	29 min	Documentary Educational Resources
First Person Plural	2000	Deann Borshay Liem	1 hr	POV/PBS
The Fog of War	2003	Errol Morris	107 min	Sony Pictures Classics
Following Sean	2005	Ralph Arlyck	1 hr, 27 min	Timed Exposures
Forest of Bliss	1986	Robert Gardner	90 min	Documentary Educational Resources
Ghost	1990	Jerry Zucker	2 hr, 7 min	Paramount Pictures
Gimme Shelter	1970	Albert Maysles, David Maysles and Charlotte Zwerin	91 min	Criterion
The Godfather	1972	Francis Ford Coppola	2 hr, 55 min	Paramount Pictures
The Good Woman of Bangkok	1991	Dennis O'Rourke	82 min	Film Australia
Goodbye CP [Sayonara CP]	1972	Kazuo Hara	1 hr, 22 min	Shisso Production
Grass [Iran]	1925	Merian C. Cooper and Ernest B. Schoedsack	71 min	Paramount Pictures
Harlan County, USA	1976	Barbara Kopple	1 hr, 43 min	The Criterion Collection
High School	1968	Frederick Wiseman	75 min	Zipporah Films
Hookers on Davie	1984	Janis Cole and Holly Dale	88 min	Pan Canadian Film Distributors

(continued)

Name	Year	Director	Running time	Production company/ distributor
Horses of Life and Death	1991	Janet Hoskins and Laura Whitney	28 min	Center for Visual Anthropology
The Human Pyramid	1959	Jean Rouch	1 hr, 30 min	Les Films de la Pléiade
The Hunters	1957	John Marshall	1 hr, 12 min	Documentary Educational Resources
The Imposter	2012	Layton, Bart	95 min	
In the Footsteps of Taytacha	1985	Peter Getzels and Harriet Gordon	30 min	Documentary Educational Resources
Jaguar	1967	Jean Rouch	88 min	Icarus Films
Jathilan: Trance and Possession in Java	2011	Robert Lemelson	27 min	Documentary Educational Resources
Jero on Jero: A Balinese Trance Seance Observed	1981	Linda Connor, P. Asch and Timothy Asch	17 min	Documentary Educational Resources
Jero Tapakan Series	1979–1983	Linda Connor, Timothy Asch and Patsy Asch		Documentary Educational Resources
A Joking Relationship	1962	John Marshall	13 min	Documentary Educational Resources
A Kalahari Family	1951–2002	John Marshall and Claire Ritchie	360 min	Documentary Educational Resources
Karba's First Years	1950	Gregory Bateson and Margaret Mead	20 min	New York University Film Library
Kites and Monsters	2012	Robert Lemelson	22 min	Documentary Educational Resources
Las Hurdes [Land Without Bread]	1933	Luis Buñuel	27 min	Les Films du Panthéon
Latah: A Culture-Specific Elaboration of the Startle Reflex	1982	Ronald C. Simons	38 min	Indiana University Audiovisual Center
Legong, Dance of the Virgins	1935	Henry De la Falaise	65 min	DuWorld Pictures (USA) and

(*continued*)

Name	Year	Director	Running time	Production company/ distributor
Les maitres fous [not capitalized] [The Mad Masters]	1954	Jean Rouch	36 min	Paramount International Editions Montparnasse
Leviathan	2012	Lucien Castaing-Taylor and Verena Paravel	1 hr, 27 min	The Cinema Guild
The Look of Silence	2014	Joshua Oppenheimer	1 hr, 43 min	Final Cut for Real
Magical Death	1973	Napoleon Chagnon and Timothy Asch	29 min	Documentary Educational Resources
A Man Called Bee	1974	Timothy Asch and Napoleon Chagnon	40 min	Documentary Educational Resources
Man on a Wire	2008	James Marsh	1 hr, 34 min	Magnolia Pictures
A Married Couple	1969	Allan King	1 hr, 37 min	The Criterion Collection
Masters of the Balafon series	2001–2002	Hugo Zemp	221 min	Documentary Educational Resources
Memory of My Face	2011	Robert Lemelson	22 min	Documentary Educational Resources
Millennium: A Thousand Years of History [TV Series]	1999			CNN
Me, A Negro	1968	Jean Rouch	70 min	Icarus Films
Mondo Cane [A Dog's World]	1962	Gualtiero Jacopetti, Paolo Cavara, and Franco Prosperi	1 hr, 48 min	Cineriz
Movements and Madness: Gusti Ayu	2006	Robert Lemelson and Dag Yngvesson	71 min	
N!ai, Story of a !Kung Woman	1980	John Marshall	59 min	Documentary Educational Resources

(continued)

Name	Year	Director	Running time	Production company/ distributor
N/um Tchai: The Ceremo-nial Dance of the !Kung Bushmen	1969	John Marshall	20 min	Documentary Educational Resources
Nanook of the North	1922	Robert J. Flaherty	1 hr, 19 min	Pathé Exchange
New Year Baby	2008	Socheata Poeuv	1 hr, 20 min	ITVS
Ngaben: Emotion and Restraint in a Balinese Heart	2012	Robert Lemelson	16 min	Documentary Educational Resources
The Nuer	1971	Robert Gardner	73 min	Documentary Educational Resources
Odyssey Series	1980–1981	Michael Ambrosino	16 hr, 42 min	Documentary Educational Resources
Primary	1960	D. A. Pennebaker	60 min	Academy Film Archive
Ritual Burdens	2011	Robert Lemelson	25 min	Documentary Educational Resources
Rivers of Sand	1974	Robert Gardner	85 min	Documentary Educational Resources
Shadows and Illuminations	2010	Robert Lemelson	35 min	Documentary Educational Resources
Sherman's March	1986	Ross McElwee	2 hr, 37 min	First Run Features
Shoah	1985	Claude Lanzmann	9 hr, 26 min	BBC
Singing Pictures	2005	Lina Fruzetti, Akos Ostor and Aditi N. Sarkar	40 min	Documentary Educational Resources
Spear and Sword: A Cere-monial Payment of Bridewealth	1989	James Fox, Tim-othy Asch and Patsy Asch	25 min	Documentary Educational Resources
The Spirit Possession of Alejandro Mamani	1973–1974	Hubert Smith and Neil Reichline	27 min	Documentary Educational Resources

(continued)

Name	Year	Director	Running time	Production company/ distributor
Standard Operating Procedure	2008	Errol Morris	118 min	Sony Picture Classics
Standing on the Edge of a Thorn	2012	Robert Lemelson	33 min	Documentary Educational Resources
Sweetgrass	2009	Lucien Castaing-Taylor and Ilisa Barbash	101 min	Cinema Guild
Tajen	2015	Robert Lemelson		
Tales of the Waria	2011	Kathy Huang	56 min	New Day Films
Tarnation	2003	Jonathan Caouette	88 min	Wellspring Media
Thin	2006	Lauren Greenfield	102 min	HBO
The Thin Blue Line	1988	Errol Morris	103 min	Miramax Films
Time Indefinite	1993	Ross McElwee		
Titicut Follies	1967	Frederick Wiseman	84 min	Zipporah Films
To Kill a Mockingbird	1962	Robert Mulligan	2 hr, 9 min	Columbia Pictures
Trance and Dance in Bali	1952	Margaret Mead and Gregory Bateson	22 min	New York University Film Library
Up Series	1964–present	Michael Apted		Granada Television
Warrendale	1967	Allan King	1 hr, 40 min	Allan King Associates
The Water of Words: A Cultural Ecology of an Eastern Indonesian Island	1983	James Fox, Timothy Asch and Patsy Asch	30 min	Documentary Educational Resources
We Know How to Do These Things: Birth in a Newar Village	1997	Barbara Johnson	40 min	Documentary Educational Resources
Welfare	1975	Frederick Wiseman	2 hr, 47 min	Zipporah Films
Were Ni: He is a Madman	1963	Raymond Prince and Francis Speed	27 min	Royal Anthropological Institute
The Yanomamo Series	1968–1971	Timothy Asch and Napoleon Chagnon	7 hr, 8 min	Documentary Educational Resources

(continued)

Name	Year	Director	Running time	Production company/ distributor
Yanomamo: A Multi-Disciplinary Study	1968	Timothy Asch, Napoleon Chagnon and James Neel	45 min	Documentary Educational Resources

INDEX

Note: Locators followed by 'n' refer to notes.

© The Author(s) 2017   297
R. Lemelson, A. Tucker, *Afflictions,* Culture, Mind, and Society,
DOI 10.1007/978-3-319-59984-7

ritual, ix, xii–xiii, 10, 20, 26, 28–9, 31, 35–6, 49, 55–6, 62, 74, 80, 82, 85, 100, 157–75, 186, 210, 218–19, 225, 228–9, 231, 233–4, 251, 274

S
salvage ethnography, 27
Satria(s), 83
scaffolding, 220, 238n4
schizoaffective disorder, 53, 54, 136, 141, 143
schizophrenia, viii, 51–4, 59, 61, 104, 140, 173, 186, 279
schizophrenia paranoid type, 102
social deviance, 117
sociological deviance theory, 128
sound, 31, 101, 161, 208–9, 229–31, 233, 235, 248, 284
soundtrack, 8, 15, 230–5, 239n6
soundtrack score, 233–4
state violence, 256
stigma, 6, 13, 16, 36, 57, 59, 62, 74, 79, 85, 88, 104, 116, 124–5, 128, 138, 145, 151, 154, 162, 169–70, 174, 179, 185, 187–8, 211, 214, 259, 262, 279, 282
subjectivity, 14, 16, 30, 32–4, 36, 38, 50, 63, 104–7, 144, 169, 204, 213–16, 227–9, 232, 266

T
teaching psychological anthropology films, 275–7
test screenings, 236
Tourette Syndrome, x, 3, 5, 74, 77
traditional healing, 56–7, 79–81
transcultural psychiatric epidemiology, 61

transcultural psychiatry [cross-cultural psychiatry], 227, 282
transient psychosis, 54
true consent, 261–3

U
UCLA [University of California, Los Angeles], xi, xiii
University of California, Los Angeles [UCLA], xi, xiii

V
violence, xiii, 19, 35, 53, 83–4, 100, 103–5, 107, 117, 120–1, 125–6, 142–4, 159, 181, 195, 233, 253–4, 256–7, 259–61, 282
visual anthropology, xiii, 8, 15, 34–5, 40, 63, 203, 230, 246, 249, 266, 268n2, 281, 284
visual ethnography, xii, 5, 15, 17–18, 38, 40, 51–2, 60, 63, 218, 249
visual person-centered interviews, ix, 4, 13, 151, 210–11, 227
visual psychological anthropology, xiv, 3–22, 25–33, 40–1, 194–5, 202, 207, 209, 237, 256–9, 262, 267, 273–85
voice hearing [hallucinations], 36, 50, 102, 106, 116, 118, 137, 139–40, 144, 204–5, 278
voice-over, 30, 207, 213, 225–7

W
Wesya(s), 83
WHO [World Health Organization], viii, ix, 16, 50, 59, 61–2, 64n2, 86, 184, 186

ADDITIONAL TV

CPSIA information can be obtained
at www.ICGtesting.com
Printed in the USA
LVHW070856091221
705729LV00002B/2